Ilkhanid Capital Cities

Edinburgh Historical Studies of Iran and the Persian World

Published in association with Elahé Omidyar Mir-Djalali, Founder and Chair, Roshan Cultural Heritage Institute

ROSHAN CULTURAL HERITAGE INSTITUTE

This series covers the history of Iran and the Persian world from the medieval period to the present. As well as its core concern with Iran, it extends its concerns to encompass a much wider and more loosely defined cultural and linguistic world, to include Afghanistan, the Caucasus, Central Asia, Xinjiang and northern India. Books in the series present a range of conceptual and methodological approaches, looking not only at states, dynasties and elites, but at subalterns, minorities and everyday life.

Published and forthcoming titles

Nationalising Oil and Knowledge in Iran: Labour, Decolonisation and Colonial Modernity, 1933–51
Mattin Biglari

Political, Social and Cultural History of Modern Iran: Essays in Honour of Ervand Abrahamian
H. E. Chehabi

The Last Muslim Intellectual: The Life and Legacy of Jalal Al-e Ahmad
Hamid Dabashi

The Persian Prison Poem: Sovereignty and the Political Imagination
Rebecca Ruth Gould

Ilkhanid Capital Cities: Transcultural Interactions
Atri Hatef Naiemi

The Art of Iran in the Twentieth and Twenty-first Centuries: Tracing the Modern and the Contemporary
Hamid Keshmirshekan

The Loneliest Revolution: A Memoir of Solidarity and Struggle in Iran
Ali Mirsepassi

Religion, Orientalism and Modernity: Mahdi Movements of Iran and South Asia
Geoffrey Nash

Remapping Persian Literary History, 1700–1900
Kevin L. Schwartz

Muslim–Christian Polemics in Safavid Iran
Alberto Tiburcio

edinburghuniversitypress.com/series/ehsipw

Ilkhanid Capital Cities

Transcultural Interactions

Atri Hatef Naiemi

EDINBURGH
University Press

Edinburgh University Press is one of the leading university presses in the UK. Publishing new research in the arts and humanities, EUP connects people and ideas to inspire creative thinking, open new perspectives and shape the world we live in. For more information, visit www.edinburghuniversitypress.com.

Edinburgh University Press Ltd
13 Infirmary Street, Edinburgh EH1 1LT

First published in hardback by Edinburgh University Press 2025

Typeset in 11/15 EB Garamond by
Cheshire Typesetting Ltd, Cuddington, Cheshire, and
Printed and bound in the UK using 100% renewable electricity by
CPI Group (UK) Ltd

A CIP record for this book is available from the British Library

ISBN 978 1 3995 1038 7 (hardback)
ISBN 978 1 3995 1039 4 (paperback)
ISBN 978 1 3995 1040 0 (webready PDF)
ISBN 978 1 3995 1041 7 (epub)

Contents

Figures

Acknowledgements

This book originated in a doctoral dissertation presented at the Department of Art History and Visual Studies, University of Victoria in 2019. I wish to express my heartfelt gratitude to my supervisor, Marcus Milwright, for his continuous support throughout my PhD studies and associated research, and for his patience and immense knowledge. I appreciate his generosity with his time and advice. I am very grateful to Evanthia Baboula and Margaret Graves for their insightful feedback on earlier drafts of this book. I also thank Tsung-Cheng Lin for his encouragement and unwavering belief in me.

The initial stages of research for this book were funded by a doctoral fellowship from the Social Sciences and Humanities Research Council of Canada. The fieldwork in Iran also received support from travel grants provided by the Barakat Trust, the Graduate Student Society and the Department of Art History and Visual Studies at the University of Victoria. The writing of this book was made possible through two post-doctoral fellowships: one from the Aga Khan Program for Islamic Architecture at MIT and the other from the Barakat Trust, hosted at the Khalili Research Centre, University of Oxford. I deeply value the hospitality I received from Nasser Rabbat, James Wescott and Jeremy Johns during my stay in Cambridge and Oxford.

Throughout my fieldwork in Iran, I was fortunate to receive invaluable support. I am grateful to the entire staff of the Sultaniyya World Heritage Site for their assistance and warm hospitality. I want to extend special thanks to Muhammad Muradi Shurchih and Parvanih Uliyaei for generously granting me access to the library and archive of Öljeytü's tomb, where I spent countless hours conducting my research. I am also grateful to Abulfazl ʿAli, the research director of Zanjan Cultural Heritage, Handicrafts and Tourism Organization, as well as to Sajjad Jaʿfari, for facilitating my first-hand examination of some of the pottery shards excavated at the site. I would like to offer profound thanks to ʿAbbas Ghadimi Gheydari at the University of Tabriz, and to Mehran Besharat Ghazani, who helped me to carry out my fieldwork in Ghazaniyya.

I am grateful to Stephanie Cronin, the editor of the Edinburgh Historical Studies of Iran and the Persian World series, for her interest in my project, and to the Series Advisory Board for their comments on the book proposal. It was enjoyable to work with Rachel Bridgewater and the editorial team at Edinburgh University Press, particularly Isobel Birks, who adeptly navigated the project through various stages of publication.

I am grateful too to Stefan Kamola for his critical comments on the book proposal. Despite my accidental sending of the sample chapter, he patiently read it with interest and provided insightful feedback. I also thank the anonymous readers for their comments on the book proposal, the sample chapter and the manuscript.

I express my sincere thanks to my parents, Zohreh and Davood, for their long-term support. Special thanks are also owed to my husband, Hamed, whose support was instrumental in completing this book. He offered me the initial spark of inspiration for the project, accompanied me on all my fieldwork trips, provided feedback on numerous earlier drafts, and dedicated countless days to caring for our infant daughter, Dena, to afford me more time to focus on the work. This book would not have been created without his love, enduring patience, boundless encouragement and brilliant comments.

Notes for the Reader

Technical vocabulary in Persian and Arabic is transliterated according to the style of the *International Journal of Middle Eastern Studies*, but I have imposed some standardisation. When the Persian silent (ه) is final, it is given as (ih). Thus, *khānih* is preferred to *khānah* or *khāna*; tappih is preferred to tappah. However, some Persian words are spelled as they commonly appear in published books. For instance, *Shāhnāma* (*Shahnama*) is preferred to *Shāhnāmih* (*Shahnamih*). The silent final (ه) in the words built according to Arabic grammar is given as (a). Thus, Sultaniyya is preferred to Sultaniyyih and Ghazaniyya is preferred to Ghazaniyyih. The short (و) is given as (v). However, some Persian words, and some words which are common to both Persian and Arabic, are spelled as they commonly appear in published books. For instance, *iwān* is preferred to *ivān* and *zāwīya* to *zāvīya*.

For the standard names of dynasties and rulers (particularly for Mongolian names), I have mainly followed Bosworth's *The New Islamic Dynasties* (1996).

For Persian and Arabic names of persons, places and primary sources, diacritical marks are omitted in the main text, except for *ʿayn* (ʿ) and *hamza* (ʾ). The reader can find the transliterated forms of these words in the Notes, Bibliography and Appendix.

The plural forms of Persian and Arabic terms are indicated by the addition of an unitalicised (s).

Chinese terms are transliterated according to the pinyin 拼音 system, but without tone symbols.

Years and centuries mentioned in the book are given according to the Anno Domini system unless otherwise noted.

Translations of Persian primary sources and Persian and Arabic inscriptions are those of the author unless otherwise noted.

Notes on Key Terms

'Persia' is an ancient term for the territory that roughly corresponds to present-day Iran. For the sake of convenience, 'Persia' and 'Iran' are used interchangeably in this book. 'Persianate world' refers to the Persian-speaking domain, which extended far beyond the borders of modern Iran. Alongside language, 'Persian' is often associated with other cultural aspects of the Persianate world (such as art and architecture). Since Iran (as a geographical and cultural entity) was a significant part of the Persianate world during the Ilkhanid period, 'Persian' and 'Iranian' are also used interchangeably in this book. Similarly, 'Iranians', referring to the people who resided within Iran's borders under the Mongols, and 'Persians' are interchangeable terms.

To My Homeland,
IRAN

Introduction
The Mongol Ilkhans Meet the Sedentary World and Enter into Dialogue with It

The period following the Mongol conquest of vast areas of Eurasia in the thirteenth century, that of the so-called *Pax Mongolica*,[1] witnessed the emergence of a new visual language in Persian art and architecture. Various Islamic and non-Islamic visual traditions that permeated the whole body of the arts of thirteenth- and fourteenth-century Iran[2] played a pivotal role in the formation of the hybrid style characterising the art and architecture of the Ilkhanid period (1256–1335). Operating as an interconnected network of people, buildings and institutions, the Ilkhanid city perfectly represents different aspects of cross-cultural encounters in medieval Iran. Along with the reconstruction of the rural and urban settlements that had been extensively destroyed during the Mongol attack on Iran, the Ilkhans (Mongol rulers) built a number of new major cities, mostly in the north-west of Iran. Both literary and archaeological evidence testifies that the foundation and development of urban centres was one of the prime objectives of the Ilkhans. The disintegration of the Ilkhanids in the mid-fourteenth century nevertheless drastically diminished the political and cultural significance of these cities. Over the succeeding decades, many of these urban areas were abandoned while hundreds of their buildings suffered structural damage. During the conflicts of the pre-modern period, many monuments and archaeological sites were plundered, and the building materials scattered. The final phase of destruction occurred in the twentieth century when the remnants of the Ilkhanid cities were covered by modern constructions, and thus nothing remained of most of these cities but some names appearing in the medieval texts.

In view of the Mongols' attachment to their nomadic lifestyle, even during the time they had established their sedentary rule across Eurasia, the cities founded following the conquest need to be analysed according to a new set of standards, different from more traditional definitions of the concept of the city. The present research examines the urban qualities of Ilkhanid cities with regard to the seasonal migrations of the Ilkhans and the fluidity of their political and administrative centres. It discusses how political and administrative centrality could have been transferred from one city to another during the year when the *ordu* (encampment) of the Ilkhans moved between different cities and seasonal camps.

Problems and Questions

The Ilkhanid city was founded in the Islamic context of medieval Iran. However, the archaeological findings, surviving buildings and textual records reveal how a complicated system of local and global forces interacted in order to form the distinct architectural and urban identity of the city. The multidimensional character of the Ilkhanid city is the outcome of communication between pre-existing traditions and received conventions. This dialogue did not incorporate simply the conquered (the Iranians) and the conqueror (the Mongols),[3] but included other cultural traditions that originated in the Eastern Islamic world, Central Asia and the Far East, most significantly in the sedentary civilisation of China. The Ilkhanid city, as will be argued in this book, was hybridised in body and spirit. Not only did various tangible formal and stylistic grounds encounter one another in these cities: also, several intangible forces shaping the identity of these urban centres, such as the motivations behind their foundation, were hybrid by nature. The synthetic identity of the Ilkhanid city, nevertheless, is poorly understood, mainly because our understanding of the city, for the most part, is confined to the studies concerning individual buildings rather than the city in its entirety. Compared with relatively well-researched Ilkhanid art and, to a lesser degree, architecture, the urban settlements founded under the patronage of the Ilkhans still remain to be fully explored.

The hybrid character of Ilkhanid art and architecture is often examined in relation to the artistic traditions of settled societies, while the cultural conventions of the steppe people are given less credit. Even today, speaking of the

Mongol invasions of Iran can arouse national sentiment. In public opinion, the Mongols are still regarded as barbarians whose widespread bloodshed in the thirteenth century destroyed a significant phase of the civilisation of Iran. Suffering the consequences of the conquest for centuries, the Iranians have barely recognised the nomadic steppe customs and beliefs of the Mongol invaders as an established form of culture. Whether this view is grounded in the historical reality or is shaped by the myths that grew up around the Mongols' violence, a rather similar mindset has been transmitted from the non-scholarly part of society to academia. For example, in a recent history of Iran, Katouzian writes:

> It is difficult to credit the Mongol regime in Persia with much positive achievement ... A few notable constructions such as Soltaniyeh [*sic*] and Holagu's [*sic*] observatory in Maragheh [*sic*] are hardly compensation for the losses they inflicted on the country. Hundreds of thousands (perhaps millions) were killed; towns were devastated; sedentary agriculture suffered tremendously from pillage, plunder and heavy taxes.[4]

While scholars from an Iranian background have put more effort into disentangling the hard fact from myth, under the influence of their nationalistic viewpoint or Islamic beliefs they have still tended to emphasise the superiority of the sedentary culture of Islamic Iran over the steppe culture of Mongol nomads. They highlight the Mongols' mass conversion to Islam or their dependence on their resourceful Persian viziers.[5] On the one hand, the scholars acknowledge the emergence of new artistic and architectural styles and techniques in the post-conquest period, while on the other, they attribute the achievements of Ilkhanid art, architecture and urbanism to the Iranian-Islamic culture of the settled society of Iran. They value this culture as a remarkable source of inspiration for artists and artisans and undermine the nomadic traditions of the Ilkhans themselves. Consequently, the Ilkhanid city is described as an arena in which the struggle between nomadic and urban tendencies eventually resulted in the supremacy of the latter.[6]

Challenging the stereotypes that have developed in earlier scholarship up to the present time, this book argues that the arts of the Ilkhanids need to be addressed as the product of the interactions between a number of cultural realms without attributing a privileged position to the well-established

Perso-Islamic culture of Iran. There is no doubt that Ilkhanid art and architecture were built on pre-Mongol artistic styles and practices such as the arts of the Seljuq period. The stylistic and technical achievements of the Iranians in different areas of art and architecture prior to the Mongol invasions formed a certain foundation for the new aesthetic idiom that came into being under the Ilkhans. Furthermore, Iran, as a result of its geopolitical situation in the medieval world, facilitated the transmission and exchange of cultural, political and economic traditions between Eastern Asia and the Eastern Islamic world. However, as we will see in the following chapters, it seems that Ilkhanid Iran should be given credit for acting as a 'contact zone' providing proper context for the encounter between different cultures rather than as a prevailing culture that deeply impressed the Ilkhans and manipulated their aesthetic taste.

While admitting the emergence of various non-Islamic/non-Iranian forms and notions in Ilkhanid art and architecture, this book specifically focuses on the dialogue between the Mongols and the Iranians and looks for the imported signs and meanings brought in by the Mongol conquerors and injected into the principles of Iranian urban architecture. It concentrates on two major urban sites in the north-west of Iran, Ghazaniyya and Sultaniyya, in order to show how the architectural and urban features of the cities were determined through the complex interaction of diverse forces. Reassessing the development of the sites, the study uncovers the imported visual, conceptual and theoretical traditions that permeated the whole structure of the cities, and examines the mechanisms through which the foreign trends were adapted to suit local values and established traditions of Perso-Islamic culture.

This project promotes understanding of Ilkhanid urbanism through scholarly reconstruction of the cities that have partially or completely vanished over the course of time. This reconstruction is intended to illuminate two aspects of the cities: first, general layout, including key architectural elements and their spatial arrangement; and second, major historical figures who contributed to the formation of the cities in the role of patrons. The identification of the Ilkhanid cities is important because they are the least-known aspect of the Ilkhans' endeavours in Iran. Moreover, the study of intercultural contacts between Mongol rulers and their subjects needs to be grounded in a body of material evidence, otherwise it will simply constitute pure speculation about a situation in the past, speculation not necessarily in accordance with the historical reality. Shaping a vivid picture of the Ilkhanid city will significantly develop this solid foundation.

A Brief Literary Overview of Studies on Ilkhanid Art and Architecture

The large number of works written on the history of the Mongol Empire have laid the foundations for more detailed studies of art and architecture that flourished in different khanates following the conquests of the Mongols.[7] Part of these studies examines Central Asian Mongols in connection with the sedentary civilisations bordering the steppe.[8] Contrary to traditional views representing the nomads as violent barbarians,[9] more recent scholarly works, exemplified by the innovative books of Thomas Allsen, draw attention to the influence of the steppe people on their neighbours and highlight their dominant role as active agents in the transcultural exchange of goods and ideas across Eurasia.[10] This unconventional opinion on the Mongols forms the basis for the main argument of this book, aiming to uncover the nomadic traditions and concepts brought in by the Mongols to the urban architecture of the Ilkhanid land. The project borrows substantially from the solid scholarship on the history of the Ilkhanate and, to a lesser degree, the Yuan dynasty. It intentionally avoids digging deeply into other sectors of the Mongol Empire, including the Golden Horde and the Chaghadaid Khanate, due to their more limited historical interactions with Ilkhanid Iran.

The book benefits from the great body of literature on Ilkhanid art and architecture. Different forms of decorative arts including textile, ceramic, metalwork, jewellery and manuscript illustration have been extensively examined.[11] Although delving into the arts of this period is not within the scope of the present research, it is noteworthy that some of the studies conducted on Ilkhanid decorative arts have raised the issue of continuous artistic communication between East and West Asia, and thus the occurrence of Far Eastern motifs and themes in Iranian art under the Mongols. They provide a methodological model, which is also applicable to urban architectural studies in the project. *Islamic Chinoiserie*[12] and '*Khita'i*: Cultural Memory and the Creation of a Mongol Visual Idiom'[13] are two significant works in this regard (see Chapter 5).

Along with the portable arts, a large number of extant architectural remains throughout the territory of the Ilkhanids have been surveyed, analysed and published over the last few decades.[14] While there are more recent analytical studies that aim to integrate Anatolia into the study of the Ilkhanate,[15] Wilber's book, *The Architecture of Islamic Iran: The Il Khānid Period*, is still considered the most comprehensive catalogue of the Ilkhanid monuments surviving within the confines of present-day Iran.[16] In addition to general surveys, in a number of newer works, such as *The Ilkhanid Shrine Complex at Natanz*,[17] architecture has been examined in greater detail in the socio-political context of Iran under the Mongols. Despite these efforts, in comparison with pictorial and decorative arts held in many museums around the world, Ilkhanid buildings have been given less attention in Western scholarship, mainly due to the smaller number of expeditions of European scholars to Iran following the 1979 Iranian revolution. The Iran Cultural Heritage, Handicrafts and Tourism Organization (ICHTO), however, has been considerably concerned with the identification and preservation of historic buildings and archaeological sites over the last forty years. In co-operation with ICHTO, extensive research and excavations have been conducted by architectural historians as well as archaeologists in numerous buildings and many historic sites, including those founded during the Ilkhanid period.[18] As a result, a large number of scholarly works published in Persian form a relatively rich body of literature on Ilkhanid architecture.

Regardless of the awareness of the formal and functional features of Ilkhanid architecture, few attempts have been made, either in Western or Iranian scholarship, to contextualise the buildings. The research conducted in this area mainly deals with major monuments with the purpose of examining their aesthetic and architectural qualities as individual buildings rather than considering them within the wider context of urban space. This approach results in the compilation of valuable catalogues, monographs and surveys of the buildings founded by the Ilkhanids, but it barely contributes to the creation of a bright image of the Ilkhanid city in its entirety. Although cities have been given least attention in the existing scholarship on the Ilkhans' architectural undertakings, there are still a few research works that deal specifically with Ilkhanid urbanism, including two remarkable articles by Isfahanian and Khaza'ili ('The Ilkhanid New Cities' and 'Urban Development in Iran during the Time of the Mongols'[19]) and Masuya's publication on the Ilkhanid capital of Takht-i Sulayman.[20] I have also published an academic article on the citadel and the outer city of Sultaniyya that complements my discussion about the imperial city in Chapter 4 of the present book.[21]

Contrary to the scant concentration on urbanism under the Mongols in Iran, there is a significant literature on the cities that developed outside the Ilkhanids' territory, contemporaneously with the Ilkhanid dynasty, in Central Asia and the Far East. Considering the distance between the capitals of the Ilkhanate and the Yuan dynasty, the socially, culturally, religiously and politically different environment of their capitals and the power disparity between the dominant host cultures (China and Iran), the Mongols' strategy in relation to Chinese culture may barely extend to the Ilkhanids. However, in view of the widespread transmission of ideas and concepts across Eurasia under Mongol rule, it is likely that the process and method through which the Yuan emperors adopted the values and customs of their host culture in China impacted their counterparts' attitude towards the native cultural elements of their sedentary host. Understanding the Mongols' strategy in China could be illuminating with regard to how the Ilkhans, like or unlike the Khaqans, mediated between what they had brought in from their homeland and what their Persian Muslim hosts offered them. As such, the examination of the architectural projects patronised by the Mongols in the East can throw light on the origin of the models employed by the Ilkhans and determine how the latter reacted to the long-established Perso-Islamic architectural conventions. In this regard, Steinhardt's extensive research on the cities founded by the Mongol rulers of the Yuan dynasty in China[22] and Masuya's studies of the settlements of the Mongols in Central Asia[23] are noteworthy examples.

Primary Sources

In view of the relative paucity of secondary literature on Ilkhanid urbanism, primary historical texts are regarded as important sources of information on the court-sponsored urban projects in the Ilkhanate. Written sources regarding the Mongol invasion and the Mongols' control over Western Asia are rich and can be found in different languages, including Persian, Arabic, Turkish, Armenian, and some Eastern languages such as Chinese and Mongolian.[24] The textual evidence includes a wide range of sources, from chronicles written by members of the royal court and the ruling elite to local histories, travel accounts and religious texts such as endowment deeds (*waqf-nāmihs*). Written records help scholars to make connections among the scattered archaeological and architectural remains which have been found at the urban sites, providing the missing link and thus contributing to the formation of an integrated picture of the city. The research, therefore, is based largely on the works of thirteenth- and fourteenth-century authors writing in Persian, specifically three historians: Rashid al-Din (d. 1318), Abu al-Qasim Kashani (d. 1337) and Wassaf al-Hazra (d. 1329). The importance of their histories is that they are the contemporary accounts of the reigns of Ghazan Khan (r. 1295–1304), Öljeytü (r. 1304–16) and Abu Saʿid (r. 1316–35), embracing first-hand information on the main case studies of this project, Ghazaniyya and Sultaniyya. The authors not only witnessed events at the time of the last three Ilkhans, but also held positions in the administrative system of the court. They were in regular contact with the Ilkhans themselves, and in this way their historical accounts also reflect their conceptions of their masters. In addition, several other significant works have been consulted – although to a lesser extent – throughout the book, such as the invaluable book of ʿAta Malik Juvayni (d. 1283), the *Tarikh-i Jahangushay*, particularly in the sections concerning the history of the Mongol Empire prior to the reign of Arghun Khan (r. 1284–91), and the remarkable works of Hamdallah Mustawfi (d. 1349), *Tarikh-i Guzidih*, which is a general history of the world, and *Nuzhat al-Qulub*.

Apart from the significance of the *Jamiʿ al-Tawarikh* as the most comprehensive extant account of the establishment and development of the Mongol Empire written by a Persian, one can find in this book one of the best representations of the Mongol–Iranian intercultural dialogue.[25] Rashid al-Din[26] extensively consulted translated Mongol texts and Mongol agents as his sources of information.[27] Those sections of the book that deal with the history of the Mongols are particularly important examples of pre-modern textual translation, because the linguistic exchange happened directly between the two cultures and the process primarily involved two agents, Rashid al-Din and Bolad Aqa (d. 1313), according to the former. Bolad, the famed Mongol tribesman, was a senior court official who arrived in Iran in 1285 during the reign of Arghun. Rashid al-Din acknowledged Bolad as his primary informant, who was as knowledgeable as Ghazan about the Mongols' genealogy[28] and provided much of the information on the cultural life and tribal history of the Mongols. Kamola, however, argues that the Mongol historical tradition was more diverse than the memory of one man.[29]

Additionally, the *Jami' al-Tawarikh* was commissioned by Ghazan Khan as an effort to record the history of the Mongols and preserve their nomadic roots, which were on the verge of oblivion as the result of the Mongols' encounters with the sedentary world. Following the death of Ghazan, the project of the *Jami' al-Tawarikh* continued under the auspices of his brother and successor Öljeytü, but substantially expanded in order to cover the whole history of the known world.[30] Ghazan's effort reveals the extent to which the preservation of the Mongols' nomadic heritage mattered to him even when he was fulfilling his new role as the padishah of Iran. The fact that the Ilkhan chose a non-Mongol figure, Rashid al-Din, to conduct the project, despite the presence of several well-informed Mongol characters in the Ilkhanid court, raises questions about the text as well as the author. One obvious reason why the work was delegated to a Persian vizier could be the absence of a historiographical tradition among the Mongols, although they had orally transmitted history.[31] The other possible reason was the position of Rashid al-Din as an 'outsider'. In the post-conquest era, more than any political and religious propaganda, Rashid al-Din's approving opinion about the Ilkhans, particularly Ghazan himself, played a significant role in the legitimisation of Mongol rule in Iran. However, in designating Rashid al-Din to oversee the project, Ghazan accepted the risk of some of the notions transferred to Rashid al-Din through his mediators and translators being misunderstood. Consequently, in spite of the importance of the *Jami' al-Tawarikh* in the study of the history of the Mongols, it should be treated first as an account written from the point of view of an Iranian, with all his biases and preferences, and second as a source compiled from the information and observations that were transported across different languages and cultures.

Kashani's history, the *Tarikh-i Öljeytü*, is a substantial book on the Ilkhanid period. While the *Jami' al-Tawarikh* concluded with the account of Ghazan's death, the *Tarikh-i Öljeytü* covers the next important phase of the history of the Ilkhans, the reign of Öljeytü. Kashani was possibly one of the scribes of the Ilkhanid court who also participated in the grand project of the *Jami' al-Tawarikh* under the supervision of Rashid al-Din.[32] In his chronicle, however, Kashani claims that he compiled the *Jami' al-Tawarikh* and Rashid al-Din took all the credit for it. He was obviously annoyed with the vizier, and expresses his displeasure via unpleasant mentions of Rashid al-Din throughout the book; for instance, Kashani calls him Rashid al-Dawla, which was the title of the vizier before converting from Judaism to Islam.[33]

Wassaf al-Hazra, the author of the *Tajziyat al-Amsar va Tazjiyat al-A'sar* [The Allocation of Cities and the Propulsion of Epochs] (known as *Tarikh-i Wassaf*), worked at the court of Ghazan Khan and Öljeytü assisting Rashid al-Din and his joint vizier Sa'd al-Din Muhammad Savaji (d. 1311) in court affairs.[34] As Wassaf states, his history is in fact the continuation of the work of 'Ata Malik Juvayni, the *Tarikh-i Jahangushay*, for whom Wassaf had the greatest admiration and respect. The *Tarikh-i Wassaf* covers the period between 1258, the siege of Baghdad, and 1328, the middle of the reign of Abu Sa'id. The work has been regarded, for the most part, as an eye-witness account of the Ilkhanids.[35] In addition to the description of historical events, Wassaf included short poems in his book. The most important piece is a relatively long ode dedicated to Öljeytü in 1312 in which he describes Sultaniyya in richly poetic language.[36]

My linguistic capacity does not extend to the primary sources in Mongolian and Chinese, in respect of which I consulted exclusively the secondary literature and relied on translations and interpretations of the original texts. Since the non-Persian sources are barely informative about the camps and cities built by the Ilkhans in Iran, language restrictions have not been a large obstacle in most of the research. Nevertheless, in the absence of English translations of some invaluable Chinese historical texts such as the *Yuan Shi*,[37] limited language proficiency has presented certain challenges in studying the urban settlements of the Mongols in the East or examining non-Persian historical figures.

European travellers' narratives recounting their journeys across Mongol territories in the Middle East, Central Asia and the Far East offer valuable insights into the dynamics of the Mongol Empire, particularly its interactions with Europe. Among travellers, the accounts of two observers, William of Rubruck (d. 1293) and Marco Polo (d. 1324), are of great importance for the purpose of this study since they provide relatively accurate reports of the Mongols' settlements in the East as well as their cultural practices and religious systems. Rubruck was a missionary sent by Louis IX of France (r. 1226–70). He was given the opportunity of meeting Möngke Khan (r. 1251–9) in his palace at Karakorum.[38] The Venetian merchant Marco Polo also recorded a great amount of interesting information about the Mongol Empire in his book, particularly on events at the court of Qubilay Khan (r. 1260–94).[39] Furthermore, several European travellers heading east paused in the realms of the Ilkhanate, where they meticulously documented the cities they encountered along their journey to Central Asia and China. The account of Ruy Gonzalez de Clavijo (d. 1412), the ambassador of Henry III of Castile to the court of Timur (r. 1370–1405), is a notable example in this regard. His description of the Ilkhanid city of Sultaniyya sheds much light on the physical structure of the city a few decades after the disintegration of the Ilkhanids.[40] In the Safavid (1501–1736) and Qajar (1789–1925) periods, many Iranian cities were visited by European ambassadors, merchants and travellers, whose reports sometimes contain important remarks on the Ilkhanid architectural remains.[41]

Methods and Theories

In comparison with historical texts, archaeological excavations usually produce more factual information on the structural features of pre-modern cities. Generating archaeological evidence, however, is associated with some challenges: for instance, the limited coverage of excavations and surveys and the unsatisfactory amount and/or quality of published data.[42] In the case of Ilkhanid cities, regrettably, the excavations have been confined to a few famous sites (notably Sultaniyya, Ujan and Takht-i Sulayman), and several other settlements, such as Ghazaniyya, despite their vital role in the political history of the Ilkhanids, have been overlooked. Moreover, even in some of the well-excavated sites, excavations have been limited mostly to archaeological digs, and documenting the unearthed layers has not been a priority. This is particularly the case for Sultaniyya, where the entire Ilkhanid citadel was unearthed over the course of sixteen seasons; however, no written records were found to accompany the discoveries. Despite the extensive excavations, in the absence of sufficient published reports it is still confusing to differentiate between different phases of construction and to understand the spatial arrangement of architectural elements of the citadel.[43]

Regardless of the limitations, excavated findings form a significant body of data for the present research. Archaeologically derived information, combined with the textual accounts of the cities, removes many ambiguities concerning their spatial structure. The combination of excavated materials and written evidence is the basis of historical archaeology,[44] which is broadly conceived as the study of societies that produced textual records.[45] Historical archaeology can also be defined as the study of the 'modern world' or the world that has shaped since around AD 1500.[46] While the archaeologists of history merge textual and material evidence, the independence between the two sources of evidence is equally significant. As Kosso argues, texts and archaeology can be used 'as independent sources of information to function in the accountability of the other as evidence'.[47]

Having examined the Ilkhanid cities through the perspective of historical archaeology, we can overlay the historical descriptions with the archaeological findings in order to reconstruct parts of the cities that developed under the Ilkhans. The integration of textual evidence and archaeological data, nevertheless, is not always fruitful, due to the disparities between the two categories of evidence. Textual sources are sometimes criticised for not being entirely unbiased. The events and figures seen and recorded from the viewpoint of a Christian missionary, for instance, might have been affected by some degree of religious or political bias. This issue is particularly the case for the accounts written by court historians, which are the primary historical documents used in this book. Their hyperbolic language for describing the architectural undertakings of their patrons could mislead architectural historians about what is being unearthed since the physical findings sometimes do not match up with what has been exaggeratedly described in the text. Additionally, their architectural descriptions might refer to the structures that were replaced with later constructions. In this case, the account of a particular site may not correspond to the results of the excavation of the same place. For example, in Kashani's report of the citadel of Sultaniyya one can find some information about the buildings built during the reign of Öljeytü. It is probable that some of them were replaced with Abu Saʿid's buildings. Although archaeologists can roughly date the uncovered structures on the basis of their stylistic and technical features, style and technique usually change slightly over a short period of time, which means that it is almost impossible to determine with certainty whether the unearthed remains belong to the time of Öljeytü or of his successor Abu Saʿid.

Another challenge faced by architectural historians of the Ilkhanid period is the fact that most of the archaeological sites are urban or rural settlements with several overlaid layers of habitation. Some of them are still active towns and cities witnessing widespread construction projects. Archaeologists are not always given the opportunity to survey sites or conduct rescue excavation in advance of construction.[48] For example, private ownership of the properties located in the middle of archaeological sites has caused some valuable physical evidence to become distorted before being documented and studied (some is not even seen by archaeologists). Sometimes the sudden removal of earth using machines has changed the order of archaeological layers or has caused some layers to be destroyed. Regardless of the scale of the construction projects, whether as large as recently developed streets and neighbourhoods or as small as individual residential units, they could have seriously damaged the archaeological and architectural integrity of the historical sites. As a result, despite the substantial archaeological discoveries in a number of Ilkhanid cities during the last couple of decades, the sites are still far from being fully understood in their entirety.

Given the dearth of adequate physical evidence, aerial archaeology, or the study of archaeological remains by examining them from altitude, is the method that could improve our understanding of the urban fabric of certain cities in the past.[49] Aerial photographs and satellite images can show the general configuration of now-vanished urban sites.[50] Older photographs are even more useful than more recent ones, since the original layout of the site could be better preserved in images from an earlier date, making it more recognisable. For instance, in the case of Ghazaniyya, the outline of the pre-modern city covered by modern constructions can be generated on the basis of the 1960s aerial image. However, it must be noted that the sketch maps drawn from aerial photographs are less accurate than what can be measured on the ground, and what is measured on the ground is less accurate than what is excavated.[51] In addition to aerial photographs and satellite images, low-level oblique shots are also significant material, providing large-area view of historical landscapes with greater clarity. The tendency to apply these images is increasing among archaeologists and architectural historians, particularly because of the wider availability of Unmanned Aerial Vehicles (UAVs)[52] over the last few years.[53]

Visual analysis of pre-modern topographical paintings is an effective method for vividly visualising the overall landscape of Ilkhanid camps and cities, which have left scarce traces in the present day. Paintings present more details than textual accounts, but they are not unbiased in communicating content and thus need to be consulted cautiously. Furthermore, they were usually generated on the basis of realistic sketches made on site, either by the painters themselves or their assistants, but to some degree they might have been affected by their creators' imagination. The interpretation of such images is also qualified by questions of style and function, that is to say, their stylistic and visual features should be considered alongside the purpose they served and the motivations of their patrons. These visual materials were often produced in the court scriptorium following the pictorial conventions of their own time. Contextualising these works with their contemporary paintings can reveal the general drawing rules followed by their painters, and hence facilitates the elucidation of their content.

Similarly, medieval miniatures, the most applicable of which is the *Great Mongol Shahnama*, are extensively consulted in the book. During the Ilkhanid period, illustrated copies of the *Shahnama*, the epic poem embodying the ethno-national identity of the Iranians, were widely produced in Iran.[54] The *Great Mongol Shahnama* is one of the surviving copies commissioned, arguably by the court, towards the end of the Ilkhanate.[55] It is held that each painting in the manuscript was intended not only to depict a story from the *Shahnama* but also to portray an episode from Mongol history.[56] In this way, Ilkhanid figures, events and traditions were represented by their fictional counterparts. This interpretation raises two possibilities regarding the main purpose of the production of the book, whether it was commissioned by Mongol rulers seeking to justify their power through the epic, or initiated by an Iranian elite attempting to validate the alien rulers.[57] Either way, the Ilkhans appear to have become increasingly similar to the national figures over the course of time, and thus to have gained greater legitimacy and acceptability among their subjects.

Regardless of the content of the paintings, they illustrate distinct physical features of the Mongols as well as their costumes. In view of the different aspects of Mongol cultural identity portrayed via the stories of the *Shahnama* and assimilated into the national culture of Iran using the epic poem,[58] the manuscript presents a shrewd case of intercultural translation, an idea which is explored further in my final chapter.

The overview of practical tools and methods can be followed with a brief mention of the theoretical framework that provides a conceptual understanding of the hybrid nature of the Ilkhanid city. Among a multitude of terms and theories analysing the intricate process of transcultural interactions, this book largely benefits from a theory of translation which discusses the concept of translation, beyond the domain of languages, in relation to the transmission of forms, meanings and ideas between different cultures. The notion of translation has been discussed by Homi Bhabha in his ground-breaking work *The Location of Culture*.[59] This book, together with his earlier publication 'The Third Space',[60] forms the basis for the main argument of the present study. Furthermore, this study is greatly enriched by the relatively recent publications of Barry Flood's *Objects of Translation* and Esra Akcan's 'Channels and Items of Translation',[61] both of which apply the concept of translation in an art/architectural history context. According to this conceptual model, the hybrid quality of Ilkhanid cities is scrutinised in order to determine how the imported ideas, themes and motifs gained a new identity under the influence of the cultural environment of Ilkhanid Iran. The theory of translation and its applicability in studying the transcultural exchanges within the Mongol Empire will be extensively examined in the final chapter of this book.

Chapter Outline

The chapters that follow explore the process during which the Mongols accustomed themselves to the practices of the sedentary world. They examine how the nomad conquerors dismounted from their horses and ascended the throne, and how their settled mentality strengthened against their nomadic background. By contrast, the following discussion investigates the extent to which the Mongols were inclined to retain their steppe conventions. Focusing on the architectural and urban projects conducted under the patronage of the Ilkhans, the emphasis is on the encounter between these two apparently opposite forces and the reflection of this encounter in the urban foundations of the Ilkhanids.

Ilkhanid cities did not form in isolation. Bearing this in mind, Chapter 1 delves into the broader setting in which Ilkhanid urbanism evolved, namely the medieval Islamic world on the one hand and Mongol Eurasia on the other. Thus, the first section of the chapter explores the major structural and conceptual transformations of the cities that developed between the twelfth and sixteenth centuries across a geographic area known as the 'central Islamic lands', including today's Egypt, Syria, Iraq, Jordan and Turkey,[62] with particular emphasis on the Ilkhanids' western frontier, Anatolia. In the second section of the chapter, the focus shifts to the urban centres built under the patronage of the Great Khans of the Mongol Empire in Central Asia and China. Karakorum, Shangdu (Kaiping Fu) and Daidu (Dadu), three major cases designated as the capitals of the Khans for a certain period during their lifetime, are studied in greater detail. While the focus of attention is the contemporaries of Ilkhanid cities, Chapter 1 touches upon the urban centres that developed under the Seljuqs (1040–1194) and the Khwarazm Shahs (1077–1231) prior to the Mongol invasion, such as Isfahan and Nishapur. This overview sheds some light on the context in which Ilkhanid cities were born.

After the Mongol conquest of Iran, along with the reconstruction of the cities that had been extensively destroyed during the course of the invasion in the 1250s, the Ilkhans founded a number of new settlements. Chapter 2 offers an overview of the projects carried out under the patronage of the Ilkhans in the second half of the thirteenth century and the early decades of the fourteenth. These projects ranged from larger settlements designated by the Ilkhans as their political and administrative centres, including Maraghih, Takht-i Sulayman and Ujan, to less ambitious projects in their seasonal quarters such as Alatagh in Azerbaijan. Furthermore, the Ilkhans generously funded construction projects and expanded infrastructure in a multitude of smaller villages and towns, some of which, over the course of time, attracted many immigrants and converted into larger cities. While the focus of attention in this chapter is major urban centres, lesser-known cases such as Aq Qalʿih in Khurasan, located far from the western headquarters of the Ilkhans in Azerbaijan, are also studied in some depth to explore how urban centres developed in the eastern sector of the Ilkhanid state.

The next two chapters focus on Ghazaniyya and Sultaniyya, the two case studies presented in this book. Chapter 3 examines Ghazaniyya in two major areas. First, it studies the spatial structure of the city during the Ilkhanid period. Given the extensive destruction of the medieval city and the scarcity of architectural and archaeological evidence, this section relies primarily on textual records and visual material such as aerial photographs and satellite images. Second, the chapter considers Ghazaniyya beyond its physical entity and studies it in relation to the socio-religious, cultural and political context in which the city was built. Great emphasis will be placed on Ghazan himself as the founder, and on his religious and political aspirations. Understanding the nature of the spiritual beliefs of the Ilkhans paves the way for the exploration of Ghazan's intention of establishing a new urban centre beside a long-established prosperous city like Tabriz. Building upon the findings of the first two sections, the last part of the chapter discusses the foundation of Ghazaniyya in connection with the main argument of this book. It challenges the assumption that the construction of Ghazaniyya was merely due to the religious orientation of Ghazan following his momentous conversion to Islam, and suggests that the city and the charitable foundation in Shanb-i Ghazan reflected the synthesis of Perso-Islamic and Mongol visual and spiritual traditions.

The layout of Sultaniyya that developed during the time of Öljeytü, Ghazan Khan's brother and successor, is reconstructed in Chapter 4. The focus of attention is the citadel that once embraced the most magnificent architectural project of the city, the tomb of Öljeytü. The outer city that expanded beyond the walls of the citadel is also studied in order to gain a better understanding of the civilian settlement of Sultaniyya, where the general population lived. In comparison with Ghazaniyya, the study of Sultaniyya is enriched by more archaeologically-derived information. The architectural evidence unearthed during the excavations reveals substantial data regarding the original layout of the medieval city. Other sources of information including chronicles describing the city, illustrations left by visitors to the site, aerial photographs and satellite images of the area, and, more importantly, findings from site surveys conducted by the present author are consulted to paint a realistic picture of the fourteenth-century city. This chapter not only serves to describe the spatial structure of Sultaniyya, but also sheds much light on the question of the encounter between Perso-Islamic concepts and Mongol nomadic conventions in the context of the built environment of the Ilkhanid city.

Building upon the discussions of the previous chapters, Chapter 5 theorises the intercultural contacts between the Mongols and the Iranians on the basis of the above-mentioned theory of translation. Benefiting from both literary and archaeological evidence, this chapter argues that the Ilkhans not only facilitated the westward transportation of cultural wares, but also intervened actively in the process of adoption and transformation of forms, ideas and traditions in the destination (Iran). Although the Ilkhans initially established their domination through the power of the sword, they gradually redefined their political aspirations in accordance with the principles of the newly conquered land of Iran. While they adhered to their nomadic conceptions of the world to some extent, they compromised a number of their steppe customs for the sake of being accepted by subject peoples. Chapter 5 articulates and discusses this strategy of conciliation in three areas: dialogues between Khans and sultans/padishahs; dialogues between tents and buildings; and dialogues between camps and cities. The Ilkhans veered between the retention of their past and an openness to new influences. The past was their nomadic selves as well as the tents and camps where they used to reside and in connection with which they had formed part of their tribal identity. The new was their sedentary selves as the sovereigns of the state, and the imperial buildings and cities which were deemed the requisites of their sovereignty. This chapter examines how the character of the Ilkhans themselves and the architectural and urban projects that developed under their patronage reflected the interaction between the past and the new.

As a concluding note, it should be emphasised that the sack of Baghdad by the Mongols and the fall of the Abbasid Caliphate in 1258 terminated the long dominance of the Arab world and stabilised the political state of Iran. After the establishment of the Ilkhanids in Iran, as one of the many consequences of the Mongol conquest, Iran became less connected with the Arab lands of the Fertile Crescent – despite their close association since the rise of Islam in the seventh century – and was reoriented towards Central Asia.[63] Artistically, Iran flourished as a centre of art and culture after the Mongol campaign. It served as a creative mediator between East and West, acting as the gateway through which Chinese motifs and themes entered the Islamic world.[64] Nevertheless, we must bear in mind that the so-called legacy of Chinggis Khan pointing to the achievements of Iranian art and architecture following the Mongol conquest was founded on the ruins of the cities that had enjoyed their highest levels of prosperity a few years prior to the invasion. Although the Mongols – possibly inadvertently – provided a context in which the extensive intercultural contacts changed the face of art and architecture in Iran, they abruptly terminated the century-long evolving process that had reached its climax in Seljuq art. This fact is usually ignored by those scholars who regard the subjugation simply as a turning point in the history of art and architecture of Iran,[65] whereas the two-sided outcome of the Mongol conquest, as Allsen concisely describes it, should always be addressed 'under the twin rubrics of "communication" and "destruction"'.[66]

Notes

1. *Pax Mongolica* refers to a period of time (c. 1280–1360), following the conquests of the Mongol Empire, during which Mongol domination stabilised the social and cultural life in most part of Eurasia and guaranteed security on the Eurasian commercial routes. See Nicola Di Cosmo, 'Black Sea Emporia and the Mongol Empire: A Reassessment of the Pax Mongolica', *Journal of the Economic and Social History of the Orient* 53, no. 1/2 (2010): 83. The term, however, can be considered problematic because of oversimplifying the complex political and cultural circumstances during the Mongol Empire and downplaying the violence and destruction associated with Mongol conquests.
2. The Ilkhanids governed present-day Iran, Azerbaijan, Eastern Anatolia and parts of Iraq. The major architectural and urban undertakings of the Ilkhans themselves, as well as their political activities, as will be discussed in the following chapters, were concentrated in the north-west of present-day Iran. Therefore, for the sake of convenience, in this book 'Iran' and 'Ilkhanid state/land/territory' in Western Asia are used interchangeably.
3. The Ilkhanids were descendants of Chinggis Khan, who was the son of Yesügei, the head of the ruling Mongol clan. Therefore, the steppe people of Central Asia who ruled Iran in the thirteenth and fourteenth century are generally called the Mongols, despite the presence of nomadic Turks and Uyghurs among the Mongols. In other words, in the context of Ilkhanid Iran the word 'Mongol' no longer serves as the name of a particular clan. On nomadic Turks and Uyghurs, see Jonathan Skaff and William Honeychurch, 'Empire Building before the Mongols: Legacies of the Türks and Uyghurs', in *Genghis Khan and the Mongol Empire*, ed. William Fitzhugh, Morris Rossabi and William Honeychurch (Washington: Dino Don, 2009), 85–9.
4. Homa Katouzian, *The Persians Ancient, Mediaeval, and Modern Iran* (New Haven, CT: Yale University Press, 2009), 106. This viewpoint is not, however, confined to Iranian scholars. As Thomas Allsen puts it, 'The long-held stereotypes in the sedentary world ... viewed ... the steppe peoples as barbarians, destroyers of civilizations, or at best children of nature and noble savages'. See Thomas Allsen, *Commodity and Exchange in the Mongol Empire: A Cultural History of Islamic Textiles* (Cambridge: Cambridge University Press, 1997), 105–6.

For more studies on this stereotype, see Allsen, *Commodity and Exchange*, 106, n. 31. Michal Biran also writes that 'representatives of the sedentary civilizations ... often portrayed them [pastoral nomads] either as a violent force that left no mark of their culture or as source of negative influence that was responsible for "all that went wrong" with their civilizations'. See Michal Biran, 'Introduction', in *Nomads as Agents of Cultural Change: The Mongols and their Eurasian Predecessors*, ed. Reuven Amitai-Preiss and Michal Biran (Honolulu: University of Hawaii Press, 2015). For more discussion on the image of Chinggis Khan in popular Western culture, see Peter Marsh and Myagmar Saruul-Erdene, 'I Conquer like a Barbarian! Genghis Khan in the Western Popular Imagination', in *Genghis Khan and the Mongol Empire*, ed. William Fitzhugh, Morris Rossabi and William Honeychurch (Washington: Dino Don, 2009), 278.

5. There is no doubt that the Mongols' conversion drastically changed the social and political conditions of the Ilkhanid state. However, the exaggerated interpretation of this historical event offered in some secondary sources sometimes contradicts the accounts of eye-witness historians. For instance, in a section of her book dealing with Ghazan Khan's conversion, Shirin Bayani writes that the Ilkhan converted to Islam in order to win the war against Baydu and to ascend the throne. While she confirms that this conversion was not entirely sincere, she adds that following the conversion, the sovereignty of Chinggisid Yasa came to an end for ever in Iran and Islam became prevalent again. See Shirin Bayani, *Dīn va Dawlat dar Iran-i 'Ahd-i Mughul* [Religion and Government in Iran during the Time of the Mongols] (Tehran: Markaz-i Nashr-i Dānishgāhī, 2002), vol. 2, 441. Despite this, as will be discussed in Chapter 3, we know that Ghazan remained committed to the Yasa until his death (Reuven Amitai-Preiss, 'Ghazan, Islam and Mongol Tradition: A View from the Mamlūks Sultanate', *Bulletin of the School of Oriental and African Studies* 59, no. 1 (1996).
6. See also Abulfazl Razavi, 'Sākhtār-i Ḥayāt-i Shahrī dar 'Aṣr-i Īlkhānān [The Structure of Urban Life during the Ilkhanid Period]', *Kitāb-i Māh-i Tārīkh va Jughrāfīyā* 123 (2008): 9; Bayani, *Dīn va Dawlat*, vol. 2, 465–6.
7. For a historiographical study of recent scholarship on the Mongols, see David Morgan, *The Mongols* (New York; Oxford: Blackwell, 1986), 27–31.
8. Two recent publications on the Mongols in Western Asia are of great importance: Bruno De Nicola and Charles Melville, *The Mongols' Middle East: Continuity and Transformation in Ilkhanid Iran* (Leiden; Boston: Brill, 2016) and Peter Jackson, *The Mongols and the Islamic World: From Conquest to Conversion* (London; New Haven: Yale University Press, 2017). On the interactions between

the Mongols and their northern and eastern neighbours, see Donald Ostrowski, *Muscovy and the Mongols: Cross-Cultural Influences on the Steppe Frontier, 1304–1589* (Cambridge: Cambridge University Press, 1998) and Gary Seaman and Marks Daniel (eds), *Rulers from the Steppe: State Formation on the Eurasian Periphery* (Los Angeles: Ethnographics Press, Centre for Visual Anthropology, University of Southern California, 1991).

9. For the literature on these stereotypes, see note 4.
10. See e.g. Allsen, *Commodity and Exchange*; Thomas Allsen, *Culture and Conquest in Mongol Eurasia* (Cambridge: Cambridge University Press, 2001); Reuven Amitai-Preiss and Michal Biran (eds), *Nomads as Agents of Cultural Change: The Mongols and their Eurasian Predecessors* (Honolulu: University of Hawaii Press, 2015). For more examples of studies with a critical approach to cross-cultural interaction, see Matthew Canepa, 'Preface: Theorizing Cross-Cultural Interaction among Ancient and Early Medieval Visual Cultures', *Ars Orientalis* 38 (2010): 21, n. 3.
11. See e.g. Ernst Grube, *Persian Painting in the Fourteenth Century: A Research Report* (Naples: Istituto Orientale di Napoli, 1978); Julian Raby and Teresa Fitzherbert, *The Court of the Il-khans, 1290–1340* (Oxford: Oxford University Press, 1996); Linda Komaroff and Stefano Carboni (eds), *The Legacy of Genghis Khan: Courtly Art and Culture in Western Asia, 1256–1353* (New York; New Haven: Metropolitan Museum of Art, 2002); Linda Komaroff, *Beyond the Legacy of Genghis Khan* (Leiden: Brill, 2006).
12. Yuka Kadoi, *Islamic Chinoiserie: The Art of Mongol Iran* (Edinburgh: Edinburgh University Press, 2009).
13. Ladan Akbarnia, '*Khita'i*: Cultural Memory and the Creation of a Mongol Visual Idiom in Iran and Central Asia' (PhD diss., Harvard University, 2007).
14. For more examples of works focusing on Ilkhanid architecture, see Lisa Golombek, 'The Cult of Saints and Shrine Architecture in the Fourteenth Century', in *Near Eastern Numismatics: Iconography, Epigraphy and History: Studies in Honor of George C. Miles*, ed. George Carpenter Miles and Dickran Kouymjian (Beirut: American University of Beirut, 1974), 419–30; Sheila Blair, 'Ilkhanid Architecture and Society: An Analysis of the Endowment Deed of the Rabʿ-i Rashīdī', *Iran: Journal of the British Institute of Persian Studies* 22 (1984): 67–90; Sheila Blair, 'The Mongol Capital of Sulṭāniyya, "The Imperial"', *Iran: Journal of the British Institute of Persian Studies* 24 (1986): 139–51; Sheila Blair, Jonathan Bloom and Richard Ettinghausen, *The Art and Architecture of Islam 1250–1800* (New Haven, CT: Yale University Press, 1994); Brigitt Hoffmann, 'The Gates of

Piety and Charity: Rašīd al-dīn Faḍl Allāh as Founder of Pious Endowments', in *L'Iran Face à la Domination Mongole*, ed. Denise Aigle (Tehran: Institut Français de Recherche en Iran, 1997), 189–201; Robert Hillenbrand, *Islamic Art and Architecture* (London: Thames & Hudson, 1999); Sheila Blair, 'Monumentality under the Mongols: The Tomb of Uljaytu at Sultaniyya', in *Text and Image in Medieval Persian Art*, ed. Sheila Blair (Edinburgh: Edinburgh University Press, 2014), 112–71.

15. Such studies consider the monuments built in Anatolia within the broader context of Mongol rule, in connection with the monuments built in the central Ilkhanid lands. See e.g. Suzan Yalman, Filiz Yenişehirlioğlu, Alev Ayaokur and Defne Karakaya (eds), *Cultural Encounters in Anatolia in the Medieval Period: The Ilkhanids in Anatolia, Symposium Proceedings, 21–22 May 2015, Ankara* (Ankara: Vehbi Koç Ankara Studies Research Center, 2019). I further discuss architecture in Anatolia under Mongol rule in Chapter 1.
16. Donald Wilber, *The Architecture of Islamic Iran: The Il Khānid Period* (New York: Greenwood, 1969).
17. Sheila Blair, *The Ilkhanid Shrine Complex at Natanz, Iran* (Cambridge, MA: Harvard University, Centre for Middle Eastern Studies, 1986).
18. For archaeological studies of Ilkhanid historic sites, see e.g. Sa'id Ganjavi, 'Kāvush-i Tappih Nur [The Excavation of Tappih-nur]', *Barrisīhā-yi Tārīkhī* 62, no. 1 (1976): 163–96; 'Abd al-Reza Muhajerinejad, *Guzārish-i Gamānih-zanī Jahat-i Ta'yīn-i Ḥarīm-i Muḥavvata-yi Tappih-nūr* [The Report of the Trial Trenching in the Area of Tappih-nur] (Zanjan: Sāzmān-i Mīrāth-i Farhangī-yi Kishvar, 2009); Abulfazl 'Ali, *Guzārish-i Faṣl-i Duvvum-i Barrisī va Shināsāyī-yi Abhar and Khurram-darra* [The Report of the Second Season of the Field Survey of Abhar and Khurram-darra] (Zanjan: Sāzmān-i Mīrāth-i Farhangī-yi Kishvar, 2006); 'Abd al-Reza Muhajerinejad, *Faṣl-i Avval-i Kāvush-i Muḥavvata-yi Jum'ih-masjid* [The First Season of Archaeological Excavation in the Area of Jum'ih-masjid] (Zanjan: Sāzmān-i Mīrāth-i Farhangī-yi Kishvar, 2009); Mehrdad 'Asgarian, Ibrahim Muhammadi and Parastou Qasemi, *Gamānih-zanī dar Qismatī az Ḥarīm-i Tārīkhī-yi Shahr-i Ghadīm-i Sultaniyya* [The Report of the Trial Trenching in the Historical City of Sultaniyya] (Zanjan: Sāzmān-i Mīrāth-i Farhangī-yi Kishvar, 2005); Rahim Velayati, *Guzārish-i Khabarī-yi Faṣl-i Avval-i Shahr-i Tārīkhī-yi Ujan* [The Report of the First Season of Excavation in the Historical City of Ujan] (Tehran: University of Tehran, 2017).

    For architectural studies of Ilkhanid historic buildings, see e.g. 'Ali-'Asghar Mirfattah, 'Pāytakht-hā-yi Īlkhānīyān: Maraghih, Tabriz va Sultaniyya

[The Ilkhanid Capital Cities: Maraghih, Tabriz, and Sultaniyya]', in *Pāytakht-hā-yi Iran* [The Capitals of Iran], ed. Muhammad Y. Kiani (Tehran: Sāzmān-i Mīrāth-i Farhangī-yi Kishvar, 1995), 517–63; Javad Shikari-Niri, 'Kankāsh dar Baqāyā-yi Raṣad-khānih-yi Maraghih [The Examination of the Architectural Remains of Maraghih Observatory]', *Pazhūhish-hā-yi Tārīkh-i Iran va Islam* 2 (2006): 61–80; Bihzad Mahdizada and Husayn Nasiri, 'Banā-hā-yi Waqfī-yi Maraghih dar Dura-yi Īlkhānī [The Endowed Buildings of Maraghih during the Ilkhanid Period]', *Waqf Mīrāth-i Jāvīdān* 89 (2015): 49–72; Homayun Rezvan and Hassan Karimian, *Sultaniyya: Ẓuhūr va Suqūṭ-i Yik Pāytakht* [Sultaniyya: The Emergence and the Decline of a Capital] (Tehran: Sāzmān-i Jahād-i Dānishgāhī-yi Tehran, 2016); Amin Muradi Rasul Musavi-Haji and Behruz 'Umrani, 'Bāz-Shināsī-yi Furm-i Miʿmārī-yi Ārām-gāh-i Ghazan dar Majmūʿa-yi Abwāb al-birrī-yi Ghazaniyya [Re-identification of the Tomb of Ghazan in the Abwāb al-birr of Ghazaniyya]', *Bāgh-e Nazar* 42 (2016): 33–44.

19. Davood Isfahanian and Alireza Khaza'ili, 'Shahr-hā-yi Tāza Bunyād dar Dura-yi Īlkhānī [The Ilkhanid New Cities]', *Nāmih-yi Anjuman* 6 (2002): 60–70; Davood Isfahanian and Alireza Khaza'ili, "Umrān-i Shahrī dar Iran-i 'Aṣr-i Mughul [Urban Development in Iran during the Time of the Mongols]', *Jughrāfiyā va Barnāmih-Rīzī* 12 (2003): 9–34.
20. Tomoko Masuya, 'The Ilkhanid Phase of Takht-i Sulaimān' (PhD diss., New York University, 1997). See also Tomoko Masuya, 'Ilkhanid Courtly Life', in *The Legacy of Genghis Khan: Courtly Art and Culture in Western Asia, 1256–1353*, ed. Linda Komaroff and Stefano Carboni (New York; New Haven: Metropolitan Museum of Art, 2002), 75–103.
21. Atri Hatef Naiemi, 'The Ilkhanid City of Sultaniyya: Some Remarks on the Citadel and the Outer City', *Iran: Journal of the British Institute of Persian Studies* 60, no. 1 (2022): 91–120.
22. See Nancy Steinhardt, 'Imperial Architecture under Mongolian Patronage: Khubilai's Imperial City of Daidu' (PhD diss., Harvard University, 1981); Nancy Steinhardt, 'The Plan of Khubilai Khan's Imperial City', *Artibus Asiae* 44, no. 2/3 (1983): 137–58; Nancy Steinhardt, 'Imperial Architecture along the Mongolian Road to Dadu', *Ars Orientalis* 18 (1988): 59–93; Nancy Steinhardt, 'Toward the Definition of a Yuan Dynasty Hall', *Journal of the Society of Architectural Historians* 47, no. 1 (1988): 57–73.
23. Tomoko Masuya, 'Seasonal Capitals with Permanent Buildings in the Mongol Empire', in *Turko-Mongol Rulers, Cities, and City Life*, ed. David Durand-Guedy (Leiden; Boston: Brill, 2013), 223–56.

24. George Lane, *Early Mongol Rule in Thirteenth Century Iran: A Persian Renaissance* (New York: Routledge Curzon, 2003), 2.
25. Flood raises a similar idea regarding the encounter between pre-modern Indic and Persianate Elites, more particularly al-Biruni and his work on Indian culture and religion, the *Kitāb fī Taḥqīq mā lil-Hind*. See Finbarr Barry Flood, *Objects of Translation: Material Culture and Medieval 'Hindu–Muslim' Encounter* (Princeton: Princeton University Press, 2009), 6.
26. For further discussion on the life and works of Rashid al-Din, see e.g. Stefan T Kamola, *Making Mongol History: Rashid Al-Din and the Jāmiʿ al-Tawārīkh* (Edinburgh: Edinburgh University Press, 2019); Atri Hatef Naiemi, 'Confronting the Foreigner: Common Policies of Rashid al-Din and Liu Bingzhong on Mongol Rule in Iran and China', *Journal of the Royal Asiatic Society* 32, no. 3 (2022): 613–33; Reuven Amitai-Preiss, 'New Material from the Mamluk Sources for the Biography of Rashid al-Din', in *The Court of the Il-khans, 1290–1340*, ed. Julian Raby and Teresa Fitzherbert (Oxford: Oxford University Press, 1996), 23–37; Brigitt Hoffmann, 'Speaking about Oneself: Autobiographical Statements in the Works of Rashīd al-Dīn', in *Rashid al-Din: Agent and Mediator of Cultural Exchanges in Ilkhanid Iran*, ed. Anna Akasoy, Charles Burnett and Ronit Yoeli-Tlalim (London: Warburg Institute, 2013), 1–14.
27. According to Rashid al-Din, Ghazan Khan himself had extensive knowledge of the history and genealogy of the Mongols from which Rashid al-Din greatly benefited. See Rashid al-Din Fazlallah Hamadani, *Jāmiʿ al-Tawārīkh* [Compendium of Chronicles], ed. Muhammad Roshan and Mustafa Musavi (Tehran: Alburz Press, 1994), vol. 2, 1,338.
28. Rashid al-Din Fazlallah Hamadani, *Tārīkh-i Mubārak-i Ghāzānī* [The Blessed History of Ghazan], ed. Karl Jahn (Hertford: Stephen Austin, 1940), 171.
29. Kamola, *Making Mongol History*, 81. See also Hatef Naiemi, 'Confronting the Foreigner', 629.
30. Rashid al-Din, *Jāmiʿ al-Tawārīkh* (Preface) 50–1.
31. Franke discusses this issue in the context of Yuan China with regard to the fact that the dynastic histories compiled under the patronage of the Mongols in China show few alien traits. The percentage of non-Chinese compilers was often lower than that of those who had a Chinese background. See Herbert Franke, 'Chinese Historiography under Mongol Rule: The Role of History in Acculturation', *Mongolian Studies* 1 (1974): 15–16.
32. Abu al-Ghasim Kashani, *Tārīkh-i Öljeytü* [The Chronicles of Öljeytü], ed. Mahin Hambly (Tehran: Bungāh-i Tarjuma va Nashr-i Kitāb, 1969) (Introduction) 16.

33. Ibid., 76, 240–1; Bayani, *Dīn va Dawlat*, vol. 2, 490. Also, in the Mamluk sources Rashid al-Din is usually called Rashid al-Dawla. In the Ilkhanid state, the title ending in al-dawla was generally applied to non-Muslims. See Amitai-Preiss, 'New Material from the Mamluk Sources', 26.
34. Wassaf presented his book in two parts to Ghazan and Öljeytü respectively in 1303 and 1312.
35. Wassaf al-Hazra and 'Abd al-Muhammad Ayati, *Taḥrīr-i Tārīkh-i Wassaf* [Wassaf's History, Rewritten] (Tehran: Bunyād-i Farhang-i Iran, 1967) (Introduction), 1–6.
36. 'Abd al-Muhammad Ayati, 'Qaṣīda-yi Wassaf al-Hazra dar Vaṣf-i Sultaniyya [The Ode of Wassaf al-Hazra describing Sultaniyya]', *Nāmih-yi Anjuman* 15 (2004): 25–30.
37. The *Yuan Shi* is the official history of the Yuan dynasty. Despite the historical importance of the source, there are no sections on the other Mongol khanates (including the Ilkhanate) in it. See Morgan, *The Mongols*, 15
38. For the biography and mission of William of Rubruck, see Willem van Ruysbroeck, *The Mission of Friar William of Rubruck: His Journey to the Court of the Great Khan Möngke, 1253–1255*, trans. Peter Jackson (Indianapolis, IN: Hackett, 2009); Morgan, *The Mongols*, 25–6.
39. For the biography and travels of Marco Polo, see Arthur Christopher Moule and Paul Pelliot, *Marco Polo: The Description of the World*, 2 volumes (London: Routledge, 1938); Marco Polo, *The Book of Ser Marco Polo, the Venetian, Concerning the Kingdoms and Marvels of the East*, 2 vols, trans. and ed. Colonel Henry Yule (London: John Murray, Albemarle Street, 1871).
40. Ruy González de Clavijo and Guy Le Strange, *Embassy to Tamerlane, 1403–1406* (London: G. Routledge, 1928). For further discussion on the visitors to Sultaniyya, see Chapter 4 and also Blair, 'Mongol Capital of Sulṭāniyya', 140–1.
41. For further discussion on European travellers to Iran in the Safavid period, see Rudi Matthee, 'The Safavids under Western Eyes: Seventeenth-Century European Travelers to Iran', *Journal of Early Modern History* 13, no. 2 (2009): 137–71.
42. Marcus Milwright, 'Imported Pottery in Ottoman Bilad al-Sham', *Turcica* 40 (2008): 122.
43. The archaeological studies of the historical city of Sultaniyya have been discussed in detail in Chapter 4.
44. Orser discusses 'historical archaeology' as 'the combination of excavated and textual information' in connection with 'global historical archaeology' and

'modern-world archaeology'. See Charles Orser, 'Historical Archaeology as Modern-World Archaeology in Argentina', *International Journal of Historical Archaeology* 12, no. 3 (2008): 182.

45. Pedro Paulo Funari, Martin Hall and Siân Jones (eds), *Historical Archaeology: Back from the Edge* (London; New York: Routledge, 1999), 1–3.
46. Charles Orser, *Encyclopedia of Historical Archaeology* (New York; London: Routledge, 2002) (Introduction), xiii–xv; Charles Orser, *Historical Archaeology*, 3rd edition (New York: Routledge, 2017), 3–11.
47. Peter Kosso, 'Epistemic Independence between Textual and Material Evidence', in *Methods in the Mediterranean: Historical and Archaeological Views on Texts and Archaeology*, ed. David Small (New York Leiden: Brill, 1995), 182. For further discussion on this topic, see Kosso's more recent work: Peter Kosso, *Knowing the Past: Philosophical Issues of History and Archaeology* (Amherst, NY: Humanity Books, 2001).
48. For a general discussion on rescue archaeology, see Jean-Paul Demoule, 'Rescue Archaeology: A European View', *Annual Review of Anthropology* 41 (2012): 611–26. For various examples of rescue archaeology in different geographical regions, see Sherene Baugher, Douglas Appler and William Moss (eds), *Urban Archaeology, Municipal Government and Local Planning: Preserving Heritage within the Commonwealth of Nations and the United States* (New York: Springer, 2017).
49. William Hanson and Ioana Oltean, *Archaeology from Historical Aerial and Satellite Archives* (New York: Springer, 2012). For more examples of the archaeological use of aerial photos, see David Kennedy and Robert Bewley, 'Aerial Archaeology in Jordan', *Antiquity* 83 (2009): 69–81; David Kennedy, Robert Bewley and F. Radcliffe, 'Aerial Archaeology in the Middle East, Progress and Achievements in Jordan (1997–2008) and the Future', *Aerial Archaeology: Studies in Archaeological Aerial Photography* 4–5 (2010): 333–7.
50. For more examples of the archaeological use of Google Earth satellite images, see David Kennedy and M. C. Bishop, 'Google Earth and the Archaeology of Saudi Arabia: A Case Study from the Jeddah Area', *Journal of Archaeological Science* 38 (2011): 1,284–93.
51. Being located in a different geographical region, however, Samarra presents a good example of the city plans generated by photogrammetric techniques from air photography. See Alastair Northedge, *The Historical Topography of Samarra* (London: British School of Archaeology in Iraq, 2005), 27–8.
52. Or 'drones', as more widely used by the public.

53. On the application of UAVs in archaeological research, see the special issue of *Drones*: '(Re)defining the Archaeological Use of UAVs'. See e.g. David Cowley, Charles Moriarty, George Geddes, Georgina Brown, Tom Wade and Caroline Nichol, 'UAVs in Context: Archaeological Airborne Recording in a National Body of Survey and Record', *Drones* 2, no. 1 (2018): 1–16.
54. Yuka Kadoi, 'Chinese and Turko-Mongol Elements in Ilkhanid and Timurid Arts, Part 1: The Mongols (c. 1250–1350)', in *A Companion to Islamic Art and Architecture*, 2 vols, ed. Finbarr Barry Flood and Gülru Necipoğlu (Oxford: Wiley-Blackwell, 2017): 643.
55. The *Great Mongol Shahnama* was completed around 1335–6, during the time of Abu Saʿid. See Eleanor Sims, 'Thoughts on a *Shahnama* Legacy of the Fourteenth Century: Four Īnjū Manuscripts and the Great Mongol *Shahnama*', in *Beyond the Legacy of Genghis Khan*, ed. Linda Komaroff (Leiden: Brill, 2006): 269–86.
56. The relationship between the illustrations of the book and events of Mongol history has been extensively examined. See e.g. Oleg Grabar and Sheila Blair, *Epic Images and Contemporary History: The Illustrations of the Great Mongol Shahnama* (Chicago: University of Chicago Press, 1980); Abolala Soudavar, 'The Saga of Abu-Saʿid Bahādor Khān, the Abu-Saʿidnāmé', in *The Court of the Il-khans, 1290–1340*, ed. Julian Raby and Teresa Fitzherbert (Oxford: Oxford University Press, 1996): 95–188.
57. Grabar and Blair, *Epic Images and Contemporary History*, 46. Drawing a parallel between the Ilkhans and the ancient Persian kings, these illustrated copies of the *Shahnama* rationalised the notion of imposed rule through the idea that the new ruler possessed the necessary *farr* (literally glory) in order to be the leader of the Iranians.
58. In addition to the Mongol figures and cultural elements, in some of the illustrations of the book Chinese motifs and designs are also visible. As Soudavar points out, the combination of culturally various pictorial components has sometimes caused odd iconographic features unrelated to the stories of the *Shahnama*, for instance Rustam painted in an imperial Chinese robe; see Soudavar, 'The Saga of Abu-Saʿid', 97.
59. Homi Bhabha, *The Location of Culture* (London; New York: Routledge, 1994).
60. Homi Bhabha, 'The Third Space', in *Identity: Community, Culture, Difference*, ed. Jonathan Rutherford (London: Lawrence & Wishart, 1990), 207–21.
61. Flood, *Objects of Translation*; Esra Akcan, 'Channels and Items of Translation', in *Art History in the Wake of the Global Turn*, ed. Jill H. Casid and Aruna D'Souza (Williamstown, MA: Sterling and Francine Clark Art Institute, 2014), 145–59.
62. Wolper calls this area 'the central Islamic land' because we are witnessing the

emergence of some of the most recognisable components of the medieval city (such as mosques, madrasas, khanqahs – and other buildings associated with Sufism – and mausoleums) in this region for the first time. See Ethel Wolper, 'Islamic Architecture and Institutions in the Late Medieval City', *History Compass* 12 (2014): 912.

63. Charles Melville, 'The Mongols in Iran', in *The Legacy of Genghis Khan: Courtly Art and Culture in Western Asia, 1256–1353*, ed. Linda Komaroff and Stefano Carboni (New York; New Haven: Metropolitan Museum of Art, 2002), 37. Over this period, a pre-Islamic concept known as *Iranzamīn* (the Land of Iran) or *Iranshahr* (the City of Iran) was revived. Under the Mongols, within the conceptual framework of *Iranzamīn*, the connections between Iran and the Central Asian world strengthened and the idea of the political and cultural autonomy of Iran was encouraged by the Mongols and their Persian administrators. See Melville, 'Mongols in Iran', 43.
64. Komaroff and Carboni, *Legacy of Genghis Khan*, 6–7.
65. *The Legacy of Genghis Khan: Courtly Art and Culture in Western Asia, 1256–1353* was the exhibition organised by Linda Komaroff and Stefano Carboni. The exhibition was held at the Metropolitan Museum of Art from November 2002 to February 2003 and at the Los Angeles County Museum of Art from April to July 2003. A publication with the same title accompanies the exhibition. In the introduction of the book Komaroff and Carboni write that 'culturally, the Mongol invasions and the so-called *Pax Mongolica* had the effect of energizing Iranian art and infusing it with novel forms, meanings, and motifs that were further disseminated throughout the Islamic world. In uniting Eastern and Western Asia for over a century, the Mongols created a unique opportunity for an unrestricted cultural exchange that forever altered the face of art in Iran and made it a focal point of innovation and synthesis for the next three hundred years. This, too, was Genghis Khan's legacy'.
66. Allsen, *Culture and Conquest*, 4.

1

The Western and Eastern Neighbours of the Ilkhanid State

Ilkhanid cities did not form in isolation. The cities built under the auspices of the Ilkhans during the post-conquest era developed in accordance with the architectural traditions that had already been established by their predecessors in Iran, as well as the patterns that were being practised by their contemporaries beyond the borders of the Ilkhanate, in Western and Eastern Asia. Thus, the concept of Ilkhanid urbanism should be considered not only in the historical context of medieval Iran,[1] but also in the broader setting of the medieval Islamic world on the one hand and Mongol Central/Eastern Asia on the other.

In this chapter, I first explore the major structural and conceptual transformation of the cities that developed between the twelfth and sixteenth centuries across a geographical area known as the 'central Islamic lands', including today's Egypt, Syria, Iraq, Jordan and Turkey.[2] I delve more deeply into the Ilkhanids' western frontier, Anatolia, as the area was part of their 'sphere of influence', and important shifts in architectural patronage occurred there during the Mongol era.[3] Then, I shift my focus to the major urban centres built under the patronage of the Great Khans of the Mongol Empire in Central Asia and China. While the focus of attention is the contemporaries of Ilkhanid cities, I am aware that the urban patterns generated in the pre-Mongol period certainly affected the course of subsequent development. Therefore, in the last section of the chapter I touch upon two cities, Isfahan and Nishapur, that flourished under the Seljuq and the Khwarazm Shahs, prior to the Mongol invasion. This overview sheds some light on the context in which Ilkhanid cities were born. The examination of Western and Eastern Asian cities may not necessarily improve our knowledge of Ilkhanid cities due to their dissimilar social, political and religious conditions. We are dealing with cities that developed across a continent over a span of several centuries. Nevertheless, unravelling the materiality and spatiality of Ilkhanid cities' antecedents or contemporaries paves the way for a better understanding of the forces that might have affected the evolution of the Mongol-sponsored cities.

The 'Islamic City'

The Arab conquests of the seventh and early eighth centuries brought changes to the spatial and temporal structure of the cities in the Middle East, Central Asia and North Africa, although the gradual process of change did not cause a sudden discontinuity with Late Antiquity during the early period.[4] From the ninth century, nonetheless, the material and visual cultures of the Islamic world moved away more noticeably from Late Antique patterns and practices.[5] A number of newly founded cities in this period denote this distance in their built environment.[6] The architectural and archaeological evidence shows that the urban and rural settlements across the Islamic world broke even more significantly with Late Antique roots during the tenth and eleventh centuries. Over the medieval period (roughly between the twelfth and sixteenth centuries), many cities throughout Muslim lands experienced a comprehensive transformation. While the changes to early Islamic pre-existing cities were mostly confined to their physical fabrics, medieval cities underwent a metamorphosis in different socio-religious, economic and political arenas, besides a change in their architectural structure.

The medieval period witnessed the formation of cities that gained a certain uniformity in terms of both institutions and architecture. Many Islamic institutions, such as mosques, madrasas, mausoleums and khanqahs, which were associated with certain architectural buildings with distinctive forms and functions, fundamentally changed the physical and mental character of Islamic cities.[7] The cities developed in response to the new needs of dynasties, which had passed the period of military expansion and were starting to show signs of stabilisation. The building of new urban centres seems to have been part of the development of the concept of Islamic kingship in which the grandeur of the constructions expressed the power and glory of their founders.[8] Contrary to early Islamic urbanism marked by the transition from pre-existing urban settlements to Islamic 'medina' (Arabic *madīna*), the medieval period should be perceived as the establishment phase of the so-called 'Islamic city'.

The 'Islamic city' is a term with 'colonialist overtones';[9] such a city does not literally exist, but has developed a life of its own in scholarship. At the beginning of the twentieth century, study of the 'Islamic city' was based on two approaches. The first, deriving from English and German Orientalist studies, attributed the structure of Islamic cities to social and religious factors.[10] The second approach, deriving from French Orientalist studies, highlighted the distinctive characteristics of the architecture and urban planning of the city in the Islamic world.[11] Both approaches attempted to establish how the structure of the traditional 'Islamic city' is different from that of the 'western city'.[12] This body of studies, however, has been heavily critiqued.[13] One of the methodological problems of these studies was that they explained the physical features of the 'Islamic city' on the basis of a few cases in a specific region (mostly North Africa),[14] and then applied the same urban model to many cities in different regions of the Islamic world. Furthermore, many of these studies focused on one particular historical phase in different cities and forgot that Islamic cities have evolved over time. In the 1950s, this Orientalist model of approaching Islamic cities was refined by some scholars.[15] In later decades more flexible models were suggested, which were applied to the study of a wide range of cities across the Islamic world in different historical periods.[16] A new phase of scholarship was begun in the 1980s proposing that every city has its own unique identity and should be analysed in its own distinct historical and geographical conditions.[17] This long process of the evolution of scholarship on the 'Islamic city' resulted in the formation of a regional approach to the study of cities in the twenty-first century.[18]

A rather vivid image of the built environment of the medieval city, as well as the socio-political and economic interactions of the city dwellers, has formed on the basis of this substantial body of literature on the evolving concept of the 'Islamic city'. Despite the formation of the notion of a medieval 'Islamic city' as a well-defined phenomenon, urban structure did not take exactly the same form in all the different regions throughout Muslim lands. Being affected by various political and socio-religious conditions in each region, medieval cities also acquired regionally diverse characters.[19] Adopting regional approaches to these cities helps us to understand different geographical and cultural forces, along with Islamic juridical and legal parameters[20] that shaped the identity of numerous urban sites spreading all over the Islamic world.

The complex and multi-layered nature of the medieval city defines distinct areas of research for different cities. In addition to the study of the urban fabric in individual cases, the socio-religious and architectural transformation of the medieval Islamic city as a whole needs to be addressed. As will be discussed in the following pages, the analysis of different processes of change will help to uncover the tangible and intangible forces shaping the distinctive nature of the medieval city. This analysis sheds light on the structural components of the cities, as well as on different social classes and urban institutions that contributed to the transition from early Islamic urban centres to medieval cities.[21]

The socio-religious transformation of medieval cities in the 'central Islamic lands'

The disintegration of the Abbasid Empire in 1258, followed by the decline of the caliphate and the rise of local princes, commenced a new era in Islamic history that is characterised by important changes in the social structure of the city. This period sees the emergence of new social players in the medieval society, such as military aristocracy, patrician families, 'ulama' (orthodox scholars) or religious elite and Sufis. These players maintained the balance of power, although they were constantly threatened by one another and sometimes lost their authority over civil bureaucracy for a while. The social transformation of the medieval Middle East is also marked by 'the transition from central control of resources to increasing private control'.[22] Hence, besides the above-mentioned social groups, the role of individuals, such as merchants, became more significant and their political and economic power increased. Powerful individuals attracted the support of commoners through the foundation of charitable institutions. The waqf, or charitable endowment, functioned as a mechanism that converted wealth and possessions into social prestige in the medieval Islamic world.[23] This function was not the claimed reason for the existence of the pious endowments, however.[24]

The religious transformation of the medieval society is characterised to a large degree by 'a popular atmosphere of religious excitement':[25] the restoration of Sunnism or the Sunni revival[26] on the one hand and the rise of Sufism and the expansion of popular religion on the other. Between the two, we should highlight the central position of Sufism. The dissemination of mysticism and Sufism alongside the rise of the khanqah significantly changed the medieval society. The foreign military elite, who were dependent on new sources of validation, regarded Sufi saints as sources of legitimation and sought to gain the blessing and spiritual protection associated with these figures through supporting living saints or by being buried within the shrine complexes around the graves of dead saints.[27] The Sufis stepped out of their traditional mystical world and established their position in the congregational life of commoners. Sermons and various religious celebrations were the occasions through which Sufi shaykhs strengthened their links with the common people. Mediating between the military regimes and their subjects, Sufi institutions, together with 'ulama', played a pivotal role in the improvement of the internal balance of these societies.

The architectural and urban transformation of medieval cities in the 'central Islamic lands'

The medieval Islamic cities were characterised by urban and architectural transformations.[28] In addition to the institutional changes mentioned above that affected the appearance of the medieval city, the drastic alterations of structural elements, particularly citadels and pious institutions, also led to the physical transformation of the Islamic urban sites. Regardless of the sociopolitical outcome, the fall of the Abbasid caliphate, as the central pillar of power, and the rise of the Turkish military states significantly transformed the architectural character of the city. The process of political decentralisation that gradually pervaded the medieval Islamic world increased the importance of military architecture in the cities. As a result, citadels were constructed in a number of major cities, such as Damascus, Aleppo and Mosul. The citadels were the new centres of power and government of the military elite, and consisted of royal mosques, palaces and places for ruling family and the military.[29] In other words, the earlier form of Islamic citadel as a military outpost was replaced by a new institution that functioned as the centre of the court and the administration in the medieval city.[30]

In the late eleventh century, the emergence of the court-citadel as the seat of government and the ruler, and the locus of his military-political power, contributed to a large degree to the architectural transformation of the medieval city. Court complexes formerly situated away from the urban centres were attached to the cities. The location of the citadel, usually on an elevated position, allowed the court to separate itself physically from the city dwellers, but consolidated visual interaction between the ruling class and their subjects. The position of the citadel highlights its symbolic role as a dominating element, not merely a defensive unit within the city.[31] The court was linked to the city in two ways: first, through the roads that led the dwellers in the citadel from the citadel gates to the congregational mosque of the city and the major markets; second, through religious institutions such as madrasas and shrines located in the citadel. Although Talmon-Heller describes the citadel as a place of interaction between rulers and their subjects, such communication was limited to particular classes of society, such as ʿulama' and Sufis and the merchants and artisans who were allowed to enter the citadel.[32]

The other urban element that underwent major changes was the madrasa. In addition to the rise in the number of madrasas, there were changes in the transmission of religious knowledge in these institutions.[33] Following the foundation of the great Nizamiyya madrasa in Baghdad by Nizam al-Mulk (d. 1092) – the Persian vizier of the Turkish Seljuq sultans Alp Arslan (r. 1063–72) and Malik Shah (r. 1072–92) – and in different parts of the Seljuq Empire thereafter, the independent religious character of madrasas diminished. Considering the various financial sources that funded the vast network of Nizamiyya madrasas (including Nizam al-Mulk, sultans and high officials), Tabbaa interprets madrasas as 'institutions for the state'. This role seems to have continued into the post-Seljuq era (the twelfth and thirteenth centuries), so that the madrasas founded by Sunni dynasties were understood by modern scholars as forming a counterweight to Shiʿism. The architectural form of the madrasa, revealing its new character as a state institution, also embodied both palatial and religious qualities.[34]

The emergence of a large number of small mosques, chapels, mausoleums (in the form of free-standing buildings or as part of charitable complexes), shrines, *ribāṭs*[35] and monasteries began another remarkable string of changes in the urban landscape of the Middle East in the twelfth century. These architectural constructions gave Islam 'an institutional importance and urban visibility' and paved the way for the urban settlements to become genuine Islamic cities.[36] Grabar suggests that such varying architectural structures were built in response to different forms of Muslim piety that started to exist, as well as the need for smaller social units (family, quarter and profession).[37]

Other socio-religious factors, such as the society's further religiosity and the growth of opposing religious trends (such as partisans of the four Sunni schools of law or diverse Shiʿa sects), were also crucial to the formation of numerous new pious institutions. In addition, Sufism and its associated architecture impacted the landscape of the city morphologically.[38]

In the twelfth and thirteenth centuries, under the Zangid (r. 1127–1251) and Ayyubid (r. 1169–1260) dynasties, urban life in Syria and the northern section of Mesopotamia prospered remarkably. Aleppo, Damascus and some other Syrian cities were transformed into 'cosmopolitan Muslim intellectual centres' due to the sudden growth of construction and the availability of hundreds of jobs, attracting a large group of teachers and students to these cities. In addition to these two groups, one should highlight the role of other classes of immigrants, including amirs (commanders), 'ulama' and bureaucrats, as a 'central catalyst' in the prosperity and architectural development of the Ayyubid cities.[39]

Under the Mamluks (r. 1250–1517), a thoroughly different pattern of architectural patronage can be seen. The Mamluk patrons focused less on the large-scale urban projects, the royal palaces and the congregational mosques that had been the centre of attention for earlier Islamic dynasties.[40] Instead, the institutions dealing with mysticism, law and theology – those which were accommodated in the buildings with more moderate proportions – benefited from the patronage of the Mamluks. Uncovering the reasons for their patronage policy, Rabbat suggests that the Mamluks, who were ethnically and linguistically different from their subjects, sought their acceptance. Therefore, they established their position as defenders of Sunni orthodoxy, supported the religious class and endowed pious structures to prove their religiosity.[41] Under the Mamluks, the Sufi movement also evolved into institutional communities. Consequently, the central position of the traditional congregational mosques was overshadowed by the emergence of other building forms, such as khanqah, madrasa and *zāwīya*, that better fulfilled their demands and purposes.[42]

The Mamluks were the heirs to the Ayyubid ideology and like their predecessors pursued the purpose of serving Sunni institutions. The architectural and urban foundations of the Mamluks manifested the grandeur and greatness of Sunni Islam, the Islam that developed with the protection and support of Mamluk amirs. The major monuments of the Mamluk period represent remarkable elements of 'palatial symbolism'.[43] The Mamluks were not creative patrons, in the sense that they did not add any new monumental types or building methods to what they had inherited from Zangid and Ayyubid architecture. However, they constructed lavishly decorated buildings with astonishing speed, which immortalised their powerful founders.[44]

While I have provided a concise broad overview of major socio-religious and architectural transformations in medieval cities across the 'central Islamic lands', the importance of delving deeper into the Ilkhanids' western frontier, Anatolia, should be emphasised. It is crucial to include the region in the examination of Ilkhanid architecture and urbanism and to analyse the monuments built there within the wider context of Mongol rule, alongside those constructed in the central domain. However, given the book's stress on the Ilkhanids' court-sponsored architectural endeavours and their scarcity in Anatolia, the following will simply constitute a brief discussion of the latest ideas concerning the architecture of the region during the Mongol period.

Anatolia under Mongol rule

When the Mongols entered the Anatolian peninsula in the 1240s, people of diverse religious, ethnic and cultural backgrounds resided there under the rule of a local Seljuk dynasty. Diversity increased during the thirteenth and fourteenth centuries as numerous scholars, religious leaders and individuals in pursuit of wealth and opportunity from across the Islamic world were drawn to the region, actively contributing to its cultural prosperity.[45] Despite the cultural and political significance of Mongol Anatolia, the region has not received sufficient scholarly attention. This is partly due to its distance from the Ilkhanid capitals in Tabriz and Sultaniyya, and partly because of traditional historiography, which diminishes the importance of the Mongol era, viewing it primarily as a transitional period between the Seljuks and the Ottomans.[46]

This section aims to counteract the marginalisation of Mongol Anatolia in scholarly discourse by highlighting the architectural atmosphere of the region under the Ilkhans. Nevertheless, here we confine our argument to brief mentions of occasions when connections between Anatolia and the central Ilkhanid lands are most evident, for three reasons: first, the focus of the book is on the construction activities of the Ilkhanid court within the borders of present-day Iran; second, in spite of the Mongol conquest of Anatolia, direct governance of the region by the Ilkhans themselves, and thus their personal involvement in architectural endeavours, rarely occurred; and third, as extensively discussed by Patricia Blessing in *Rebuilding Anatolia after the Mongol Conquest*,[47] while being affected by the historical, economic and cultural conditions of Western Asia, architecture in Mongol Anatolia was connected more with local dynamics than with the imperial dynamics of Ilkhanid rule.

To emphasise the significance of integrating Anatolia into the study of the Ilkhanate, it is important to note that, as with Ilkhanid Iran, recent scholarship describes medieval Anatolia as a space where negotiations between newcomers and locals encouraged cultural exchange.[48] In this regard, Mongol Anatolia could serve as a significant point of comparison for future research addressing transcultural interactions across the Ilkhanate and beyond.

Throughout much of the Ilkhanid period, architectural projects in Anatolia were chiefly sponsored by two emerging groups of patrons: individuals affiliated with the Seljuk sultan (who lacked authority and resources at that time) and those aligned with Ilkhanid rulers.[49] Among the prolific new patrons in the second half of the thirteenth century, the names of two political figures stand out: Mu'in al-Din Sulayman Parvanih (d. 1277) and Sahib 'Ata Fakhr al-Din 'Ali (d. 1285), who sponsored various types of monuments, including madrasas, mosques, khanqahs and caravanserais across Anatolia. The nature of architectural patronage, however, underwent a slight change after the death of these two. Modest constructions such as mausoleums and *zāwīya*s (or *zawāyā*) funded by Sufi communities replaced the large foundations financed by individual wealthy patrons.[50]

Conducting stylistic analyses of numerous cases constructed throughout Anatolia by patrons with diverse intentions and motivations is obviously beyond the scope of this section. Instead, given my aim of establishing more direct links between Anatolian architecture and what was commonly practised in the Ilkhanid central domain, I focus on Sivas, where one of the few examples of buildings directly funded by patrons from Iran still exists.

The Çifte Minareli Medrese was built in 1271/2 during the decade when the Ilkhanids attempted to strengthen their military control over Anatolia. The patron was Shams al-Din Juvayni (d. 1284), a senior official in the Ilkhanid court and the brother of the famous historian and statesman 'Ata Malik Juvayni. Only the lavishly decorated façade of the medrese has survived, embracing a noteworthy foundation inscription. The latter displays the name of the patron, accompanied by royal titles such as the great stateman, the king of the viziers of the world, the *ṣāḥib dīwān*.[51] Interestingly, it includes neither the name of the powerless Seljuk sultan nor that of the seated Ilkhanid ruler, Abaqa Khan (r. 1265–82), who had not yet converted to Islam, and thus could not be appropriately fitted into the foundation inscription of a religious building.

Blessing draws our attention to an intriguing dichotomy here: an innovation alongside a continuation of established traditions. The former is exemplified by the foundation inscription of the building including the name of an Ilkhanid patron while excluding the name of a ruler, thus diverging from a common practice observed in earlier Seljuk buildings in Anatolia. The latter is demonstrated through robust local architectural references, such as the plastic vegetal motifs present in earlier monuments across the region of Sivas.[52] Despite the appearance of the Ilkhanid patron's name in the text, which may seem to justify the presence of imported components such as the brick and tile decoration, elements belonging to the 'stylistic vocabulary of Sivas' are strong enough to overshadow Iranian influences.

The Çifte Minareli Medrese vividly exemplifies the prevailing tendency towards localism in architecture in Anatolia during the latter decades of the thirteenth century. This inclination is further evident in subsequent monuments erected in the region during the early fourteenth century, following the Ilkhans' conversion to Islam. In spite of occasional mentions of ruling Ilkhans in endowment inscriptions, the buildings themselves barely display the style of Ilkhanid architecture in Iran. Notably, the hallmark feature – monumentality – found no resonance in Anatolia.[53]

The preference for local forms and materials extends past the Mongol period. On a broader scale, in medieval Anatolia, there existed multiple architectural styles rather than one single style imposed by imperial patronage. However, among different designs, materials and working methods made available to craftsmen due to increased mobility, and in the absence of a unified style promoted by imperial patronage, local patrons and craftsmen turned to local traditions while also incorporating non-native elements.[54]

Despite the centrality of localism in architecture in Mongol Anatolia and the absence of significant traces of Iranian architectural influence, according to this brief study of Anatolian architecture, it remains important to consider this region when examining Ilkhanid architecture and urbanism in this book. Architectural and urban projects located outside the heartland, traditionally regarded as peripheral, play a vital role in helping us to understand the dynamics between the capital/centre and the provinces/peripheries.

Major Urban Projects of the Mongols in Central Asia and China

Paralleling the temporal and spatial transformation of the cities in the 'central Islamic lands', the construction activities of the Mongols, who had been expanding the Great Mongol Empire since the early decades of the thirteenth century, increased in Central Asia and China. Many new urban centres emerged, due to the imperial expansion of the Mongols and the sudden arrival of wealth and a sedentary population into the Mongolian steppe and the adjacent lands.[55] Contrary to the above brief survey of the 'Islamic city', what will be presented in the following pages is an in-depth study of Mongol cities in Eastern Asia. What necessitates such different approaches to the urban foundations of the eastern and western neighbours of the Ilkhans? Apart from certain visual elements (such as dragons, phoenixes, lotuses and clouds) pointing towards the dominant existence of East Asian visual culture in the Ilkhanate, what other reasons lead us to prioritise Mongol architectural projects in Central and Eastern Asia over other concurrent movements happening across the Islamic world?

The material evidence associated with the presence of the Ilkhans in Iran attests to the emergence of non-Iranian elements in the material culture of this period.[56] While the traces of several Western and Eastern cultures can be uncovered in Ilkhanid art and architecture, the Ilkhans' cousins in China and Central Asia, who had come from the same cultural background as the Mongol rulers of Iran, seem to have been the most influential source of inspiration for their subordinates in Iran. The Yuan dynasty, established by Mongol nomads in 1271, was the most powerful khanate after the division of the Mongol Empire. The extensive interactions between the Yuan dynasty and the Ilkhanids in different fields provided an ideal context for the transfer of ideas from East Asia to the West and vice versa. Furthermore, in view of the fact that the Ilkhans, at least during the first decades of their presence in Iran, were subordinates to the Khans of Yuan China, one can raise the possibility that they might have been obligated to follow some aspects of the Yuan dynasty's royal protocol, if there was any, such as an official system of rules overseeing their architectural activities.

Whether the Mongol emperors of Yuan China were more prolific builders or whether, simply, a larger amount of archaeological material has been unearthed in the East, we have a clearer picture of their urban foundations than we have of those of their relatives in Ilkhanid Iran. Examination of these projects is enlightening about possible common roots from which some of the features of Ilkhanid architecture grew. It could also throw light on the mechanisms through which the interaction between native traditions of the Mongols and the long-established architectural conventions of their sedentary hosts (China, and subsequently Iran) might have occurred. What will be understood about Yuan cities is expected to be illuminating as regards the urban centres that developed under the auspices of their counterparts in the Ilkhanate.

A brief overview of Mongol urban settlements

Prior to the foundation of the Mongol Empire, the residential architecture of the Mongols consisted mainly of tents, although more permanent elements were gradually added to the structure of their tents; for instance, by the thirteenth century Mongol tents had wooden doors. Archaeological findings and written sources reveal that around this time, seasonal quarters of the Mongols were formed of both temporary and permanent structures. For example, while Chinggis Khan continued his nomadic lifestyle, he moved between three fixed seasonal quarters, the most important of which was the Great *Ordu* or Chinggis Khan's Palace.[57] The Great *Ordu* was possibly located in a permanent place, the Avraga site in North Mongolia. The focal element of the site was a large platform on which Chinggis's tent was probably pitched. Archaeological excavations uncovered two layers of construction on the platform, suggesting two phases of development in the site: Chinggis Khan's Great *Ordu* and a shrine built later in his memory in the exact location of his *ordu*. Historical texts report that many important *qūrīltāys*[58] as well as rituals to commemorate the imperial ancestors were held at the site.[59]

The Mongol conquest of China in the thirteenth century affected the residential architecture in the Central Asian steppes to a remarkable degree and changed the shape of the Mongols' settlements. Following the conquest, the Mongols camped outside the pre-existing cities because of the availability of water and space. These encampments evolved over the years into their new cities. Some of these newly founded cities retained part of their qualities as seasonal camps, and some of them amalgamated with other cities and formed larger urban centres. There were also pre-existing cities which were either modified by the Mongols or re-used by them without any change.[60]

The settlements that developed under Mongol patronage gradually found their distinctive characteristics and fulfilled different needs and expectations of their patrons. They ranged from major urban sites to smaller walled villages where farmers resided. For instance, the capitals of *uluses*[61] functioned as residences and administrative centres of the rulers of the Great Mongol Empire. Karakorum, the capital of the Empire, founded by Chinggis Khan in 1220 (in Mongolia), Shangdu, the summer capital of Qubilay Khan established in 1256 (in Inner Mongolia Autonomous Region, China) and Daidu, the capital of the Yuan dynasty from 1272 to 1363, founded by Qubilay Khan in 1267 (in Beijing, China), are the most remarkable settlements of this type (Figure 1.1). In addition to the capitals, there were regional government centres where the local administrative units were placed. In the regional capitals, located at the sites of the capitals of the earlier dynasties, the government used the pre-existing buildings. The regional centres mostly consisted of governmental buildings, but possibly lacked palaces. There were also pleasure-palace complexes (*xinggong* in Chinese),[62] which were the sites of hunting and feasts for the Mongol emperors located in hunting grounds usually near a lake. Urban structures gradually formed around these complexes in order to accommodate those who were engaged in maintaining the palaces. Chaghan Na'ur was one of these pleasure residences, built by Qubilay Khan in 1280 (in Guyuan County, China). In the course of their seasonal migrations, the emperors divided their nomadic life between different pleasure palaces. Besides enjoyment, important political and administrative matters as well as different royal and religious ceremonies were organised in these centres. The Chinggisid family and high-ranking officials resided in 'aristocratic cities'.[63] They were private cities built by members of the royal family or by those notables who had important positions in the government. The land the cities were built on was usually bestowed on them by the emperors. Finally, the humblest Mongol settlements

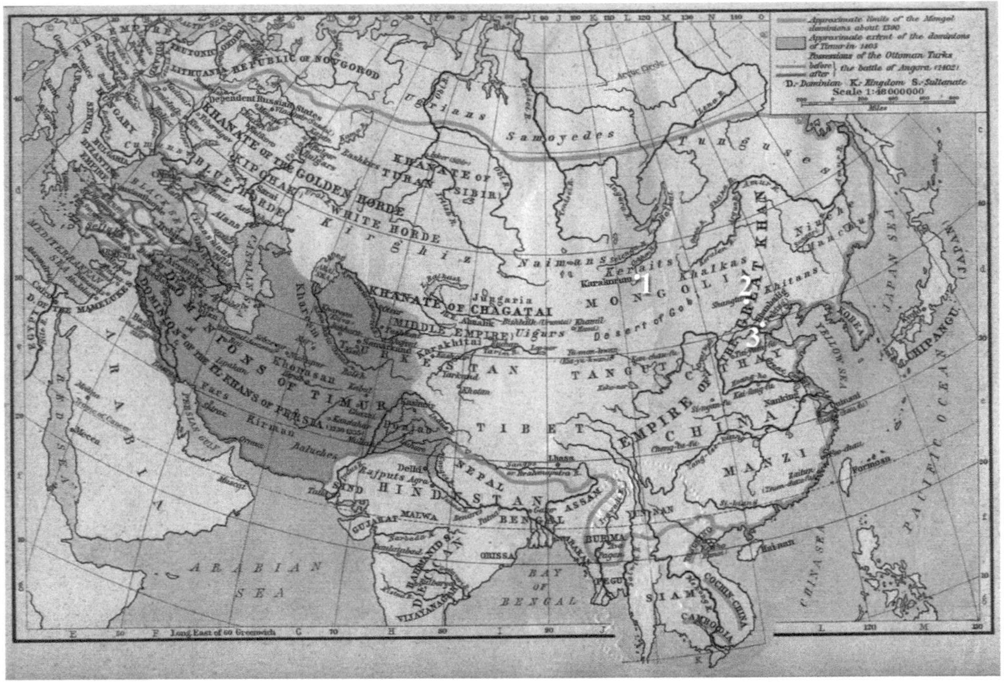

Figure 1.1 The Mongol Dominions, 1300–1405. From *The Historical Atlas* by William R. Shepherd, 1923.
1. Karakorum
2. Shangdu
3. Daidu
Courtesy of the University of Texas Libraries, University of Texas at Austin

were agricultural centres where archaeological excavations have revealed no remains of large buildings. Simple objects used in daily life and traces of streets on the grounds are the only evidence unearthed in these sites.[64]

We have a clearer idea of the general layout of the Mongols' imperial cities than of their individual structures, due to the nature of available textual and archaeological evidence. For example, the descriptions offered by contemporary observers, as well as the material uncovered during the excavations, suggest that Mongol cities were usually oriented cardinally. Their main axis ran north-north-west to south-south-east. Masuya proposes that this orientation must have been related to the orientation of Mongol tents, which was based on the direction of sunlight and its significance for the Mongols.[65] In his report to King Louis, William of Rubruck says that the Mongols pitched their dwellings with the doorway towards the south while they placed the master's couch at the northern end.[66] The same arrangement is also observed by William in Möngke's palace at Karakorum. He says that the palace had three doors on the south side and that the Khan sat opposite the doors at the northern end.[67] In the palatial enclosures of Mongol cities, such as Karakorum and Daidu, the private residence of the Khan was usually located behind this audience hall.

Inside their tents, they situated the women's position on the eastern (left) side of the master and the men's position on his western (right) side. Similarly, within their encampments, the tents of the chief wife were pitched to the left and the residences of the eldest son were erected to the right of the Khan's tent. This feature seems to appear later in the palatial enclosures of Mongol cities. In Daidu the residence of the Crown Prince was built to the west (right) of the emperor's residence. Contrary to the Chinese tradition of placing the residence of the Crown Prince to the east of the imperial residence, this feature of Daidu must have been proposed by the Mongol patrons of the city.

In several palatial complexes, there were round or polygonal structures that worked as pleasure palaces. Their form may have been derived from the circular shape of their tents, and thus is regarded as a sign of the long-lasting loyalty of the Mongols to their nomadic conventions.[68] Temples and churches associated with various religions were the other elements of the cities. While the Mongols showed a willingness to build Chinese-style halls and chambers, they still allocated restricted areas of imperial cities to their tents. Regardless of the scale of the urban site, whether as large as the outer city of Shangdu or as small as the enclosure at Daidu, the 'tent dwelling section' was a standard feature of imperial Mongol city planning.[69]

In the formation of the thirteenth- and fourteenth-century imperial Mongolian cities, Steinhardt attributes a pivotal role to Chinese imperial urban planning, whose fundamental principles such as 'four-sided enclosure,[70] gates, corner towers, defensive projections, clearly articulated and directed space, axial orientation and alignment, wards of restricted population or function, accessibility by water, vast size and huge population' are clearly observable in Mongolian imperial urbanism. This influence is also noticeable in architectural decoration such as glazed ceramic roof tiles, animal-faced stone sculpture[71] and turtle-based and entwined dragon-headed stele. Therefore, in addition to the nomadic culture partially retained by Mongol khans in their newly founded cities in China, one can observe the distinct presence of Chinese traditions brought by Chinese officers, architects and urban planners who were designated by the Mongols to design and build their cities.

Among the numerous settlements founded by the Mongol emperors throughout the eastern sectors of the vast territory of the Empire of the Great Khans, the focus of the following discussion will be on three major imperial cities: Karakorum, Shangdu and Daidu. The selection of the cases is based on two criteria. First, the cities, for a period during their lifetime if not the whole of it, were designated as the capitals of the Mongols, and thus they are believed to share a considerable number of characteristics with the Ilkhanids' administrative and political capitals in Iran. Second, all the above-mentioned cases were founded, or simply expanded, during almost the same time period as the Ilkhans undertook their major urban projects in the north-west of Iran.

Karakorum

Karakorum is the first known imperial walled town constructed by the Mongols. The city was located several kilometres east of the bank of the Orkhon River, north of Ulan Bator, the present capital of the Mongolian People's Republic (Figure 1.2). Karakorum was known as a city of tents throughout its history, but by the mid-1230s the tent city was converted into a walled settlement by Ögedey (the third son of Chinggis Khan, r. 1229–41). In the south-western part of the site, there is a walled area oriented along a

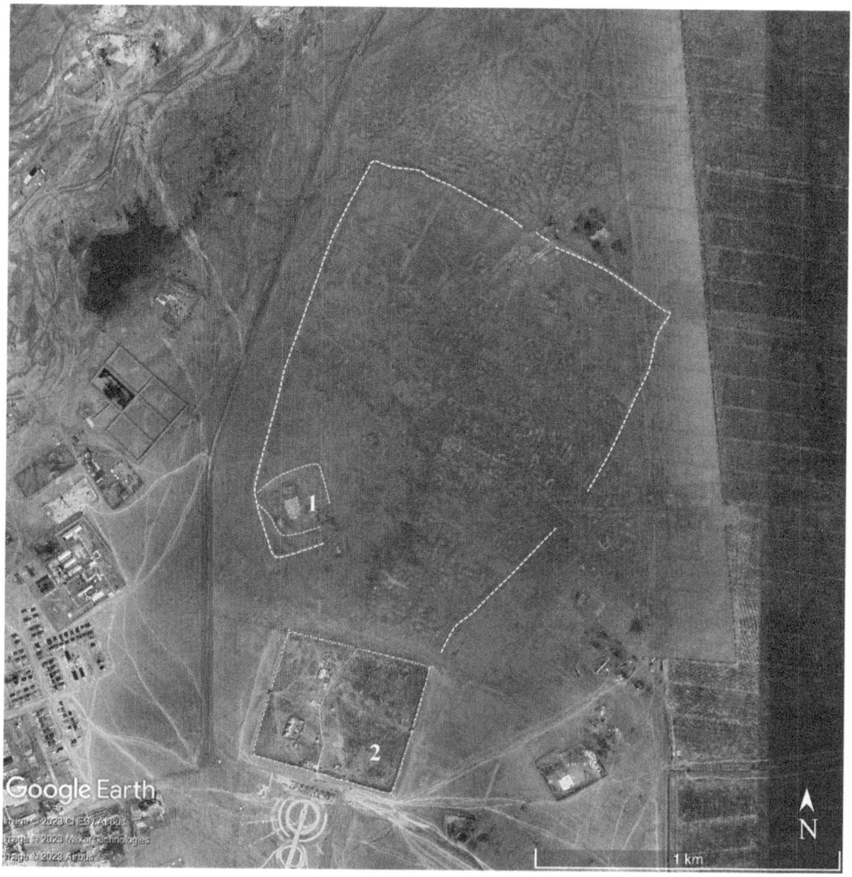

Figure 1.2 Satellite image of Karakorum and its surroundings. The dashed line shows the approximate area of the city.
1. Ögedey's 'palace area', later known as a Buddhist temple
2. Erdene Zuu monastery
Google Earth (imagery date: 31 May 2022)
47° 12′ 34.21″ N, 102° 50′ 48.12″ E, eye alt 2.39 km
CNES/Airbus 2023, Maxar Technologies 2023, Airbus 2023. Accessed 4 September 2023

north-east–south-west axis, which was investigated by the Russian archaeologist Sergej Kiselev in 1949 and was supposed to be Ögedey's 'palace area' (Figure 1.3). However, German-Mongolian collaborative examination of Kiselev's so-called 'palace area' in 2001 revealed that this sector of the site contains the remains of a Buddhist temple contemporary with the imperial city of Karakorum.[72] Excavation continued in the walled Erdene Zuu monastery that

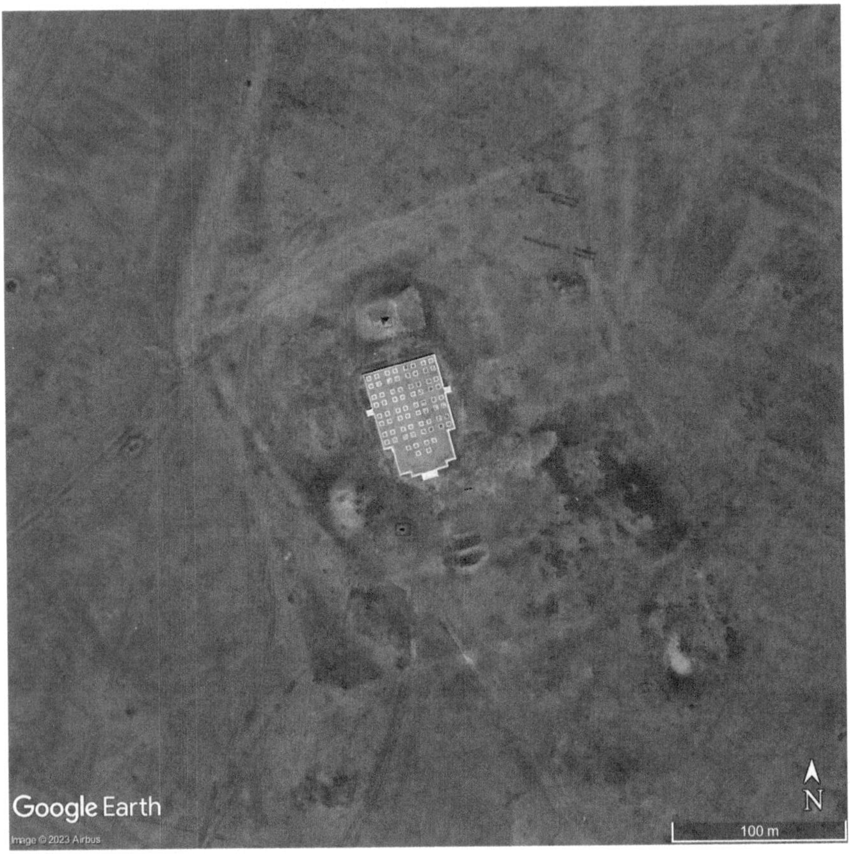

Figure 1.3 Satellite image of Ögedey's 'palace area', later known as a Buddhist temple in Karakorum. The halls have been unearthed.
Google Earth (imagery date: 31 May 2022)
47° 12′ 25.13″ N, 102° 50′ 28.31″ E, eye alt 375 m.
Airbus 2023. Accessed 4 September 2023

lies to the south of Karakorum in order to locate the palace of the Great Khan. The walls unearthed below the monastery possibly belonged to the palace of Ögedey and Möngke.[73]

Literary sources are rather illuminating regarding the general physical features of Karakorum. In his description of the city, Rashid al-Din briefly writes about some of the structures founded by Ögedey. He mentions that in the yurt (*ordu*) of Karakorum an exceedingly tall palace was built that embraced a tall pavilion in the middle. The edifice was lavishly decorated and was named *qarshī*.[74] Ögedey designated the complex as his auspicious residence (*takhtgāh-i mubārak*) and ordered his brothers, sons and other princes to erect their splendid buildings around it. All the foundations gradually formed the city of Karakorum.[75] The description of Karakorum offered by Rubruck as a contemporary observer is also of great significance. He writes:

> It [Karakorum] contains two quarters: one for the Saracens, where there are bazaars and where many traders gather due to the constant proximity of the camp and to the great number of envoys; the other is the quarter of the Cataians, who are all craftsmen. Set apart from these quarters lie large palaces belonging to the court secretaries. There are twelve idol temples belonging to different peoples, two mosques ... and one Christian church at the far end of the town. The town is enclosed by a mud wall and has four gates. At the east gate are sold millet and other kinds of grain ... at the western, sheep and goats are on sale; at the southern, cattle and wagons; and at the northern, horses.[76]

William's description of Karakorum is the first that is currently available to us from a visitor to the place.[77] The report contains interesting information on the general physical characteristics of the city, part of which, however, has been questioned in view of the most recent archaeological findings at Karakorum. For instance, despite Rubruck's remark on the wall of Karakorum, the Mongolian-German expedition to the site reveals that the city itself had no clear limits, and built areas developed beyond the city wall, although they became less dense with distance from the centre.[78] Rubruck's account is also enlightening about the inside relations of the household of Möngke Khan and their customs.

The archaeological remains of Karakorum display the characteristics of the 'international style' of the twelfth to fourteenth centuries.[79] The combination of Chinese, West Asian and native influences is recognisable in the fragments of frescoes and small finds, such as beads, uncovered in the site.[80] The existence of several distinct artistic styles attests to the activities of artists and artisans from various parts of Asia who came to the capital of a cosmopolitan empire. Even some of the archaeological finds which follow a unified tradition, such as the ceramics and tiles showing Chinese influence, were made locally. This fact supports the claim that many non-Mongol craftsmen were resettled in Karakorum and were accommodated in certain quarters of the city. In addition, some evidence, such as numismatic finds as well as weighing scales, confirms the presence of the merchants in Karakorum, as William mentions in his passage too.[81]

Steinhardt mentions that ceramics, decorative arts and architecture were produced for different purposes in Karakorum. Different craftsmen provided the artefacts that were previously absent in the nomadic life of the Mongols. Among them, Chinese ceramics were of great significance. They were produced to improve the Mongols' perception of themselves as Chinese-style rulers. The visual splendour of Chinese wares was foreign to Mongol patrons of the city, but the wares may have served to remind the Mongols about a Chinese standard model that they were supposed to fit as the non-Chinese ruling dynasty of China.[82] Also in architecture, the Mongols chose Chinese visual imperial symbols rather than international architectural vocabulary in order to express their imperial ambitions. For instance, dragon and phoenix designs, as the most popular mythical animals in Chinese culture, were extensively used in the decoration of Mongol-sponsored buildings.[83] Like Chinese ceramics, the use of Chinese decorative motifs can be interpreted as the effort of Mongol rulers to adapt to their new role as the emperors of China.

Although the Mongols constructed new cities, they retained the nomadic tradition of seasonal migrations. Despite the significance of Karakorum as the political, cultural and economic centre of the Mongol Empire, it was not the permanent residence of the Great Khans. They lived in Karakorum for short lengths of time in early spring and early summer and spent the rest of the year at their seasonal palaces in the environs of the city.[84] These palaces, together with pastoral lands, hunting grounds, agricultural lands and craft workshops, shaped 'the peri-urban area of Karakorum', in Shiraishi's words.[85]

Alongside the emergence of new economic sources in Mongol cities, pastoral nomadism continued to develop successfully in the steppe throughout the thirteenth and fourteenth centuries. On the one hand, archaeological examination of the court of Karakorum confirms 'the existence of a permanent grain market, local agriculture and the virtual absence of wild animal bones in the thirteenth-century ruins of the city', all pointing towards the urbanised qualities of Mongol life at that time.[86] On the other, statistical analysis of the skeletal remains of domesticated animals proves the flourishing state of the Mongolian herd during the imperial period. The percentage of herd animals (sheep, goats, cattle and camels) in fourteenth-century Karakorum is very close to their percentage in the twentieth century.[87] Therefore, parallel with urbanism in the city, the nomadism connected with this economic activity (herding) still existed. The archaeological data led Soviet scholars to suggest that the economy of the Mongols in the early thirteenth century consisted of a mixture of nomadic and settled elements.[88] The fact that the pre-conquest Mongols were not mere tent-dwelling nomads depending only on a herd-based economy supports the claim that they were semi-urbanised people who had been familiar with the idea of founding permanent settlements even before their encounter with the sedentary civilisations of Iran and China, a hypothesis which will be considered further in the discussion of Ilkhanid cities in the following chapters.[89]

Shangdu (Kaiping Fu)

Shangdu was situated five kilometres north-west of Dolon-nor in present-day Inner Mongolia. The city was built by order of Chinggis Khan's grandson Möngke Khan. His younger brother, Qubilay Khan, became Khaqan in 1264, and elevated the status of the city to a walled capital and called it Shangdu, 'the upper capital'.[90] After the foundation of Daidu as the new capital of Qubilay, Shangdu was converted into the summer residence of the Khaqan and a private pleasure area. Rashid al-Din says that Qubilay erected his *yaylāq* (summer quarter) in the environs of the city of Keymin Fu [*sic*] and built a palace (*qarshī*) called Lang-ten to the east of the city.[91] Shangdu and Daidu functioned as twin centres of government and power in Qubilay's new administration.[92]

Shangdu, designed by Qubilay's Chinese advisor Liu Ping-chung,[93] was intended to be a Chinese-style imperial city.[94] Closely corresponding to typical mid-thirteenth-century Chinese imperial urban plans, the city was formed from three walled areas that were identified as Outer, Imperial and Palace Cities (Figure 1.4). Administrative offices and some monasteries were located within the Imperial City. The Palace City of Shangdu was enclosed by two layers of walls. The main palace building, Da'an Ge, was attached to the northern side of the innermost wall, facing south. Textual records state that Chinese craftsmen and painters supervised the construction of Da'an Ge. In addition to Da'an Ge, monasteries are the only building types whose remains have been found among the ruins of the city of Shangdu.[95]

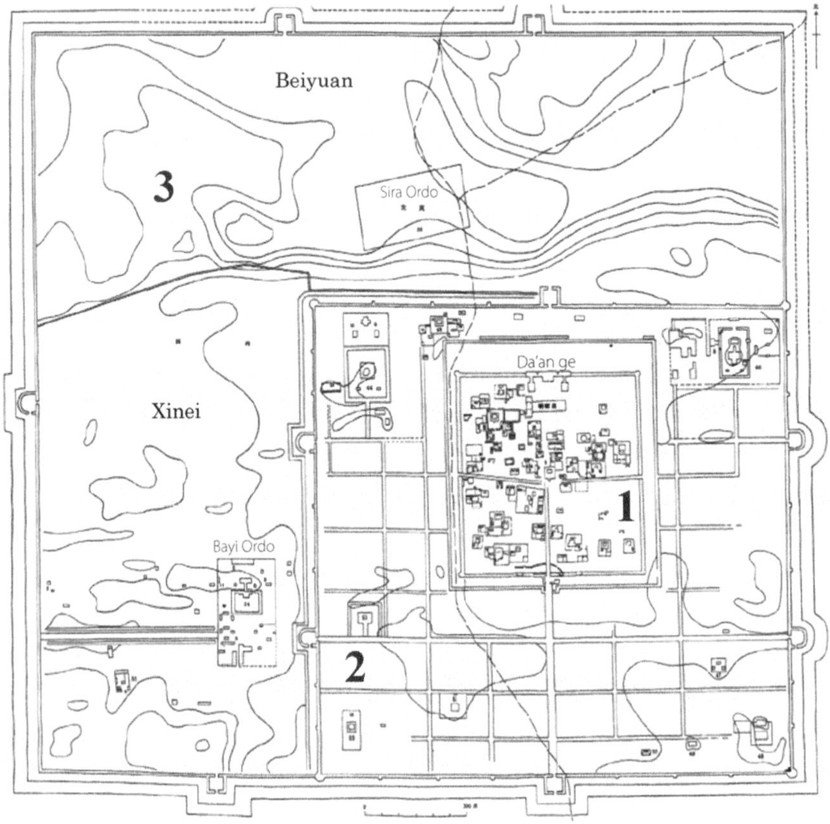

Figure 1.4 Mongol city of Shangdu.
1. Palace City
2. Imperial City
3. Outer City
Drawing by Tomoko Masuya, used with permission, Masuya, 'Seasonal Capitals', 240; for the original drawing, see Wei Jian, *Yuan Shangdu* 元上都 [Shangdu site of the Yuan Dynasty] (Beijing: publisher not identified, 2008), vol. 1, figure 2

The activities related to the Great Khans' recreations happened within the Outer City. According to the excavation reports, two areas of the Outer City, the 'Northern Garden' (Beiyuan) and the 'Western Inner Space' (Xinei), were separated by a mud wall. The pleasure palaces mentioned in the written sources, the Sïra Ordu and the Bayi Ordu, were possibly located in these two areas.[96] Marco Polo describes the Outer City as a fortified castle in which were

> fountains and rives of running water and very beautiful lawns and groves enough. And the great Kaan keeps all sorts of not fierce wild beasts which can be named there ... And the great Kaan often goes riding through this park which is surrounded with a wall ... And ... in the middle place of that park thus surrounded with a wall, where there is a most beautiful grove, the great Kaan has made for his dwelling a great palace or loggia which is all of canes, upon beautiful pillars gilded and varnished, and on the top of each pillar is a great dragon ... The roof of this palace is also all of canes gilded and varnished so well ... Moreover the great Kaan had made it so arranged that he might have it easily taken away and easily set up, put together and taken to pieces, without any harm whenever he wished, for when it is raised and put together more than two hundred very strong ropes of silk held it up in the manner of tents all round about ... the great Kaan stays there in that park three months of the year ... sometimes in the marble palace and sometimes in this one of cane.[97]

Polo's description strengthens the possibility that the pleasure palaces located in the outer walled area of Shangdu were semi-permanent structures built on the model of the Mongols' tents. The juxtaposition of portable tents and permanent buildings in Shangdu denotes the adherence of the Mongol emperors to their former nomadic life. They continued to pitch their splendid tents on the grass lands which were surrounded by the walls of their Chinese-style city. The pattern used in Shangdu is observable in many Mongolian cities, which are now fields of ruins covered with mounds and depressions. The empty pieces of land uncovered among the remains of buildings often show the space occupied by tents which were erected in the vicinity of permanent structures.[98]

Daidu (Dadu or Khan Baliq)

In 1267 Qubilay Khan founded a greater capital city located about 315 kilometres south-west of Shangdu and called it Daidu or Dadu, 'great walled capital'. Daidu functioned as the winter capital of the Khaqan.[99] During Qubilay's reign, people from many different ethnic, religious and cultural backgrounds resided in the city and brought in their native conventions from different lands of Mongolian conquest. Although Chinese officials played a substantial role in the formation of Daidu, the city attracted a wide variety of cultural traditions not only from China and Mongolia, but also from Central Asia and beyond.

Daidu was built, from the outset, as a centre of power. In comparison with the two earlier capitals of the Mongols, Karakorum and Shangdu, Daidu is considered a more significant example of imperial architecture and urbanism, for two reasons. First, it was located inside China, and thus must have been deeply influenced by long-established Chinese architectural and urban traditions. Second, the more organised layout of the city consisted of a larger number of permanent residential, religious and administrative buildings.[100]

Daidu is also a well-documented case. While the city was extensively destroyed by the Ming army and the surviving sections were buried under the Ming city of Beijing, archaeological excavations have revealed considerable parts of the Outer City. More remarkable than the archaeological material are textual sources describing the imperial sectors of the city in great detail. Two fourteenth-century texts, both written in Chinese, represent the most comprehensive architectural descriptions of Qubilay's city. The earlier text is a chapter of the *Zhougeng Lu* published by the Chinese official Tao Zongyi, possibly on the basis of a first-hand account. The second, *Gugong Yilu*, written by the official Xiao Xun, is the only surviving eye-witness account of the Imperial City.[101]

Like Shangdu, Daidu was composed of three walled areas in a concentric arrangement. The non-imperial Mongols and the non-Mongol population lived and worked within the outer wall. Eleven gates built in this wall provided access to the city. The gates were connected with straight lines. The main layout of the city was largely shaped on the basis of these strong north–south and east–west axes, although they were interrupted by water channels or buildings. Several waterways moved into the city, three of which supplied water for different palatial and administrative sections of the city and eventually flowed into a large pond (Figure 1.5). The imperial sector, enclosed by the second wall, consisted of the Palace City, administrative buildings and two palaces for crown princes (Figure 1.6).[102] Textual sources attest to the elegance of the internal decoration of the palaces located to the west of the pond within the Imperial City. For instance, the late fourteenth-century official Xiao Xun describes the halls of the palaces as being covered with white silk and decorated with dragons and phoenixes.[103] The Palace City of Qubilay Khan, the most private zone of Daidu, was a walled city formed from those buildings that exclusively belonged to the Khaqans, such as reception and audience halls, sleeping chambers and private worship rooms. While Daming dian, the main building of the Palace City, was completely built in the Chinese style, the thrones of the Great Khan and the empress were arranged next to each other following Mongol convention.[104]

Tradition says that Qubilay Khan brought grass from the Mongolian steppe to Daidu as a nostalgic symbol of the Mongols' homeland and planted

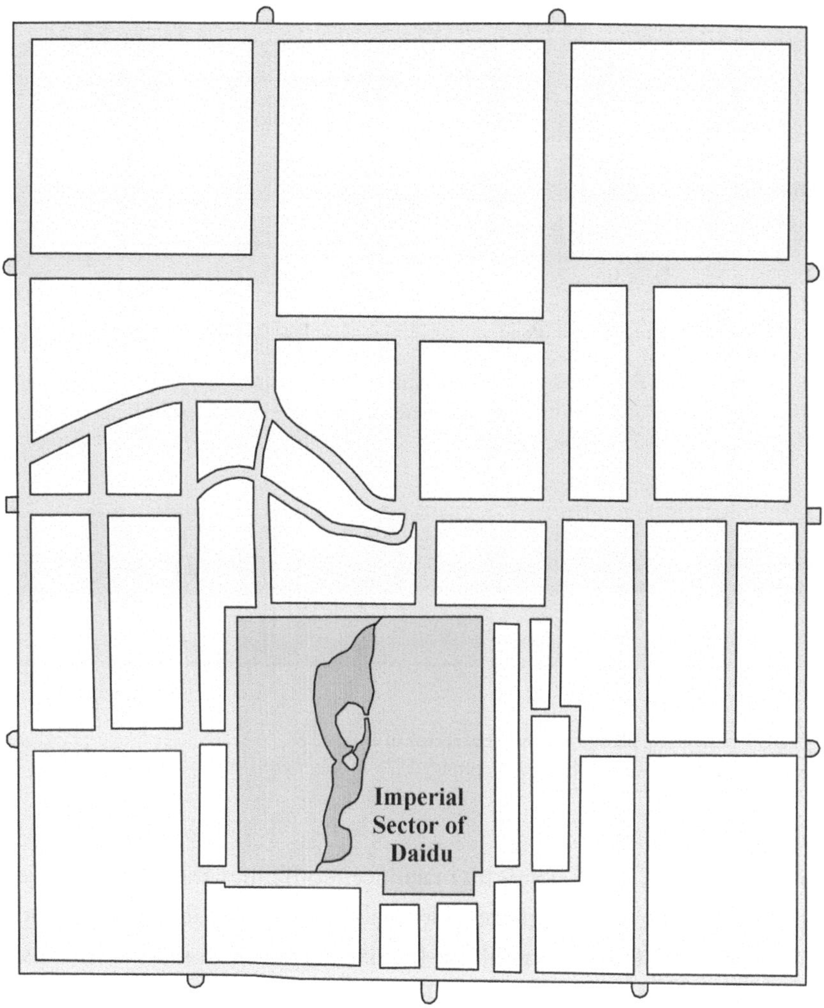

Figure 1.5 Schematic plan of Yuan Daidu.
Regenerated after Steinhardt, *Chinese Imperial City Planning*, 157

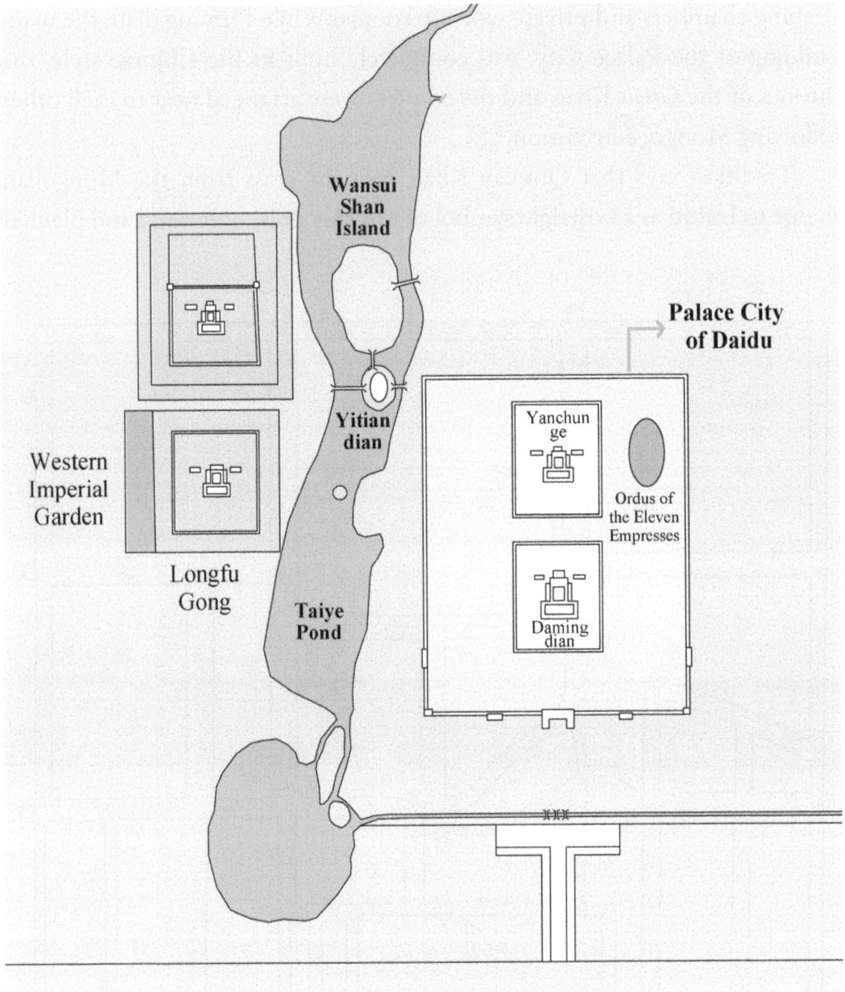

Figure 1.6 Schematic plan of the imperial sector of Daidu.
Regenerated after Masuya, 'Seasonal Capitals', 237

it in the Imperial City.[105] Beside his magnificent buildings, the moveable dwellings were erected in these grasses. Not only the Chinese imperial halls bore signs of Mongolian native traditions (for instance, animal skins replaced silk wall paintings that decorated the palaces of former Chinese emperors), but these tents built in the open spaces of the city also represented the Mongols' insistence on preserving their nomadic lifestyle. Nevertheless, while the juxtaposition of tents and palaces in the Imperial City reveal native Mongolian taste and sensibilities, there are some other features suggesting how the Khans partially compromised their nomadic conventions for the sake of being accepted by their Chinese subjects as the legitimate rulers of China.

Liu Ping-chung, Qubilay's confidant, was given the task of founding the capital city of Daidu. Liu chose a suitable site and submitted a city plan to the Khaqan. The suggested place was the seat of the imperial cities of the previous dynasties, and thus several splendid buildings were still present at the site. Furthermore, the location of the city was believed to be at the centre of heaven and earth.[106] It is proposed that the principles of auspicious *feng shui* (Chinese geomancy) might have been employed in the city planning and construction of Daidu.[107] Some scholars also suggest that Daidu was planned on the basis of the model of the ideal capital described in the classical Confucian text the *Zhou Li*, the *Rituals of the Zhou dynasty*.[108] In an illustrated version of the *Zhou Li*, the description of the City of State of the King of Zhou is accompanied by a drawing of the city depicting a square-shaped plan with the royal structures at the city centre (Figure 1.7). The construction of Buddhist temples and Confucian shrines in Yuan capitals, including Daidu, is another example of the Mongols' willingness to follow certain Chinese social and religious norms.[109]

Daidu was built as a new city in the vicinity of the existing Jin capital. As Chan puts it, this new capital legitimised the Mongol ruler as the Son of Heaven ruling from the centre of the Universe.[110] The metropolis designed by Liu in Daidu was a traditional Chinese imperial capital (both in general plan and in style of individual structures), although its architecture and decorations represented certain Mongolian tribal and pastoral features. In addition to Liu, several Chinese officials and engineers, and a few artisans of Central Asian origin, are mentioned in the textual sources, who conducted different sections of the grand project of Daidu: for example, Zhao Bingwen (d. 1232), a knowledgeable official in city building,[111] and Guo Shoujing (d. 1316), a famous astronomer and mathematician.[112]

In view of both the general plan and the style of individual structures in Daidu, textual references and archaeological findings support the claim that the city was part of the mainstream of Chinese imperial architecture and urban tradition. Despite the themes and concepts pointing towards the non-Chinese origins of the rulers of Daidu, the city is usually considered a Chinese-style

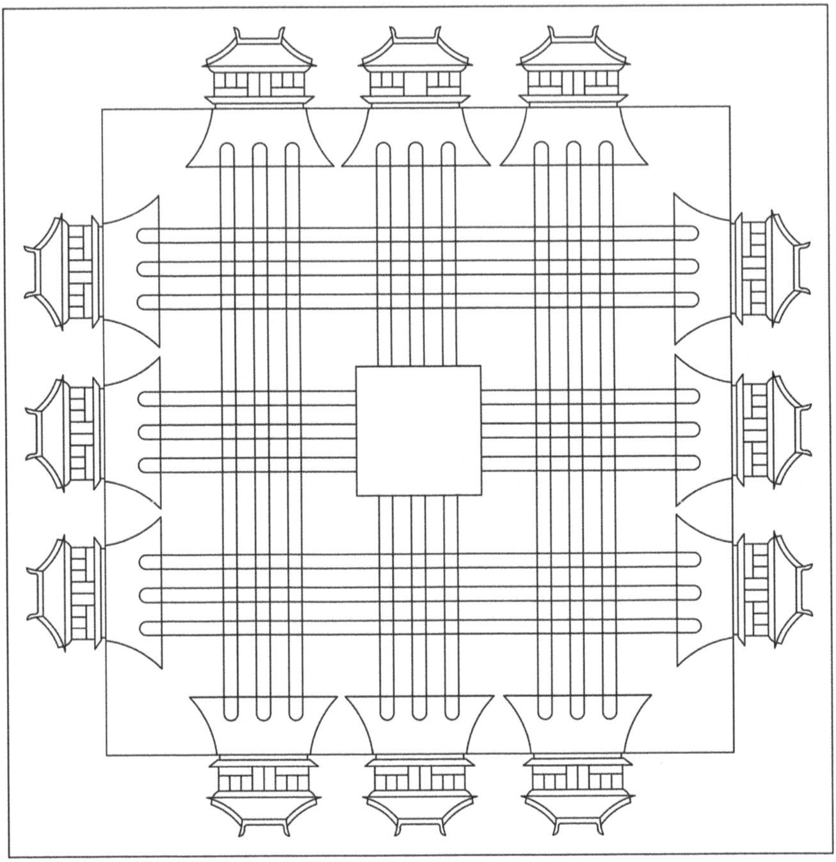

Figure 1.7 Plan of the City of State of the King of Zhou.
Regenerated after Steinhardt, 'Plan of Khubilai Khan's Imperial City', 146

Imperial City. This quality of the city is explained by two factors: the idea of symbolism and the concept of adaptability. Historically, in East Asia, an Imperial City was one of the attributes of a world empire. Qubilay Khan, who came from Central Asia and identified himself as a world emperor in China, as a foreign-born ruler lacked such a native imperial symbolism. Thus, he benefited from the symbolism of Chinese architecture and adopted the elements of a Chinese Imperial City in his foundations at Daidu in order to legitimise his own rule as a non-Chinese emperor in China.[113] In terms of adaptability, the Chinese architectural system enabled the former tent dwellers to erect their tents behind the walls of their palatial complexes and revive their native decorative system in Chinese post-and-lintel structures.[114] Furthermore, the imperial family could practise their nomadic rituals in the private sectors of their palaces, while the Chinese-style walls and roofs of the public sections presented a Chinese palatial complex to the outside world. The simplicity of Chinese architectural form[115] and the availability of builders and craftsmen easing the construction were the other factors encouraging the Mongols to choose this architectural system. Despite the Mongols' loyalty to some aspects of their nomadic lifestyle, Daidu played a significant role in the transformation of the Mongols from tent-dwelling nomads to the dominant emperors of the sedentary civilisation of China.

Among several settlements constructed by Mongolian rule in Central Asia and China during the imperial period (thirteenth and fourteenth centuries), Karakorum, Shangdu and Daidu are considered the most significant imperial urban foundations of the Khans. In addition to the major urban centres, there were a large number of settlements of different sizes that served different purposes; for instance, the satellite villages constructed around Karakorum worked as rest stops for travellers to the Mongol capital.[116] Examination of the smaller residences sheds light on the question to what extent the cities sponsored by Mongolian rule were impacted by native Mongolian taste on the one hand and Chinese architectural traditions on the other. Such settlements are not the focus of this section; however, Khara Khoto is an interesting example that is worth a quick mention here. The site, with large amounts of archaeological findings, is a lesser-known yet significant Mongol city that found a special place in the post-conquest sedentary world. Khara Khoto in western Inner Mongolia was a major trade centre throughout the mid-imperial period. Marco Polo refers to the site as the city of Etzina.[117] Russian explorers, particularly P. K. Kozlov, uncovered hundreds of manuscripts written in Tangut, Chinese and Mongolian, paintings on silk, coins and artefacts at the site.[118] Later investigations on the site carried out by Lubo-Lesnichenko showed that, besides commercial activities, Khara Khoto functioned as an important crafts centre, to the extent that the artisans of the city are considered key players in the development of the blue and white porcelain ware.[119] In addition to the rich collection of portable objects, architectural remains at the site are also worth attention. Outside the south-west corner of the wall of the city, Kozlov described a building with a small dome and a humble portal, possibly an Islamic mausoleum or a mosque, which follows the architectural style of similar buildings constructed in the Middle East in the eleventh and twelfth centuries. The presence of the building might be explained in relation to Muslim merchants who controlled trans-Eurasian trade during the Mongol era and played an important role in the economic life of the Mongol Empire.[120]

Chinese imperial cities were the proper choice for the Mongol khans fulfilling their needs for imperial symbolism and adaptability. The khans' desire to emulate the imperial architecture of China can also be discussed in relation to a general pattern of adoption of ideas, concepts and traditions of the sedentary world by nomadic people in order to fit the requirements of their new role as the emperors of a settled empire. Although Chinese imperial architecture, as the most influential visual tradition in Eastern and Central Asia, fascinated the Mongols, the architecture and urban planning of the imperial cities, Daidu in particular, reflect the encounter between native traditions of the Mongolian steppe on the one hand and the long-established architectural conventions of China on the other. Examination of the imperial cities provides insights into the Mongol patrons' motivations for the foundation of a Chinese-style city in the non-Mongol context of China. Two reasons seem to have been more significant. First, for the non-Chinese rulers, following Chinese established standards in architecture and urbanism worked as a means of legitimisation. Second, not only did the influential Chinese ministers of Yuan Khaqans lead the aesthetic taste of the Mongols in their favoured direction, they also propagated Chinese methods and ideas by conducting certain architectural projects.[121] The two factors can be discussed in relation to other divisions of the Mongol Empire, including Ilkhanid Iran. I expand on them later in the book, when the Iranian–Mongol transcultural encounters in the Ilkhanid imperial cities will be analysed. While these key factors form the basis of my discussion, they will be adapted to fit the distinct socio-political and religious context of the Ilkhanid court.

Major Urban Projects in pre-Mongol Iran

Mongol campaigns in Iran caused extensive destruction to different aspects of the Iranians' social life and built environment. It took them several decades to get over the shock of the widespread devastation. Focusing on the architecture and urbanism that began to revive under the first Ilkhan, Hülegü (r. 1256–65), one may discern in them the traces of the monuments and urban complexes of eleventh- and twelfth-century Iran. After the conquest, when the dust settled, large groups of master builders came back to their homeland. These architects and craftsmen, who had inherited the skills and abilities of the previous generation, contributed to the transfer of motifs, styles and techniques of the earlier centuries to the architectural undertakings of the post-conquest period and bridged the gap caused by several years of bloodshed. Looking into the major achievements of Iranian architecture and urbanism under the Seljuqs and the Khwarazm Shahs who ruled Iran prior to the Mongol invasion can shed some light on the context in which Ilkhanid cities were born. The urban patterns generated in the pre-Mongol period affected the course of subsequent development.

The Seljuq Empire was a Turko-Persian Sunni Muslim empire that ruled vast areas of Mesopotamia, Syria, Palestine and most of Iran during the eleventh and twelfth centuries. Under the Seljuqs, Anatolia and Iran gradually overshadowed the political centrality of the Arab territories. Islamic power was shared among the traditional centres in Damascus and Baghdad and Seljuq capitals in the Iranian world, Marv, Nishapur, Rayy and Isfahan.[122] Following the Seljuqs, the Khwarazmian dynasty, which was a Persianate Sunni Muslim dynasty, controlled large parts of Central Asia and Iran during the twelfth century and the early years of the thirteenth. The importance of Iran as a centre of artistic production increased with these political changes.

The concept of Seljuq art and architecture[123] in Iran is usually discussed in relation to the artistic production between the middle of the eleventh century, when the Turkish dynasties established themselves in Eastern Persia, and the beginning of the Mongol invasion. Persian art and architecture of the Seljuq period flourished in a multi-centred landscape in which not only the major urban centres of the Persian plateau, but also smaller towns and cities attracted the attention of patrons, artists and craftsmen. The Seljuq period is often regarded as one of the most important phases of Persian art due to the development of techniques (of design, construction and decoration) and the establishment of formal solutions after the long process of trial and error undergone in the first centuries after Islam.[124] Comparable to the Ilkhans, the Turkish Seljuqs, who had slight artistic and literary heritage of their own, were deeply influenced by the cultural environment of Iran. Nonetheless, the occasional appearance of Central Asian-Turkic motifs and elements affirms that the Seljuqs, despite patronising various forms of Persian art and literature, retained some aspects of their ethnic identity and tribal culture.

Among numerous figures sponsoring construction projects, some names shine out in particular. One of them is the Persian vizier Nizam al-Mulk, who was given full authority over the empire's organisation. Remarkable architectural undertakings were conducted under the supervision of Nizam al-Mulk, such as the network of Nizamiyya madrasas discussed earlier in this chapter, and the expansion of the congregational mosque of Isfahan.[125] In spite of the large number of individual religious and secular monuments of the cities that have remained, the extent of the destruction caused by natural and human factors, particularly during the Mongol period, makes it difficult to present a vivid image of the Seljuq city as an integrated whole. To obtain a general idea of the layout of Seljuq cities, the Seljuq phase of development in the life of the two well-studied cities of Isfahan and Nishapur will be discussed in the following section. The aim is to understand the spatial structure of the cities between the eleventh and thirteenth centuries by locating the key structural elements and reconstructing their arrangement in the urban landscape of the cities.

Seljuq Isfahan

It should not be difficult to identify the individual monuments built during the Seljuq period in Isfahan, thanks to the literary sources and the architectural/archaeological data. It is, however, challenging to distinguish between several earlier phases of construction intertwining to form the Seljuq and post-Seljuq layout of the city. Isfahan under the Seljuqs encompassed a pre-existing urban fabric that communicated actively with the newly founded monuments. Extensive archaeological excavation is needed to uncover the Seljuq development of the city and the spatial organisation of the urban elements during this period.

Tughril Beg (r. 1037–63), the founder of the Seljuq Empire, conquered Isfahan in 1051 and transferred the seat of government from Rayy. Under the governorship of Abu al-Fath Nishapuri, appointed by Tughril, Isfahan began a period of rapid urban revival.[126] The description of the city by Nasir-i Khusraw's (d. 1088) in 1052 testifies to the prosperity of Isfahan under the Seljuqs. He writes:

> The city has a high, strong wall with gates, embrasures and battlements all around. Inside the city are courses for running water, fine tall buildings and a beautiful and large Friday Mosque ... everything inside [the city] is in a flourishing state, as I saw nothing in ruins. There were many bazaars; one I saw was only for money changers and contained two hundred stalls. Every bazaar has doors and gates, as do all quarters and lanes. The caravanserais are exceptionally clean, and in one lane ... there were fifty fine caravanserais, in each of which were retail merchants and shopkeepers ...[127]
>
> ... Of all the Persian-speaking cities, I never saw a finer, more commodious, or more flourishing city than Isfahan ...[128]

The urban development of Isfahan continued during the reign of Tughril's successors, Alp Arslan and his son Malik Shah. The reign of Malik Shah is particularly remarkable for the number of architectural undertakings conducted inside and outside the city. The old fort was restored and a new fortress, named Dizh-kuh or Shah-dizh, which served as the treasure house of the sultan, was built around thirty kilometres south-east of Isfahan.[129] On the north shores of the Zayandih Rud, outside the walls, the Seljuqs founded numerous garden-palaces. In addition to the extramural gardens and pleasure palaces, there were several 'green belts' within the walled city, some of which became the ground of the later foundations, for instance, the Seljuq Garden of Naqsh-i Jahan on which the Safavid palatial complex was built. Furthermore, the congregational mosque was extensively renovated and expanded at that time. The hypostyle mosque was transformed into a four-*iwān* structure, which became the typical style of the mosques built across Iran in the eleventh and twelfth centuries.[130] The most important Seljuq extensions to the mosque were two domed structures, the dome of Taj al-Mulk (or Gunbad-i Khagi) and the dome of Nizam al-Mulk, which were built respectively in the north and south of the central courtyard. According to the foundation inscriptions running around the interior of the domes, the former was built by order of Taj al-Mulk in 1088–9 and the latter was constructed under the patronage of Nizam al-Mulk, possibly a year or two earlier.[131]

Taking into account the general layout of the city, it seems certain that Seljuq Isfahan retained the Buyid configuration. Under the Buyids (934–1062), a defensive wall with twelve gates was built around part of the city and a citadel was placed in its south-east quadrant. Axial bazaars or roads divided the area of the walled city into four quarters. In the Seljuq city, a public square known as the Old Maydan (Maydan-i Kuhnih or Maydan-i Qadim) lay at the intersection of the roads, just south of the congregational mosque (the Masjid-i Jamiʿ), which had been founded in the eighth century. The *maydān*, in the centre of the city, had possibly been the focus of public life since Seljuq times, if not earlier. Monuments relating to the royal families and notables, as well as major buildings such as madrasas and mosques, were often constructed in the area surrounding the city centre;[132] for example, the Malik Shahi madrasa was built by Malik Shah in the Karan quarter and the Nizamiyya madrasa was built by Nizam al-Mulk in the Dardasht quarter.[133] The *maydān* kept its importance until the Safavid period, when Shah ʿAbbas built the Maydan-i Shah and made it a religious, administrative and commercial focal point in the life of the city (Figure 1.8).

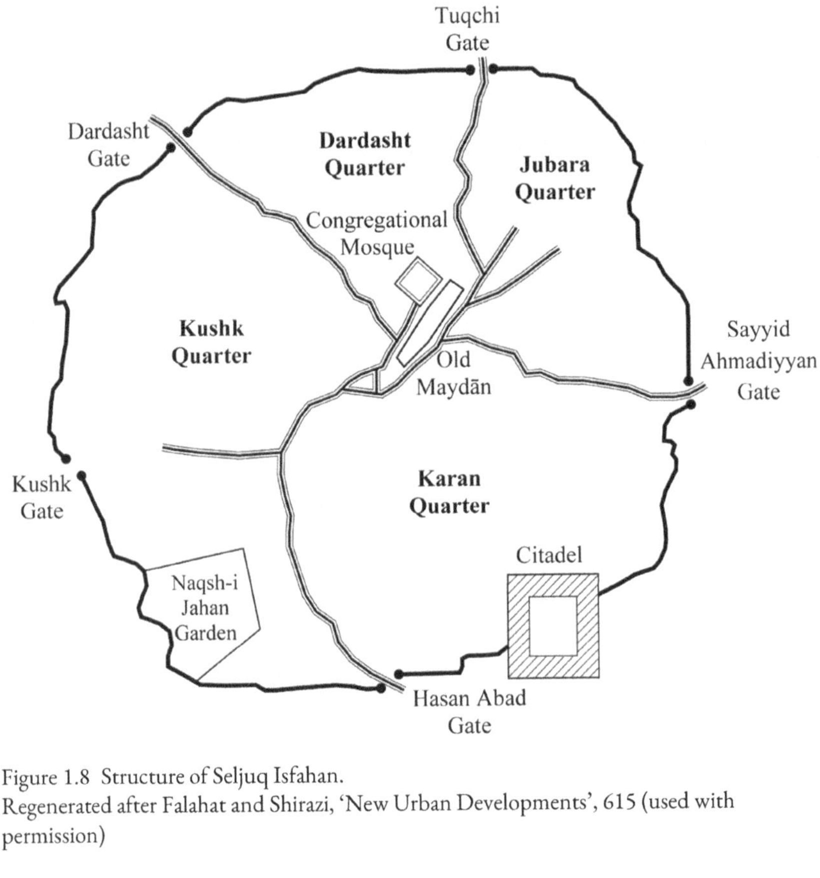

Figure 1.8 Structure of Seljuq Isfahan.
Regenerated after Falahat and Shirazi, 'New Urban Developments', 615 (used with permission)

In many Iranian cities, *maydāns* were located on the outskirts, serving as horse-racing courses and polo fields. Since horse races were not daily activities, the courses were sometimes converted into markets or commercial centres. In a similar way, the Old Maydan of Isfahan seems to have been located at the edge of the old city up to the eighth century, but it was gradually surrounded by later constructions, and was placed in the centre of the Buyid city. Gaube suggests that the Old Maydan in Seljuq Isfahan became the religious and administrative centre of the city while the *maydān* partially retained its original function as a sports and commercial site. The central bazaar of the city formed around the Old Maydan and the smaller ones gradually grew near the city gates. In addition, the linear bazaars developed outwards along the intra-urban routes. The residential quarters, usually with high building density, filled the space around the *maydān* and between the communication axes.[134]

Seljuq Nishapur

During the Mongol invasion of Nishapur in 1221, the city was devastated and many buildings were levelled. As Yaqut al-Hamawi (d. 1229) puts it, 'the Mongols left not one stone standing upon another'.[135] Nishapur, however, recovered again and became a populous centre in the fourteenth century. Mustawfi calls it *umm al-bilād* (the mother of cities) of Khurasan, which denotes the important position of the city even after the Mongol conquest.[136] Despite the late thirteenth-century revival, repeated earthquakes (in 1389, 1405 and 1673) afterwards severely affected the spatial structure of the city and forced the residents to build a new city at another location.[137] Considering the multiple phases of construction and destruction of the city that happened through the medieval period, the reconstruction of the Seljuq city must remain highly speculative. Nevertheless, in view of the significance of Nishapur as the *dār al-mulk*[138] of Khurasan under the Seljuqs, and the possible influence of the city over its contemporary urban centres throughout eastern Iran, it is crucial to uncover the pieces that shaped the outline of Seljuq Nishapur by digging into the literary sources and physical remains of the city.

In the *Nuzhat al-Qulub*, Mustawfi writes that the *dār al-ʾimāra* (the seat of government) of Khurasan was in Marv and Balkh until the end of the Tahirid dynasty (821–73), but that during the Saffarid dynasty (861–1002) Nishapur became the *dār al-mulk* of Khurasan.[139] However, Mustawfi seems to be slightly inaccurate in dating the transfer of the capital to Nishapur, since at the time of the earthquake of 856 the city had become the capital of Khurasan and was governed by Tahir ibn 'Abdallah (r. 845–62).[140] The Seljuqs captured Nishapur twice, first in 1038 when Tughril was enthroned in Nishapur and chose the city as his capital, and secondly in 1040 when the Seljuqs defeated Sultan Mas'ud Ghaznavi (r. 1030–40), who had reoccupied the city. The third Seljuq sultan, Alp Arslan, resided in Nishapur for a period of time. Eventually Sultan Sanjar (r. 1097–1157), the last prominent sultan of the Seljuq dynasty, transferred his court from Nishapur to Marv out of strategic considerations. Marv was considered a suitable place for the sultan's military purposes, such as the defence of the north-eastern border of Iran and his campaigns against the Khwarazm Shahs and the Qara Khitay.[141]

During the medieval period the city of Nishapur was formed from three parts: the citadel (*quhan-dizh*), the inner town (*ḥākim-nishīn*) and the outer town (*rabaż*).[142] The citadel and the inner town were fortified in pre-Islamic times, but the walls were being destroyed in the early Islamic centuries and the main body of the city shifted to the outer town. From the late tenth century the citadel seemed to begin a period of abandonment and depression, while the outer town became the central part of the city, economically and politically, containing key urban elements such as the congregational mosque, most of the bazaar, the *dār al-'imāra* or government building, the houses of the notables and the popular residential quarters. At the time of the Seljuq invasion of Nishapur, the outer town seemed not to be fortified or, even if the walls and gates existed, they might have been a superficial barrier aimed at impressing invaders rather than working as effective defensive structures.[143] Bulliet suggests that the reason the outer town was not suburban but contained the functional core of the city might be that Nishapur became a major Muslim administrative centre after the Arab conquest and developed significantly. The growth happened outside the inner town, which was small and possibly remained the residence of the old population of the city.[144]

Ibn Hawqal (d. 988) calls Nishapur 'Abrshahr',[145] and mentions some of the structural components of the city. According to his account, the citadel, the inner town and the outer town of Nishapur were flourishing in the tenth century. The citadel was situated outside the inner town, both of which were embraced by the outer town. The citadel and the inner town had two and four gates respectively. The outer town also had several gates and Ibn Hawqal names just four of them: Bab al-Qubab towards Iraq and Gurgan; the gate of Jik (also read as Jig or Jang) towards Balkh, Marv and Transoxiana; the gate of Ahvasabad towards Fars and Quhistan; and the fourth gate towards Tus. The congregational mosque of the city, built by the successor of the famous Yaʿqub Layth-i Saffari (r. 861–79), ʿAmr-i Layth (r. 879–901), was located in the outer town at a place called al-Muʿaskar (army camp). The *dār al-ʾimāra*, also founded by ʿAmr-i Layth, opened onto a square called the Maydan al-Husayniyn, and not far from this was the city's prison. The bazaars were also located in the outer town. The most splendid bazaars were Murabbaʿat al-Kabira (Chahar-Suq-i Buzurg, or Large Crossroads Market) and Murabbaʿat al-Saghira (Chahar-Suq-i Kuchak, or Small Crossroads Market) (Figure 1.9).[146] There were numerous shops in the bazaars allocated to various types of crafts, and also a number of caravanserais where the merchants ran their businesses.[147]

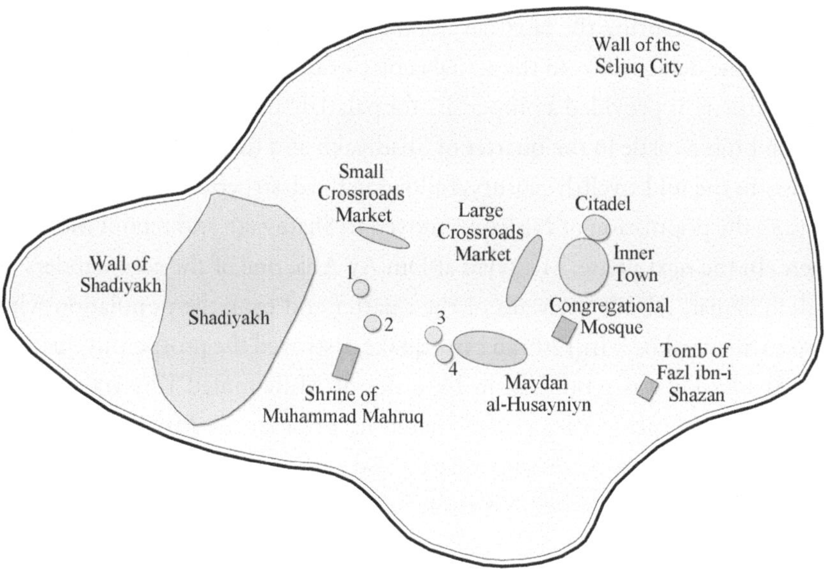

Figure 1.9 Main structural elements of Seljuq Nishapur.
1. Tappih Sabz Pushan
2. Vineyard Tappih
3. Tappih Madrasa
4. *Dār al-ʾimāra*
Regenerated after Muhammad-Reza Riyazikesheh, 'Nishabur from an Archaeological Perspective [Nishabur az Dīdgāh-i Bāstān-Shināsī]', *Bāstān-Shināsī va Tārīkh* 1, 2 (1990): 25

According to Hakim-i Nishapuri (d. 1014), Nishapur had forty-seven quarters,[148] while Maqdisi (d. 991) reports forty-two.[149] Half of these quarters are now nothing but names, and there is no evidence to mark their locations. Bulliet, however, speculates on the location of the remainder on the basis of photographic and written sources.[150]

The quarter of Shadiyakh was a dominant element in the urban landscape of Nishapur through the medieval period. The quarter was originally a garden area outside the city. Hakim-i Nishapuri attributes the foundation of Shadiyakh to ʿAbdallah ibn Tahir al-Khurasani (r. 830–44), the Tahirid governor of Khurasan. This site was first used as a military structure, but it rapidly became an urban political centre enclosed by a rampart.[151] The palaces constructed by the Tahirids were destroyed by Yaʿqub-i Layth. Hakim writes that Yaʿqub built gardens there and that Shadiyakh was converted into a city (*shahr*)[152] during his time.[153] Under the Samanids (819–999), Shadiyakh was integrated into the urban area and was considered one of the quarters of the city.[154] During the later developments of Nishapur, Shadiyakh gradually became detached from the actual centre of the city. Being covered mainly with gardens, it provided a proper site for palatial buildings. For example, Alp Arslan built a castle in the quarter of Shadiyakh and fortified it as his treasure house. In the mid-twelfth century, following the destruction of the city by the Ghuzz, the population of Nishapur moved to Shadiyakh and rebuilt the town there. In the next phase, Mu'ayyid al-Din Ay Aba, one of the commanders of Sultan Sanjar, rebuilt the walls of the quarter and took the population with him to Shadiyakh.[155] In 1209 an earthquake destroyed the prosperous quarter, but Shadiyakh was rebuilt again by order of Muhammad Khwarazm Shah (r. 1200–20) quickly afterwards. Therefore, prior to the Mongol invasions, Shadiyakh was a prosperous city quarter and a centre of the population.[156]

Nasir-i Khusraw visited Nishapur in 1046. He referred to a madrasa that was being constructed by order of Tughril near the Saddlers' Bazaar.[157] Nizam al-Mulk also founded his Nizamiyya madrasa in Nishapur, which was his original home. In addition to Nizamiyya, on the basis of literary sources Bulliet lists thirty-eight madrasas that operated in Nishapur between the tenth and twelfth centuries.[158] This piece of historical information, alongside part of the city unearthed during the excavations conducted by the Metropolitan Museum in the 1930s (more specifically in the mounds known as the Vineyard Tappih,

Tappih Madrasa, Tappih Sabz Pushan and the Qanat Tappa), attests to the importance of Nishapur as 'a cosmopolitan, polyglot city, a famed centre of learning' through the early Islamic and medieval period.[159] The brickwork, wall painting and carved stone and plaster decoration found across the excavated mounds show exquisite craftsmanship, which reveals that not only the rulers of Nishapur and their palatial complexes but also the commoners and their residential quarters benefited from a carefully executed architecture.

The study of pre-Mongol Isfahan and Nishapur showed that, despite the presence of some common urban elements such as mosque, madrasa, bazaar and *maydān*, the two cities varied in layout. In view of the dissimilar socio-political and environmental conditions of Isfahan and Nishapur, they seemed to follow different processes of development through the medieval period. The examination of the two cases suggests that we should expect the existence of several local/regional methods of urban planning under the Seljuqs rather than the emergence of one single style used in different parts of the country. In other words, unlike the individual buildings described with certain formal and technical features, Seljuq urbanism hardly fits into a well-defined frame. This is partly because of the ever-changing nature of the organic cities that prevents the formation of a constant arrangement. Such urban centres developed over a long period of time, and inherited, in each phase of development, certain structural components that previously existed.

The lengthy survey of cities under the Ilkhans' predecessors and contemporaries in Western and Eastern Asia provides us with a clearer picture of the temporal and mental context in which Ilkhanid cities were founded. However, it barely provides a benchmark for comparison, primarily because of the dissimilar circumstances in which each of the cases flourished. With no intention of proposing a prototype or a single source of inspiration for the Ilkhanid city, the survey sought to underline the major movements in architecture and urban planning that might have impacted the Ilkhans' tastes and preferences with regard to their own cities in Iran. It would be challenging to unravel the Ilkhans' mentality towards cities while they were oscillating between their nomadic conception of a permanent settlement and the sedentary world's expectations of a ruler's residence. Although their mindset is far from clear, delving deeply into the network of major cities that the Mongols encountered in the broader landscape of medieval Asia prior and subsequent to the invasion may throw some light on how the Ilkhans envisaged developing their imperial capitals. Our current understanding of the urban activities of the Ilkhans' antecedents and contemporaries across Asia forms the basis for our discussion on Ilkhanid urban centres in the next chapter.

Notes

1. On the interchangeable usage of Iran and Ilkhanid state/land/territory in Western Asia in this book, see the Introduction, note 2.
2. See the Introduction, note 62.
3. Patricia Blessing, 'Building a Frontier: Architecture in Anatolia under the Ilkhanid Rule', in *Cultural Encounters in Anatolia in the Medieval Period: The Ilkhanids in Anatolia, Symposium Proceedings, 21–22 May 2015, Ankara*, ed. Suzan Yalman, Filiz Yenişehirlioğlu, Alev Ayaokur and Defne Karakaya (Ankara: Vehbi Koç Ankara Studies Research Center, 2019), 68.
4. In modern scholarship, Late Antiquity is defined as the period between the third/fourth and the seventh century, during which profound transformation can be witnessed in the physical layout of the cities of the Middle East. See Marcus Milwright, *An Introduction to Islamic Archaeology* (Edinburgh: Edinburgh University Press, 2010), 29–34.
5. Although the cities in the Islamic world, in a general sense, experienced a process of transformation from the classical city to the Islamic city between the sixth and eleventh centuries, the urban change, in Avni's words, 'was more complex and involved a wide regional variability of intensification and abatement of settlements'. See Gideon Avni, '"From Polis to Madina" Revisited – Urban Change in Byzantine and Early Islamic Palestine', *Journal of the Royal Asiatic Society* 21, no. 3 (2011): 328.
6. Marcus Milwright, 'Early Islamic Urbanism', unpublished. Samarra, founded in the ninth century, is a good example in this regard. For further discussion on Samarra, see Northedge, *Historical Topography of Samarra*; Thomas Leisten, *Excavation of Samarra. Volume 1: Architecture. Final Report of the first Campaign, 1910–1912* (Mainz am Rhein: Von Zabern, 2003).
7. Wolper, 'Islamic Architecture and Institutions', 912. According to Wolper, these institutions could be found in most cities across the Islamic world during the medieval period.
8. Michael Rogers, 'Samarra: A Study in Medieval Town-Planning', in *The Islamic City: A Colloquium*, ed. Albert Hourani and Samuel Miklos Stern (Oxford: Cassirer; Philadelphia: University of Pennsylvania Press, 1970), 120.

9. Wolper, 'Islamic Architecture and Institutions', 920.
10. Giulia Annalinda Neglia, 'Some Historiographical Notes on the Islamic City with Particular Reference to the Visual Representation of the Built City', in *The City in the Islamic World*, ed. Salma Jayyusi, Renata Holod, Attilio Petruccioli and André Raymond (Leiden; Boston: Brill, 2008), vol. 1, 3.
11. Milwright, *Introduction to Islamic Archaeology*, 75.
12. For further discussion on early twentieth-century studies of the 'Islamic city', see Masashi Haneda, 'An Interpretation of the Concept of Islamic City', in *Islamic Urban Studies: Historical Review and Perspectives*, ed. Masashi Haneda and Toru Miura (London: Kegan Paul International, 1994), 1–10; Michael Bonine, *The Middle Eastern City and Islamic Urbanism: An Annotated Bibliography of Western Literature* (Bonn: Ferd. Dümmlers Verlag, 1994).
13. See e.g. Albert Habib Hourani and Samuel Stern (eds), *The Islamic City: A Colloquium* (Oxford: Bruno Cassirer and University of Pennsylvania Press, 1970); Janet Abu-Lughod, 'The Islamic City: Historic Myth, Islamic Essence, and Contemporary Relevance', *International Journal of Middle East Studies* 19 (1987): 155–76.
14. See, among others: Georges Marçais, 'L'Urbanisme Musulman [Muslim Urbanism]', *5e Congrès de la Fédération des Sociétés Savantes de l'Afrique du Nord*, Algiers, 1940. The article was reprinted on pp. 219–31 of the collection of his works, *Mélanges d'Histoire et d'Archéologie de l'Occident Musulman*, tome I, articles et conférences de Georges Marçais, Algiers, 1957.
15. See, among others: Edmond Pauty, 'Villes Spontanées et Villes Crées en Islam [Spontaneous Cities and Created Cities in Islam]', *Annales de l'Institut d'Études Orientales* 9 (1951): 52–75.
16. See, among others: Ira Lapidus, *Muslim Cities in the Later Middle Ages* (Cambridge, MA: Harvard University Press, 1967).
17. See, among others: Abu-Lughod, 'Islamic City'; Janet Abu-Lughod, 'What Is Islamic about a City? Some Comparative Reflections', in *Urbanism in Islam: The Proceedings of International Conference on Urbanism in Islam (ICUIT)* (Tokyo: The Middle Eastern Culture Centre, 1989), vol. 1, 193–217.
18. For more studies dealing with this approach, see Neglia, 'Some Historiographical Notes', 18–46.
19. For a brief bibliography on the regional approach, see Neglia, 'Some Historiographical Notes', 18–25. Also see Paul Wheatley, *The Places Where Men Pray Together: Cities in Islamic Lands, Seventh through the Tenth Centuries*, Part II (Chicago: University of Chicago Press, 2001).

20. For example, Abu Lughod discusses three 'Islamic' forces that played an important role in the creation of the traditional Islamic city: the juridical distinction between the *Umma* population and the outsiders, gender segregation, and the legal system of property laws. See Abu Lughod, 'Islamic City', 162–3.
21. Different aspects of this transformation have been tackled in different studies. For instance, Wolper looks at the transformation of urban space in medieval Anatolia in connection with a series of newly built dervish lodges. See Ethel Wolper, *Cities and Saints: Sufism and the Transformation of Urban Space in Medieval Anatolia* (University Park: Pennsylvania State University Press, 2003.

    Addressing the concept of religious transformation in the medieval Islamic society, Mulder also mentions the emergence of 'religious effervescence' and the foundation of hundreds of new religious buildings in this era. See Stephennie Mulder, *The Shrines of the 'Alids in Medieval Syria: Sunnis, Shi'is and the Architecture of Coexistence* (Edinburgh: Edinburgh University Press, 2014).

    Focusing on Aleppo, Tabbaa examines the transformation of the urban structure of the city in the eleventh and twelfth centuries in the larger context of the urban and architectural transformations that characterised Islamic cities of the medieval period. See Yasser Tabbaa, 'Circles of Power: Palace, Citadel, and City in Ayyubid Aleppo', *Ars Orientalis* 23 (1993): 181–200; Yasser Tabbaa, *Constructions of Power and Piety in Medieval Aleppo* (University Park: Pennsylvania State University Press, 1997).
22. Alison Gascoigne, 'The Water Supply of Tinnis: Public Amenities and Private Investments', in *Cities in the Pre-Modern Islamic World: The Urban Impact of State, Society and Religion*, ed. Amira Bennison and Alison Gascoigne (New York: Routledge, 2007), 173.
23. Tabbaa, *Constructions of Power*, 32.
24. During the medieval period, Muslim rulers altered the legal parameters of waqf on some occasions in order to achieve their own political or financial goals. In this regard, Tabbaa discusses the concept of 'state waqf', which was possibly introduced by Nur al-Din Zangi (r. 1146–74). He diverted monies from the treasury (*bayt al-māl*) into *awqāf* in a way that served his purposes; see Tabbaa, *Constructions of Power*, 33.
25. Mulder, *Shrines of the 'Alids*, 3.
26. For further discussion on the movement of the Sunni revival, see Yasser Tabbaa, *The Transformation of Islamic Art during the Sunni Revival* (Seattle: University of Washington Press, 2001), 11–23.
27. Wolper, 'Islamic Architecture and Institutions', 916.

28. Tabbaa, *Constructions of Power*, 1.
29. Wolper, 'Islamic Architecture and Institutions', 918. For further discussion on the transformation of citadels in the medieval Islamic world, see Nasser Rabbat, *The Citadel of Cairo: A New Interpretation of Royal Mamluk Architecture* (New York; Leiden: Brill, 1995); Nasser Rabbat, 'The Militarization of Taste in Medieval Bilād al-Shām', in *Muslim Military Architecture in Greater Syria: from the Coming of Islam to the Ottoman Period*, ed. Hugh Kennedy (Leiden; Boston: Brill Academic, 2006), 84–105.
30. Tabbaa, *Constructions of Power*, 56.
31. Peter Pentz, *The Medieval Citadel and its Architecture* (Copenhagen: Nationalmuseet, 1997), 30.
32. Daniella Talmon-Heller, *Islamic Piety in Medieval Syria: Mosques, Cemeteries and Sermons under the Zangids and Ayyūbids (1146–1260)* (Leiden; Boston: Brill, 2007), 10.
33. Although early medieval madrasas were built as individual buildings, by the end of the medieval period they were joined to mosques, tombs and other structures and formed monumental complexes.
34. Tabbaa, *Constructions of Power*, 125–9.
35. *Ribāṭ* was a term originally used for small fortifications. It was later used for a place where travellers could stay, and also a centre for the Sufis and their gatherings.
36. Mulder, *Shrines of the ʿAlids*, 251.
37. According to Grabar, archaeological findings suggest that the alliance of the individual Muslim was parochial in the twelfth century, although no evidence of a parish-like organisation in Islam has been found. He questions 'whether the parochialism was related to quarters, or whether certain city-wide organizations took precedence over topographical proximity'. See Talmon-Heller, *Islamic Piety*, 23. For the original discussion, see Oleg Grabar, 'The Architecture of the Middle Eastern City from Past to Present: The Case of the Mosque', in *Middle Eastern Cities: A Symposium on Ancient, Islamic, and Contemporary Middle Eastern Urbanism*, ed. Ira Lapidus (Berkeley: University of California Press, 1969), 38–9.
38. Focusing on Central Anatolia, Wolper argues that the growth of Sufism and the formation of dervish lodges were influential in the massive physical changes of Anatolian cities during the thirteenth and fourteenth centuries. For instance, the location and orientation of dervish lodges altered the configuration of space within the city. See Wolper, *Cities and Saints*.

39. Talmon-Heller, *Islamic Piety*, 44–5.
40. There are some exceptions to this pattern, however. The Mamluk Sultan al-Zahir Baybars is a good example in this regard. The large number of buildings he founded (including monumental mosques and shrines) is recognised as the means utilised by the sultan to legitimise his rule in the eyes of his Muslim subjects. For further discussion on Baybars, see Yehoshua Frenkel, 'Baybars and the Sacred Geography of Bilād al-Shām: A Chapter in the Islamization of Syria's Landscape', *Jerusalem Studies in Arabic and Islam* 25 (2001): 153–70.
41. Rabbat, *Citadel of Cairo*, 284.
42. The construction of religious and funerary monuments served two different purposes for the Mamluks. In addition to pious motivations, they sought material benefits that could be achieved through the waqf system. See Doris Behrens-Abouseif, *Cairo of the Mamluks: A History of the Architecture and its Culture* (London; New York: I. B. Tauris, 2007), 12. Taking into account the problems of inheriting wealth in the Mamluk system, the waqf functioned as a means whereby Mamluk amirs could pass on some wealth to their families while expressing conspicuous piety. Also see Doris Behrens-Abouseif, 'The Mamluk City', in *The City in the Islamic World*, ed. Salma Khadra Jayyusi, Renata Holod, Attilio Petruccioli and André Raymond (Leiden: Brill, 2008), 295–316.
43. Stephen Humphreys, 'The Expressive Intent of the Mamluk Architecture of Cairo', *Studia Islamica* 35 (1972): 80.
44. Behrens-Abouseif, *Cairo of the Mamluks*, 45.
45. Bruno De Nicola, 'Letters from Mongol Anatolia: Professional, Political and Intellectual Connections among Members of a Persianised Elite', *Iran: Journal of the British Institute of Persian Studies* 56, no. 1 (2018): 77.
46. Bruno De Nicola, 'On the Outskirts of the Ilkhanate: The Mongols' Relationship with the Province of Kastamonu in the Second Half of the 13th Century', in *Cultural Encounters in Anatolia in the Medieval Period: The Ilkhanids in Anatolia, Symposium Proceedings, 21–22 May 2015, Ankara*, ed. Suzan Yalman, Filiz Yenişehirlioğlu, Alev Ayaokur and Defne Karakaya (Ankara: Vehbi Koç Ankara Studies Research Center, 2019), 118. It is noteworthy that, despite traditional narrative highlighting Seljuk continuity in style and patronage running from the late eleventh century to the emergence of the Ottomans in the early fourteenth century, more recent studies place Anatolia within the context of the Mongol Empire and describe the technical and stylistic characteristics of the monuments of this period. See Blessing, 'Building a Frontier', 81.

47. Patricia Blessing, *Rebuilding Anatolia after the Mongol Conquest: Islamic Architecture in the Lands of Rum, 1240–1330* (London: Routledge, 2016).
48. Ibid., 4.
49. Ibid., 19.
50. Ibid., 67. It is important to note that there were close relationships between leading Anatolian Sufis and the Ilkhanid elite in the late thirteenth and early fourteenth centuries; however, direct patronage of the monuments related to Sufi communities from the Ilkhanid centre barely happened. See A. C. S. Peacock, 'Two Sufis of Ilkhanid Anatolia and their Patrons: Notes on the Works of Mu'yyid al-Din Jandi and Da'ud al-Qasari', in *Cultural Encounters in Anatolia in the Medieval Period: The Ilkhanids in Anatolia, Symposium Proceedings, 21–22 May 2015, Ankara*, ed. Suzan Yalman, Filiz Yenişehirlioğlu, Alev Ayaokur and Defne Karakaya (Ankara: Vehbi Koç Ankara Studies Research Center, 2019), 11 and Blessing, *Rebuilding Anatolia after the Mongol Conquest*, 183.
51. Blessing, 'Building a Frontier', 67.
52. Blessing, *Rebuilding Anatolia after the Mongol Conquest*, 77–89.
53. Ibid., 187.
54. Blessing, 'Building a Frontier', 69.
55. Thomas Allsen, 'Archaeology and Mid-Imperial History: The Chin and Yuan', in *Soviet Studies of Pre-Modern China: Assessments of Recent Scholarship*, ed. Gilbert Rozman (Cambridge: Cambridge University Press. Ann Arbor, MI: Centre for Chinese Studies, University of Michigan, 1984), 89.
56. The occurrence of the Chinese elements in the art of Mongol Iran has been discussed in great detail by Yuka Kadoi (Kadoi, *Islamic Chinoiserie*). For further discussion on the cultural exchange between the Ilkhanids and the eastern Islamic world, see e.g. Donald Little, 'Diplomatic Missions and Gifts Exchanged by Mamluks and Ilkhans', in *Beyond the Legacy of Genghis Khan*, ed. Linda Komaroff (Leiden: Brill, 2006), 30–42; Robert Hillenbrand, 'The Art of the Books in Ilkhanid Iran', in *The Legacy of Genghis Khan: Courtly Art and Culture in Western Asia, 1256–1353*, ed. Linda Komaroff and Stefano Carboni (New York; New Haven: Metropolitan Museum of Art, 2002), 135–67; Robert Hillenbrand, 'Mamluk and Ilkhanid Bestiaries: Convention and Experiment', *Ars Orientalis* 20 (1990): 149–87.
57. Noriyuki Shiraishi, 'Avraga Site: The "Great Ordū" of Genghis Khan', in *Beyond the Legacy of Genghis Khan*, ed. Linda Komaroff (Leiden: Brill, 2006), 85.
58. *Qūrīltāy* describes an assembly of Mongol princes and nobles at which important decisions, such as the election of the new khans and Ilkhans, were made.

59. Masuya, 'Seasonal Capitals', 230–1.
60. Masuya, 'Ilkhanid Phase of Takht-i Sulaimān', 204–6.
61. *Ulus* in Mongolian means a union of different tribes. *Ulus* was first used to refer to the Great Empire of Chinggis Khan, but then was used to refer to the sectors given to his four sons. See Rashid al-Din, *Jāmiʿ al-Tawārīkh*, vol. 3, 2,296–7.
62. *Xinggong* (行宮) is composed of two parts: *xing* (moving) and *gong* (palace). *Xinggong* usually means an imperial palace used for short stays. The first part (*xing*) in fact emphasises the temporary nature of residency in these pleasure-palace complexes.
63. Allsen suggested the title 'aristocratic cities' for the settlements of this group. See Allsen, 'Archaeology and Mid-Imperial History', 91.
64. Masuya, 'Ilkhanid Phase of Takht-i Sulaimān', 166–77.
65. In almost all the excavated Mongol cities built during the first half of the thirteenth century, the buildings have a north-north-west to south-south-east orientation. See Masuya, 'Ilkhanid Courtly Life', 89–90.
66. Ruysbroeck, *Mission of Friar William Rubruck*, 74–5.
67. Ibid., 210.
68. Masuya, 'Ilkhanid Phase of Takht-i Sulaimān', 219.
69. Steinhardt, 'Imperial Architecture along the Mongolian Road', 68.
70. Most 'Mongolian' architecture is quadrangular. However, there are some exceptions, such as the site excavated on the Kondui River in the 1950s that was cross-shaped. See Allsen, 'Archaeology and Mid-Imperial History', 91.
71. Animal-faced stone sculpture, as an architectural component, is one of the most prevalent remains of imperial Mongolian construction. See Steinhardt, 'Imperial Architecture along the Mongolian Road', 70.
72. In many recent publications on Karakorum, Kiselev's so-called 'palace area' is still known as an imperial palace rather than a temple. See e.g. Noriyuki Shiraishi, 'Seasonal Migrations of the Mongol Emperors and the Peri-Urban Area of Kharakhorum', trans. Tomoko Masuya and Gaynor Sekimori, *International Journal of Asian Studies* 1, no. 1 (2004): 106.
73. Hans-Georg Hüttel, 'The Search for Khara Khorum and the Palace of the Great Khan', in *Genghis Khan and the Mongol Empire*, ed. William Fitzhugh, Morris Rossabi and William Honeychurch (Washington: Dino Don, 2009), 147–9.
74. *Qarshī* is a generic name for these imperial buildings, which in Mongolian means palace and palace hall. See Rashid al-Din, *Jāmiʿ al-Tawārīkh*, vol. 3, 2,385.

75. Rashid al-Din, *Jāmiʿ al-Tawārīkh*, vol. 1, 670.
76. Ruysbroeck, *Mission of Friar William Rubruck*, 221.
77. Ibid. (Introduction by Jackson and Morgan), 49–50.
78. Jan Bemmann, Sven Linzen, Susanne Reichert and Lkh Munkhbayar, 'Mapping Karakorum, the Capital of the Mongol Empire', *Antiquity* 96, no. 385 (2022): 159–78; Jan Bemmann and Susanne Reichert, 'Karakorum, the First Capital of the Mongol World Empire: An Imperial City in a non-Urban Society', *Asian Archaeology* 4, no. 2 (2021): 121–43.
79. Hüttel, 'Search for Khara Khorum', 148.
80. In addition to Karakorum itself, literary and physical evidence attest to the existence of diverse foreign motifs and styles in the seasonal palaces built in the environs of Karakorum. For instance, Juvayni (who visited Mongolia not long after Rubruck) and Rashid al-Din mention that one of the palaces of Ögedey was built by Muslims. The blue-glazed square floor tiles unearthed in excavations also suggest that the palace was possibly in the architectural style of the Muslims. The absence of roof tiles, which were common in the Chinese architectural style, supports this hypothesis. See Masuya, 'Seasonal Capitals', 233. For an example of fragments of a mural with figures recovered from the ruins of Karakorum, see James Watt, *The World of Khubilai Khan: Chinese Art in the Yuan Dynasty* (New Haven; London; New York: Metropolitan Museum of Art, 2010), 22.
81. Allsen, 'Archaeology and Mid-Imperial History', 89. Also see the results of the excavation of Karakorum conducted by a team of Soviet and Mongolian archaeologists under the direction of Sergej Kiselev in Sergei Kiselev, *Drevnemongol'skie goroda* [Ancient Mongolian Cities] (Moscow: Nauka, 1965). The chapters of *Drevnemongol'skie goroda* on the construction materials of Karakorum, the frescoes found in the court of Ögedey in Karakorum, and the ceramics, beads, coins and artefacts of various handicraft industries excavated in Karakorum are particularly worth studying. For more recent findings, see the results of the Mongolian-German expedition to Karakorum in Jan Bemmann, Ulambayar Erdenebat and Ernst Pohl, *Mongolian-German Karakorum Expedition, Vol. 1: Excavations in the Craftsmen Quarter at the Main Road* (Wiesbaden: Reichert Verlag, 2010) and the reports of the field research of Noriyuki Shiraishi around Karakorum in Shiraishi, 'Seasonal Migrations'.
82. Steinhardt, 'Imperial Architecture along the Mongolian Road', 62.
83. Masuya, 'Ilkhanid Courtly Life', 96.

84. Interestingly, two Persian sources, the *Jāmiʿ al-Tawārīkh* and the *Tārīkh-i Jahāngushāy*, are particularly enlightening about these seasonal palaces. See Shiraishi, 'Seasonal Migrations', 107–8.
85. Ibid., 117.
86. Elizabeth Endicott-West, 'The Yuan', in *Soviet Studies of Pre-Modern China: Assessments of Recent Scholarship*, ed. Gilbert Rozman (Cambridge: Cambridge University Press/Ann Arbor, MI: Centre for Chinese Studies, University of Michigan, 1984), 103.
87. On the basis of the studies of V. I. Tsalkin in Karakorum. See Allsen, 'Archaeology and Mid-Imperial History', 90. For further discussion, see V. I. Tsalkin, 'Fauna from the Excavations at Khara Khorum [in Russian]', *Kratkie Soobshcheniia Instituta Arkheologii* 114 (1968): 16–23.
88. The emphasis of Soviet scholars on the early urban culture of the Mongols may be discussed in relation to their national sensitivities. For further discussion on this topic, see Endicott-West, 'The Yuan', 103.
89. Archaeological studies suggest that the first truly urban settlements in Central Asia were built at the end of the third millennium BC. For further discussion on early urbanism in Central Asia, see Y. A. Zadneprovsky, 'Early Developments in Central Asia', *Iran* 33 (1995): 155–9. Shiraishi's studies of the Great *Ordu* of Chinggis Khan and the seasonal palaces of the Mongol emperors also shed light on the permanent structures built by the Mongols prior to the foundation of their major cities; see Shiraishi, 'Seasonal Migrations'; Shiraishi, 'Avraga Site'.
90. Nancy Steinhardt, *Chinese Imperial City Planning* (Honolulu: University of Hawaii Press, 1990), 153.
91. Rashid al-Din, *Jāmiʿ al-Tawārīkh*, vol. 2, 903.
92. Hok-lam Chan, *Legends of the Building of Old Peking* (Seattle; Hong Kong: University of Washington Press, 2008), 37.
93. On the role of Liu in the foundation of Shangdu, see Hatef Naiemi, 'Confronting the Foreigner', 14.
94. Steinhardt, 'Imperial Architecture under Mongolian Patronage', 163.
95. Steinhardt, *Chinese Imperial City Planning*, 151–3.
96. Masuya, 'Seasonal Capitals', 239–43.
97. Moule and Pelliot, *Marco Polo*, vol. 1, 185–7.
98. Masuya, 'Ilkhanid Phase of Takht-i Sulaimān', 209.
99. According to Rashid al-Din, Qubilay Khan designated the city of Khan Baliq, which is called Jungdu in Chinese (*khitāʾī*), as his winter camp (*qishlāq*). Next to Khan Baliq, he founded another city called Dai-Du, whose wall had seventeen

towers. In the middle of the city he built his *ordu*, which was a grand building (*sarāy*), and called it *qarshī*. See Rashid al-Din, *Jāmi' al-Tawārīkh*, vol. 2, 901.

100. Steinhardt, 'Imperial Architecture under Mongolian Patronage', 4.
101. For more information on different sorts of texts encompassing some details of Daidu as well as those publications that deal with the textual accounts of the city, see Steinhardt, 'Imperial Architecture under Mongolian Patronage', 5–8.
102. Steinhardt, *Chinese Imperial City Planning*, 154–8. For more information on the concentric triple-walled architectural model (or the classical Wangcheng model) and the astral-geographical precept of *fatian xiangdi* employed in the city building of Daidu, see Chan, *Legends of the Building*, 44–57.
103. Xiao Xun, *Gugong Yilu* (*Record of the Remains of the Imperial Palace*) (Taibei: Shijie Press, 1963), cited in Steinhardt, 'Imperial Architecture under Mongolian Patronage', 31–2.
104. Masuya, 'Seasonal Capitals', 238.
105. Steinhardt, 'Imperial Architecture under Mongolian Patronage', 46.
106. Chan, *Legends of the Building*, 45.
107. *Xijin zhi* (compiled by Xiong Mengxiang (1213–?)), 33, cited in Chan, *Legends of the Building*, 57. For further discussion of the impact of the *Yijing* (*Book of Changes*) on city planning in the Mongol-Yuan era, particularly in the two capitals of the Mongols, Daidu and Shangdu, see Chan, *Legends of the Building*, 192.
108. Masuya, 'Ilkhanid Phase of Takht-i Sulaimān', 214; Steinhardt, 'Plan of Khubilai Khan's', 137–58. The *Rituals of Zhou* (*Zhou Li*) became one of the nine Confucian Classics during the Tang dynasty (618–907). The text had been written in early classical Chinese. The *Rituals* is an idealised blueprint for government organisation; see B. Elman and M. Kern, *Statecraft and Classical Learning: The Rituals of Zhou in East Asian History* (Leiden and Boston, 2010), 1–29.
109. Steinhardt, 'Imperial Architecture under Mongolian Patronage', 60.
110. Ibid., 48.
111. Although Zhao Bingwen is mentioned as a person who accompanied Liu to inspect the site of Daidu and submitted a city plan to Qubilay Khan, his death date accords neither with Qubilay Khan's reign nor with the dates reported in other sources for the foundation of the city.
112. See Zhao Bingwen's biography in the *Yuan Shi* 150: 3,555, cited in Hok-lam Chan, 'Exorcising the Dragon: A Legend about the Building of the Mongolian Upper Capital (Shangdu)', *Central Asiatic Journal* 55, no. 1 (2011): 6, and Guo Shoujing's biography in the *Yuan Shi* 164: 2,852, cited in Chan, 'Exorcising the Dragon', 19.

113. Steinhardt, 'Imperial Architecture under Mongolian Patronage', 199–205.
114. Steinhardt, *Chinese Imperial City Planning*, 158.
115. The simplicity of Chinese architectural form is connected with its adaptability. Chinese structures – for instance the Chinese hall, as one of the simplest – can be erected quickly. They are adaptable to change and thereby can suit different conditions and tastes.
116. Allsen, 'Archaeology and Mid-Imperial History', 91.
117. Chapter 45 of the *Book of Ser Marco Polo*, trans. Colonel Henry Yule (Marco Polo, *Book of Ser Marco Polo*), contains a short description of the city of Etzina: 'When you leave the city of Campichu you ride for twelve days, and then reach a city called Etzina, which is towards the north on the verge of the Sandy Desert; it belongs to the Province of Tangut'. Allsen suggests that in Marco Polo's nomenclature Khara Khoto is referred to as Etzina. See Allsen, 'Archaeology and Mid-Imperial History', 91.
118. The site of Khara Khoto was extensively investigated by P. K. Kozlov in 1908 and 1926. For a history of the archaeological research conducted in Khara Khoto, see E. I. Lubo-Lesnichenko, 'Historical and Archaeological Investigation of the City of Khara Khoto [in Russian]', *SNV* 6 (1968): 115–24, cited in Allsen, 'Archaeology and Mid-Imperial History'.
119. E. I. Lubo-Lesnichenko, 'Porcelain Artifacts from Khara Khoto [in Russian]', *SNV* 18 (1976): 199–208, cited in Allsen, 'Archaeology and Mid-Imperial History'.
120. G. A. Pugachenkova, 'A Monument of Islamic Architecture in Khara Khoto [in Russian]', *SA* 3 (1965): 258–62, cited in Allsen, 'Archaeology and Mid-Imperial History'.
121. Ibid., 141–2.
122. Hillenbrand, *Islamic Art and Architecture*, 89–90.
123. As Akimushkin and Ivanov mention, the classification of art by dynasties is too artificial. This approach should serve merely as chronological guide. See Oleg Akimushkin and Anatol Ivanov, 'The Art of Illumination', in *The Arts of the Book in Central Asia, 14th–16th Centuries*, ed. Oleg Akimushkin and Basil Gray (London: Serindia, 1979), 35. However, despite the rejection of dynastic names, the use of rulers' names is sometimes justified since rulers played a central role – as patrons – in the formation of the arts, such as Timurid art. See Lisa Golombek and Donald Wilber, *The Timurid Architecture of Iran and Turan* (Princeton, NJ: Princeton University Press, 1988), xviii.
124. Lorenz Korn, 'Saljuqs: Art and Architecture', *Encyclopædia Iranica*, http://www.iranicaonline.org/articles/saljuqs-vi (last accessed 15 August 2023).

125. The Editors of *Encyclopaedia Britannica*, 'Seljuq, Turkish Dynasty', *Encyclopaedia Britannica*, https://www.britannica.com/topic/Seljuq (last accessed 10 July 2023).
126. Husayn Kamaly, 'Isfahan: Medieval Period', *Encyclopædia Iranica*, http://www.iranicaonline.org/articles/isfahan-vi-medieval-period (last accessed 10 July 2023).
127. Nasir-i Khusraw, *Nāṣer-e Khosraw's Book of Travels: Safarnāma*, trans. Wheeler M. Thackston (Albany, NY: The Persian Heritage Foundation, Bibliotheca Persica, 1986), 98.
128. Ibid., 99.
129. Kamaly, 'Isfahan: Medieval Period'.
130. Oleg Grabar, *The Great Mosque of Isfahan* (New York: New York University Press, 1990), 56. For further discussion on the meaning and origins of four-*īvān* mosques, see Edward Keall, 'Some Thoughts on the Early Eyvan', in *Near Eastern Numismatics, Iconography, Epigraphy, and History: Studies in Honor of George C. Miles*, ed. Dickran Kouymjian (Beirut: American University of Beirut, 1974), 123–30.
131. Sheila Blair, *The Monumental Inscriptions from Early Islamic Iran and Transoxiana* (Leiden; New York: Brill, 1992), 162.
132. Lisa Golombek, 'Urban Patterns in Pre-Safavid Isfahan', *Iranian Studies* 7, no. 1/2 (1974): 28–32; Somaiyeh Falahat and M. Reza Shirazi, 'New Urban Developments in Safavid Isfahan: Continuity or Disjuncture?', *Planning Perspectives* 27, no. 4 (2012): 614–16.
133. Nurallah Kasayi, 'Isfahan and the Nizamiyya Madrasa [Isfahan va Madrasa-yi Nizamiyya]', *Farhang-i Isfahan* 4 (1996): 7.
134. Heinz Gaube, *Iranian Cities* (New York: New York University Press, 1979), 76–82.
135. Guy Le Strange, *The Lands of the Eastern Caliphate; Mesopotamia, Persia, and Central Asia, from the Moslem Conquest to the Time of Timur* (Cambridge: Cambridge University Press, 1905), 385.
136. Hamdallah Mustawfi, *Nuzhat al-Qulūb* [Hearts' Bliss], ed. Muhammad Dabir-Siyaqi (Qazvin: Hadith-i Imruz, 2002), 212.
137. Charles Melville, 'Earthquakes in the History of Nishapur', *Iran: Journal of the British Institute of Persian Studies* 18 (1980): 117.
138. The term *dār al-mulk* utilised in historical texts refers to a city with political, economic and administrative centrality. It is usually used as the equivalent of 'capital'.

139. Mustawfi, *Nuzhat al-Qulūb*, 212.
140. Melville, 'Earthquakes', 104.
141. Clifford Edmund Bosworth, 'Nishapur: Historical Geography and History to the Beginning of the 20th Century', *Encyclopædia Iranica*, http://www.iranicaonline.org/articles/nishapur-i (last accessed 28 June 2023).
142. Ibn Hawqal, *Ṣūrat al-'Arḍ* [The Face of the Earth], ed. and trans. Ja'far Shu'ar (Tehran: Amir Kabir Press, 1987), 167.
143. Jürgen Paul, 'The Seljuq Conquest(s) of Nishapur: A Reappraisal', *Iranian Studies* 38, no. 4 (2005): 583–4; Rocco Rante, 'Nishapur: Archeology', *Encyclopædia Iranica*, http://www.iranicaonline.org/articles/nishapur-06-archeology (last accessed 29 July 2023).
144. Richard Bulliet, 'Medieval Nishapur: A Topographic and Demographic Reconstruction', *Studia Iranica* 5 (1975): 72–3.
145. Ibn Hawqal, *Ṣūrat al-'Arḍ*, 166. There are different versions of this name in different historical texts, such as Abrashahr (Le Strange, *Lands of the Eastern Caliphate*, 383). Although the origin of the word is still unknown, it is possibly derived from the name of the Sasanian province of Abharshahr or Abarshahr.
146. The large cruciform mound identified by P. M. Sykes as 'ruins of Bazaars' in 1911 was presumably the Large Crossroads Market. See Bulliet, 'Medieval Nishapur', 74–5.
147. Ibn Hawqal, *Ṣūrat al-'Arḍ*, 166–9; Le Strange, *Lands of the Eastern Caliphate*, 383–5.
148. Hakim-i Nishapuri, *Tārīkh-i Nishābūr* [The History of Nishapur], ed. Muhammad R. Shafiei Kadkani (Tehran: Agah Press, 2005), 200.
149. Le Strange, *Lands of the Eastern Caliphate*, 384.
150. Bulliet, 'Medieval Nishapur', 77–85. Following the excavations made at a number of places in Nishapur, some of Bulliet's speculations have been criticised. See Charles Wilkinson, *Nishapur: Some Early Islamic Buildings and their Decoration* (New York: The Metropolitan Museum of Art, 1986); Rocco Rante and Annabelle Collinet, *Nishapur Revisited: Stratigraphy and Ceramics of the Qohandez* (Oxford: Oxbow Books, 2013).
151. Rante, 'Nishapur: Archeology'.
152. The word 'city' applied by Hakim may refer solely to the flourishing state of Shadiyakh during the time of the Saffarids.
153. Hakim-i Nishapuri, *Tārīkh-i Nishābūr*, 201.
154. Melville, 'Earthquakes', 106.
155. Ibid., 105.

156. On the history of Nishapur, see also Wilkinson, *Nishapur*, 37–44.
157. Nasir-i Khusraw, *Book of Travels*, 2.
158. Richard Bulliet, *The Patricians of Nishapur: A Study in Medieval Islamic Social History* (Cambridge, MA: Harvard University Press, 1972), 249–55.
159. Wilkinson, *Nishapur*, 290.

2

'Let our Capital be our Saddle':[1] The Foundation of Urban Centres under the Ilkhanids

The Mongols, at least during the early years of their presence in Iran, showed little interest in the traditional system that had been used by previous dynasties. Instead, they returned to their own traditions, perfectly exemplified by the Yasa of Chinggis Khan. They founded their seasonal capitals and camps in Khurasan and Azerbaijan, although military, ecological and economic factors persuaded them to concentrate in the north-west. As an essential part of their nomadic life, they kept on the move between their seasonal camps even after establishing themselves as the rulers of the sedentary world. Living on horseback and in tents, while migrating between summer and winter capitals, not only harked back to earlier times but was also essential to pastoral nomadism, which was deemed a pivotal element in the Mongol economy.[2] Despite the allegiance of the Ilkhans to the Yasa and their dependence on the portable settlements throughout the Ilkhanid period, they gradually realised that they would not be able to achieve political stability merely through following this traditional doctrine and lifestyle. Therefore, they started seeking other methods of governing the country. In the same way, the history of the Mongols in Iran is characterised, in Melville's words, by their oscillation between two poles: adjusting to Persian ways in some circumstances and retaining their own customs within the Persian context in others.[3]

The Construction Activities of the Ilkhans

The textual and physical evidence testify that the Ilkhanid rulers pursued the foundation of new settlements as one of their prime ambitious objectives throughout the thirteenth and fourteenth centuries. The flourishing state of construction under the Ilkhanids was the product of the relative stability that started to grow around the mid-thirteenth century. Although the picture of the Ilkhanid settlements is extremely blurred, if we take into account the archaeological and architectural remains as well as the sporadic references to these sites found in written sources, the Ilkhans' enterprises seem to fall loosely into three categories: seasonal camps, permanent capitals and pre-existing smaller towns and villages developed by the Ilkhans.

Seasonal camps

Ilkhanid courtly life, particularly during the reign of the early Ilkhans, was deeply affected by Mongolian traditions. The Ilkhanid court retained the pivotal feature of the nomadic life of their ancestors and adhered to the foundation of seasonal camps and seasonal migration between summer camps (*yaylāq*s) and winter camps (*qishlāq*s) around which their first settlements formed. Seasonal camps were the temporary residences of the Mongols. They usually consisted of the royal tents erected in the centre during the annual presence of *ordus*[4] in the site and a few permanent buildings constructed around the tents. Since the Ilkhans resided in these encampments for certain months, the administrative body of their court was inevitably transferred there. In some cases, to supply the *ordu*, small groups of artisans and traders gradually shaped their neighbourhoods around the camps. However, the settlements were usually abandoned after the death of the ruler or the permanent departure of his camp, since the social and economic life of the city dwellers was mainly dependent upon the presence of the camp. Nothing remained of most of the Ilkhanid royal camps but some names appearing in the historical texts of the fourteenth century such as Alatagh in Azerbaijan founded by Hülegü and Qutlugh-Baligh built by Gaykhatu (r. 1291–5) in the region of Arran.[5]

We should approach this group of Ilkhanid residences cautiously, since our modern perceptions of urban centres might affect how we evaluate these foundations. In the eyes of the thirteenth-century nomad Mongols, their seasonal camps possibly stood in the same, if not higher, position as their permanent capitals. As we will see later in the book, the Ilkhanids founded their permanent political capitals, consisting of numerous magnificent buildings, on the basis of the patterns and criteria of the sedentary world. Nevertheless, they still valued their camps as the headquarters of their courts. Mentions of the grand assemblies of the Mongol princes (*qūrīltāys*) who gathered in these encampments to make important administrative and military decisions support this claim. For instance, in the *Tarikh-i Mubarak-i Ghazani*, Rashid al-Din refers to one of these assemblies held in the yurt of Sayin (located between Sarav and Ardabil), which lasted two days.[6]

Permanent capitals

The idea of establishing a governmental centre as the permanent capital of the Ilkhan formed during the reign of the fourth Ilkhan, Arghun Khan, in the palatial city of Arghuniyya (Arghun's city). However, his son Ghazan Khan was the first Ilkhan to have founded a true capital and administrative centre, the complex of Ghazaniyya (Ghazan's city) in the suburb of Tabriz. This tradition was followed by his brother and successor, Öljeytü, in Sultaniyya.[7] While these capital cities were established as permanent settlements, they were often the residence of the court for only a few months during the year. Since the later Ilkhans continued the practice of seasonal migration, in fact, they supplanted their seasonal camps with cities, consisting of monumental buildings, around which they still camped and erected their royal tents.

The cities were built on the basis of predetermined plans while their location, layout, material and requisite sources of finance had been arranged in advance. The royal court was accommodated in the central core of the city or the citadel. The citadel, in most cases, was composed of a multi-functional complex known as *abwāb al-birr*.[8] The complex was formed from individual buildings and charitable foundations enclosing the tomb of the Ilkhanid sultans, their viziers or Sufi shaykhs. The citadel was surrounded by the edifices, gardens and various public, governmental and imperial buildings built by the viziers and the notables. The complex of buildings, along with the houses of the city dwellers, were encompassed by a fortified wall.

Isfahanian discusses the foundation of Ilkhanid administrative and political centres and suggests that while many public and private buildings were patronised by statesmen or Mongol princes, in fact they were built by order of the Ilkhan. Wealthy officials were forced to contribute to the development of the cities that had been intended to fulfil the political aspirations of the Ilkhans. Much of the workforce in these architectural undertakings consisted of artists, artisans and workers who were also compelled to leave their homelands and take part in these large-scale urban projects. Although this compulsion increased the speed and volume of the construction work, it jeopardised the future of the cities. Many of the citizens who had been resettled in these newly founded cities left them immediately after the death of the Ilkhan. Despite the centrality and prosperity of the cities in their heyday, they were mostly left as unfinished projects by the successors of the deceased Ilkhan, gradually declining after the fall of the Ilkhanid dynasty.[9]

Pre-existing smaller towns and villages

The Ilkhans provided a proper context for the development of smaller villages and towns through the construction of public buildings and expanding infrastructure such as water systems and roads. Over the course of time, they attracted many immigrants and converted into larger cities. Since this type of settlements developed on the basis of the social, cultural and economic needs of the residents of the region, they mostly continued to thrive even after the disintegration of the Ilkhanids, unlike the settlements of the first and second groups. Many of the urban undertakings in this category are associated with Ghazan Khan's reforms. As an example, one can refer to the large group of villages founded along the Ghazani River in Iraq. Ghazan Khan constructed a channel between Baghdad and Hillah and led a branch of the Euphrates to it. Following the development of the region, he founded a city there and called it Ghazaniyya.[10] The city of Rayy that had been destroyed during the Mongol invasion was rebuilt by order of the Ilkhan. A new wall and a moat were also constructed around Shiraz. A number of charitable complexes, khanqahs and *dār al-sīyāda*s (a residence for *sayyid*s and *sādāt*s, the descendants of the Prophet Muhammad) were founded across the country due to the religious beliefs of the Ilkhan and his devotion towards dervishes and the descendants of the Prophet.[11]

Leafing through the textual sources of the Ilkhanid period, one comes across the name of several sites from the three above-mentioned categories. Some of them still exist, but many of them are mere names, barely connected with an existent site: for instance, the unknown seasonal quarters named in the itineraries of the Ilkhans, particularly those of Ghazan Khan and Öljeytü.[12] While the descriptions of the cases in the historical texts are mostly brief, they are still informative regarding the location and, in few cases, the general characteristics of each site. According to these scattered pieces of information, we can make a list of more famous settlements (including camps, villages, towns and cities) associated with the Ilkhans. The list, although incomplete, gives us an idea of what prolific patrons the Ilkhans were (Figure 2.1):[13]

- Maraghih.
- Takht-i Sulayman (Suqurluq)[14] in Azerbaijan.
- Tabriz, Arghuniyya and Ghazaniyya: in addition to the urban complexes constructed in Ilkhanid Tabriz, two smaller settlements, Arghuniyya and Ghazaniyya, developed in the suburbs of Tabriz.
- Sultaniyya (called Qunqur Öläng during the reign of Arghun).
- Sharuyaz was possibly the same area as that in which the city of Sultaniyya was later built by Öljeytü. Rashid al-Din mentions the grand city of Sharuyaz initiated by Arghun but left as an incomplete project.[15]
- Khabushan, in Khurasan, was rebuilt by Hülegü and was expanded by his grandson Arghun[16] and his great-grandson Ghazan.[17]
- Alatagh, in Azerbaijan, was the summer camp of Hülegü where he built a grand building.[18]
- Qishlaq-i Zarrinih-rud, or the winter camp of Hülegü in Zarrinih-rud, in the south of Lake Urmia in Azerbaijan, was called Chaghatu and Naqatu by the Mongols.[19]
- Siyah Kuh, in Azerbaijan, along with Alatagh, was designated by Abaqa Khan as his summer camp.[20]
- Sujas is a region located about five *farsang*s to the south of Sultaniyya. Arghun was secretly buried in Mount Sujas. However, his daughter Öljey Khatun revealed his grave, built a khanqah there and resettled people in the site.[21] In addition, Bulughan Khatun the Elder died beside the Kur River in 1286 and her coffin was taken to Mount Sujas.[22] She was the wife of Abaqa Khan and married his son Arghun Khan after his death (according to a Mongolian tradition).
- Ujan or Shahr-i Islam (City of Islam) in the south-east of Tabriz was founded by Ghazan Khan.[23]
- Qutlugh-Baligh was built by Gaykhatu in the region of Arran, at Qarachali, which was his old yurt,[24] beside the Kur River.[25]

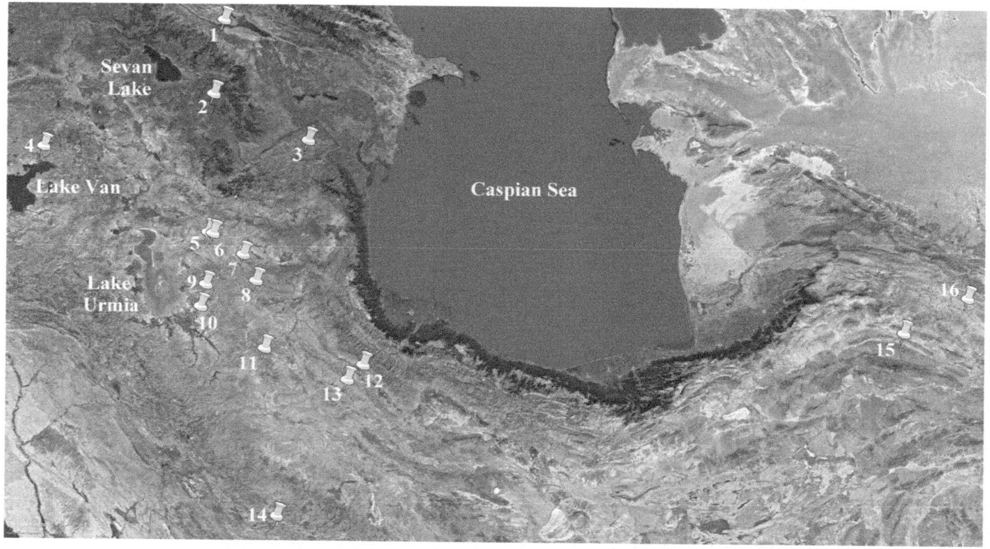

Figure 2.1 Location of the camps and cities of the Ilkhans.
Safely identified locations:

2. Arran Region	8. Hasht-rud	13. Sujas
5. Tabriz	9. Maraghih	15. Aq Qalʿih
6. Ghazaniyya	11. Takht-i Sulayman	
7. Ujan	12. Sultaniyya	

Possibly identified locations:

1. Qutlugh-Baligh	4. Alatagh	14. Sultanabad-i Chimchal
3. Mahmudabad	10. Chaghatu and Naqatu	16. Khabushan

The locations of Siyah Kuh, Ghazaniyya of Iraq, the yurt of Hulan Muran, and Sultanabad (Öljeytüabad) are unknown
Google Earth
Landsat/Copernicus

- Mahmudabad was founded by Ghazan Khan on the plain of Gavbari, on the Mughan Plain that was one of his winter camps.[26] Öljeytü led a branch of Aras River to Gavbari and made it a cultivated field.[27]
- Ghazaniyya of Iraq, founded by Ghazan Khan.[28]
- The yurt of Hulan Muran,[29] in Azerbaijan, which was called Buynuq by Öljeytü.[30]
- Hasht-rud, in Azerbaijan, has repeatedly been mentioned in the historical texts as one of the stopping points of Ghazan Khan in the course of his seasonal migrations between summer and winter camps.[31]
- Sultanabad-i Chimchal: in the *Tarikh-i Öljeytü*, Kashani mentions that Öljeytü founded the city of Sultanabad in Sultan-Maydan around Chimchal and Mount Bisutun in Kermanshah in 1312.[32]
- Sultanabad or Öljeytüabad, founded by Öljeytü in the Mughan plain.[33]
- Arran was the winter camp of the Ilkhans. The lands between the Kur and Aras rivers are called *vilāyat-i Arran* by Mustawfi.[34] The palace of Mansuriyya was located in Arran.[35]
- Baghdad was one of the winter camps of the Ilkhans where they conducted several construction projects.
- Aq Qalʿih in Khurasan (the site is not mentioned in any pre-Modern text).[36]

Locating and examining all the sites that contributed to the generation of a new landscape of Mongol settlements in north-western Iran is neither within the scope of this book nor practically feasible, mainly because of the extent of destruction in most cases and the scarcity of archaeological and architectural evidence. While acknowledging the importance of the study of different types of Ilkhanid sites, the focus of the present research is the second group: the larger settlements designated by the Ilkhans as their administrative and political capitals. Therefore, a fleeting overview of their major urban foundations is here offered first, and the enterprises of five successions of the Ilkhans, Hülegü, Abaqa Khan, Arghun Khan, Ghazan Khan and Öljeytü, are analysed next. The study of three capital cities in the north-west of Iran – Maraghih, Takht-i Sulayman and Ujan – will be followed by a brief discussion of a lesser-known urban project in Khurasan, Aq Qalʿih. The most prominent urban centres of the Ilkhans in Ghazaniyya and Sultaniyya will be examined thoroughly in the next two chapters.

Ilkhanid Urban Foundations: A Brief Overview

Urban development in Iran during the Ilkhanid dynasty was largely influenced by fluctuations in the political, economic and cultural environment of the country. After the conquest of Iran, the Mongol rulers and princes, who were designated as the representatives of the Great Khans, began the revitalisation of the towns and cities that had been extensively destroyed in the course of the invasion in the 1250s. Although establishing security and stabilising commerce across the country were the Mongols' primary objectives, their undertakings indirectly resulted in the recovery of urban life. Many cities in Azerbaijan and Greater Khurasan, particularly Marv and Tus, flourished significantly during the first years of Ilkhanid rule, to the extent that the latter was promoted to the capital or *dār al-mulk* of Khurasan.[37] In addition, within the cities, the emergence of new patrons breathed new life into art, architecture and historiography.

The political stability occurring after the arrival of Hülegü and the foundation of the Ilkhanid dynasty intensified the process of urban development. Under Hülegü the architectural and urban projects were mostly conducted in the western regions of the country, with some exceptions, for instance the city of Khabushan in Khurasan which was largely rebuilt by Hülegü and the notables of his court. According to Juvayni, the city and its infrastructure, such as the underground water system (*kārīz*), were restored by order of Hülegü, who also covered the entire cost of the construction work.[38]

In western Iran, Hülegü first focused his attention on the reconstruction of Baghdad, but his urban development activities extended to Azerbaijan following the designation of this region as the headquarters of the Mongols. Maraghih was chosen as the first capital of the Mongols, and the best-known architectural project of Hülegü, the observatory, was founded there through the efforts of Nasir al-Din al-Tusi (d. 1274), the famous scientist and astronomer. In addition to the cities, Hülegü erected several buildings in his seasonal camps, where he resided for most of the year; for example, Rashid al-Din refers to a splendid house (*sarā*) in Alatagh and an idol-temple (*but-khānih*) in Khuy, both in Azerbaijan, that were built by the Ilkhan.[39] Rabban Sawma (d. 1294) also writes about a church in Alatagh which had been built by Doquz Khatun (d. 1265), the Christian wife of Hülegü.[40] The other example is a fortified structure reported to have been built by order of Hülegü to protect his mythical treasure gathered in Baghdad and other campaigns. Rashid al-Din states that Hülegü ordered Majd al-Din-i Tabriz to construct a strong building in a mountain called Tillih[41] on the shore of Lake Urmiya and Salmas,[42] while some scholars speculatively suggest that the building was located on the rocky island of Shahi in Lake Urmiya, although no archaeological work has ever been undertaken to support this claim.[43]

The local powers in the south, particularly Fars, Kerman and Yazd, retained their place by submitting themselves to Hülegü. They even strengthened their connections with the Mongol court via marriage. There is no evidence of the physical presence of the Ilkhans in central and southern Iran, possibly because the hot and dry climate of these regions did not attract Mongol pastoralists.[44] However, the historical accounts reveal that they controlled these areas by supporting certain groups of local princes. Interestingly, in several cases, in lieu of princes who were of young age, their powerful mothers acted as regents intervening in political and economic affairs.[45] These women were often active patrons who financed extensive architectural projects. Qutlugh Tarkan Khatun in Kerman region is an outstanding example in this regard.[46] During her reign she initiated a vast architectural project, consisting of five major buildings, and ordered the construction of underground water channels. In addition, approximately sixteen charitable foundations bear witness to her philanthropy.[47] Wealthy provincial families also extensively supported the religious classes, both the 'ulama' and Sufi shaykhs, by conducting architectural programmes and constructing religious buildings in the cities. These families contributed to strengthening the values of Islamic communal life that had been severely damaged during the Mongol invasions.[48]

Tabriz and Takht-i Sulayman developed during the reign of Hülegü's successor, Abaqa Khan. In addition to the Mongols, Persian families also started to take part in the urban and architectural projects. The most famous of these is the Juvayni family, which was promoted to the higher political positions in the Ilkhanid court, particularly under Abaqa Khan. Several members of this family invested significant amounts of their wealth in construction works and patronised several projects in Khurasan, 'Araq-i 'Arab, 'Araq-i 'Ajam, or Persian 'Araq (particularly Isfahan) and Rum.[49]

Despite the cases mentioned earlier, it is noteworthy that the Mongols' policy of urban development, especially during the period of the earlier

Ilkhans, was confined to the cities designated as their major urban centres. Many smaller cities and towns continued to suffer from the consequences of the Mongol invasions in the first half of the thirteenth century. During the reign of Abaqa Khan's successors, Arghun Khan and Gaykhatu, the Ilkhanids broadened their construction activities and founded several new cities rather than focusing on the renovation of the existing ones. The best-known case was the city of Arghuniyya in the vicinity of Tabriz, which will be discussed later. Nevertheless, nothing remains of most of these cities since they were mainly built near the location of their seasonal camps without consideration for the infrastructures essential to urban life.

Under Ghazan Khan, a comprehensive construction programme was implemented which, despite the earlier schemes, took into consideration all the necessary components of a prosperous city and the welfare of its inhabitants. Rashid al-Din praises Ghazan Khan for this programme and confirms that the system designed by the Ilkhan was better than anyone would have thought possible since all the technical and financial issues involved were handed over to the most reliable experts.[50] While the architectural undertakings led by Ghazan Khan culminated in the city of Ghazaniyya, construction activities were not confined to the capital but were extended to almost all the regions of the country, beyond the areas where the Ilkhans resided. In addition to the undertakings initiated by Ghazan himself, he issued a decree (*yarlīgh*) that compelled the local rulers and governors to conduct architectural and urban projects in their domains.[51]

Blair raises an interesting point about the network through which 'Ghazan's reforms were diffused vertically through the society and horizontally into the countryside'. The Iranian civil bureaucracy, whose fortune was mainly based on land tenure, became wealthier, mostly due to the financial reforms of Ghazan's vizier, Rashid al-Din, especially regarding the system of taxation. As a result, along with the buildings patronised by the royals and the notables in the Ilkhanid capitals, this economic improvement enabled the local officials to finance many architectural projects in their home towns.[52] The considerable number of construction projects expanded the movement of craftsmen and materials among different urban centres, an important point which will be analysed further in the following chapters.

The development plans of Ghazan Khan were pursued by his successor Öljeytü. The most ambitious urban project of the Ilkhanids, the city of

Sultaniyya, was founded by order of Öljeytü. Although the city did not finish during his lifetime and his son Abu Saʿid did not complete the work left unfinished by his father, the architectural remains of Sultaniyya attest to the stylistic and technical excellence of the city patronised by Öljeytü. After the death of the Ilkhan, during the reign of Abu Saʿid, the process of urban development significantly decelerated. By the time the Ilkhanids disintegrated in the mid-fourteenth century, construction activities had almost ceased.

The great interest of the Ilkhans in urban and architectural activities encouraged the Persian elites to become involved in the construction projects all over the country. While the Mongol invasions of the thirteenth century had left urban life in ruins, the development programmes pursued by the Mongols, particularly during the time of Ghazan Khan and Öljeytü, gave the Iranians the opportunity to reclaim their lost social position and economic success through the patronage of various construction projects. Among them, those notables who had penetrated the Mongol court encouraged the Ilkhans to invest in the urban development even more, and they themselves became the most prolific patrons. Rashid al-Din and Taj al-Din ʿAli Shah (d. 1324) shine out as two important figures in this regard who financed several projects in different cities.[53] As a result, one can suggest that the flourishing urban development under the Ilkhans was the product of an environment in which not only the sultan but also a diverse group of patrons, including Mongol princes and amirs, Persian viziers and nobles and local rulers and governors, underwrote construction projects. Although the real motivation behind their actions is not still entirely transparent, this enthusiastic patronage was successful in partly compensating for the extensive destruction caused by the Mongols.

Major Urban Foundations of the Ilkhans

Maraghih

In 1258, Ilkhanid forces led by Hülegü Khan besieged and captured Baghdad, the capital of the Abbasid Caliphate. The disintegration of the Sunni caliphate that had lasted for more than five centuries left most parts of the Islamic world in a state of political turmoil. Several claimants attempted to fill the power vacuum left by the execution of the last caliph, Al-Mustaʿsim (r. 1242–58), who was believed by Sunnis to be the true successor of the Prophet Muhammad.

The struggle began between Buddhist/Christian-oriented Mongol Hülegü, who had conquered much of Western Asia, and the Mamluk sultans, who were the successors of the Ayyubids who had defended the Islamic world against the Christian world and the Crusaders. Although this conflict continued through the Ilkhanid period, in comparison with other Ilkhans, Hülegü faced more challenges both inside and outside his domain. He had to establish his reign in a foreign land and ensure its durability for his successors.[54]

When the Ilkhans stabilised themselves as the rulers of the south-western sector of the Mongol Empire, they founded two headquarters, one in the north-west/west and the other in the north-east/east of present-day Iran. Throughout the Ilkhanid period, the western headquarters was the residence of the Ilkhan/sultan (*sulṭan-nishīn*) and the eastern headquarters was the residence of the crown prince (*valī'ahd-nishīn*). Maraghih, Tabriz and Sultaniyya in Azerbaijan, and Marv and Tus in Khurasan, were the headquarters or capitals of the Ilkhans, which are usually called *dār al-mulk* in their contemporary accounts. Many of the large-scale construction projects patronised by Mongol khans were concentrated in their capitals, among which Maraghih, the capital of Hülegü, contains the smallest number of surviving Ilkhanid structures.[55]

Maraghih lies beside the Sufi-Chay River, which rises at Mount Sahand in north-west Iran. The fertile soil and fine pastures, mild weather and the strategic location of the city, which was on the route connecting 'Araq-i 'Ajam to Azerbaijan, persuaded Hülegü to designate Maraghih as the first capital of the Ilkhans and the *dār al-mulk* of Azerbaijan. Furthermore, Maraghih was a significant centre of Islamic education in Azerbaijan prior to the Mongol invasion of Iran. Historical texts confirm that at least seven important madrasas had been built in this city up to the thirteenth century.[56] Alongside educational institutions, the extant architectural structures from the Seljuq period, such as Gunbad-i Surkh (1147), Gunbad-i Kabud (possibly 1197) and Burj-i Mudavvar (1167), attest to the prosperity of the city in earlier centuries.[57]

The best-known component of the Ilkhanid city was an astronomical observatory, built in 1259 under the patronage of Hülegü and the directorship of Nasir al-Din al-Tusi. Prominent scientists from Damascus, Mosul, Tbilisi and Qazvin were summoned to Maraghih by Hülegü's decree. The observatory of Maraghih is believed to be the first Islamic observatory to have benefited from extensive endowments, and in this regard it established a new tradition which was later imitated in the Ulugh Beg Observatory in Samarqand and the Observatory of Sultan Murad III in Istanbul.[58] Wassaf writes that the observatory was located to the north of Maraghih on the top of a hill. The structure had a dome, and the rays of the sun entered it through a slit in its upper part.[59] Along with the observatory, there was a library in the complex for manuscripts plundered at Baghdad and elsewhere.

The excavations carried out at the site revealed interesting points regarding the outline of the observatory. The most important component of the complex was a circular tower whose internal space consisted of a long passage along the diameter of the circle with six rooms on either side. Alongside the remains of the tower, which measured around 23.6 metres in external and 22 metres in internal diameter, the foundations of five other circular structures were found whose function is yet unclear. Some other parts of the complex have been uncovered by archaeologists, including the foundries where the astronomical devices were produced, a madrasa, a library and residential units.[60]

To the west of the hill, there are a number of cells and tunnels that were carved out and called locally the temple of Rasad-daghi (Figure 2.2).[61] It is unlikely that these spaces were connected with the structures of the observatory; however, they were possibly built during the same period as the main complex. Shikari-Niri speculatively associates the rooms with Chinese and Mongolian religious ceremonies. Considering the altar-like elements and the stone platforms in the rooms, he suggests that they were possibly part of a Buddhist temple.[62] A historical account given by Rashid al-Din supports this claim since it affirms the presence of Buddhists in Maraghih during the Ilkhanid period. The vizier writes that in 688/1289 Arghun arrived in Maraghih and paid a visit to the observatory. He began to take the 'black drug' (*dārū-yi sīyāh*) there. The drug was, in fact, an elixir promising eternal life. It was prescribed by a Buddhist priest (*bakhshī*) from India in whom Arghun had great faith. Rashid al-Din believed that taking that drug eventually resulted in the death of the Ilkhan.[63] A more recent report written by Arnold Wilson, who visited the site in the early twentieth century, connects the rooms cut into the rock with a Nestorian monastery. Wilson was told by the locals of Maraghih that Christian monks had lived in the cells of this monastery a long time ago.[64]

The observatory continued to exist until the reign of Abu Sa'id, but during the Aq Qoyunlu and Jalayirids invasions of Azerbaijan the complex

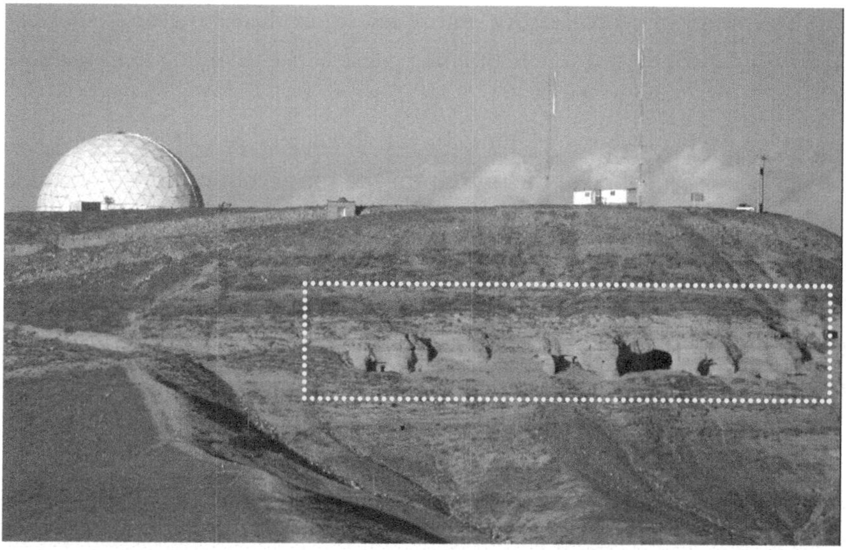

Figure 2.2 Observatory of Maraghih and the temple of Rasad-daghi. The archaeological remains of the observatory are conserved under the white half-sphere. The cells of the temple of Rasad-daghi are marked on the photo.
© Atri Hatef Naiemi

suffered massive destruction and its grand library was plundered. Nevertheless, some individual elements of the building remained at the site. Ghiyath al-Din Jamshid Kashani (d. 1429), a Persian astronomer and mathematician who was invited to Samarqand by Ulugh Beg to work at his observatory, mentions one of these. In a letter he wrote to his father, he describes a 'geometric circular pulpit' (*minbar-i mustadīr-i hindisī*) in the middle of the Maraghih observatory, whose nature and function were not known to anyone.[65]

Although Nasir al-Din's fame to a large degree rests on his scientific activities, he was also an influential politician assisting Hülegü with his decision-making. The Ilkhan delegated to him complete authority over endowments (*awqāf*) throughout the country. In order to control the large incomes earned from the donated properties, Nasir al-Din designated one deputy to each city. It is reported that one tenth of the revenues was allocated to Maraghih observatory to cover the expenses of the residents and the equipment.[66] Furthermore, Nasir al-Din was a leading supporter of Shiʿa beliefs, who provided a proper context for the political and social activities of the Shiʿis.[67]

Except for the observatory and a few individual structures, such as Gunbad-i Ghaffariyya, a square building constructed according to its inscription during the reign of Abu Saʿid, the main body of the city has been massively destroyed over the course of time. In the absence of proper archaeological data on the urban fabric of the thirteenth- and fourteenth-century Maraghih, textual sources are rather enlightening. What will be offered in the following section is a brief overview of the buildings – mentioned in the historical texts – that existed in the urban landscape of Ilkhanid Maraghih. Such random remarks on the Ilkhanid foundations may not provide us with a transparent picture of the first capital of the Mongols, but they do enhance our understanding of the spatial structure of the city.

Juvayni refers to an idol-temple (*but-khānih*) in Maraghih.[68] In the endowment deed of the Rabʿ-i Rashidi, Rashid al-Din writes about several plots of land in Maraghih endowed by the vizier for a madrasa he built in the same city.[69] Ibn al-Fuwati (d. 1323) refers to Majd al-Din Muhammad al-Sivasi al-Rumi, who resided in Maraghih around 1280 and had a madrasa next to the congregational mosque.[70] In another entry of his book, Ibn al-Fuwati mentions ʿIzz al-Din Abu al-Fazl al-Maraghi, who was a famous preacher in the congregational mosque of Maraghih, and Nasir al-Din had great faith in him.[71] *Zāwīya* of al-Shaykh Suvab[72] and Suq al-Bazzazin[73] (the bazaar of textile sellers) are two other buildings that existed, according to Ibn al-Fuwati, in Ilkhanid Maraghih.

Rabban Sawma was a Turkic Chinese monk and later a Nestorian priest who was dispatched to Europe as Arghun's envoy in 1287. The purpose of the journey was to seek help in defeating the Mamluks.[74] In his long journey from China to West Asia, he was accompanied by his fellow cleric, Mar Yaballaha, who was later elected Patriarch of the Nestorian Church in West Asia. They benefited from the tolerant policies of Abaqa, Arghun and Gaykhatu towards Nestorians. For example, Abaqa authorised the Patriarch to levy a tax for the upkeep of the churches and monasteries, or, during the reign of Arghun, the power of the Patriarch increased, and several churches were built under his supervision.[75] What is important for our discussion is the construction of the churches and monasteries in Maraghih associated with these two historical figures. The first case is the church of Mar Shalita. During the reign of Arghun, Mar Yaballaha pulled down the old building and spent large sums of money on rebuilding it.

Sawma emphasises that 'instead of using [the old] beams [and making a single roof] he made [the new church] with two naves; and by the side of it he built a cell in which to live'.[76] Before the consolidation of power in the hands of Ghazan Khan, enmity towards non-Muslims, including towards Christians, encouraged by Amir Nowruz resulted in the destruction of this church.

After accomplishing his mission and returning from Europe, Sawma won Arghun's favour and received great rewards from him. Remarkably, Arghun made a pledge to build him a church at the Gate of his Kingdom (i.e. the Ilkhanate palace). In 1288, by order of the Ilkhan and at Sawma's request, Mar Yaballaha came to the camp, whose location is still unknown to us, to consecrate the church. Arghun erected a tent-like church, which 'was so close to the Door of the Throne that the ropes of the curtains of the church intermingled with those of his [Arghun's] house' and made a great feast. When the camp moved, Sawma, who was designated the chief and director of the church, alongside the priests moved the church and all its belongings.[77] In 1289, as another sign of favour, Arghun went to the residence/cell of the Patriarch in Maraghih and asked Mar Yaballaha to baptise his son Öljeytü.[78]

The next case is a permanent church built by Sawma in the names of Mar Mari and Mar George under the direct patronage of Gaykhatu in Maraghih. Sawma, who had grown old and tired of the seasonal migrations of the Mongols, completed the building and resided in the cell he had built by the side of the church until 1293, when he went to Baghdad in the service of Mar Yaballaha for the last year of his life. The church was located near the site of Mar Yaballaha's private residence/cell, where Gaykhatu visited him twice and remained there as his guest for short periods. Furthermore, with the help of Mar Yaballaha, Sawma founded a series of endowments in order to provide the church with an income covering the cost of the building's upkeep.[79] The last case is the holy monastery of Mar John the Baptist built by Mar Yaballaha on the north side of the city of Maraghih, at a distance of about two miles from the city, in 1294. He started building the monastery with the money he had received from Gaykhatu. Sawma writes that 'he built up the wall nearly to the top, and the nave up as far as the spring of the roof', but we are not sure whether he succeeded in completing the building.[80]

Maraghih was a political and administrative centre under Hülegü. After his death, the *dār al-mulk* was transferred to Tabriz. Hülegü died in Maraghih but his coffin, according to Mongolian traditions, was carried to Mount Shahu in Dih-kharigan where his *quruq* (forbidden burial precinct) had already been built.[81]

Takht-i Sulayman (Suqurluq)

The dates found on the lustre-painted tiles unearthed during the excavations of Takht-i Sulayman suggest that the construction of the Ilkhanid palatial complex goes back at least to the reign of Abaqa Khan.[82] Mustawfi's report on the site also supports this claim.[83] However, neither Rashid al-Din nor Wassaf clearly write about the foundation of the town by the Ilkhan, although they mention other quarters where he spent his summers and winters.[84] It is also noteworthy that Rashid al-Din refers to Takht-i Sulayman as Suqurluq but does not specifically attribute the construction of its complex to Abaqa Khan. The name Takht-i Sulayman appeared only after the Timurid conquest of Persia.[85]

The site includes the remains of the sanctuary of Azar Gushnasp, which literally means the 'fire of the warriors and kings' (one of the three most revered fires of the Sasanian period, AD 224–651[86]), and the other related contemporary buildings. Although archaeological excavations conducted at the site revealed materials that date back to the Achaemenid period (550–330 BC), the monumental architecture on the site was begun later during the Sasanian dynasty. The arrangement of the extant buildings in relation to the open spaces suggests that the site was originally laid out on a master plan which determined all later building activities.[87] After the Mongol conquest, Abaqa Khan built his palace on the ruins of the ancient sanctuary and palatial complex. In addition to natural resources and the intact strong fortification available at the site of Takht-i Sulayman,[88] the re-use of a pre-Islamic site might be explained with regard to the Ilkhans' intention to associate themselves with the ancient history of Iran. This possibility is strengthened by the fact that the Ilkhanid palace was decorated with tiles depicting scenes and verses from the *Shahnama* (Book of Kings), the Persian national epic. The transformation of the Ilkhans into religious and national heroes intensified during the reign of later Ilkhans (see Chapters 3 and 4), particularly Ghazan Khan, who was idealised, in Melville's words, as a 'second Alexander, a philosopher king, and a Persian emperor'.[89]

The Ilkhanid constructions in Takht-i Sulayman were mainly based on the original Sasanian layout. The palatial complex seemed to function as a summer residence for the Ilkhans. It was smaller and possibly less important than their other quarters in Alatagh or Arran since no enthronement at the site is reported in the textual sources.[90] It is recorded that Ghazan Khan was raised by Bulughan Khatun the Elder, Abaqa Khan's wife, in Suqurluq, and that the Ilkhan bequeathed his *ordu* to Ghazan Khan.[91]

The southern gate cut through the oval wall was the principal entrance to the complex during the Ilkhanid period, and the main Sasanian gate to the north-north-west became a secondary entrance. The Sasanian secondary gate in the south-east was not re-used by the Mongols. The most dominant component of the Ilkhanid constructions in the site is a courtyard with the lake in the centre surrounded by arcades. On the north side of the courtyard, the fire temple is located, whose *iwān* was enlarged under the Ilkhans (Figure 2.3). Huff suggests that the upper floor of this building possibly worked as a 'Chinese throne hall' during the Ilkhanid period. The lack of large quantities of debris on the floor of the Mongol hall supports the idea that this space had been a hypostyle hall with wooden columns. Huff attributes the construction of a Chinese hall in Takht-i Sulayman to the close relationships between the Ilkhans and the Great Khans, and, thus, to the influence of the Chinese courtly architecture of the Khans on their subordinates in Iran.[92]

To the left of the temple (the north-west corner of the courtyard), there was a Sasanian palace to which a central hall and two adjacent octagonal structures were added. The northern octagon may have been the Ilkhan's private living room for dining. Parallel to the western side of the arcade, there was a line of buildings in different shapes and types. Inside the oval wall, to the north of the central courtyard, there is an area that possibly functioned as the civilian settlement of Takht-i Sulayman. Also, the remains of kilns uncovered there suggest that workshops must have been built in this part during the construction of the complex. Masuya proposes that the general layout of the Ilkhanid phase of the palatial complex in Takht-i Sulayman is based on the concept of a four-*iwān* plan. Despite the fact that the scheme was commonly used in Ilkhanid monuments, it is difficult to locate the source of influence since there are no surviving secular or religious four-*iwān* buildings from the late twelfth and early thirteenth centuries.[93] However, it is possible that the Ilkhanid monuments adopting the scheme had their roots in earlier times (i.e. the Seljuq period, when the four-*iwān* plan was widely used in western and central Iran for religious buildings and in eastern Iran for secular buildings).

The Ilkhans not only retained their portable tents as pivotal elements of their seasonal quarters under the influence of their former nomadic lifestyle, but also considered their Mongolian traditions while founding their

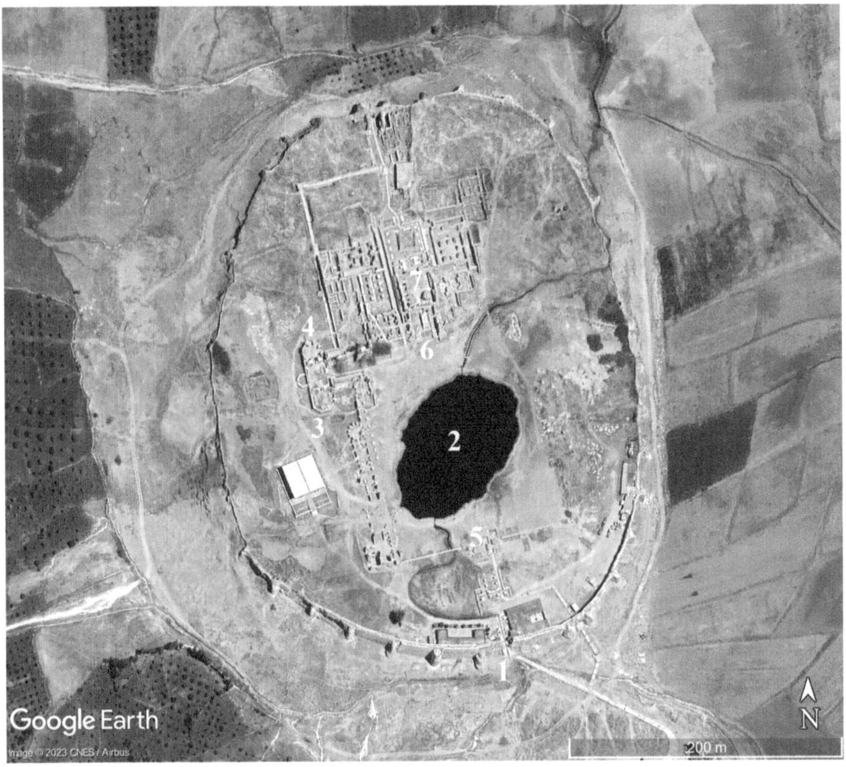

Figure 2.3 Ilkhanid palatial complex in Takht-i Sulayman.
1. Ilkhanid south gate
2. Lake
3. South octagon
4. North octagon
5. Entrance *iwān*
6. North *iwān*
7. Throne Hall
Google Earth (no imagery date)
36° 36′ 16.55″ N, 47° 14′ 05.03″ E, eye alt 530 m
CNES/Airbus 2023. Accessed 4 September 2023

permanent structures. Takht-i Sulayman, the only extant Ilkhanid palatial complex, reveals some specific Mongolian features incorporated into the architecture of its buildings. For instance, erecting the palace over the ruins of Sasanian structures was based on a practice which was common among the Mongols; as the city of Karakorum in Mongolia, the first capital of the Mongol Empire, was built on the remains of an Uyghur fortress, or Daidu, the capital of the Yuan dynasty was founded on the site of Zhongdu, one of the capitals of the Jin dynasty (1115–1234).[94] It is noteworthy that in the case of Takht-i Sulayman, the pre-existing Sasanian structures were re-used as the main residence of the Ilkhan and his family, whereas in Yuan China, as was mentioned earlier, the pre-existing complexes and cities were usually re-used by the Mongols as the capital cities of regional governments (see Chapter 1). The Mongol emperors of China and their court resided only in the new buildings, which had been designed and built from the outset as imperial constructions.[95]

Furthermore, locating important buildings in the centre of the city, or the centre of its northern part, facing south, can be traced back to Mongol customs in city planning.[96] The north-north-west to south-south-east orientation of the Ilkhanid palace was also one of the notable qualities of Mongol tents, and that was based on the direction of sunlight. Moreover, the Mongol enthusiasm for polygonal or round buildings reflected in several polygonal structures in the site of Takht-i Sulayman was probably affected by the form of their traditional residential tents.[97]

Ujan (Shahr-i Islam)

Although Ujan was never officially designated the capital of the Ilkhans, it frequently appears in their contemporary accounts and thus deserves to be studied in some depth. Mustawfi refers to Ujan as the *dār al-mulk* of Ghazan Khan,[98] but Rashid al-Din calls it the honourable encampment (*ordu-yi muʿaẓẓam*)[99] and the golden encampment (*ordu-yi zarrīn*),[100] and uses *dār al-mulk* exclusively for Tabriz. Ujan was not comparable with major cities such as Tabriz and Sultaniyya, but was still an important camp for the Ilkhans where the assemblies of Mongol princes were occasionally held[101] and some significant decisions were made, such as the enthronement of Öljeytü.[102] In addition to historical reports of the city, the fruitful archaeological excavations conducted at the site provide us with a substantial amount of information on its spatial structure.

The Ilkhanid city of Ujan was located in the middle of the meadow of Ujan (*marghzār-i Ujan*) in the province of west Azerbaijan.[103] The city was possibly founded by the Seljuqs.[104] Ujan was rebuilt and expanded by Ghazan Khan in 1299 and was renamed Shahr-i Islam (City of Islam). Yaqut al-Hamawi's account of the site is one the few reliable texts, if not the only one, that mentions the existence of the city before the Ilkhanids. Yaqut describes Ujan as a town (*shahrak*), located about ten *farsang* (c. 60 kilometres) from Tabriz, that still had a wall and a bazaar, but had been extensively destroyed.[105]

One of the main motivations for the foundation of an imperial city in Ujan was the strategic location of the site. Four important routes radiated from Ujan towards Rayy, Tabriz, Maraghih and Sarab.[106] In addition, the geographical features of the region, such as the fertility of the soil and the existence of lush green pasturelands, made it an ideal place for a royal residence in the eyes of the Mongol rulers.

Among contemporary sources, the accounts of Wassaf, Rashid al-Din and Mustawfi throw more light on the urban foundation of the Ilkhanids in Ujan. Wassaf says that in the spring of 698/1299, Ghazan Khan ordered the foundation of the 'City of Islam' in Ujan with several bazaars and public baths. The lands of the city were divided between the relatives of the Ilkhan and the notables of the court. They built their houses, gardens and bazaars on these properties.[107] According to Rashid al-Din, however, as Ghazan Khan had ordered, a group of skilful masters and engineers worked for three years to build a golden tent (*khargāh-i zarrīn*) and all the necessary equipment for the Ilkhan in Ujan. He adds that the city was founded in 701/1302. Rashid al-Din gives us more details regarding the general layout of the site. He says that a wall was built around the meadow of Ujan that formed a square-shaped enclosure. The square was divided into equal sections, and rows of willows and poplars were planted on the sides to define the borders of the city and to prevent people from passing through the area. Several pavilions, towers, public baths and magnificent edifices were built, and the golden tent was erected in the garden. It took the handymen (*farrāshān*) and engineers (*muhandisān*) one month to set up the grand tent and the jewelled throne. In the opening ceremony for the city, Ghazan Khan threw a public feast (*ṭuy-i ʿām*), and a great amount of gold and garments were bestowed on the audience.[108] Mustawfi also clearly says that Ghazan Khan rebuilt Ujan and constructed the 'Wall of

Ghazan' (*bārū-yi Ghāzānī*) with a perimeter of 3,000 paces around the city. He mentions that Ujan was a wealthy city and that part of its income was endowed to the *abwāb al-birr* of Ghazan Khan (*abwāb al-birr-i Ghāzānī*).[109] However, whether this reference relates to the *abwāb al-bir* of Ujan or the charitable complex of Ghazaniyya (see Chapter 3) is not certain.

As well as in contemporary textual sources, the names of a few buildings in Ujan are mentioned by later historians. For example, Khwandmir (d. 1534) refers to the pavilion of Ghazan Khan (*kūshk-i Ghāzānī*) in Ujan.[110] Although the building is destroyed, as we will see below, the mere fact that it existed in the city during the Ilkhanids would aid us in decoding the pictorial and textual evidence more logically.

The textual and visual descriptions of Ujan presented by two Ottoman historians who visited the site during the Safavid period shed some light on the spatial structure of the Ilkhanid city. Evliya Çelebi (d. 1682), a celebrated Ottoman polymath, describes Ujan as a square-shaped castle[111] with a perimeter of 2,000 paces (*gām*) (1,220 m)[112] and a metal gate on its eastern side. Çelebi says that the castle consisted of 3,000 earthen houses, seven mosques, three public baths, seven guesthouses and 600 shops.[113] The details of his account might not necessarily be accurate; however, it may convey how the general physical layout of the medieval city looked. The second document is a drawing made by Matrakçi Nasuh (d. 1564) presenting a general view of the city (Figure 2.4).[114] While the picture seems too simplified to be considered an authentic illustration of the Ilkhanid city, it depicts two buildings that must have been the most significant architectural elements of Ujan. Some speculations about the identity of the structures will be put forward at the end of this section.

Three seasons of excavations have been conducted in Ujan, in 2006, 2013 and 2017.[115] On the basis of the archaeological finding,[116] the archaeologists have speculated that the Ilkhanid city of Ujan was founded in the vicinity of the current city of Bustanabad. The main area of the city possibly consisted of three parts: the citadel (*arg*), the inner town (*shāristān*) and the outer town (*rabaż*). The remains of two historical cemeteries,[117] in the north-west and south-west of the inner city, were discovered during the field survey of the site. The remnants of the stone and brick walls on the ground suggest that the inner town had a non-rectangular wall (Figure 2.5). During the last season of excavation, a tower

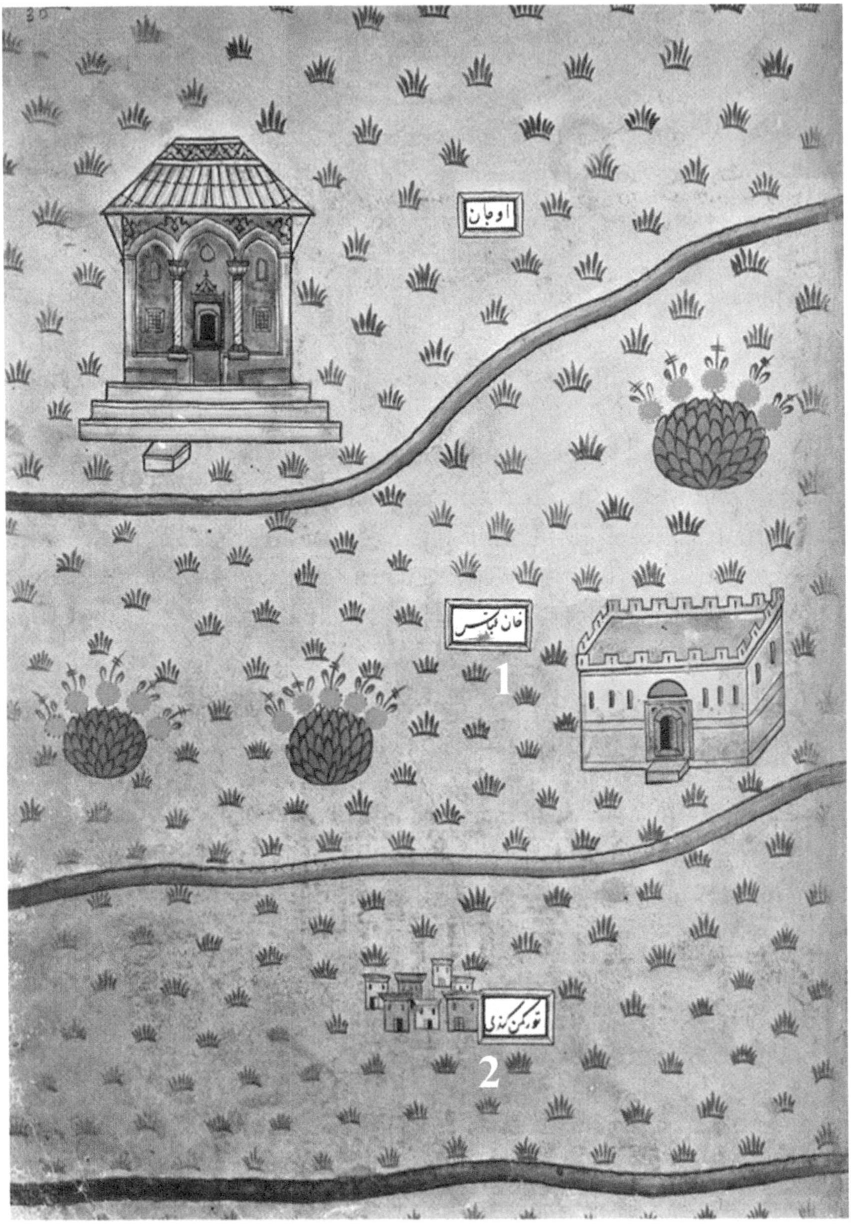

Figure 2.4 Matrakçi Nasuh's miniature of Ujan, sixteenth century.
1. Khan ʿAbbas
2. Turkman Kandi
Courtesy of Istanbul University Library

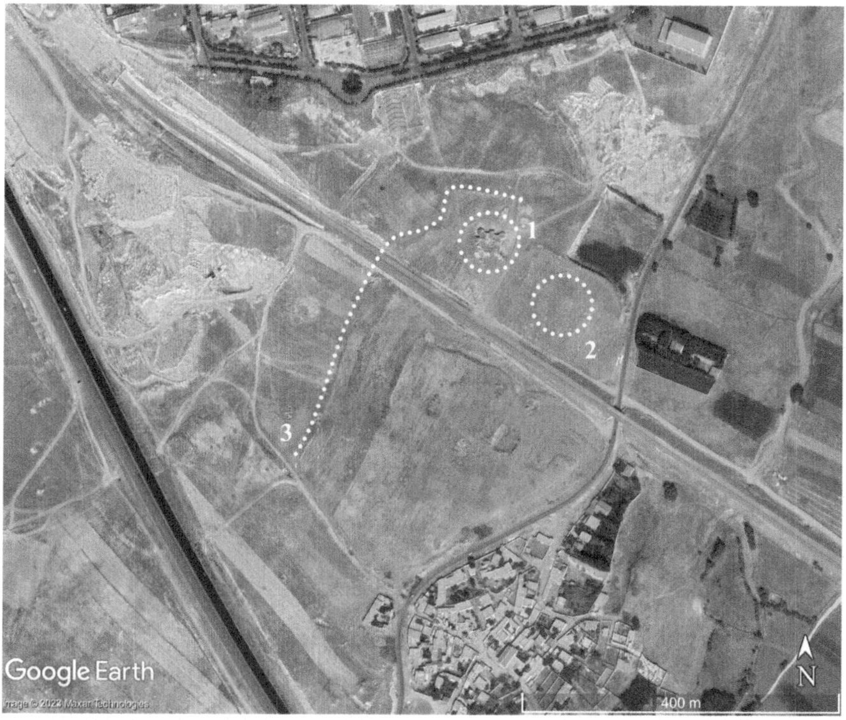

Figure 2.5 Archaeological site of Ujan.
1. Castle of Ujan
2. Possible location of the pavilion of Ghazan Khan
3. Traces of the wall of the inner town of Ujan
Google Earth (imagery date: 2 October 2020)
37° 48′ 39.56″ N, 46° 49′ 29.09″ E, eye alt 916 m
Maxar Technologies 2023. Accessed 4 September 2023

and part of the wall of a building, which is temporarily called the castle of Ujan, were uncovered inside the town. The surface debris found in the south-east of the castle raises the possibility that the pavilion/palace of Ghazan Khan might have been located around this area (Figure 2.6).[118]

Within the area of the inner town, there is a hill locally known as Qizil-kushk (a Turkish name that means 'Red Pavilion/Palace') around which a large amount of red pottery shards and bricks as well as glazed potteries and glasses have been observed. The hill might have been formed from the debris of the building known as the pavilion of Ghazan Khan. In the south of Qizil-kushk, there is another hill, called Tappih-ʿimarat (the edifice hill), whose

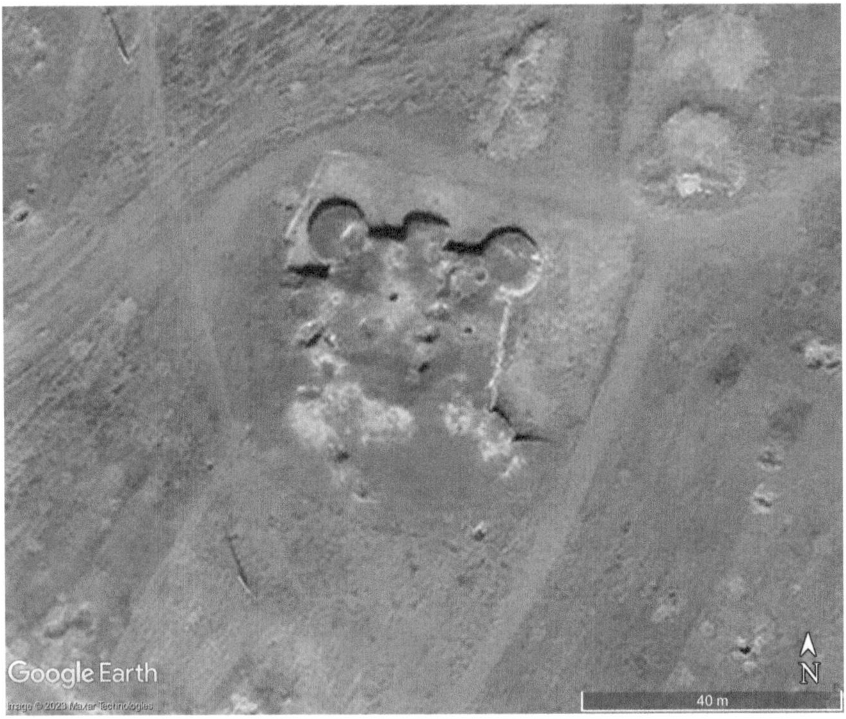

Figure 2.6 Castle of Ujan. The tower and part of the wall uncovered during the excavation are visible in the image.
Google Earth (imagery date: 2 October 2020)
37° 48′ 44.01″ N, 46° 49′ 32.59″ E, eye alt 112 m
Maxar Technologies 2023. Accessed 4 September 2023

surface is covered with a mass of broken bricks and glazed-pottery shards. The hill marks the location of an edifice built by order of the Qajar ruler Fath 'Ali Shah (r. 1797–1834). The stone foundation of the building is still visible on the ground. The Qajar building must have been built on the ruins of an earlier Ilkhanid building.[119] Traces of a square-shaped pond (each side measuring c. 500 metres) were found in the pasture of Ujan that is locally called Ghazan-guli (a Turkish name that means 'Ghazan's pool').

Taking into account the field findings and the local appellations, as well as the textual description of the city, one can speculate about the possible identity of the monuments depicted in Matrakçi's illustration of Ujan. In the picture, three architectural elements are recognisable: a group of modest buildings in the bottom centre, a castle (or castle-like building) centre-right and a pavilion at the top left. The last item is perhaps the most interesting. The building stands on a stepped platform. It has a Chinese-style roof covered with blue glazed tiles. The decorated façade of the building is overlaid with red plaster. The pavilion seems to have a small *iwān* at the front. There are two windows, covered with metal grille work, on either side of the main portal. The physical characteristics of the building suggest that it could be the pavilion of Ghazan Khan, that had been located in the same spot as that called Qizil-kushk today. The castle-like structure, entitled 'Khan 'Abbas' in the illustration, could be the building unearthed during the excavation and called the castle of Ujan. The group of small buildings at the bottom, entitled 'Turkman kandi',[120] might represent the civilian settlement of Ujan.

Urban Projects of the Ilkhans in Eastern Iran

The eastern headquarters of the Ilkhanids was the residence of the crown princes (*valī'ahd*s). Thus, the projects carried out under their patronage in the cities of Khurasan seemed unable to rival the imperial enterprises in western Iran. That said, the Ilkhans as well as the Mongol princes left their mark on many eastern towns and cities, whether in the form of splendid buildings or infrastructure projects. Some areas benefited from the more generous attention of the court, for example Khabushan. As we saw earlier, during his campaign against the Isma'ilis in 1256, on his way to the west Hülegü Khan stopped in Khabushan and ordered that the entire city should be repaired and that its residents who had been expatriated years ago should be recalled.[121] In addition to Hülegü, Ghazan Khan also erected magnificent buildings in Khabushan. After Abaqa Khan's death, when Arghun acceded to power, Ghazan, as the crown prince, was sent to the east.[122] He constructed great idol-temples in Khabushan. According to Rashid al-Din, the way in which he performed the Buddhist rituals in the temples of the city surprised even the Buddhist priests (*bakhshīyān*) who lived there.[123]

Notwithstanding the above-mentioned cases, the architectural legacy of the Ilkhans in their eastern headquarters is confined to a few standing structures and some names in the historical texts. While the occasional remarks of the medieval historians on the Ilkhans' architectural and urban projects suggest that they were active patrons in the east too, the scarcity of textual and material evidence prevents us from conducting thorough research on their construction activities there. Considering such constraints, Aq Qalʿih – despite its obscurity – deserves more exhaustive description here, since the site is one of the few (if not the only) surviving examples of the Ilkhans' urban projects in the east that has still retained its architectural integrity.

The isolated remains of Aq Qalʿih are located in the fertile plain of Juvayn, about eighty kilometres north-west of Sabzivar in Khurasan-i Razavi. The field survey of the site and the examination of the architectural components and archaeological fragments confirm that the city must have been founded during the Ilkhanid period. Among the surviving physical material, the inscriptions of a mosque known locally as Masjid-i Sifid (White Mosque), situated within the walls of the city, strengthened this hypothesis (Figure 2.7). The hall of the mosque is decorated with an inscription band that began in the south-west corner and ran counter-clockwise around the room (Figure 2.8). The inscription contains Qur'an 62, the Sura of al-Jumuʿa, and the date 712/1313 for the construction of the building.[124] Unfortunately, some parts of the band have been destroyed or poorly restored.[125] The appellation of the mosque (White Mosque) was possibly

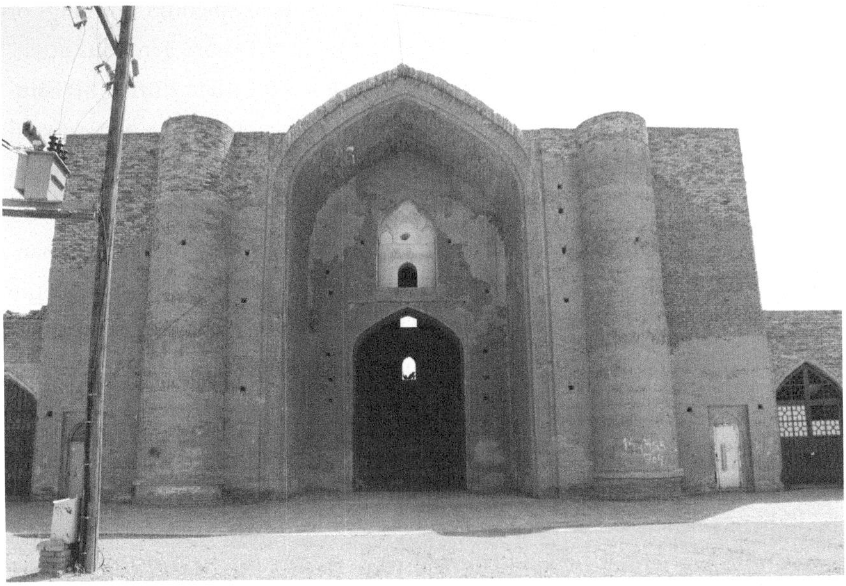

Figure 2.7 Portal of Masjid-i Sifid (White Mosque) of Aq Qalʿih.
© Atri Hatef Naiemi

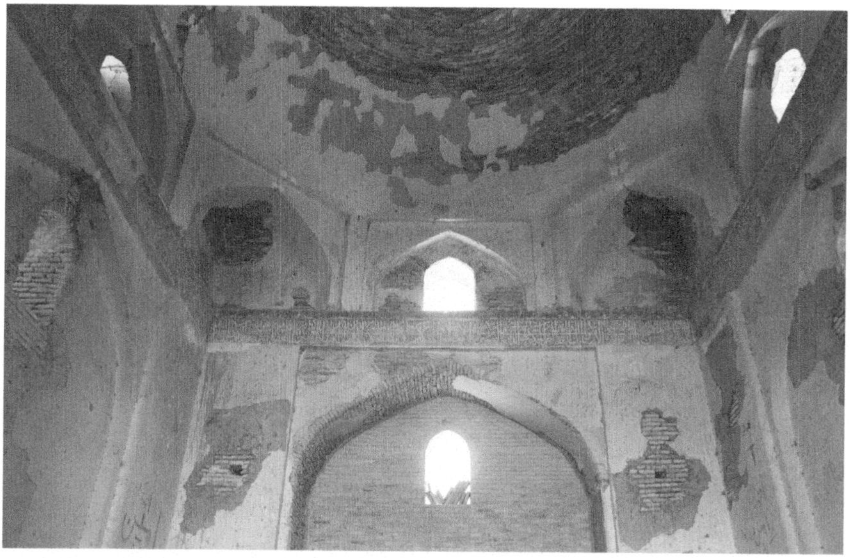

Figure 2.8 Interior of Masjid-i Sifid (White Mosque) of Aq Qalʿih.
© Atri Hatef Naiemi

derived from the colour of the painted plaster covering the internal walls of the building. Alternatively, it could relate to the name of the city, Aq Qalʿih, which means 'white castle', although it is still unclear whether the city was originally named Aq Qalʿih or whether the locals loaned the title to the enclave because of the presence of the grand white mosque on the site.

To the best of my knowledge, there is no reference to the city in contemporary textual sources. However, the study of this Ilkhanid site is important, for two reasons: first, the dated inscription of the mosque is contemporary with the reign of Öljeytü; and second, the general layout of the city resembles the form of his capital, the city of Sultaniyya. The plan is clearly visible in the aerial photos: a square-shaped citadel attached to a rectangular area surrounded by fortified walls and moats (Figure 2.9). The concentration of archaeological and architectural remains in the southern half of the site suggests that this part was more densely populated than the northern half during the Ilkhanid rule. The residents had possibly abandoned the city by the end of the period. Larger groups of people, however, built their houses on the Ilkhanid ruins and resided in the city during the Safavid period. The complex was habitable until the middle of the Qajar era.[126]

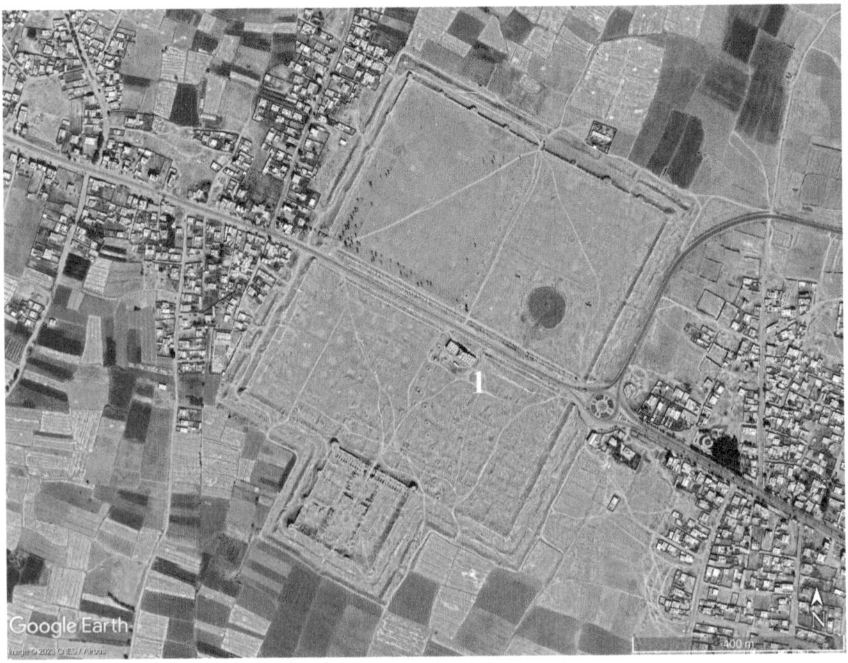

Figure 2.9 Citadel and fortified wall of the city of Aq Qalʿih.
1. Masjid-i Sifid (White Mosque)
Google Earth (imagery date: 14 September 2019)
36° 43′ 12.79″ N, 57° 22′ 43.08″ E, eye alt 1.45 km
CNES/Airbus 2023. Accessed 5 September 2023

The intention towards permanence and the establishment of capital cities came into being in the time of the first Ilkhan, Hülegü, and was continued by his son Abaqa Khan. Both Ilkhans chose pre-existing settlements, Maraghih and Takht-i Sulayman, as their political and administrative base, but conducted their own extensive construction projects. The idea of founding an urban centre as a royal residence from the outset formed during the reign of Arghun Khan and was pursued by his successors Ghazan Khan and Öljeytü in Ghazaniyya and Sultaniyya respectively. The fact that the later Ilkhans had a preference for new towns while there were many major prosperous cities in their territory raises some key questions about their political aspirations. In order to tackle these questions, the next two chapters will focus on Ghazaniyya and Sultaniyya and will examine the physical and functional features of the cities in connection with socio-political and religious parameters that impacted their creation and development during the Ilkhanid period. The study of the two cities can provide insights into the main thesis of this book, which argues that the Ilkhanid city as a physical entity represented the interaction between Perso-Islamic concepts and Mongolian native traditions

Notes

1. Quoted words of Shaybani Khan, Uzbek ruler c. 1451–1510. See Monika Gronke, 'The Persian Court between Palace and Tent: From Timur to 'Abbas I', in *Timurid Art and Culture: Iran and Central Asia in the Fifteenth Century*, ed. Lisa Golombek and Maria Subtelny (Leiden: Brill, 1992), 20.
2. Melville, 'Mongols in Iran', 45; Morgan, *The Mongols*, 32. On the general importance of pastures and horses in the economy of the steppe people of Central Asia, see Denis Sinor, 'Horse and Pasture in Inner Asian History', *Oriens Extremus* 19, no. 1/2 (1972): 171–83.
3. Melville, 'Mongols in Iran', 49–50.
4. *Ordu* 'can mean "headquarters", "encampment", "imperial camp", or "palace", as well as referring to a unit of horde under the management of a legitimate wife of a Mongol ruler'. See Masuya, 'Seasonal Capitals', 224.
5. For more information on the seasonal capitals of the Mongols, see Isfahanian and Khaza'ili, 'Shahr-hā-yi Tāza Bunyād dar Dura-yi Īlkhānī'; Masuya, 'Seasonal Capitals'.

   The PhD dissertation of Alireza Khaza'ili on the Ilkhanid cities is a good source on this topic to which, unfortunately, I could not gain access during my fieldwork in Iran. See Alireza Khaza'ili, 'Rushd va Zivāl-i Shahr-hā-yi Iran dar dura-yi Ilkhānān [The Development and Fall of the Iranian Cities during the Ilkhanid Period]' (PhD diss., University of Tabriz, 2003).
6. Rashid al-Din and Jahn, *Tārīkh-i Mubārak-i Ghāzānī*, 102. My understanding of the passage is that the meadow (*marghzār*) of Sayin and the yurt of Sayin both refer to the same place.
7. The practice of founding of urban centres was transmitted from the Ilkhans to their viziers. The charitable foundation of Rab'-i Rashidi patronised by Ghazan's vizier, Rashid al-Din, outside Tabriz is a prominent example of such centres.
8. These pious foundations are generally named *abwāb al-birr*, an Arabic term that means 'the gates of piety'.
9. Isfahanian and Khaza'ili, 'Shahr-hā-yi Tāza Bunyād dar Dura-yi Īlkhānī', 64–5.
10. Ibid., 68–9. The city of Ghazaniyya in Iraq should not be confused with the city of Ghazaniyya founded by Ghazan Khan in the vicinity of Tabriz.

11. Isfahanian and Khaza'ili, "Umrān-i Shahrī dar Iran-i 'Aṣr-i Mughul', 24.
12. The *Tārīkh-i Mubārak-i Ghāzānī* and the *Tārīkh-i Öljeytü* are particularly enlightening in this regard.
13. The list of the Ilkhanid sites offered here is largely based on Isfahanian and Khaza'ili, 'Shahr-hā-yi Tāza Bunyād dar Dura-yi Īlkhānī'.
14. For further discussion of the etymology of Suqurluq, see Masuya, 'Ilkhanid Phase of Takht-i Sulaimān', 77; Qadir Ja'fari, 'Takht-i Sulayman ya Sughūrlūq dar Zamān-i Mughul va Ba'd az Ān [Takht-i Sulayman or Sughūrlūq during the Mongol Period and Afterwards]', *Vaḥīd* 215 (1977): 34.
15. Rashid al-Din, *Jāmi' al-Tawārīkh*, vol. 2, 1,179.
16. Mustawfi, *Nuzhat al-Qulūb*, 214.
17. Rashid al-Din, Roshan, and Musavi, *Jāmi' al-Tawārīkh*, vol. 2, 1,254.
18. Ibid., 1,048.
19. Ibid.
20. Qazi Ahmad Tattavi and Asef Khan Qazvini, *Tārīkh-i Alfī* [Millennial History], ed. Ghulam-Reza Tabatabaei Majd (Tehran: Intishārāt-i 'Ilmī va Farhangī, 2003), vol. 6, 4,033.
21. Mustawfi, *Nuzhat al-Qulūb*, 98, 106.
22. Rashid al-Din, *Jāmi' al-Tawārīkh*, vol. 2, 1,162.
23. Wassaf al-Hazra and Ayati, *Taḥrīr-i Tārīkh-i Wassaf*, 231. See also Bahram Amirahmadi, 'Ujan 1 [Ujan 1]', *Rushd-i Āmūzish-i Jughrāfīyā* 25 (1991): 49–53; Bahram Amirahmadi, 'Ujan 2 [Ujan 2]', *Rushd-i Āmuzish-i Jughrāfīyā* 26 (1991): 50–6; Velayati, *Guzārish-i Khabarī-yi Faṣl-i Avval-i Shahr-i Tārīkhī-yi Ujan*.
24. 'Yurt' refers both to one single portable, round tent and to the place where a group of tents are put. In the case of Qarachali, Rashid al-Din possibly considers the latter and uses the word 'yurt' as an equivalent for camp, encampment or *ordu*.
25. Rashid al-Din, *Jāmi' al-Tawārīkh*, vol. 2, 1,192.
26. Mustawfi, *Nuzhat al-Qulūb*, 139. The Mughan Plain is located in the north-west of Iran and the south of the Republic of Azerbaijan.
27. Kashani, *Tārīkh-i Öljeytü*, 238.
28. Wassaf al-Hazra and Ayati, *Tahrīr-i Tārīkh-i Waṣṣāf*, 242.
29. Referring to Mustawfi, Le Strange mentions that the Sifid Rud, or White River, in Azerbaijan was known to the Mongols as the Hulan Mulan (more exactly Ulān Mören), which in Mongolian means 'Red River'. See Le Strange, *Lands of the Eastern Caliphate*, 169.

30. Rashid al-Din and Jahn, *Tārīkh-i Mubārak-i Ghāzānī*, 158.
31. Ibid., *passim.*
32. Kashani, *Tārīkh-i Öljeytü*, 133. See also ʿAbbas Mutarjim and Yaʿqub Muhammadifar, ʻPīshnahādī Barāy-i Taʿyīn-i Maḥall-i Shahr-i Īlkhānī-yi Sultanabad-i Chimchal (Baghdad-i Kūchak) dar Bisotun-i Kermanshah [Some Speculations on the Location of the Ilkhanid City of Sultanabad-i Chimchal (Little Baghdad) in Bisotun, Kermanshah]', *Payām-i Bāstān-shinās* 3 (2005): 95–104.
33. Hamdallah Mustawfi, *Tārīkh-i Guzīdih* [Excerpt History], ed. ʿAbd al-Husayn Navaei (Tehran: Amir Kabir Press, 1985), 607.
34. Mustawfi, *Nuzhat al-Qulūb*, 140.
35. Rashid al-Din, *Jāmiʿ al-Tawārīkh*, vol. 4, 2,942.
36. I exclude Rabʿ-i Rashidi from this list since the urban complex was founded during the Ilkhanids, but was built under the patronage of a Persian vizier, Rashid al-Din (see e.g. Brigitt Hoffmann, ʻIn Pursuit of Memoria and Salvation: Rashīd al-Dīn and his Rabʿ-i Rashīdī', in *Politics, Patronage and the Transmission of Knowledge in 13th–15th Century Tabriz*, ed. Judith Pfeiffer (Leiden; Boston: Brill, 2014), 171–85. This issue can be discussed in connection with other towns, cities and urban compounds that benefited from the sponsorship of Persian patrons. Aveh, located in Markazi province, is an important but lesser-known example in this regard. The recent excavation carried out in the site revealed that Aveh was a prosperous city during the Ilkhanid period. The most significant aspect of the archaeological findings was the star-shaped lustre tiles uncovered in the site. The considerable number of lustre tiles as well as the traces of tile kilns found in the site raise the possibility that Aveh worked as a centre for the production of lustre tiles under the Ilkhans; for more information on the site, see Arash Lashkari, Hamid Khatib Shahidi and Somaye Muhajer Vatan, ʻA Preliminary Report of Excavations at Aveh Plain, Islamic Period', *Iranian Journal of Archaeological Studies* 3 (2013): 21–37.
37. Isfahanian and Khaza'ili, "ʿUmrān-i Shahrī dar Iran-i ʿAṣr-i Mughul', 13.
38. ʿAta Malik Juvayni, *Tārīkh-i Jahāngushāy* [The History of The World Conqueror], ed. Muhammad Qazvini (Tehran: Hermes, 2008), vol. 1, 23.
39. Rashid al-Din, *Jāmiʿ al-Tawārīkh*, vol. 2, 1,048.
40. Rabban Sawma, *The Monks of Kublai Khan, Emperor of China*, trans. Sir E. A. Wallis Budge (London; New York: I. B. Tauris, 2014), 75.
41. Tilla possibly means hillside.

42. Rashid al-Din, *Jāmiʿ al-Tawārīkh*, vol. 2, 1,022. According to Rashid al-Din, Abaqa Khan also was buried beside the Great Ilkhan (*Ilkhan-i buzurg*) in Shahu-tilla. See ibid., 1,118.
43. Wilber, *Architecture of Islamic Iran*, 9.
44. The Mongols' long-lasting reliance on their herds of mares and horses, and the key role of the extended grasslands of Central Asia in their pastoral economy, are well recognised. See Morgan, *The Mongols*, 32. The loyalty of the Ilkhans to their nomadic customs persuaded them to build their settlements, whether seasonal quarters or permanent cities, in the natural landscapes that resembled the steppes of Central Asia and supported their nomadic economy. Therefore, they preferred regions with grasslands.
45. Bruno De Nicola, *Women in Mongol Iran: the Khātūns, 1206–1335* (Edinburgh: Edinburgh University Press, 2017), 65–82.
46. Melville, 'Mongols in Iran', 46.
47. Karin Quade-Reutter, 'Qotloḡ Tarkān Ḵātun', *Encyclopædia Iranica*, http://www.iranicaonline.org/articles/qotlogh-tarkan-khatun (last accessed 28 July 2023).
48. Melville, 'Mongols in Iran', 61.
49. Isfahanian and Khaza'ili, ''Umrān-i Shahrī dar Iran-i 'Aṣr-i Mughul', 16.
50. Rashid al-Din, *Jāmiʿ al-Tawārīkh*, vol. 2, 1,370.
51. Isfahanian and Khaza'ili, ''Umrān-i Shahrī dar Iran-i 'Aṣr-i Mughul', 19–20.
52. In Sheila Blair's words, 'the extensive reforms of ... Rashid al-Din ... produced an economic upswing ... and shifted the balance of power in favor of the Iranian civil bureaucracy at the expense of the nomadic Turko-Mongolian aristocracy', a fact that deeply influenced the mechanism of patronage under the two Ilkhans, Ghazan Khan and Öljeytü, and expanded the construction projects all across the country. See Blair, *Ilkhanid Shrine Complex*, 52.
53. Isfahanian and Khaza'ili, ''Umrān-i Shahrī dar Iran-i 'Aṣr-i Mughul', 30.
54. For further discussion on this topic, see Bayani, *Dīn va Dawlat*, vol. 1, 343.
55. The lesser number of surviving Ilkhanid structures in Maraghih compared with that of newly founded cities like Ghazaniyya or Sultaniyya can be attributed in part to the presence of monuments dating back to the Seljuq period in the city. This factor resulted in fewer architectural projects being undertaken during the Ilkhanid dynasty.
56. Shikari-Niri, 'Kankāsh dar Baqāyā-yi Raṣad-khānih-yi Maraghih', 63.
57. For more studies on Seljuq buildings in Maraghih, see Raya Shani, *A Monumental Manifestation of the Shīʿite Faith in Late Twelfth-Century Iran:*

The Case of the Gunbad-i 'Alawyān, Hamadān (Oxford: Oxford University Press for the Board of the Faculty of Oriental Studies, University of Oxford, 1996), vol. 11; Carol Bier, 'The Decagonal Tomb Tower at Maraghih and its Architectural Context: Lines of Mathematical Thought', *Nexus Network Journal* 14, no. 2 (2012): 251–73; Shakiba Sharifian and Sadeq Khudaparast, 'Nigāhī bar Gunbad-i Kabūd-i Maraghih [The Examination of Gunbad-i Kabud of Maraghih]', *Kitāb-i Māh-i Hunar* 180 (2013): 72–6.

58. Shikari-Niri, 'Kankāsh dar Baqāyā-yi Raṣad-khānih-yi Maraghih', 64.
59. Wassaf al-Hazra and Ayati, *Taḥrīr-i Tārīkh-i Wassaf*, 29; Wilber, *Architecture of Islamic Iran*, 10.
60. Parviz Varjavand, *Kāvush-i Raṣad-khānih-yi Maraghih va Nigāhī bi Pīshīna-yi Dānish-i Sitāra-shināsī dar Iran* [The Excavation of Maraghih Observatory and A Brief Study of the History of Astrology in Iran] (Tehran: Amir Kabir Press, 1987); Javad Shikari-Niri, 'Ta'yīn-i 'Amalkard va Ṭarḥ-i Mi'mārī-yi Vāḥid-hā-yi Nujūmī-yi Makshūfa dar Raṣad-khānih-yi Maraghih [Suggesting the Function and Architectural Design of the Unearthed Astrological Units in Maraghih Observatory]', *Muṭāli'āt-i Bāstān-shināsī* 8, no. 2 (2016): 91–109.
61. Rasad-daghi is a Turkish name that means mountain of observation. The name describes the hill on top of which the remains of Maraghih Observatory are located.
62. Shikari-Niri, 'Kankāsh dar Baqāyā-yi Raṣad-khānih-yi Maraghih', 70.
63. Rashid al-Din, *Jāmi' al-Tawārīkh*, vol. 2, 1,176, 1,179. For the whole passage, see the Appendix, section 1.
64. Sir Arnold Talbot Wilson (1884–1940) was a British soldier, explorer, author and politician who served in Iran for a few years. I was not able to find the travel account in which his visit to Maraghih has been described, but it has been mentioned by Shikari-Niri in Shikari-Niri, 'Kankāsh dar Baqāyā-yi Raṣad-khānih-yi Maraghih', 72.
65. Muhammad Baqiri, *Az Samarqand bi Kashan: Nāmih-hā-yi Ghiyath al-Din Jamshid Kashani bi Pidarash* [From Samarqand to Kashan: The Letters of Ghiyath al-Din Jamshid Kashani to his Father] (Tehran: Intishārāt-i 'Ilmī va Farhangī, 1996), 65.
66. Mahdizada and Nasiri, 'Banā-hā-yi Waqfī-yi Maraghih', 59. It is noteworthy that Nasir al-Din was later criticised for using the revenues of the endowments in his observatory project. See George Saliba, 'Horoscopes and Planetary Theory: Ilkhanid Patronage of Astronomers', in *Beyond the Legacy of Genghis Khan*, ed. Linda Komaroff (Leiden: Brill, 2006), 366.

67. Bayani, *Dīn va Dawlat*, vol. 1, 351.
68. Juvayni, *Tārīkh-i Jahāngushāy*, vol. 1, 35.
69. Rashid al-Din Fazlallah Hamadani, Mujtaba Minuvi and Iraj Afshar, *Waqf Nāmih-yi Rabʿ-i Rashīdī* [The Endowment Deed of Rabʿ-i Rashīdī] (Tehran: Anjuman-i Āthār-i Millī, 1971), 113.
70. Mahdizadih and Nasiri, 'Banā-hā-yi Waqfī-yi Maraghih', 63; see the original passage in Ibn al-Fuwati, *Majmaʿ al-Ādāb fī Muʿjam al-ʾAlqāb*, ed. Muhammad al-Kazim (Tehran: Ministry of Culture and Islamic Education, 1995), vol. 4, 512.
71. Ibid., 512. Ibn al-Fuwati also refers to four other schools in Ilkhanid Maraghih, madrasa of al-Ghazi Kamal al-Din, madrasa of al-Ghazi ('Izziya), madrasa of al-Khalifa, and madrasa of al-Muhiyya, some of which had been built in earlier times.
72. Ibn al-Fuwati, *Majmaʿ al-Ādāb*, vol. 1, 506.
73. Ibid., 386.
74. Morris Rossabi, *Voyager from Xanadu: Rabban Sauma and the First Journey from China to the West* (Berkeley: University of California Press, 2010), 99.
75. Sawma, *Monks of Kublai Khan*, 72.

    It is noteworthy that the above-mentioned source, *The Monks of Kublai Khan*, officially known as *The History of Yahballaha III*, is a translation of the Syriac History of the two Nestorian Chinese monks Rabban Sawma and Mar Yaballaha. A Nestorian cleric translated the original Persian text (consisting of Rabban Sawma's accounts, memoirs and diaries) into Syriac twenty years after Sawma's death. In addition to the translation of the documents, he added a report on the persecution of Nestorian Christians during the reign of Ghazan Khan, as well as a survey of Mar Yaballaha's career. Besides translating, the cleric edited the account and added his own comments to the narrative. See Rossabi, *Voyager from Xanadu*, 171.
76. Sawma, *Monks of Kublai Khan*, 165.
77. Ibid., 197–9.
78. Rossabi, *Voyager from Xanadu*, 173.
79. Ibid., 176; Sawma, *Monks of Kublai Khan*, 203–4.
80. Sawma, *Monks of Kublai Khan*, 76, 208.
81. Rashid al-Din, *Jāmiʿ al-Tawārīkh*, vol. 2, 1,051.
82. Masuya, 'Ilkhanid Phase of Takht-i Sulaimān', 72.
83. Mustawfi, *Nuzhat al-Qulūb*, 106; Mustawfi calls the site Saqurliq (Saturiq), which is apparently a misreading of Suqurluq. See Jaʿfari, 'Takht-i Sulayman', 34.

84. Masuya, 'Ilkhanid Phase of Takht-i Sulaimān', 86.
85. Dietrich Huff, 'Tak̲t-e Solaymān', *Encyclopædia Iranica*, http://www.iranicaonline.org/articles/takt-e-solayman (last accessed 14 October 2022).
86. In Zoroastrianism, fire is revered as a symbol of the presence of Ahura Mazda, the supreme god.
87. Ibid.
88. Dietrich Huff, 'The Ilkhanid Palace at Takht-i Sulayman: Excavation Results', in *Beyond the Legacy of Genghis Khan*, ed. Linda Komaroff (Leiden: Brill, 2006), 96.
89. Melville, 'Mongols in Iran', 54.
90. Masuya, 'Ilkhanid Phase of Takht-i Sulaimān', 96.
91. Rashid al-Din and Jahn, *Tārīkh-i Mubārak-i Ghāzānī*, 7.
92. Huff, 'Ilkhanid Palace at Takht-i Sulayman', 103.
93. Masuya, 'Ilkhanid Phase of Takht-i Sulaimān', 150.
94. Masuya, 'Ilkhanid Courtly Life', 88.
95. Masuya, 'Ilkhanid Phase of Takht-i Sulaimān', 209.
96. Michael Danti, *The Ilkhanid Heartland: Hasanlu Tepe (Iran) Period I* (Philadelphia: University of Pennsylvania Museum of Archaeology and Anthropology, 2004), 45.
97. Masuya, 'Ilkhanid Courtly Life', 88–90.
98. Mustawfi, *Nuzhat al-Qulūb*, 127.
99. Rashid al-Din, *Jāmiʿ al-Tawārīkh*, vol. 1, 4. Banakati also refers to Ujan as *ordu-yi muʿaẓẓam*. See Davood Banakati, *Tārīkh-i Banākatī* [Banakati's History], ed. Jaʿfar Shuʿar (Tehran: Anjuman-i Āthār-i Millī, 1969), 474.
100. Rashid al-Din, *Jāmiʿ al-Tawārīkh*, vol. 2, 1,303.
101. Ibid., 1,288, 1,296–7.
102. Hafiz-i Abru, *Dhayl-i Jāmiʿ al-Tawārīkh-i Rashīdī* [The Continuation of Rashid Al-Din's Jāmiʿ al-Tawārīkh], ed. Khan-Baba Bayani (Tehran: Anjuman-i Āthār-i Millī, 1971), 66.
103. Rashid al-Din and Jahn, *Tārīkh-i Mubārak-i Ghāzānī*, 138.
104. Velayati, *Guzārish-i Khabarī-yi Faṣl-i Avval-i Shahr-i Tārīkhī-yi Ujan*, 3.
105. Yaqut al-Hamawi, *Muʿjam al-Buldān* [Dictionary of Countries], ed. Alinaqi Munzavi (Tehran: Sāzmān-i Mīrāth-i Farhangī-yi Kishvar, 2001), vol. 1, 123.
106. In the eastern side of the pasture of Ujan, the remains of a building can be seen that is locally called *qarāvul-khānih* (the station of road guards). The existence of the building reveals the significance of the roads connecting Ujan to other cities. See Amirahmadi, 'Ujan 2', 52.

107. Wassaf al-Hazra and Ayati, *Taḥrīr-i Tārīkh-i Wassaf*, 231.
108. Rashid al-Din, *Jāmiʿ al-Tawārīkh*, vol. 2, 1,303–5. For the whole passage, see the Appendix, section 2.
109. Mustawfi, *Nuzhat al-Qulūb*, 127. For the whole passage, see the Appendix, section 3.
110. Khwandmir, *Tārīkh-i Ḥabīb al-Sīyar fī Akhbār Afrād al-Bashar* [The Beloved of Careers Reporting on the Multitudes of People], ed. Jalal al-Din Humayi (Tehran: Khayyam Press, 2001), vol. 3, 501.
111. In the Ottoman text, Çelebi uses the term *qalʿih* to refer to the castle.
112. For the value of each pace (*qadam* or *gām*), see Chapter 4, n. 42.
113. Rahim Velayati, Behzad Mahdizada, and Hamid Khanali, 'Makān-yābī-yi Shahr-i Tārīkhī-yi Ujan bar Asās-i Manābiʿ-i Tārīkhī va Barrisī-hā-yi Bāstān-shinākhtī [Locating the Ilkhanid City of Ujan on the Basis of Historical Sources and Archaeological Surveys]', *Bāgh-e Nazar* 34 (2015): 85.
114. Matrakçi Nasuh was a historian, geographer and cartographer in the Ottoman Empire. He accompanied the Ottoman sultan Sulayman (r. 1520–66) in his campaign to Persia.
115. Evliya Çelebi, 'The Sīyāḥat-nāmih of Evliya Çelebi [Travel Account of Evliya Çelebi]', trans. Haj Husayn Nakhjavani, *Nashrīyih-yi Dānishkadih-yi Adabīyyāt-i Tabriz* (1959): 291–2.
116. Among the potteries and metal objects found during the excavations, an Ilkhanid coin minted in Tabriz is considered an important proof that the site was a settlement under the Ilkhans.
117. The historical graves scattered around the pasture of Ujan are locally called the 'graves of strangers' (*gharīblar qabrī* in Turkish), possibly because the locals were not able to associate the graves with any of the surrounding villages or towns. See Amirahmadi, 'Ujan 1', 52.
118. Rahim Velayati, Homayun Rezvan and Qadir Ibrahimi, 'Miʿmārī-yi Īlkhānī dar Bastara-yi daw Shahr-i Tārīkhī Islāmī-yi Ujan va Sultaniyya [Ilkhanid Architecture in the Historical Cities of Ujan and Sultaniyya]', *Bāgh-e Nazar* 55 (2017): 20.
119. Amirahmadi, 'Ujan 2', 53–4.
120. Since the meaning of the phrase is still vague, it can also be pronounced as 'Turkman kindi' or 'Turkman kundi'.
121. Juvayni, *Tārīkh-i Jahāngushāy*, vol. 1, 23.
122. Rashid al-Din, *Jāmiʿ al-Tawārīkh*, vol. 2, 1,332.
123. Ibid., 1,254.

124. The first section of the inscription reads as follows:

بسْمِ اللهِ الرَّحْمَنِ الرَّحِيم

يُسَبِّحُ لِلَّهِ مَا فِى السَّمَاوَاتِ وَمَا فِى الأَرْضِ الْمَلِكِ الْقُدُّوسِ الْعَزِيزِ الْحَكِيمِ (1) هُوَ الَّذِى بَعَثَ فِى
الأمِّيِّينَ رَسُولا مِنْهُمْ يَتْلُو عَلَيْهِمْ آيَاتِهِ وَيُزَكِّيهِمْ وَيُعَلِّمُهُمُ الْكِتَابَ وَالْحِكْمَةَ وَإِنْ كَانُوا مِنْ قَبْلُ لَفِى
ضَلالٍ مُبِينٍ (2) وَآخَرِينَ مِنْهُمْ لَمَّا يَلْحَقُوا بِهِمْ وَهُوَ الْعَزِيزُ الْحَكِيمُ (3) ذَلِكَ فَضْلُ اللهِ يُؤْتِيهِ
مَنْ يَشَاءُ وَاللَّهُ ذُو الْفَضْلِ الْعَظِيمِ (4) مَثَلُ الَّذِينَ حُمِّلُوا التَّوْرَاةَ ثُمَّ لَمْ يَحْمِلُوهَا كَمَثَلِ الْحِمَارِ يَحْمِلُ
أَسْفَارًا بِئْسَ مَثَلُ الْقَوْمِ الَّذِينَ كَذَّبُوا بِآيَاتِ اللهِ وَاللَّهُ لا يَهْدِى الْقَوْمَ الظَّالِمِينَ (5) قُلْ يَا أَيُّهَا الَّذِينَ
هَادُوا إِنْ زَعَمْتُمْ أَنَّكُمْ أَوْلِيَاءُ لِلَّهِ مِنْ دُونِ النَّاسِ فَتَمَنَّوُا الْمَوْتَ إِنْ كُنْتُمْ صَادِقِينَ (6) وَلا يَتَمَنَّوْنَهُ
أَبَدًا بِمَا قَدَّمَتْ أَيْدِيهِمْ وَاللَّهُ عَلِيمٌ بِالظَّالِمِينَ (7) قُلْ إِنَّ الْمَوْتَ الَّذِى تَفِرُّونَ مِنْهُ فَإِنَّهُ مُلاقِيكُمْ ثُمَّ
تُرَدُّونَ إِلَى عَالِمِ الْغَيْبِ وَالشَّهَادَةِ فَيُنَبِّئُكُمْ بِمَا كُنْتُمْ تَعْمَلُونَ (8) يَا أَيُّهَا الَّذِينَ آمَنُوا إِذَا نُودِىَ لِلصَّلاةِ
مِنْ يَوْمِ الْجُمُعَةِ فَاسْعَوْا إِلَى ذِكْرِ اللَّهِ وَذَرُوا الْبَيْعَ ذَلِكُمْ خَيْرٌ لَكُمْ إِنْ كُنْتُمْ تَعْلَمُونَ (9) فَإِذَا قُضِيَتِ
الصَّلاةُ فَانْتَشِرُوا فِى الأَرْضِ وَابْتَغُوا مِنْ فَضْلِ اللهِ وَاذْكُرُوا اللَّهَ كَثِيرًا لَعَلَّكُمْ تُفْلِحُونَ (10) وَإِذَا
رَأَوْا تِجَارَةً أَوْ لَهْوًا انْفَضُّوا إِلَيْهَا وَتَرَكُوكَ قَائِمًا قُلْ مَا عِنْدَ اللهِ خَيْرٌ مِنَ اللَّهْوِ وَمِنَ التِّجَارَةِ وَاللَّهُ
خَيْرُ الرَّازِقِينَ (11)

(Qur'an, 62:1–6)

Whatever is in the heavens and whatever is on the earth is exalting Allah, the Sovereign, the Pure, the Exalted in Might, the Wise (1) It is He who has sent among the unlettered a Messenger from themselves reciting to them His verses and purifying them and teaching them the Book and wisdom – although they were before in clear error (2) And [to] others of them who have not yet joined them. And He is the Exalted in Might, the Wise (3) That is the bounty of Allah, which He gives to whom He wills, and Allah is the possessor of great bounty (4) The example of those who were entrusted with the Torah and then did not take it on is like that of a donkey who carries volumes [of books]. Wretched is the example of the people who deny the signs of Allah. And Allah does not guide the wrongdoing people (5) Say, 'O you who are Jews, if you claim that you are allies of Allah, excluding the [other] people, then wish for death, if you should be truthful' (6) But they will not wish for it, ever, because of what their hands have put forth. And Allah is Knowing of the wrongdoers (7) Say, 'Indeed, the death from which you flee – indeed, it will meet you. Then you will be returned to the Knower of the unseen and the witnessed, and He will inform you about what you used to do' (8) O you who have believed, when [the adhan] is called for the prayer on the day of Jumu'ah [Friday], then proceed to the remembrance of Allah and leave trade. That is better for you, if you only knew (9) And when the prayer has been concluded, disperse within the land and seek from the bounty of Allah, and remember

> Allah often that you may succeed (10) But when they saw a transaction or a diversion, [O Muhammad], they rushed to it and left you standing. Say, 'What is with Allah is better than diversion and then a transaction, and Allah is the best of providers' (11)
>
> ('English Translation of Sura al-Jumuʿah', King Saud University, https://quran.ksu.edu.sa/index.php?l=en#aya=62_1 (last accessed 25 May 2023))

The rest of the inscription is as follows (as read and translated by the author):

'صدق الله العلی العظیم و صدق رسول الله النبی الکریم و نحن علی ذلک من الشاهدین
(الشاکرین و الحمد لله رب العالمین) ... هذه عمارته ... فی یوم ... شهر ربیع الثانی 712 ...'

The section in parentheses has been destroyed and is illegible. The last few words of the sentence mention the date of construction of the mosque, which is Rabīʿ al-Thānī of 712/1312, but the day is illegible.

125. The plan of Aq Qalʿih is comparable with the plan of Khar Balgas (Ordubalik), an urban site in the Orkhon Valley, Mongolia. Khar Balgas was the capital of the eighth- and ninth-century Uyghur Empire. For the low-level oblique photo of the site, see Fitzhugh, Rossabi and Honeychurch, *Genghis Khan and the Mongol Empire*, 147.
126. Mahmud Bakhtiyari-Shahri, *Guzārish-i Thabtī-yi Shahr-i Īlkhānī-yi Aq Qalʿih dar Fibrist-i Āthār-i Millī* [The Inscription Report of the Ilkhanid City of Aq Qalʿih for Iran National Heritage List] (place of publication not identified: Sāzmān-i Mīrāth-i Farhangī-yi Khurasan, 1996).

3

The Architectural and Urban Projects of Ghazan Khan in Ghazaniyya

The neighbourhood of Ghazaniyya in modern-day Tabriz marks the site of the grand architectural and urban project carried out by Ghazan Khan outside the walls of Tabriz in the last years of the thirteenth century. Although a few buildings had already been constructed by Arghun Khan in the same area, the project substantially developed during the reign of Ghazan. Ghazaniyya was planned and built by the Ilkhan from the outset, and thus mirrors his political and religious doctrines, he being the primary patron of the operation. While the last vestiges of the medieval city were all flattened in the early twentieth century, Ghazaniyya still presents a significant case study of an Ilkhanid urban centre which is worth special attention. The foundation of Ghazaniyya should be considered a turning point in the history of the presence of the Mongols in Iran. The project demonstrates how the Mongol conquerors, in spite of their nomadic heritage, came to appreciate the importance of establishing a permanent urban centre fulfilling their political, administrative and commercial purposes.

There is very little literature on Ghazaniyya. The extensive destruction of the city over the course of time, the scarcity of remarks on the site in the historical texts and the lack of archaeologically derived information cause the presence of Ghazaniyya in scholarly works dealing with Ilkhanid architecture and urbanism to be unimpressive in scale. In comparison with the material aspects of the city, in the available studies, even less attention is devoted to the motivations leading Ghazan to build Ghazaniyya and its charitable complex in the immediate vicinity of the capital Tabriz. Therefore, this chapter considers Ghazaniyya beyond its physical entity and studies it in relation to the socio-religious, cultural and political context in which the city was built. Great emphasis will be placed on Ghazan himself, as the founder, and on his religious and political aspirations. Understanding the nature of the spiritual beliefs of the Ilkhan paves the way for the exploration of Ghazan's intention of establishing a new urban centre exactly beside a long-established prosperous city like Tabriz. In addition, I examine how the city and the charitable complex (*abwāb al-birr*) of Shanb,[1] patronised by Ghazan, a newly converted Ilkhan, reflected the synthesis of Perso-Islamic and Mongolian visual and spiritual traditions. I argue that the construction of Ghazaniyya was not merely due to the religious orientation of Ghazan following his momentous conversion to Islam.

While myriads of pottery shards, brick pieces and architectural fragments are being uncovered in every corner of the site, the current cityscape of Ghazaniyya barely brings back the memory of Ghazan's urban project covered beneath modern constructions. Nevertheless, interestingly enough, looking at the urban fabric from a height rather than walking through the site on the ground is a fruitful practice, unravelling the general configuration of the medieval city. It is astonishing to observe that, despite the severe process of destruction and reconstruction, the layout of Ilkhanid Ghazaniyya, as it is reflected in the textual and pictorial records of this period, is still recognisable in the 2023 satellite image of the area (Figure 3.1). Therefore, along with historical texts, this chapter relies on aerial photographs and satellite images in order to visualise the physical and spatial structure of Ghazaniyya during the reign of Ghazan.

The Foundation of the City of Ghazaniyya and the *abwāb al-birr* of Shanb-i Ghazan

In the third section of Ghazan Khan's history in the *Jamiʿ al-Tawarikh*, Rashid al-Din describes the character, deeds and words of the Ilkhan in forty short accounts (*ḥikāyat*). In the twelfth account, the vizier refers to the Ilkhan's great interest in architectural activities (*ʿimārat-dūstī*) and enumerates a number of construction projects that were being conducted under the auspices of Ghazan in Iraq and in the capital (*dār al-mulk*) Tabriz. He reports that the walls of Tabriz had been destroyed and that many houses had been built far from the main body of the city. By order of the Ilkhan, the new wall was constructed enclosing Old Tabriz and its surrounding buildings and gardens.[2] Ghazaniyya

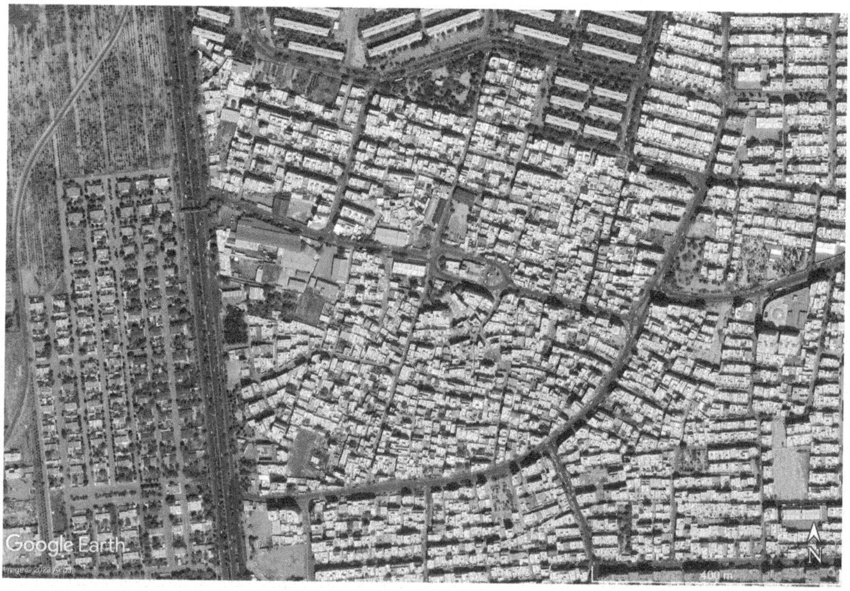

Figure 3.1 Satellite image of Ghazaniyya, 2023.
Google Earth (imagery date: 22 April 2023)
38° 04′ 51.52″ N, 46° 14′ 10.04″ E, eye alt 1.17 km
Airbus 2023. Accessed 5 September 2023

was founded around the same time as Ghazan was expanding the encompassment of Tabriz. Rashid al-Din writes that Ghazan

> has founded another city (*shahr*), larger than the encompassment of Old Tabriz, in Shanb, also called Shamm, where [he] had built the *abwāb al-birr*, in such a way that [the city] encompasses the *abwāb al-birr* and most of its gardens, and [he] called it Ghazaniyya, and ordered the merchants, who arrive from Rum and Afranj, to unload there, but the toll-collector (*tamghāchī*) [of Ghazaniyya] and the one of Tabriz should be the same [person] to prevent hostility (*tā munāzi'at nayuftad*).[3]

Along with the general layout of Ghazaniyya, this short yet informative passage raises two considerable points about the project. First, Ghazan built Ghazaniyya and its pious foundation in the suburb of Tabriz while the city had recently expanded and, thus, more space had become available for new constructions inside the city walls. Second, by order of Ghazan, trade caravans coming from Byzantine and Europe[4] unloaded their goods in Ghazaniyya, although they paid their tolls to the same toll-collectors of Tabriz.

Rashid al-Din's remarks on Ghazaniyya lead us to the problem of the location of Ghazaniyya; a newly founded urban centre on the outskirts of commercially thriving Tabriz. Did Ghazan envisage that Ghazaniyya, with its distinct architectural and urban character, would live independently from Tabriz? If that was the case, involving Ghazaniyya in the trade network of north-western Iran and developing its commercial relations with faraway lands could have been part of Ghazan's larger policy for reinforcing the political and economic position of his new city in competition with prosperous Tabriz. I will return to this question shortly.

Mustawfi also recounts how Ghazan founded a small city (*shahrchih*) beyond the new fortifications of Tabriz (*bārū-yi Ghāzānī*) in a place called Sham (pronounced Shām), and built lofty edifices there with the aim of using them as his own tomb (*khābgāh*, which literally means bedchamber).[5] To describe Ghazan's foundation in Shanb, Mustawfi does not differentiate between the city and the pious foundation, but clarifies that the Ilkhan chose Shanb as his eternal home from the outset. Ghazan's tomb was located at the centre of a pious complex, about which Rashid al-Din says:

> Since [Ghazan] was in the capital Tabriz, he chose it as the site and laid the foundation himself outside the city to the west in Shanb. They have been working on it for several years now, and it is planned to be much more magnificent than the dome of Sultan Sanjar the Seljuq in Merv, which is the most magnificent building in the world and which he saw.[6]

According to eye-witness observation, we are dealing with two separate projects: the central charitable foundation and the surrounding urban area, both of which were built in Shanb. While the boundaries between the two projects are rather blurred in the texts, for the sake of convenience in this book the former is called Shanb-i Ghazan and the latter is referred to as the 'city' (*shahr*) of Ghazaniyya.

In comparison with Shanb-i Ghazan, Ghazaniyya is poorly mentioned in the historical accounts. Passing references to the area of Shanb, particularly in the works of post-Ilkhanid historians, often point at the architectural complex surrounding Ghazan's tomb, whereas the residential neighbourhoods of the city are barely described. As I shall point out later in this chapter, Shanb-i Ghazan's fame, which outlived the Ilkhanid dynasty, rested primarily on the grandeur of the central charitable complex and the spirituality attributed to the place, while Ghazaniyya, despite Ghazan's ambitious expansion plans for the city, seemed to decline after the death of the founder.

While only a vague picture of Ghazaniyya is offered by textual sources, the *abwāb al-birr* is a relatively well-known architectural complex thanks to the accounts of Ilkhanid historians, particularly Rashid al-Din and Wassaf, the random remarks found in the reports of later visitors to the site, and the miniature paintings depicting general views of the compound. However, our understanding of the physical and spatial structure of the complex is rather fragmentary. While we are aware of the name and general function of the main components of the foundation, the layout of the buildings and their architectural features are still unknown to us. The tomb is the only element that has been described in great detail.

On Saturday 16 Dhu al-Ḥijja 696 (5 October 1297), Ghazan laid the foundations for a lofty dome (*qubbih-yi ʿālī*) in the midst of the ʿAdiliyya Garden (Bagh-i ʿAdiliyya) in Shanb,[7] beside Arghun's pavilion.[8] Rashid al-Din and Wassaf, slightly discrepantly, enumerate the twelve buildings encircling the Lofty Dome as follows:[9] mosque, khanqah, Shafiʿiyya (a residence and theology school based on the Shafiʿi school of Islamic law), *dār al-shafāʾ* (where the physicians treated patients), *bayt al-mutivallī* (superintendent's house), *kitāb-khānih* (library), *raṣad-khānih* (observatory),[10] *ḥukmīyya* (a residence for philosophers (*ḥukamā*) and philosophy teaching (*ḥikmat*)),[11] Hanafiyya (a residence and a theology school based on the Hanafi school of Islamic law), *ḥuż-khānih* (cistern), *bayt al-sīyāda* and *garmābih-yi sabīl* (public bath).[12] Interestingly, a surviving miniature painting from the *Jamiʿ al-Tawarikh*, probably produced a century later in Herat, depicts the circular layout of the complex.[13] The miniature portrays the tomb-tower located in a courtyard and enclosed by a row of buildings the façades of which are decorated by tile works and inscriptions. The enclosure is encircled by a wall fortified with towers. Although it seems unlikely that the painter copied the actual components of the *abwāb al-birr*, the painting sheds some light on the arrangement of the buildings inside the compound and their spatial relation with the tomb of Ghazan.[14]

Wassaf expands on the construction details and dimensions of the tomb as well as on the quality and quantity of the materials used in the building. He records that the twelve-sided building[15] had a circular foundation built of cut stone, on which walls were erected which were thirty-three bricks thick with each brick weighing ten *man*.[16] The thickness of the walls was fifteen *gaz*. In each row of the wall, 14,400 mud bricks were used, of which 13,000 were full and 1,400 half.[17] The height to the crown of the dome was 130 *gaz*. The vertical heights of the walls, cornice and the dome itself were 80, 10, and 40 *gaz* respectively.[18] Wassaf also offers brief information about the engineers (*muhandisīn*) and artisans (*ṣan'atgarān*) employed in the project and the rough cost of erecting the walls. His mentions of the fittings and ornaments reveal some of the glory of the tomb: 'Golden and silver lamps and candlesticks were set for that [*qubbih*]. One of the lamps was made of 1,000 *mithqāl* of gold.[19] To colour the roof of that *qubbih*, 300 *man*s of lapis (*lājvard*) were used.'[20]

Wassaf refers to a lengthy Arabic inscription encircling the dome. The inscription begins by praising God and the Prophet Muhammad and continues by expressing admiration for Ghazan Khan, who is called by the epithets of 'Exalted Qa'an', 'Greatest Ilkhan', 'Lord of the Khaqans of the World' and 'Sultan of the Sultans', among several other honorific titles. The Ilkhan is introduced as the son of the Exalted Qa'an, the Greatest Ilkhan Arghun Khan who was the son of the Greatest Qa'an, the Exalted Ilkhan Abaqa Khan. In the last segment of the inscription, Ghazan is praised for establishing the charitable institution around the tomb.[21] No date is given in the inscription for the completion of the tomb or the charitable complex.

With what was legally in his possession, Ghazan assigned an extensive endowment, called *awqāf-i khāṣṣ* (special endowments),[22] to the foundation in Shanb-i Ghazan and delegated the judicial custodianship (*tawlīyyat*)[23] of the endowment to Rashid al-Din. He also allocated the revenues of the properties in other states to the institution.[24] Wassaf reports that each year, the income from the estates exceeded one hundred *tumān*s of gold. Ghazan founded an agency (*dīwān-i khāṣṣih*) conducted by two of his amirs, Gur-Timur and Tarmtaz, to collect and manage the annual income earned from the endowment of the *abwāb al-birr*.[25]

According to Rashid al-Din, by order of Ghazan seven copies of the endowment deed were made to be held in seven different places, four of which are known to us: one with the superintendent of the complex, one in the Honourable Ka'ba (Ka'ba-yi Sharif) in Mecca, one in the *dār al-qażā'* (the seat of the judiciary) of the *dār al-mulk* of Tabriz, and one in the *dār al-qażā'* of Baghdad, the City of Peace (Madinat al-Salam-i Baghdad). All the religious scholars and jurists of Islam verified the authenticity of the document.[26]

None of the copies of the deed, alas, survives. Nevertheless, in the *Jami' al-Tawarikh*, Rashid al-Din gives a relatively vivid description of the endowed outlays for the tomb and each of the twelve charitable buildings in the vicinity, the salaries of the personnel, workers and residents of the institution, and the alms and offerings distributed among the poor and orphans, all of which were apparently detailed in the endowment deed of Shanb-i Ghazan.[27] Rashid al-Din's account also provides insights into the rituals associated with the *abwāb al-birr*, which will be discussed later. While, in the absence of the deed, many questions regarding the form and function of the complex as well as the financial resources assigned to it remain to be answered, the small portion of the endowment that is evident to us certainly denotes the grandeur of the foundation and the complexity of its administration.

Tracing Ilkhanid Ghazaniyya in present-day Tabriz

Despite the ambiguities concerning the layout of Ghazaniyya, textual and pictorial evidence discussed so far points towards the circular configuration of the city and the central pious complex. The aerial photograph taken in 1967 provides even more solid evidence that Ghazan's architectural and urban projects were arranged according to a concentric pattern. The image depicts two circles distorted by agricultural fields and later urban constructions (Figure 3.2). The inner circle possibly marks the approximate area of the pious foundation of Shanb-i Ghazan with the tomb of the Ilkhan at its core, and the outer circle shows the encompassment of the city of Ghazaniyya. The edge of the circles working as main arteries of the town in 1967, possibly indicate the track of the ruined walls that enclosed the charitable complex and the Ilkhanid city.

Close examination of the photograph reveals the traces of a radial system on the basis of which the road network of Ghazaniyya had possibly been shaped. The roads seemed to connect the pious complex and the main city to the suburbs through the gates located in the outer wall. At the time the

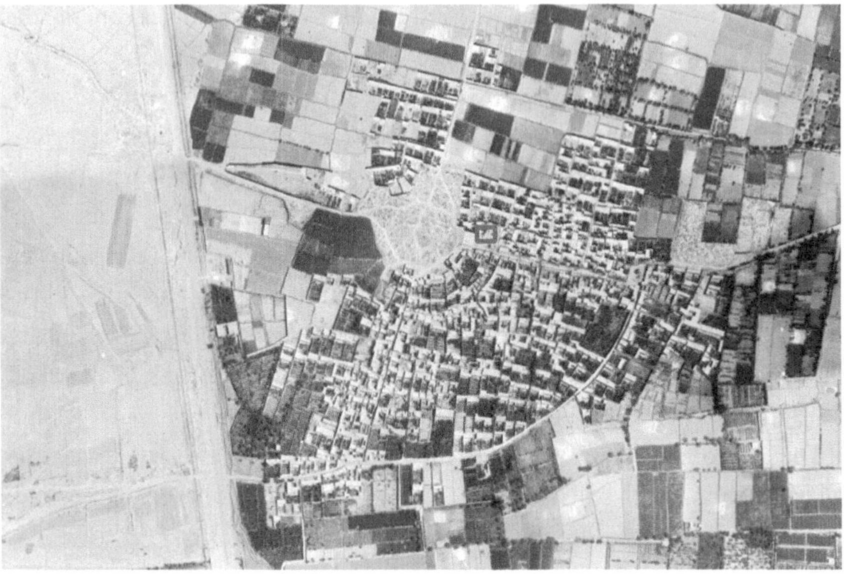

Figure 3.2 Aerial photo of Ghazaniyya, 1967. The location of the Grand Mosque of al-Mahdiyya is marked on the photo.
Iran National Cartography Centre

photograph was taken, only two perpendicular roads had survived which divided the city into four quarters (Figure 3.3).

The 1967 aerial photograph shows the area prior to the development of Tabriz, when Ghazaniyya and the city were separated by agricultural lands. With the development of Tabriz in the second half of the twentieth century, Ghazaniyya was joined to the city and became one of the neighbourhoods of modern-day Tabriz. Gardens and agricultural lands that are observable in the photograph as well as the ruins of medieval buildings were gradually overlaid with new constructions. Despite all the drastic changes during the last few decades, the most recent satellite image of Ghazaniyya, taken in April 2023, still represents the same configuration as that described in the 1967 photograph.

In approximately the same place as Ghazan's tomb is believed to have been located the Grand Mosque of al-Mahdiyya stands today (Figure 3.4). The mosque is also visible in the 1967 photograph. According to the inscription installed on the portal of the mosque, the building was built on the ruins of an earlier mosque. Part of the inscription reads as follows (Figure 3.5):

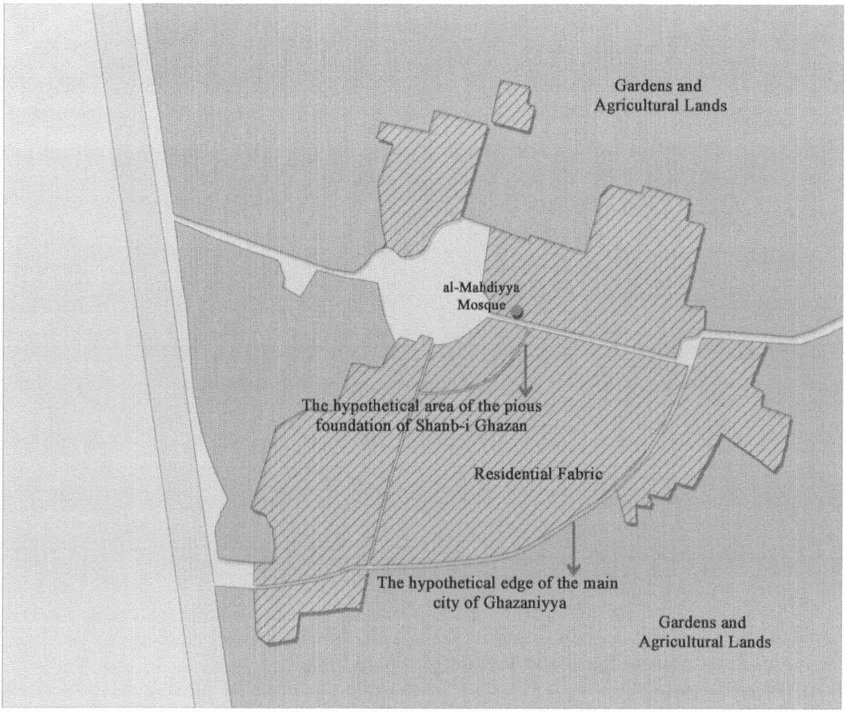

Figure 3.3 Outline of Ghazaniyya based on the 1967 aerial photo of the site.
© Atri Hatef Naiemi

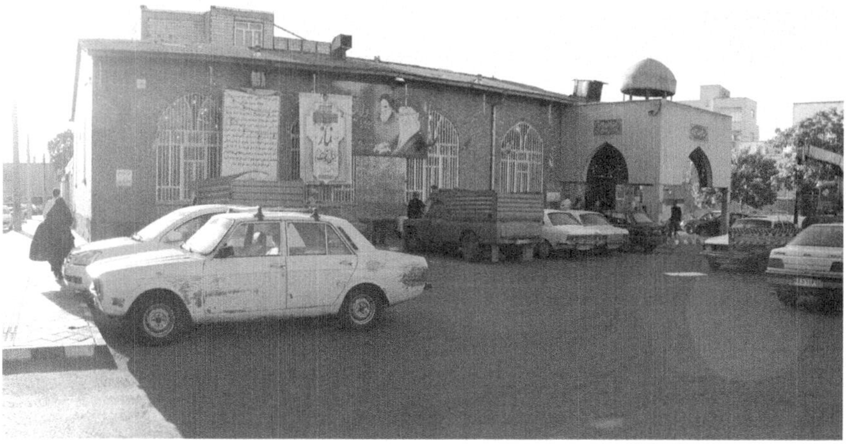

Figure 3.4 Grand Mosque of al-Mahdiyya. According to the inscription, the new mosque was built on the ruins of the Ilkhanid mosque.
© Atri Hatef Naiemi

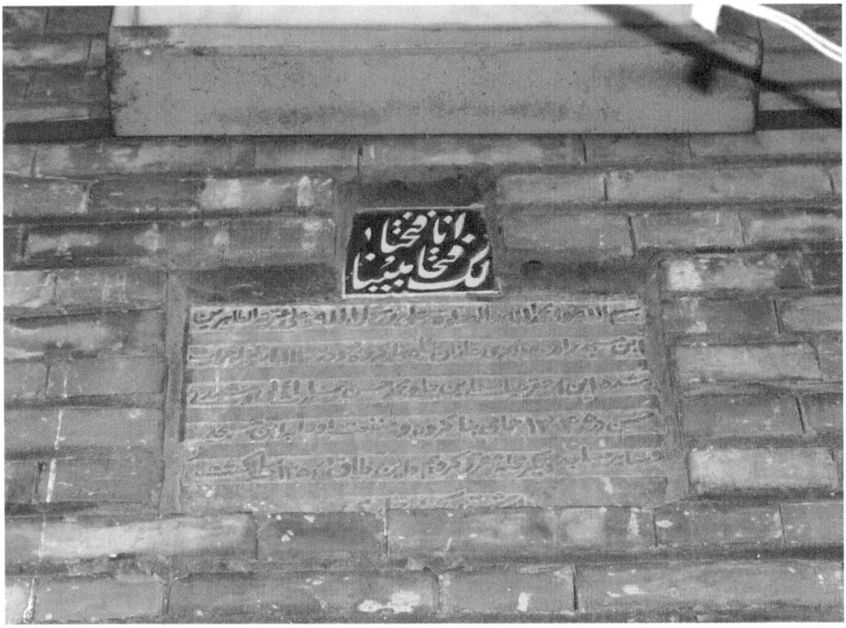

Figure 3.5 Inscription of the Grand Mosque of al-Mahdiyya.

> In the name of God, and Praise be to God, and *Ṣalawāt* be upon the prophet of God and his innocent descendants. Ghazan Shah founded this mosque in 700/1300. The building was destroyed by earthquake in 1133/1721. This humble servant, ʿAbbas-ʿAli [i]bn Haji Muhammad-Hassan, built a public bathhouse in 1345/1926 with the aid of Mashhadi Hassan and the locals and endowed it (dedicated its revenue) to this mosque and the other mosques of the neighbourhood, and this cupola (*ṭāq*) was built in 1351/1932 ...[28]

The dark stones re-used in the lower parts of the mosque's external walls seem to belong to the earlier building (Figure 3.6). Some of the stones carry marks which were possibly made by the stone carvers in the carving workshops (Figures 3.7 and 3.8). The content of the inscription of the portal and the location of the building lead us to speculatively suggest that the earlier mosque must have been part of the central pious complex of Shanb-i Ghazan.

In addition to the circular layout of the neighbourhood which corresponds to the spatial arrangement of medieval Ghazaniyya, a large number

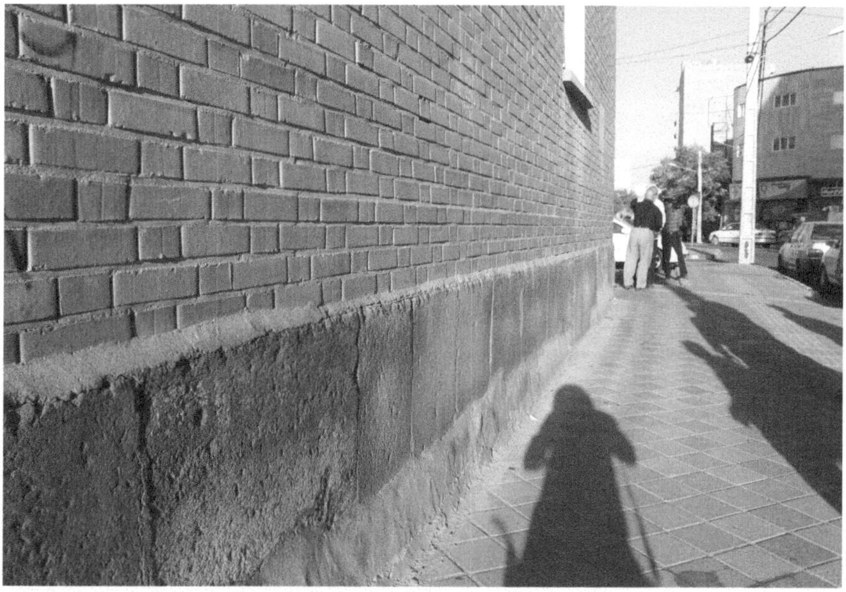

Figure 3.6 Grand Mosque of al-Mahdiyya. The dark stones used in the lower parts of the walls must have belonged to an earlier building.

of Ilkhanid architectural fragments and shards of potteries, bricks and tiles are still being unearthed here and there (Figure 3.9). Some of the remnants of historical structures are being re-used by the locals. For instance, in the old cemetery surviving in the midst of the neighbourhood, there are nameless graves adorned (and perhaps sanctified) with small shards of the tiles that once decorated the buildings of Ghazaniyya (Figure 3.10). Brick fragments inscribed with the words 'Allah' and 'Ghazan Qa'an' (Figures 3.11 and 3.12) or larger pieces such as stone plinths are also noticeable vestiges of the city which was razed to the ground (Figures 3.13 and 3.14).

The analysis of the aerial views enabled us to achieve a better understanding of the authentic layout of the Ilkhanid city concealed underneath the new buildings. Nonetheless, in view of the fragmentary nature of archaeological and textual data, our knowledge of the architectural and urban features of Ghazaniyya is still far from complete. While a full reconstruction of Ghazan's urban projects is neither feasible nor a priority in this chapter, identifying his undertakings, as far as is possible, is enlightening with regard to the spiritual

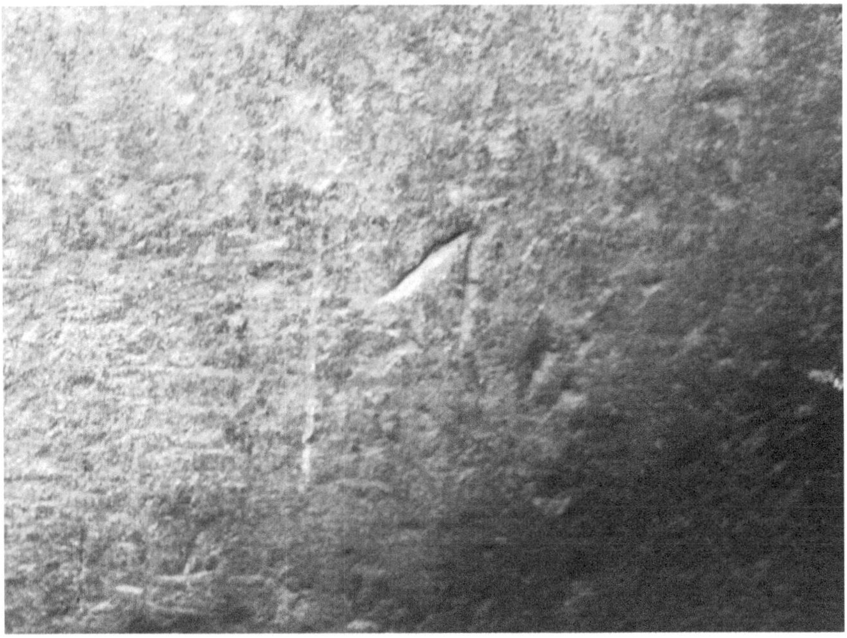

Figure 3.7 Grand Mosque of al-Mahdiyya. One example of the marks possibly made by stone carvers in the carving workshops.

mindset of the Ilkhan, who was actively involved in the process of design and construction. This is particularly the case with the tomb and the surrounding *abwāb al-birr*, which were expected to represent the Ilkhan's perception of his worldly life as well as the afterlife. In order to understand how Ghazan's ideology influenced the material and conceptual attributes of the buildings, one needs to dig deeper into the former. What will be offered next is a brief overview of the spiritual beliefs of the Mongols in general, with a focus on the religious eclecticism of Ghazan Khan.

The Religious Eclecticism of Ghazan Khan

There are numerous complexities surrounding the issue of the religion, or on a broader scale the spiritual beliefs, of the Mongols. After achieving dominion over much of Eurasia, they were exposed to a wide range of religions practised across their vast territories. Following the disintegration of the Mongol Empire in the mid-thirteenth century, in each of the autonomous khanates formed

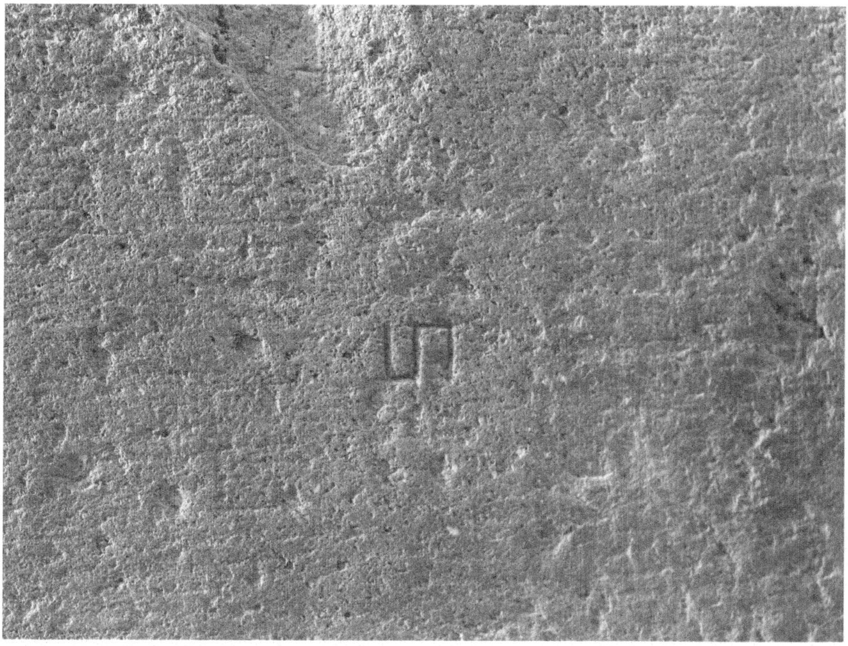

Figure 3.8 Grand Mosque of al-Mahdiyya. One example of the marks possibly made by stone carvers in the carving workshops.
© Atri Hatef Naiemi

afterwards the Mongols dealt with the religion of their subjects almost without hostility. In the same way, the Ilkhans tolerated, if not encouraged, religious diversity in Iran until the conversion of Ghazan Khan in 1295. At the time of the Mongolian conquest of Iran, Sunnism was the religion of the majority of Iranians. The fall of the Abbasid Caliphate in 1258 and the killing of the last Sunni caliph al-Mustaʿsim Billah by order of Hülegü, however, strengthened the spread of Shiʿism in Iran. In the socio-political circumstances after the Mongols' invasion, other non-Muslim communities, such as Shamanists, Buddhists, Nestorian Christians and Jews, were also widespread. [29] Needless to say, the Sufis also had a prominent presence in the Ilkhanid court and elite circles.[30]

With the accession of the neophyte Ghazan to the throne in 1295, Islam was known as the imperial religion in Western Asia.[31] Following the death of the Great Khan Qubilay, Ghazan became more determined to form a political identity that was more independent from the Khaqans of the Yuan dynasty.

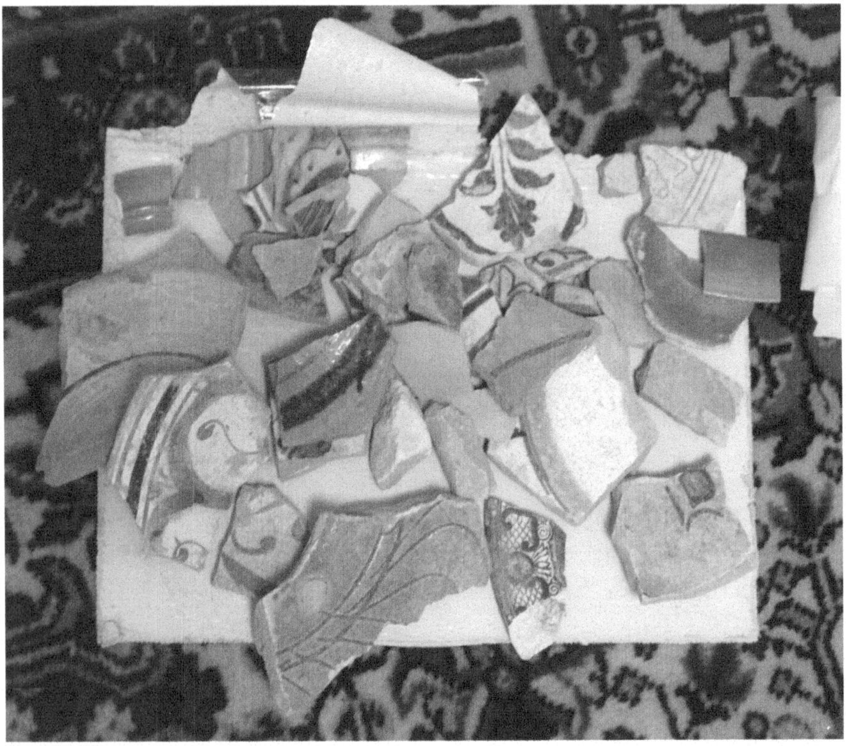

Figure 3.9 Shards of the potteries and tiles found in the modern neighbourhood of Ghazaniyya.
© Atri Hatef Naiemi (courtesy of M. Besharat Ghazani)

Therefore, he gradually loosened his ideological connections with the Great Khans in China in order to obtain the support of the Iranians. He officially called himself sultan, a propagator and defender of the faith, instead of Ilkhan, a subordinate to the Great Khan.[32] This ideological shift, however, seemed to fulfil primarily local conditions and did not result in a political break between Ilkhanid Iran and Yuan China since the two courts kept up their continuous military and diplomatic co-operation until the mid-fourteenth century.[33] The Islamisation of the Ilkhanid court under Ghazan can also be considered one of the policies pursued by the Iranian elite, Rashid al-Din in particular, in order to transform the Mongol rulers and fit them into their own ideal mould.[34] The vizier played a major role, as Johnson puts it, 'in the transformation of Ilkhanid government from a nomadic Central Asian regime into a sedentary Islamic polity'.[35]

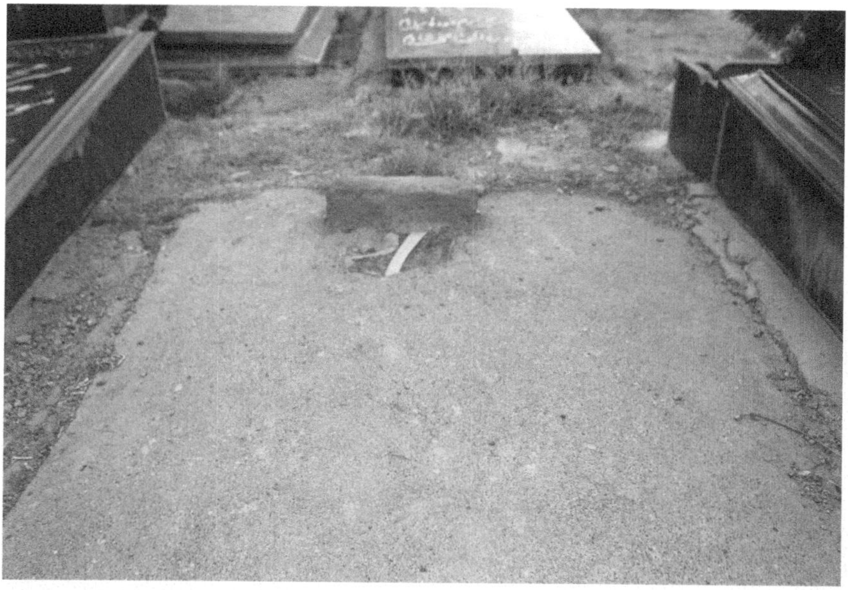

Figure 3.10 A nameless grave in the old cemetery of Ghazaniyya adorned with a small fragment of tile.
© Atri Hatef Naiemi

Ahmad Tegüder was the first Ilkhan who had officially embraced the Muslim religion.[36] However, his conversion is often deemed personal, contrary to Ghazan's conversion which caused a large group of the Mongols in Iran to convert to Islam.[37] Apart from Ahmad, Ghazan's predecessors never converted to Islam, although there is substantial evidence suggesting that they were willing to appropriate the existing Islamic themes and combine them with their own political and spiritual ideologies. The Muslim *shahāda* that appeared on all the coins minted by the first Ilkhan Hülegü and on some of the coins struck by Chinggis Khan and Möngke Khan is an interesting example in this regard.[38] Despite their willingness, it is noteworthy that the Mongols acted selectively in their encounter with the spiritual elements of the sedentary world. In other words, the appropriation of unfamiliar notions happened insofar as they were not in opposition to Mongolian customs.[39]

Whether the converted Ilkhans had sincere faith in Islam or not, their conversion certainly pleased their Muslim subjects and thus strengthened the legitimacy of their reign. While they clearly expressed their loyalty to Mongolian

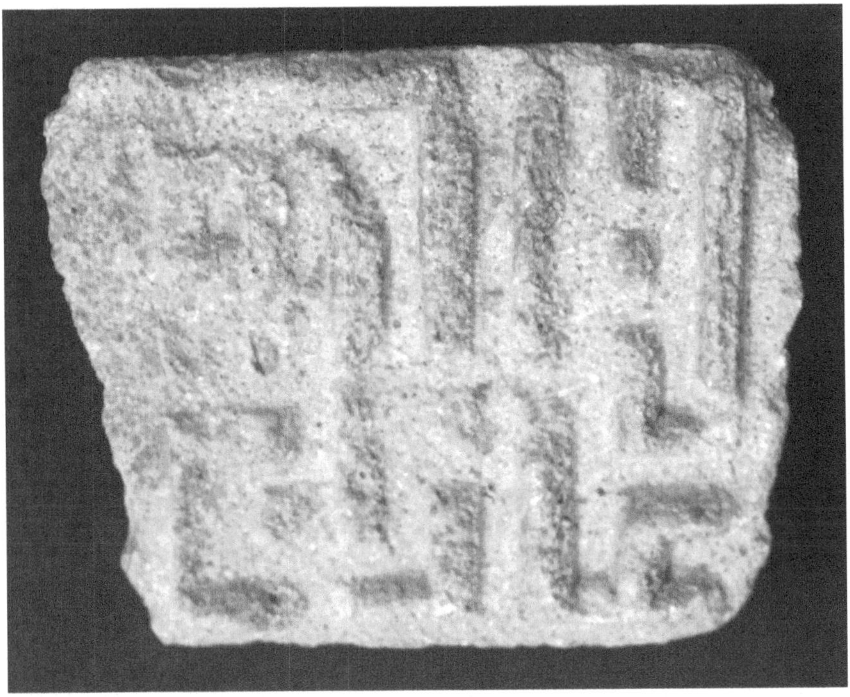

Figure 3.11 A fragment of a brick found in the modern neighbourhood of Ghazaniyya. The words 'Ghazan Qa'an' are inscribed on the brick.
© Atri Hatef Naiemi (courtesy of M. Besharat Ghazani)

traditions in their words and deeds even after conversion, their responding to the religious sensibilities of the majority of the Iranians is considered to be a gesture intended to 'domesticate' or 'diversify' the bases of their legitimation rather than representing radical changes in their ideology.[40]

The religious eclecticism of the Mongols is often explained in relation to their exposure to different spiritual realms, which enabled them to develop a greater tolerance towards various religions.[41] Looking at the issue from a different perspective, Thomas Allsen argues that, along with organising resources, people and commodities, the Mongols attempted to control the spiritual forces found in the natural world, those possessed and monopolised by their ancestors or former dynasties, and those owned by ritual specialists, skilled artisans and scholars, among whom they particularly relied on clergymen of all faiths. As a result of such an approach, while declaring belief in one specific sect or

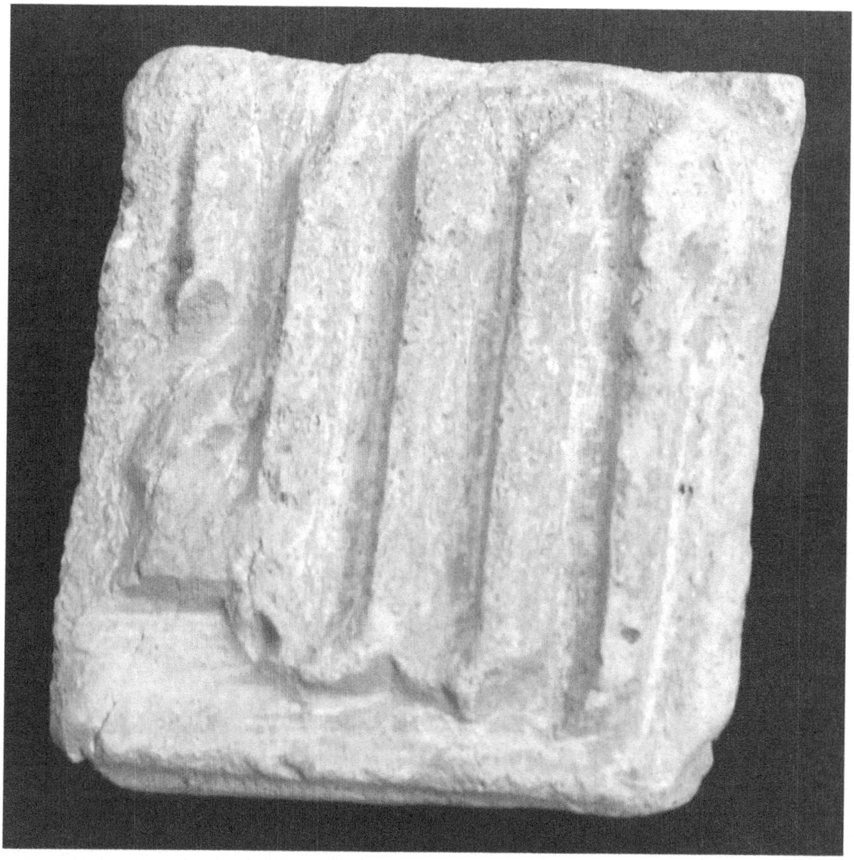

Figure 3.12 A fragment of a brick found in the modern neighbourhood of Ghazaniyya. The word 'Allah' is inscribed on the brick.
© Atri Hatef Naiemi (courtesy of M. Besharat Ghazani)

school, they arranged theological debates in their courts and showed interest in other religious principles and practices. This enthusiasm often persuaded the supporters of different religious groups to believe that the Khan/Ilkhan was 'one of them'.[42] The Mongols also welcomed diverse spiritual traditions, since they 'believed in taking out as much celestial insurance as possible', in Morgan's words.[43]

Ghazan's conversion to Islam nevertheless brought an end to the long years of religious tolerance among the Mongols. The religious eclecticism drawing upon multiple ideas and conventions was abruptly replaced with a

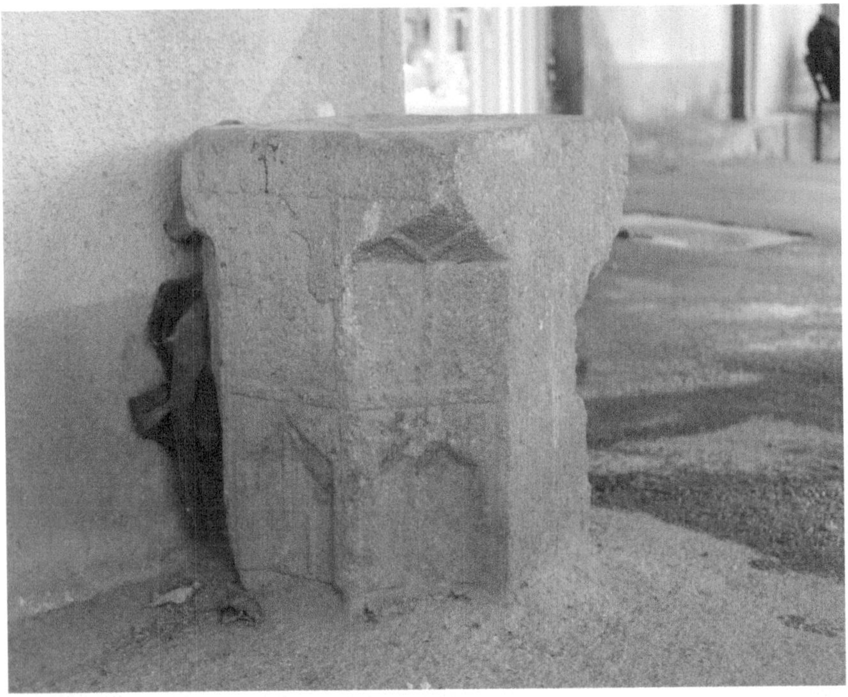

Figure 3.13 One example of the last vestiges of Ilkhanid Ghazaniyya, which was razed to the ground. The plinth is currently kept in the cemetery of Ghazaniyya.
© Atri Hatef Naiemi

growing tendency to revive Islamic teachings.[44] Although Ghazan announced his religious fidelity as a faithful Muslim by destroying idols, monasteries and temples right after the conversion,[45] within the realm of his new set of Islamic beliefs, the Ilkhan continued roaming around different branches and schools of Islam. In other words, Ghazan's Islam was an inconsistent amalgamation of various Islamic beliefs and practices. While he built amicable relations with Sufis,[46] he chose the Hanafi School following his conversion, according to Rashid al-Din.[47] Kashani, on the other hand, states that Ghazan was devoted to ʿAli and the family of the Prophet Muhammad (*ahl al-bayt*). On one occasion he decreed that the names of the Rashidun (the first three caliphs: Abu Bakr, ʿUmar and ʿUthman) should be removed from sermons since mention of their names in the sermons was an innovation (*bidʿa*) while mentioning the name of the *ahl al-bayt* and ʿAli was a religious duty

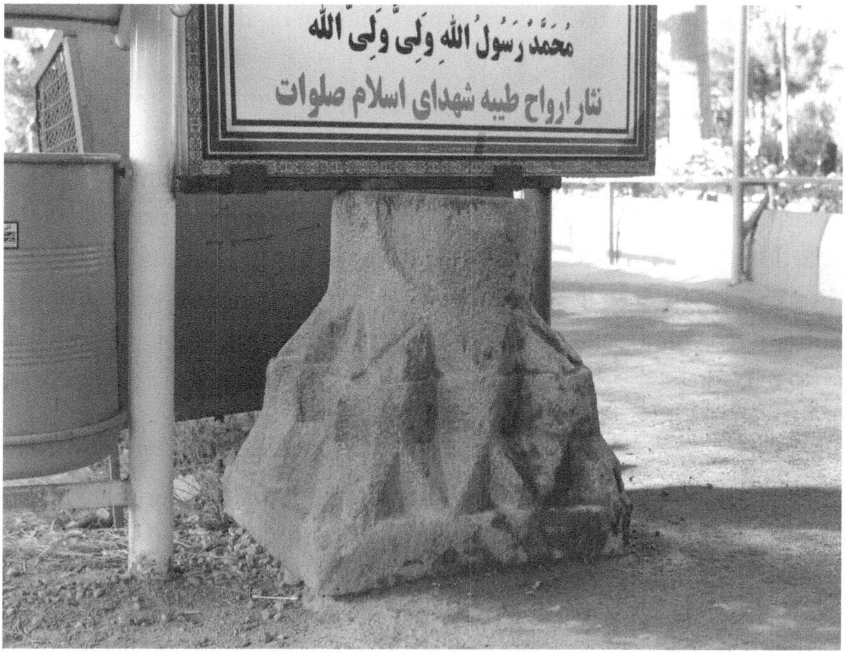

Figure 3.14 One example of the last vestiges of Ilkhanid Ghazaniyya, which was razed to the ground. The plinth is currently kept in the cemetery of Ghazaniyya.
© Atri Hatef Naiemi

(*vājib*).[48] Although Rashid al-Din eventually dissuaded Ghazan from carrying out this order, the story denotes the Ilkhan's deviation from Sunnism to Shiʿism.[49]

Ghazan's conversion was not an entirely spiritual experience after all. Gaining the support of the Muslims in his struggle against Baydu (r. 1295) is considered to be an important motive behind his conversion.[50] The Ilkhans' amir and closest advisor Nowruz convinced him to adopt Islam.[51] Wassaf describes Nowruz as 'the warrior Mahdi, the reviver (*muḥay*) of the religion of the Arabs, the representative of the divinity, the second Abu Muslim, the promoter of the religion'.[52] Although the Mongol amir appears to have been a faithful Muslim, his role in Ghazan's conversion suggests that the Ilkhan's inclination towards the new faith was encouraged by both political and spiritual motives from the outset.[53] Despite the fact that Ghazan's conversion deeply impacted the socio-political atmosphere of post-conquest Iran, it must be borne in mind that the conversion per se did not fundamentally change the Ilkhan's spiritual ideology.

Following his conversion to Islam, Ghazan continued to believe in Mongol traditions and customs. Amitai-Preiss argues that Ghazan and the Mongol elite followed the pattern of 'communal conversion' in which they adopted the new religion but retained their own cultural identity and ethnic affiliation. Ghazan remained committed to the Chinggisid Yasa and loyal to the Great Khan in China. He maintained a belief in the Mongol imperial ideology, which stated that a mandate from heaven had been bestowed upon Chinggis Khan to bring the world under his control, the mandate which was supposed to be continued by his successors.[54] The Ilkhan participated in Mongolian traditional ceremonies and consulted with his Mongolian advisors in his native language.[55] The rituals of the Mongol folk religion, shamanism, were maintained among the Ilkhanid Mongols even in the post-Ghazan period, although the Ilkhan himself had almost no adherence to it.[56]

All the evidence discussed so far points towards the fact that Ghazan's belief system consisted of a number of differing and sometimes contradictory principles and precepts. Perhaps this is the reason for the absence of explicit statements about Ghazan's religious affiliation in his contemporary textual records. He oscillated between being a Mongol Ilkhan and a Muslim sultan, and thus it would be challenging to determine which aspect of his hybrid identity influenced his decisions and undertakings more.

Referring to the main thesis of the book, in this chapter we speculatively suggested that the city of Ghazaniyya and the *abwāb al-birr* of Shanb reflected the dialogue between Perso-Islamic sedentary ideas and Mongolian nomadic traditions. Traces of the interaction between the two seemingly opposite entities are detectable in both temporal and spiritual features of Ghazan's urban enterprise. Thus, to uncover the dialogue, we first examined the physical and functional features of the city and the complex. Then we scrutinised Ghazan's – the patron's – religious beliefs, which proved to be a syncretic fusion, particularly after his historic conversion. Building on our knowledge of Ghazan's architectural and urban undertakings on the one hand, and his eclectic taste in religion on the other, what will be presented next is a reconsideration of the foundation and development of Ghazaniyya and Shanb-i Ghazan, aimed at determining how the spiritual ideology of Ghazan affected the project, and also highlighting the areas where the encounter/dialogue happened.

The Encounter between Perso-Islamic Concepts and Mongolian Traditions in Ghazaniyya and Shanb-i Ghazan

Given the fluidity of the religious beliefs of the Mongols and their 'bewildering variety of attachment', in Peter Jackson's words,[57] textual and material evidence of their acts and decisions could be open to misinterpretation. In the same way, in the case of Ghazan and his architectural and urban projects in Ghazaniyya, the ambiguity over the Ilkhan's spiritual orientation may not allow us to reach a firm conclusion about his intention of building the city and the charitable foundation. Nevertheless, what we can suggest with more certainty is that the architectural undertakings patronised by the Ilkhan following his conversion represented an arena where various visual and conceptual traditions converged, to the extent that in the eyes of modern commentators they are not effortlessly differentiable.

In the account of the construction of the pious complex of Shanb-i Ghazan, Rashid al-Din writes that Ghazan Khan had visited the holy shrine of Imam Riza and the tomb complexes of Sultan Bayazid, Abu al-Hassan Kharaqani and Shaykh Abu Sa'id Abul Khayr in Khurasan. After his conversion to Islam, he went on a pilgrimage to the mausoleum of 'Ali in Najaf and the tombs of other holy figures in Baghdad. This spiritual journey led the Ilkhan to follow the actions of the religious leaders and build an *abwāb al-birr* that would accommodate him in the hereafter (*jāy-i ākhirat*).[58] The Ilkhan said:

> How can one consider a person who has died in this manner and has a shrine or visitation site like this to be among the dead? Dying like this is better than other people's living. Even though we do not possess the rank of pious people, nonetheless in imitation of them we can build a charitable institution to spend eternity in, and in that manner, there will be charity and alms, the blessings of which will attract God's mercy, and there will be an eternal reward stored up.[59]

Thus, it would appear that the mentality and materiality associated with the institution in Shanb were in accordance with Islamic ideas and themes.

In view of the conversion of a large group of the Mongols, Ghazan possibly had little difficulty justifying his religious architectural projects which culminated in Ghazaniyya. However, as discussed earlier, despite the communal conversion of the Mongols, Islam was not willingly adopted by all the Mongols, and they largely retained their cultural identity, remaining committed to their Mongolian customs. In nomadic societies, as Allsen puts it, 'power is derived from the acquisition and retention of followers not the acquisition of land'.[60] Therefore, even if Ghazan had adopted the new faith, he had no choice but to ensure the loyalty of his extended household as well as the Mongol army through respecting their nomadic traditions. Dedicating himself too much to protecting the principles of the new religion could have caused the Ilkhan to lose the support of at least the fanatical members of his Mongol entourage. On the other hand, he inevitably needed to be trusted by his Iranian (primarily) Muslim subjects and therefore acknowledged their ideological values in his decrees and acts.

Furthermore, Ghazan had to face the issue of legitimisation in relation to both the Mongols and the Persian population. He might have benefited from the construction projects in demonstrating his authority over his subjects and supporting his claims to legitimacy. To enhance the effectiveness of this tool, the Ilkhan had to choose a visual language that was comprehensible to both groups. Although Ghazan conducted his architectural projects as the Muslim sultan of Iran, as a legitimate Ilkhan he still had to impress his Mongol followers by his operations and convey a message of power to them by means of architecture. Obviously, there would be no point in him constructing magnificent structures if the visual vocabulary used in the buildings was unfamiliar to the Mongols. As a result, the city of Ghazaniyya and the charitable foundation in Shanb must have represented, in their form and function, the combination of the cultural components introduced by the Mongols and what they were offered by their Iranian host. However, this coexistence did not always happen through the contribution of obvious elements of each cultural sphere; rather, as will be discussed shortly, in some cases it was confined to themes that were subtle but effective, and familiar enough to be understood by their target audience.

Identifying the architectural traditions which were brought together in Ghazaniyya presents a major difficulty. As mentioned earlier, the statements of the medieval historians suggest that construction of the pious complex in Shanb was derived from the religious enthusiasm of the newly converted Ilkhan Ghazan. Taking into account the architectural features of the buildings presented in the available textual and pictorial sources, the complex can be placed within the framework of pre-Mongol Muslim religious architecture, numerous examples of which have survived. The polygonal mausoleums, for instance, were familiar structures built in Iran at least four centuries prior to Shanb-i Ghazan.[61] The tomb itself is also compared to the tomb of Sultan Sanjar in Merv (built in 1157), although the former was apparently much more magnificent than the latter.[62] It would be less problematic if we considered Ghazan's constructions in Shanb exclusively in the well-known context of Perso-Islamic architecture and attributed all their physical characteristics to this set of traditions. The fact that Ghazan was born and raised in Iran, converted to Islam and, later in his career, was surrounded by his Persian advisory circle provides us with enough reasons to suggest that what was built by the Muslim Ilkhan in Ghazaniyya must have been in accordance with his Islamic beliefs as well as the dominant architectural traditions of the time. Nevertheless, there is a counter-argument to this idea. The syncretic nature of Ghazan's cultural and spiritual identity on the one hand and his wish to meet specific requirements for legitimacy on the other, as discussed above, lead us to look for non-Persian, non-Islamic components in the Ilkhan's architectural projects.

Unravelling the alien themes could be challenging. They may have been hidden in the guise of more familiar local elements. They could have partially lost their original character and have been substantially adapted to suit the taste and sensibilities of their host. In addition, there are ideas and traditions which were common to the receiving culture (the Persians) and the guest culture (the Mongols). While some concepts fit perfectly into only one specific culture, there are other notions that can be explained in connection with both Persian and Mongol cultural spheres. Therefore, the visual and conceptual attributes of the buildings that seem meaningful in the Persian/Islamic context at first glance can have different meaning when they are interpreted according to the ideological framework of the Mongols. Between the two, the latter is usually given less attention and credit, due to our fragmentary knowledge of the practices brought in by the Mongols. It must also be borne in mind that the innovative combination of pre-existing traditions and alien elements could have generated hybrid products which were barely recognisable to the participants: the Persians and the Mongols.[63] I will expand on this idea in the final chapter of the book.

What will be offered below is an extended discussion of two major areas in which the encounter between Perso-Islamic themes and Mongolian conventions can be identified with more clarity in the context of Ghazan's architectural and urban projects in Shanb-i Ghazan and Ghazaniyya: the choice of location and the practice of visitation of the ancestors and the offering of alms. Keeping the two elements in mind, I observe Ghazan's enterprise first from a Mongol and then from a Perso-Islamic perspective to unravel the ideas associated with each of the two cultural realms. As we shall see, there are also concepts which have their roots in both realms. The centre of the discussion will be the pious foundation rather than the city, due to the better-known characteristics of the former.

Observing Ghazaniyya and Shanb-i Ghazan from a Mongol perspective

The Inner Asian nomads believed in the sky-god Tengri.[64] Tengri bestowed a heavenly mandate to govern on a Qa'an who had possessed good fortune and charisma, a quality characterised 'as the manifestation of exemplary, superhuman or supernatural [divine] attributes and powers'.[65] The possessor of charisma was therefore legitimised to assume power and leadership. Following the political notions of the earlier nomads, Chinggis Khan and his successors retained two principles of their predecessors' ideology: heavenly mandate, and royal charisma (*suu* in Mongolian).[66]

According to the nomads' political ideology, the good fortune existed permanently in some specific territories in the eastern steppe, and their Qa'ans acquired royal charisma, and thus legitimacy, through occupying these lands. For instance, Burkhan Khaldun, an important ritual and political centre in north-eastern Mongolia during the thirteenth and fourteenth centuries, was believed to carry such a quality. It borrowed its spiritual power from the unknown burial site of Chinggis Khan as well as from his *ordu*s in the region. All the major Toluid princes,[67] whose right to rule had been partly questioned by other branches of the Mongols and who thus sought legitimation, were buried in the Great Forbidden Precinct (*quruq*) at Burkhan Khaldun. As a result, the region was established as an ancestral shrine for the Chinggisid family as a whole and then as the sanctuary of the branch of the Toluids.[68]

The two principles of this ideology are reflected in a coin minted in Tbilisi in 1252, during the reign of Möngke Khan, the fourth Khaqan of the Mongol Empire. The inscription written in Persian reads, 'By the Might of God/By the Good Fortune of the Emperor/of the world, Munku Qa'an'.[69] Interestingly, a similar motto appears years later on Ghazan's standard double-dirham. The coin carries a pentagonal cartouche with the profession of faith (*shahāda*) in Arabic, the mint and the date on one side, and a phrase in Uyghur and the Ilkhan's name in Persian on the other.[70] The phrase reads '*Tngri-yin küčüntür/ Kasan-u deledkegülüg-sen*', which means 'By the power of Tngri [Tengri]/ Kasan [Ghazan] had a coin struck'. The fact that the Muslim convert and the *Padishah-i Islām* (King of Islam)[71] reveals his belief in a source of divinity outside the world of Islam, the nomads' deity Tengri, supports our above-mentioned claim regarding Ghazan's religious eclecticism.[72] Besides the coin, in my opinion, Ghazan showed his appreciation of the nomads' ideology on at least two other crucial occasions: at the time of his conversion to Islam in a pavilion (*kūshk*) which was the residence (*takhtgāh*) of his father Arghun, and at the time of the selection of Shanb as the site of his burial complex as well as his city.

Ghazan became Muslim in Lar-i Damavand and repeated the profession of faith (*kalamih-yi shahādat*) after the Kubrawiyya Sufi, Shaykh Sadr al-Din Ibrahim Hammuya.[73] Although it seems that the place of conversion had not been planned in advance, the fact that Ghazan converted to Islam in the pavilion of his father is of great importance. As Charles Melville mentions, Ghazan's gesture could have emphasised his claims to Arghun's inheritance and strengthened his legitimacy among the Mongol elite.[74] One might suggest that Ghazan possibly had one more reason for the choice of location for his conversion: he wished to obtain the good fortune and royal charisma of the deceased Ilkhan Arghun which had been left at the site. In fact, while he decided to adopt a new faith, he asked for blessing for himself, at the time of his difficult decision, from another source of spirituality.

Ghazan erected his tomb and its surrounding charitable buildings in Shanb. Later, he built the city of Ghazaniyya that enclosed the burial complex. The idea of founding a new urban centre beside the *dār al-mulk* of Tabriz could be explained in connection with the aforementioned ideology of the Mongols.

Ilkhanid historians, particularly those who report the events of Arghun's early years, do not highlight one certain political and administrative centre. The accounts describe the movements of the Ilkhan among a number of seasonal camps including Tabriz, Baghdad, Maraghih and Arran.[75] Rashid al-Din, however, records that Arghun, who had a great interest in constructing buildings (*bi kār-i ʿimārat aẓīm māyil būd*), founded a grand city in Shamm (Shanb) near Tabriz in 1290, building splendid houses there, and called it Arghuniyya.[76] The vizier does not expand on the motivation behind Arghun's decision to found his city in the immediate vicinity of the capital Tabriz, but it is likely that, in Arghun's eyes, Shanb was one of the areas where the primordial good fortune existed. Ghazan captured this quality through possessing the land that had already been claimed by his father, and via establishing his own tomb, the surrounding charitable foundation and the city of Ghazaniyya. In addition, for Ghazan, as an outsider, founding a splendid urban centre in the same area as that in which Arghuniyya had been built, rather than in the developed city of Tabriz, seemed like a reasonable policy towards legitimation.

Furthermore, Arghun was buried in Mount Sujas near Sultaniyya,[77] which was called Obyr by the Mongols.[78] The Ilkhan's attendants concealed his burial site, as was the Mongol custom, and made the mountain a *quruq*. Arghun's burial site was kept secret until years later when Arghun's daughter, Öljey Khatun, revealed it and built a khanqah at the site.[79] Considering the Mongols' political ideology, one could hypothesise that, in the absence of Arghun's tomb, the Ilkhan's constructions in Arghuniyya, of which only a certain pavilion and garden are known to us, bestowed good fortune on the site of Shanb. Ghazan in fact honoured the memory of his father and obtained his royal charisma via revering his former residence rather than his unknown tomb.

This practice was not unprecedented in the spiritual culture of the Mongols. Following the death of Chinggis Khan, in the absence of the actual burial site of the Khan, his encampments were venerated as shrines where his relics were kept, and incense was continuously burnt in his honour. Textual records describe the visits of Chinggis Khan's successors to his *ordu*s in Burkhan Khaldun in search of the good fortune and royal charisma of the deceased Khan, the qualities which ensured his followers' political and military victories in their future campaigns. These visits were usually accompanied by making sacrifices to the drum and the banner of Chinggis Khan. The latter represented the Khan's good fortune and contained his charisma after his death.[80]

The practice of making offerings was not confined to the zealous successors of Chinggis Khan. The Mongols generally had the custom of distributing food, *kūmīss*[81] and meat at the graves of their ancestors.[82] They also burnt clothes, food and silk as a present to their dead.[83] Beyond their cemeteries, the notion of making offerings was one of the principles of the Mongol society. Mongol Khans provided their people with food and clothes in order to ensure their support and obedience. The receivers of the Khan's favour ranged from his immediate entourage, servants, guards and officials to envoys, travellers, and all his soldiers and poor subjects. Qubilay, for instance, established agencies in his capital of Daidu to supply clothing and food to the poor.[84]

Ögödei, the second Khaqan of the Mongol Empire, built the Yingjia dian, 'the Palace welcoming carriages', a seasonal palace at Tusuhu cheng near Karakorum. This palace is possibly the same as the Tuzghu Baligh mentioned by the Iranian authors Juvayni and Rashid al-Din. Juvayni relates that the Turghu Baliq (Tuzghu Baligh) was a pavilion where Ögödei stayed on his way to and from winter camps.[85] Rashid al-Din describes the palace as a sublime pavilion (*kūshkī ʿālī*).[86] The significance of the building for the present discussion is that it is associated with the Mongol custom of *tuzghū*, that is, the offering of food to passing travellers.[87] Juvayni also mentions that some foods (*nuzl*) called *turghū* were brought from the city to the palace.[88]

Regardless of the specific purposes of distributing food and clothing – whether it was intended to display the majesty and power of the ruler or simply represented an act of charity and generosity – the gesture itself, as we will see shortly, seems to have been adopted and adapted in later times by Muslim Ilkhans in their charitable complexes in Iran.

While we discussed the significance of the location of Shanb-i Ghazan and Ghazaniyya from a spiritual perspective, more practical factors contributing to the selection of a suitable site for the tomb of Ghazan and its associated buildings were taken into consideration. For instance, the gardens and pastures of Shanb, which met the needs of the nomadic lifestyle of the Mongols, as opposed to the dense urban fabric of Tabriz formed mostly from narrow winding lanes and packed neighbourhoods, made the outskirts of the city a proper place for the architectural projects of Arghun and his successor Ghazan.[89]

In addition, positioning Ghazaniyya apart from Tabriz could be discussed in connection with the notion of maintaining racial purity, which was of great importance to the Central Asian Mongols as a nation. This concept, in the form of blood purity, was also important to individual tribes. They tried not to distort their tribal integrity through intermarriage with neighbouring tribes whose lineage was perceived to be vague. They highlighted their tribal identity by clarifying the borders of their territory so that the precinct covered by the tents of each tribe was a well-defined (and sometimes isolated) area of land which belonged to that particular group of people.[90] In the case of Ghazaniyya, as an independent city beside Tabriz, even if the new city founded by Ghazan did not in practice remain a residence exclusively for the Mongols, it is possible that its isolation symbolically represented the different ethnic identity of its founder. Moreover, Ghazan's motive for constructing a new architectural complex in Ghazaniyya, in the environs of Tabriz, a major city with many splendid buildings, can also be explained with regard to a tradition which was common among the Mongols in Eastern Asia. As was discussed in Chapter 1, pre-existing buildings were barely re-used as the residence of the Mongol emperors and the members of the Chinggisid royal family in Yuan China, since they had a tendency to reside in new buildings which had been designed and built from the outset as imperial constructions.[91]

In terms of the shape of the city, Ghazaniyya is comparable to the satellite encampments that had been gradually laid out around Karakorum, whether or not Ghazan was familiar with the earlier settlements of the Mongols in Central Asia (Figure 3.15).[92] The circular layout of the city encircling the tomb of the Ilkhan and the surrounding charitable buildings resembled the arrangement of Mongolian *ordu*s with the yurt (portable round tent) of the Khan in the centre and the tents of the rest of the tribe around it. In a section of the *Jami' al-Tawarikh* reporting events of the time of Chinggis Khan, Rashid al-Din depicts one of these encampments. He uses the word *kura'ān*, which means 'ring' (possibly of Mongolian origin), in order to describe the circle of the tribes gathering around the Khan. He clarifies that in the past, when a tribe arrived at a place to erect its encampment, the group of people formed a circle with their tents, and the tent of their master was located in the centre. In Chinggis's time, when the enemy army was close, the tribe shaped a *kura'ān* to block the enemy.[93] Muradi – rightly in my opinion – compares Shanb-i

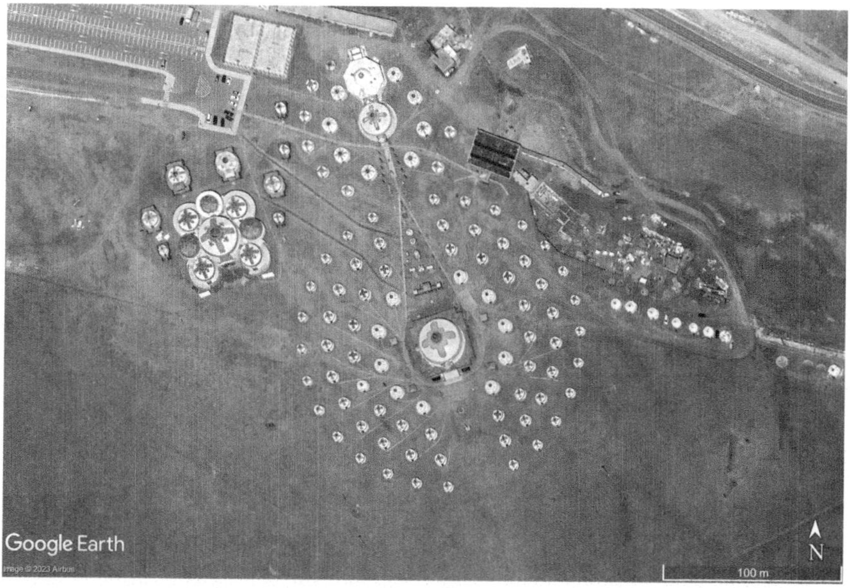

Figure 3.15 Satellite image of a tourist camp near Ulaanbaatar, capital of Mongolia. The camp has been designed on the basis of traditional Mongolian camps, the main tent in the centre, surrounded by a group of smaller tents.
Google Earth (imagery date: 8 June 2023)
47° 48′ 34.27″ N, 106° 49′ 02.26″ E, eye alt 406 m
Airbus 2023. Accessed 5 September 2023

Ghazan to a Mongolian *kura'ān*. Shanb, consisting of permanent structures rather than tents and chariots, encircled the tomb of Ghazan Khan, which was in fact the location of the master.[94] The same interpretation can be proposed in relation to Ghazaniyya, which surrounded the complex of Shanb-i Ghazan.

In his account of the reforms conducted during the reign of Ghazan, Rashid al-Din mentions the construction projects carried out under the patronage of the Ilkhan in Tabriz, namely the erection of several bazaars, caravanserais, public baths and the new walls and gates of the city, as well as the development of orchards and farms whose saplings and seeds were brought in from faraway lands.[95] However, apart from the projects sponsored by the Persian elite in Tabriz and its outskirts, such as the famous Rabʿ-i Rashidi, the large-scale architectural projects conducted by Ghazan himself seemed to have been concentrated mostly in the district of Ghazaniyya.

Contemporary historians of the reign of Ghazan place great emphasis on Tabriz as the *dār al-mulk* of the Ilkhanids. Despite the autonomy of Ghazaniyya, we must bear in mind that Tabriz was a major administrative and political centre, and the prosperity of the city was important to Ghazan too. Thus, the Ilkhan's architectural operation in Shanb could be seen in connection with the idea of creating a place of pilgrimage in the vicinity of Tabriz that promoted the commercial and economic life of the city.[96] The tomb of Ghazan and its surrounding charitable buildings attracted a large number of visitors from both nomadic and urban populations. Taking into consideration all the evidence offered so far, one might suggest that Tabriz was the locus of life and commercial activities of the general populace while Ghazaniyya was built to address primarily the needs and sensibilities of the Mongols.

Observing Ghazaniyya and Shanb-i Ghazan from a Perso-Islamic perspective

We saw that the practice of honouring the encampments of a deceased Khan as a shrine was common among the Mongols. Similar ceremonies are reported in relation to Ghazan's tomb and ʿAdiliyya Pavilion in Shanb. During his seasonal migrations between his summer camps and winter camps, Ghazan's brother and successor, Öljeytü, visited the tomb in Shanb on multiple occasions and performed the rites of visitation including weeping, reciting an invocation (*duʿā*), praying and almsgiving. According to the *Tarikh-i Öljeytü*, on one of his visits to Shanb, Öljeytü stayed at Arghun's pavilion for two days and distributed plentiful alms among the poor.[97] In addition to Öljeytü, there are some references to the pilgrimage performed by Rashid al-Din and Bulughan Khatun Muʿazzama, Ghazan's consort, to the Ilkhan's tomb.

One can suggest that in Shanb, the aforementioned Mongol tradition encountered the practice of venerating the shrines of Shiʿi and Sufi saints in the Islamic world. The charitable foundation of Shanb, as discussed above, was modelled on the shrines of the Shiʿi imams and Sufi shaykhs, which had caught Ghazan's attention in his earlier trips to Iraq and Khurasan.

The Sufi shrine complexes, or 'Little Cities of God' as they are called by Lisa Golombek, were built around the tombs of the shaykhs by their devotees and disciples. The phenomenon of the foundation, or merely restoration and redecoration, of the Sufi shrine complexes in Iran during the fourteenth century was due to a 'climate' that encouraged the development of such compounds regardless of the power, influence and spiritual importance of the saints and the popularity of their cults. The availability of financial resources as well as the power and wealth of the Sufi community in the Mongol period are two crucial factors that contributed towards establishing this climate.[98] The Muslim Ilkhans were inspired by the 'Little Cities of God' in the construction of their own tomb complexes. In Ghazaniyya, and almost a decade later in Sultaniyya, the tomb and its adjacent buildings gradually formed the central core of the city, the area that was later identified as a citadel. Unlike the typical citadel in medieval Islamic cities, which was often the seat of the government and the residence of the court, within the citadel of the two major Ilkhanid cities there emerged monumental complexes formed from charitable institutions enclosing the tomb of the Ilkhanid sultans and their household.

In addition to the act of commemorating the memory of the deceased Ilkhan, which is justifiable from both Mongolian and Perso-Islamic perspectives, Shanb represents another shared practice among the Iranians and the Mongols. Almsgiving is an Islamic religious obligation that formed one of the pillars of the pious ensemble of Shanb-i Ghazan, but as we saw earlier, this act possibly originated in part in the Mongols' nomadic beliefs.

Apart from some individuals from Ghazan's household, the tomb was the pilgrimage destination for larger groups of visitors/pilgrims. In the endowment deed of the charitable institution, the endower, Ghazan Khan, allotted the ingredients for a meal called *āsh-i bīrūnī*.[99] According to Rashid al-Din, Mongol and Tazik amirs and those who came to visit might go to the 'Adiliyya Pavilion and partake of the pottage there.[100] He also mentions another meal called *āsh-i buzurg* (grand pottage), which was given once a year on the day Ghazan passed away. On that occasion, those in residence in the institutions of Shanb, as well as the imams, the nobles and the deserving of Tabriz and other places, gathered in the foundation, recited the Qur'an, and partook of the pottage. Alms were also distributed on that day as stipulated.[101]

In addition to the locals, passing travellers enjoyed the meals distributed extensively in the *abwāb al-birr*. Ibn Battuta (d. 1369), who visited Tabriz during the reign of the last Ilkhan, Abu Sa'id, makes reference to a place outside the city called al-Sham (pronounced al-Shām), at which the grave of Ghazan, the 'King of al-Iraq', was located. He mentions that alongside the grave there was 'a fine madrasa and a hospice in which food is supplied to all wayfarers, consisting of bread, meat, rice cooked in ghee and sweetmeats'.[102]

Along with the votive meals, Rashid al-Din describes abundant endowments made over to the complex. A detailed discussion of the items given to different components of the foundation goes beyond the confines of this chapter. I mention, however, a few points that are relevant to the idea of supplying the poor with life's basic necessities. According to Rashid al-Din, in the khanqah foodstuffs were provided for making morning and evening meals and alms were available to cover the cost of the clothes and footwear of the poor. In the *dār al-sīyāda* money was provided for the cost of living of the *sādāt*s who resided there or for those who stayed there temporarily. In the *dār al-shafā'* patients were supplied with medications and clothes. Every year two thousand coats made from sheepskin were purchased and offered to the poor.[103]

While distributing votive offerings in a devotional site was customary in the Islamic tradition, interestingly, the same ritual was performed for Ghazan's Buddhist father. According to Wassaf, after his death, Arghun's attendants offered pottage (*āsh*) for three days to honour his soul, as this was the custom of the Mongols (*bar 'ādat-i Mughul*).[104] This event, alongside other examples of donating goods in the Mongol society mentioned earlier, supports our initial hypothesis about the shared roots of the practice. Thus, the act of almsgiving at Shanb, which seems to be an Islamic practice on the surface, could be the same Mongol convention presented in the guise of a familiar Islamic custom.

Given the extensive destruction of the Ilkhanid city, material evidence concerning the physical features of Shanb-i Ghazan and Ghazaniyya is scant. Thus, to explore the encounter between Perso-Islamic concepts and Mongolian traditions, I have largely focused on the conceptual aspects of Ghazan's architectural and urban projects. Scrutinising the mentality of Ghazan as the chief patron, this chapter has sought to uncover the synthetic ideology on the basis of which Ghazaniyya was founded. This study, inevitably, has dealt with non-material remnants of Ghazaniyya in search of some indications of the ideas offered by the Iranians as well as the nomadic concepts brought in by the Mongols. Hence, instead of hybrid signs, it has looked for hybrid motivations behind the formation of these signs. While our understanding of the coexistence of the concepts and conventions of the two sides (the Iranians and the Mongols) is rather fragmentary and partly speculative, what is offered in this chapter forms the basis for future studies that presumably will benefit from further archaeological findings. This problem, as we shall see in the next chapter, would be less considerable in the case of Sultaniyya, due to the greater availability of architectural material and archaeological data

Notes

1. The meaning of the words Shām, Shamm, Shamb or Shanb is not yet understood. Muhammad Roshan suggests that 'Shamb' is the shortened version of the Mongolian word 'Shamb(h)ala', which means Paradise or Utopia. See Rashid al-Din, *Jāmiʿ al-Tawārīkh*, vol. 3, 2,258. Evliya Çelebi writes that Shām-i Ghazan was known by the appellation 'Shām' since it resembled Shām (Damascus). Evliya Çelebi (Evliya Efendi), *Narratives of Travels in Europe, Asia, and Africa in the Seventeenth Century*, trans. Joseph Von Hammer (London: Oriental Translation Fund of Great Britain and Ireland, 1834), vol. 2, 143.
2. Rashid al-Din, *Jāmiʿ al-Tawārīkh*, vol. 2, 1,369–74. Mustawfi mentions that the construction of the wall remained unfinished due to Ghazan's death. See Mustawfi, *Nuzhat al-Qulūb*, 122–3.
3. Rashid al-Din, *Jāmiʿ al-Tawārīkh*, vol. 2, 1,374. For the whole passage, see the Appendix, section 4.
4. The mention of Rum and Afranj (Byzantine and Europe) in Rashid al-Din's account shows the significance of Tabriz and Ghazaniyya in the commercial network of the thirteenth and fourteenth centuries. For further discussion, see Johannes Preiser-Kapeller, '*Civitas Thauris*: The Significance of Tabriz in the Spatial Frameworks of Christian Merchants and Ecclesiastics in the 13th and 14th Centuries', in *Politics, Patronage and the Transmission of Knowledge in 13th–15th Century Tabriz*, ed. Judith Pfeiffer (Leiden; Boston: Brill, 2014), 251–99; Sheila Blair, 'Tabriz: International Entrepôt under the Mongols', ibid., 321–56.
5. Mustawfi, *Nuzhat al-Qulūb*, 123. For the whole passage, see the Appendix, section 5.
6. Rashid al-Din Fazlallah Hamadani (Rashiduddin Fazlullah) and Wheeler M. Thackston, *Jamiʿu't-Tawarikh: A History of the Mongols* (Cambridge, MA: Harvard University Press, 1998), vol. 3, 685 (trans. by Thackston, slightly modified); Rashid al-Din, *Jāmiʿ al-Tawārīkh*, vol. 2, 1,376.
7. Rashid al-Din, *Jāmiʿ al-Tawārīkh*, vol. 2, 1,282. Wassaf records 697 and 702 as the start and end dates of the project respectively. Wassaf al-Hazra and ʿAbd al-Muhammad Ayati, *Taḥrīr-i Tārīkh-i Wassaf* (Tehran: Pazhūhesh-gāh-i ʿUlūm-i Insānī va Muṭāliʿāt-i Farhangī, 2004), 210.

8. Kashani, *Tārīkh-i Öljeytü*, 179.
9. Wassaf al-Hazra and Ayati, *Taḥrīr-i Tārīkh-i Wassaf*, 211.
10. According to Rashid al-Din, after visiting the observatory of Maraghih, Ghazan Khan ordered that an observatory be built next to the *Gunbad-i ʿĀlī* and the *abwāb al-birr* of Shanb. See Rashid al-Din, *Jāmiʿ al-Tawārīkh*, vol. 2, 1,296.
11. In the list of charitable buildings surrounding the tomb of Ghazan, Rashid al-Din replaces *ḥukmīyya* with *bayt al- qānūn* (the house of tax rolls). See Rashid al-Din, *Jāmiʿ al-Tawārīkh*, vol. 2, 1,380.
12. In the *Jāmiʿ al-Tawārīkh*, Rashid al-Din enumerates the twelve charitable buildings, while in the copy of the *Tārīkh-i Wassaf* published in Bombay the names of only eleven buildings are recorded. Wassaf does not mention the public bath. See Rashid al-Din, *Jāmiʿ al-Tawārīkh*, vol. 2, 1,380 and Wassaf al-Hazra, *Kitāb-i Mustaṭāb-i Wassaf al-Hazra* (Bombay: n.p., 1853), 383.
13. See the *Pious Foundation of Shanb-i Ghazan* (a miniature from the *Jāmiʿ al-tawārīkh*, Herat, 1425 Bibliothèque Nationale de France).
14. Muradi attributes the number of the buildings surrounding the tomb of Ghazan to the Twelve Imams and the Shiʿi tendencies of the Ilkhan. See Muradi, Musavi-Haji and ʿUmrani, 'Bāz-Shināsī-yi Furm-i Miʿmārī-yi Ārām-gāh-i Ghazan', 36–7. However, to the best of my knowledge, there is neither textual evidence supporting this interpretation nor enough reason to believe that, among the different sects and schools of Islam in which Ghazan showed interest after his conversion, Shiʿism had a special place in the spiritual life of the Ilkhan.
15. Despite Wassaf's reference to the twelve-sided structure of the tomb, there is some disagreement over the geometry of the building. See e.g. Muradi, Musavi-Haji and ʿUmrani, 'Bāz-Shināsī-yi Furm-i Miʿmārī-yi Ārām-gāh-i Ghazan', 37–42.
16. *Man* is a historical unit of mass, usually equal to 3 kg.
17. For the value assumed for the *gaz*, see Wilber, *Architecture of Islamic* Iran, 125–6.
18. Although Wassaf mentions that the diameter of the dome's circle is 50, he mistakenly records the area of the dome as 530 square *gaz*. Wassaf al-Hazra and Ayati, *Taḥrīr-i Tārīkh-i Waṣṣāf*, 210–11.
19. 1 *mithqāl* is equal to 4.25 g.
20. Wassaf al-Hazra and Ayati, *Taḥrīr-i Tārīkh-i Waṣṣāf*, 210–11.
21. Wassaf al-Hazra and Ayati, *Taḥrīr-i Tārīkh-i Wassaf*, 211–12. The text of the inscription reads as follows:

الحمد الله القديم الّذی بقاءه دائم و وجوده واجب الكريم الّذی نعماءه على العالمين فيّاض وجوده
صائب. الصانع الّذی دلالات وجوده بدائع الاشياء و روايع الغرايب و آيات جوده صنائع الآلاء
و سوابغ الرغايب. القادر الذی رفع السماء مزينة بزينة الكواكب و دها الارض وطّدها بمراسی
الاطواد الرّواسی الرّواسب و زيّنها بانوار الانبياء المجتبی منهم محمّد المصطفی: المبعوث الی
المشارق و المغارب صلی الله عليهم ذوی المكارم و المناقب. ما طلع طالع و غرب غارب. حمدا
لنعمه حالب و لفضله و كرمه جالب. ثم الحمد له ثانيا على ما ايّد الدين و اعزّ الاسلام و المسلمين
بسلطنة من هو كافل لارزاق العباد و حافل در الاموال لاحيا و البلاد و صارت عتبته العليه مقبّلة
بشفاه الاعاظم السلاطين و اضحت شهب سطوته على سماء الملك رجوما للشياطين و اصبح
تراب سدته المنيفة مسجدا للجباه و امسى زلال نعمته الهنّية مورد الافواه و هو القآن المعظّم،
الايلخان الاعظم، مولا خواقين العالم، مالك رقاب الامم، سلطان السلاطين ظل الله فی الارضين،
مطاع اهل الماء و الطين، محرز ممالك الدنيا، مظهر كلمة الله العليا المنصور من السماء، المظفر
على الاعداء، كهف الثقلين، لطف الله فی الخافقين، الناصر لدين الله، القاهر لاعداء الله، حافظ
الارض بالسيف و السّنان شامل الخلق بالامن و الامان، باسط بساط العدل و الاحسان، معين الدّولة
القاهره، مغيث المّلة الزّاهره، نصرة الدنيا و الدين، غازان محمود بن القآن المعظم، الايلخان
الاعظم ارغون خان بن القآن الاعظم، الايلخان المعظم آباقا خان حرس الله ظلال ايّامه على
القريب و البعيد و جعل النصر و الظفر حافين بلوائه عن اليمن و عن الشمال قعيد. ثم نحمده ثالثا
على ما وفّقه الله تعالى لبناء هذه الخيرات و تأسيس هذه المبرات المتصله المحيطة بهذه الرّوضة
العليا الرفيعة البناء المنيعة الفناء الواسعة الارجاء كالقبة الخضراء، حتى استصغر فی جنبه
الهرمان و استحقر لديه النسر و السرطان المجعول شرفاتها كقصور الافلاك منازل و ابراجا و
عواطفها من انوار النيرين سراجا و هّاجا، اوجها يساوی السماك و قطرها يضاهی الافلاك بل هی
روضة من رياض الجنان و فيها مغفرة و رحمة و رضوان. قد اتّفق الابتداء بابتناءها فی اول شهر

22. Rashid al-Din, *Jāmiʿ al-Tawārīkh*, vol. 2, 1,383.
23. The *mutavallī* or custodian of the endowment of Shanb-i Ghazan was a person with responsibility for taking care of the endowment, whose characteristics had been assigned by Ghazan (the endower) in the endowment deed. This role seems to be different from that of the *mutavallī* or superintendent of the charitable complex at Shanb, who was possibly responsible for keeping the complex in good condition.
24. For instance, in his account of Ghazan's constructions in Karbala Plain, Rashid al-Din mentions that the Ilkhan purchased several villages that had previously been constructed with his own money and endowed them to the '*abwāb al-birr* of Tabriz', by which he probably meant the charitable foundation of Shanb-i Ghazan. See Rashid al-Din, *Jāmiʿ al-Tawārīkh*, vol. 2, 1,371.
25. Wassaf al-Hazra and Ayati, *Taḥrīr-i Tārīkh-i Wassaf*, 212.
26. Rashid al-Din, *Jāmiʿ al-Tawārīkh*, vol. 2, 1,384.
27. Ibid., 1,377–83.
28. There is one misspelling at the beginning of the inscription (الصلوة instead of الصلاة). The end of the inscription is slightly illegible:

’بسم الله و الحمدالله و الصلوة علی رسول الله و علی عترته الطاهرین
این مسجد را در 700 هجری غازان شاه بنا کرده بود. در 1133 با زلزله خراب
شده. این احقر عباسعلی بن حاجی محمدحسن به مساعدت اهالی و مشهدی
حسن در 1345 حمامی بنا کرده و منفعت او را به این مسجد
و سایر مساجد دیگر محله مقرر کردیم و این طاق در 1351 ساخته گشت ...‘

29. A. Bausani, ‘Religion under the Mongols’, in *The Cambridge History of Iran*, ed. J. Boyle (Cambridge: Cambridge University Press): 538–49.
30. The relationship between the Sufis and the Mongol ruling elite has been subjected to an excellent study by Amitai-Preiss. See Reuven Amitai-Preiss, ‘Sufis and Shamans: Some Remarks on the Islamisation of the Mongols in the Ilkhanate’, *Journal of the Economic and Social History of the Orient* 42, no. 1 (1999): 27–46.
31. On the Islamisation of the Ilkhans, see Jackson, *The Mongols and the Islamic World*, 352–80. On the conversion of Ghazan Khan, see Michael Hope, *Power, Politics, and Tradition in the Mongol Empire and the Īlkhānate of Iran* (Oxford: Oxford University Press, 2016), 159–81; Amitai-Preiss, ‘Ghazan, Islam and Mongol Tradition’, 1–10.
32. Ghazan Khan omitted the name of the Khaqan from the coins and inscribed his own name alone. ‘Ruler of the World/Sultan, the Supreme/Ghazan Muhammad/May God Prolong his Reign’ is one example of the inscriptions on the coins. For more examples, see Thomas Allsen, ‘Changing Forms of Legitimation in Mongol Iran’, in *Rulers from the Steppe: State Formation on the Eurasian Periphery*, ed. Gary Seaman and Daniel Marks (Los Angeles: University of Southern California, 1991), 223–41. See in particular 230 and 231.
33. Thomas Allsen, ‘Biography of a Cultural Broker: Bolad Ch’eng-Hsiang in China and Iran’, in *The Court of the Il-khans, 1290–1340*, ed. Julian Raby and Teresa Fitzherbert (Oxford: Oxford University Press, 1996), 11; Thomas Allsen, ‘Notes on Chinese Titles in Mongol Iran’, *Mongolian Studies* 14 (1991): 27–39.
34. Melville, ‘Mongols in Iran’, 54.
35. Boyd Johnson, ‘Rashid al-Din’, Grove Art Online, https://doi.org/10.1093/gao/9781884446054.article.T070807 (last accessed 12 March 2023).
36. Long before the first convert Ilkhan Ahmad Tegüder, there were individuals among the Mongol amirs who had converted to Islam. See Judith Pfeiffer, ‘Reflections on a “Double Rapprochement”: Conversion to Islam among the Mongol Elite during the Early Ilkhanate’, in *Beyond the Legacy of Genghis Khan*, ed. Linda Komaroff (Leiden: Brill, 2006), 375.

37. Bausani, 'Religion under the Mongols', 542. In Persian sources different figures have been mentioned as the number of Mongol amirs and army officers who adopted Islam on the day Ghazan converted. For further discussion, see Charles Melville, 'Pādshāh-i Islām: The Conversion of Sultān Maḥmūd Ghāzān Khān', *Pembroke Papers* 1 (1990): 171.
38. Pfeiffer, 'Reflections on a "Double Rapprochement"', 370. For further discussion on the emergence of the Ilkhans' titles on the coinage of this period, see Allsen, 'Changing Forms of Legitimation in Mongol Iran', 225–8. The political self-perception of the Ilkhans after conversion was also reflected in the establishment of a new coinage system in which the traditional Islamic coin names dinar and dirham were used. See Bert Fragner, 'Ilkhanid Rule and its Contributions to Iranian Political Culture', in *Beyond the Legacy of Genghis Khan*, ed. Linda Komaroff (Leiden: Brill, 2006), 68–80.
39. Pfeiffer, 'Reflections on a "Double Rapprochement"', 372.
40. Allsen, 'Biography of a Cultural Broker', 11; Allsen, *Culture and* Conquest, 26.
41. Sheila Blair, 'The Religious Arts of the Ilkhanids', in *The Legacy of Genghis Khan: Courtly Art and Culture in Western Asia, 1256–1353*, ed. Linda Komaroff and Stefano Carboni (New York; New Haven: Metropolitan Museum of Art, 2002), 105–17.
42. Allsen, *Culture and Conquest*, 200.
43. Morgan, *The Mongols*, 44.
44. Morris Rossabi, 'The Mongols and their Legacy', in *The Legacy of Genghis Khan: Courtly Art and Culture in Western Asia, 1256–1353*, ed. Linda Komaroff and Stefano Carboni (New York; New Haven: Metropolitan Museum of Art, 2002), 34.
45. Rashid al-Din, *Jāmiʿ al-Tawārīkh*, vol. 2, 1,356. Despite the extensive destruction, the remains of a few Ilkhanid structures still exist, which are believed to have been non-Islamic religious monuments, for instance an unfinished rock-cut complex locally known as Dash Kassan (possibly a Buddhist temple) near Sultaniyya. For further discussion on Dash Kassan, see Chapter 4 and also Hatef Naiemi, 'The Ilkhanid City of Sultaniyya', 23–5. For more examples of non-Islamic structures (whether Nestorian or Buddhist), see Warwick Ball, 'Two Aspects of Iranian Buddhism', *Bulletin of the Asia Institute of Pahlavi University* (1976): 1–4; 'Some Rock-Cut Monuments in Southern Iran', *Iran: Journal of the British Institute of Persian Studies* 24 (1986): 95–115.

46. Amitai-Preiss, 'Sufis and Shamans', 33–4.
47. Rashid al-Din and Jahn, *Tārīkh-i Mubārak-i Ghāzānī*, 76. Rashid al-Din does not expand on the motivations behind Ghazan Khan's preference for the Hanafi School.
48. Kashani's original text reads as follows: 'Ẕikr-i khulafā-yi sih-gānih dar khuṭba bidʿa ast va az ān-i ahl al-bayt va ʿAli ki muqaddam-i īshān ast vājib'. See Kashani, *Tārīkh-i Öljeytü*, 94.
49. Ibid., 94.
50. Wassaf al-Hazra and Ayati, *Taḥrīr-i Tārīkh-i Wassaf*, 179, mentioned in Hope, *Power, Politics, and Tradition*, 160. See also Bayani, *Dīn va Dawlat*, vol. 2, 437–41.
51. Melville, 'Pādshāh-i Islām', 159–60.
52. '*Mahdī-yi ghāzī, muḥay-yi dīn-i tāzī, nimūdār-i yazdānī, Abu Muslim-i thānī-yi dīn-parvar*'. Wassaf al-Hazra, *Tajzīyat al-Amṣār*, vol. 3, 313, mentioned by Bayani, *Dīn va Dawlat*, vol. 2, 451.
53. Amitai-Preiss, 'Sufis and Shamans', 33.
54. Amitai-Preiss, 'Ghazan, Islam and Mongol Tradition', 8–9.
55. Allsen, *Culture and Conquest*, 31–4.
56. Amitai-Preiss, 'Ghazan, Islam and Mongol Tradition', 9.
57. Peter Jackson, 'The Mongols and the Faith of the Conquered', in *Mongols, Turks, and Others: Eurasian Nomads and the Sedentary World*, ed. Reuven Amitai-Preiss and Michal Biran (Leiden; Boston: Brill, 2005), 273.
58. Rashid al-Din and Jahn, *Tārīkh-i Mubārak-i Ghāzānī*, 208.
59. Rashid al-Din and Thackston, *Jamiʿu't-Tawarikh*, vol. 3, 685 (trans. by Thackston); Rashid al-Din, *Jāmiʿ al-Tawārīkh*, vol. 2, 1,375–6.
60. Allsen, *Commodity and Exchange*, 103.
61. Sheila Blair, 'Monumentality under the Mongols', 136–7.
62. Rashid al-Din, *Jāmiʿ al-Tawārīkh*, vol. 2, 1,376.
63. The idea is discussed in Bhabha, 'The Third Space', 211 and Bhabha, *The Location of Culture*, 38.
64. Tengri (Tngri) was the sky-god of the Turko-Mongols and other Central Asian peoples. See David Leeming, 'Tengri', in *The Oxford Companion to World Mythology*, ed. David Leeming (Oxford: Oxford University Press, 2006).
65. Max Weber, Guenther Roth and Claus Wittich, *Economy and Society: An Outline of Interpretive Sociology* (New York: Bedminster, 1968), vol. 1, 241, cited in Thomas Allsen, 'Spiritual Geography and Political Legitimacy in the

Eastern Steppe', in *Ideology and the Formation of Early States*, ed. Henri J. M. Claessen and Jarich G. Oosten (Leiden: Brill, 1996), 116.

66. Allsen, 'Spiritual Geography', 116.
67. Möngke Khan, Ariq Böke (r. 1259–64) and Qubilay Khan.
68. Allsen, 'Spiritual Geography', 118–21.
69. Ibid., 117.
70. Sheila Blair, 'The Coins of the Later Ilkhanids: A Typological Analysis', *Journal of the Economic and Social History of the Orient* 26, no. 3 (1983): 296.
71. In his writings, Rashid al-Din frequently refers to Ghazan Khan as *Padishah-i Islām*. See Rashid al-Din, *Tārīkh-i Mubārak-i Ghāzānī*, *passim*.
72. For further discussion on this subject, see Mark Whaley, 'A Rendering of Square Script Mongolian on the Îlkhân Ghâzân Maḥmûd's Coins', *Mongolian Studies* 26 (2003–4): 55–8.
73. Banakati, *Tārīkh-i Banākatī*, 454–5.
74. Melville, 'Pādshāh-i Islām', 167–8.
75. For instance, according to Wassaf, Arghun ascended the throne for the first time at a summer camp called Qamisiyun (between Hashtrud and Qurban-Shira). Banakati writes that he ascended the throne the second time in Arran, when Bolad Aqa delivered his *yarlīgh* from Qubilay Khan. In the spring of the same year he went to Tabriz, and then moved towards Surluq (Suqurluq or Takht-i Sulayman). See Wassaf al-Hazra and Ayati, *Taḥrīr-i Tārīkh-i Wassaf*, 81 and Banakati, *Tārīkh-i Banākatī*, 443.
76. Rashid al-Din, *Jāmiʿ al-Tawārīkh*, vol. 2, 1,179.
77. Prior to Arghun Khan, Bulughan Khatun the Elder, Abaqa Khan's consort, had been buried in Mount Sujas in 1286. See Rashid al-Din, *Jāmiʿ al-Tawārīkh*, vol. 2, 1,162.
78. 'Obyr' literally means the upper part of the body or the chest in Mongolian, but the Mongols also use the word for the southern side of a mountain or the side facing the sun. See Pedram Jam, 'Qiydar-i Nabi: Īlkhān-i Būdāyī dar kisvat-i Payāmbar-i Ibrāhīmī [Qiydar-i Nabi: A Buddhist Ilkhan in the Guise of an Abrahamic Prophet]', *Pazhūhish-hā-yi Tārīkh-i Iran va Islam* 15 (2014): 90. Nevertheless, Barthold reads the Mongol name of Arghun's burial place as Oir, which means forest, and connects it to the Mongol tradition of planting a forest or grass over royal burials in order to conceal them. See V. V. Barthold and J. M. Rogers, 'The Burial Rites of the Turks and the Mongols', *Central Asiatic Journal* 14, no. 1/3 (1970): 210.
79. Mustawfi, *Nuzhat al-Qulūb*, 106.

80. Allsen, 'Spiritual Geography', 119.
81. Fermented mare's milk. The Mamluks also had a tradition of drinking *kūmīss* or *qumiz* despite their conversion to Islam. See Reuven Amitai-Preiss, 'Echoes of the Eurasian Steppe in the Daily Culture of Mamluk Military Society', *Journal of the Royal Asiatic Society* 26, no. 1–2 (2016): 265.
82. Urgunge Onon, *The Secret History of the Mongols: The Life and Times of Chinggis Khan* (Taylor & Francis e-Library, 2005), 64, n. 159.
83. Ibid., 137, n. 356.
84. Allsen, *Commodity and Exchange*, 56.
85. Juvayni, *Tārīkh-i Jahāngushāy*, vol. 1, 273.
86. Rashid al-Din, *Jāmiʿ al-Tawārīkh*, vol. 1, 672.
87. Masuya, 'Seasonal Capitals', 234. *Tuzghū* in Turkish consists of two parts: *tuz*, which means salt, and *ghū*, which means a food offered as a gift to a traveller. *Tuzghū* was later used to describe a food offered to a master or a Khan. See Rashid al-Din, *Jāmiʿ al-Tawārīkh*, vol. 3, 2,338.
88. Juvayni, *Tārīkh-i Jahāngushāy*, vol. 1, 273. In Persian, *nuzl* has different meanings: beneficence, blessing, and a food offered to a guest. See Hassan ʿAmid, *Farhang-i Fārsī-yi ʿAmīd* [Persian-Persian ʿAmid Dictionary], ed. ʿAzizallah ʿAlizadih (Tehran: Rāh-i Rushd, 2010), 1,016.
89. Masashi Haneda, 'The Pastoral City and the Mausoleum City: Nomadic Rule and City Construction in the Eastern Islamic World', in *Islamic Urbanism in Human History: Political Power and Social Networks*, ed. Sato Tsugitaka (London: Kegan Paul International, 1997), 151–2.
90. Boris Yakovlevich Vladimirtsov, *Niẓām-i Ijtimāʿī-yi Mughulān* [The Social System of the Mongols], trans. Shirin Bayani (Tehran: Intishārāt-i ʿIlmī va Farhangī, 2007), 87; Muradi, Musavi-Haji and ʿUmrani, 'Bāz-Shināsī-yi Furm-i Miʿmārī-yi Ārām-gāh-i Ghazan', 36.
91. Masuya, 'Ilkhanid Phase of Takht-i Sulaimān', 209.
92. For instance, Sïra Ordu in Örmögatü was a satellite camp founded by Ögödei about fifteen to twenty kilometres south-east of Karakorum, the imperial capital. See Allsen, *Commodity and Exchange*, 13. For other satellite camps and seasonal residences around Karakorum, see John Andrew Boyle, 'The Seasonal Residences of the Great Khan Ögedei', *Central Asiatic Journal* 16, no. 2 (1972): 125–31; Shiraishi, 'Seasonal Migrations', 105–19.
93. Rashid al-Din, *Jāmiʿ al-Tawārīkh*, vol. 1, 329.
94. Muradi, Musavi-Haji and ʿUmrani, 'Bāz-Shināsī-yi Furm-i Miʿmārī-yi Ārām-gāh-i Ghazan', 36.

95. Rashid al-Din, *Jāmiʿ al-Tawārīkh*, vol. 2, ed., 1,373–5.
96. Parviz ʿAliasl and Shahram Yusefifard, ʻGhazaniyya-yi Tabriz: Namād-i Taḥavvul-i Farhangī-yi Mughulān [Ghazaniyya of Tabriz: The Symbol of the Cultural Revolution of the Mongols]', *Tārīkh va Tamaddun-i Islāmī* 13 (2011): 76.
97. Kashani, *Tārīkh-i Öljeytü*, 179.
98. Golombek, ʻCult of Saints', 419–30. On the power of the Sufi community in the Ilkhanid period, also see Sheila Blair, ʻThe Epigraphic Program of the Tomb of Uljaytu at Sultaniyya: Meaning in Mongol Architecture', *Islamic Art: An Annual Dedicated to the Art and Culture of the Muslim World* 2 (1987): 67.
99. *Āsh-i bīrūnī*, which literally means ʻexternal pottage', was possibly a kind of votive pottage which was made to be given out to visitors to the complex.
100. Rashid al-Din, *Jāmiʿ al-Tawārīkh*, vol. 2, 1,380.
101. Rashid al-Din and Thackston, *Jamiʿu't-Tawarikh*, vol. 3, 686.
102. Ibn Battuta and H. A. R. (Hamilton Alexander Rosskeen) Gibb, *The Travels of Ibn Battuta, A. D. 1325–1354* (Abingdon: Routledge, 2016), vol. 2, 344.
103. Rashid al-Din and Jahn, *Tārīkh-i Mubārak-i Ghāzānī*, 209–14.
104. Wassaf al-Hazra and Ayati, *Taḥrīr-i Tārīkh-i Wassaf*, 138.

4

The Grand Capital of Öljeytü in Sultaniyya

The Ilkhanid city of Sultaniyya was founded by Arghun Khan and expanded by his son Öljeytü. Nothing has remained of the city on the ground, except for the tomb of the Ilkhan and a few semi-ruined buildings standing nearby. However, the available textual and physical evidence, including travel accounts, eye-witness chronicles, archaeological remains, and myriads of pottery shards found on every corner of the site, all attests to the existence of an extensive urban centre (approximately 350 hectares) surrounding the tomb during the Ilkhanid period. The examination of Sultaniyya is of great importance. In common with Ghazaniyya, Sultaniyya was built from the outset under the patronage of the Ilkhanids and therefore the two sites are expected to represent the Mongols' perception of a city and of urban life more vividly than several other urban centres which were only expanded by the Mongol rulers of Iran.

Following the pattern of Ghazan Khan's urban foundation in Ghazaniyya, Sultaniyya takes one further step towards the distinctive model of an 'Ilkhanid city'. The city is not a mere royal camp despite most of the examples of settlements that were founded and flourished under the previous Ilkhans. It possessed all the elements of a medieval Islamic city, although in its own particular way, as will be clarified shortly.

There is a considerable body of textual material on Sultaniyya. The Ilkhanid and Timurid chroniclers' narratives, as well as the accounts presented by Islamic and European travellers, ambassadors and merchants, provide important insights into the architectural identity of the capital. The first-hand description of Sultaniyya, occasionally accompanied by drawings, maps and illustrations, is highly informative about the architecture, function and location of the major elements of the city. Apart from repetitive texts gathering information from earlier sources or fictional chronicles that need to be treated cautiously, these textual and visual records are influential as regards reconstruction of the past.[1] Along with the scrutinising of written material, several seasons of archaeological excavation have been conducted at the site of Sultaniyya and its surrounding settlements. They have offered valuable insights into the spatial structure of the Mongol capital.

This chapter intends to reconstruct the layout of the city that developed during the time of Öljeytü on the basis of textual, visual and physical material.[2] The focus is the citadel, whose outline was uncovered almost in its entirety during the extensive excavations at the site. The area used to embrace the most magnificent buildings of the capital. The outer city lying beyond the central core of the city will also be studied, in the hope of gaining a better understanding of the civilian settlement of Sultaniyya that accommodated the commoners, the majority of the population of the city, who have barely been mentioned in the historical accounts. In addition to the impressive monuments patronised by the Ilkhans and the ruling elite, archaeological excavation of the residential neighbourhoods has unearthed some humble constructions. They are possibly the remnants of a larger group of similar structures that covered the area of the outer city.

As we will see below, multiple sources of information have been overlaid to create a vivid picture of the citadel and the outer city of Sultaniyya in the fourteenth century. These include historical chronicles describing the city, illustrations left by visitors to the site during that time, aerial photographs and satellite images of the area, remnants of the buildings that have endured the test of time, and findings from site surveys and excavations conducted at the site. Given the limitations involved in the process, the picture painted of the Ilkhanid city of Sultaniyya is partly speculative. However, the result, which is the topographical reconstruction of the city, grows out of the solid examination of all the available evidence concerning the temporal and spiritual features of the city, and such thorough study would certainly throw some light on the main question of this book: would the encounter between the nomadic beliefs of the Ilkhans, and more particularly of Öljeytü, and their later Perso-Islamic doctrines be reflected in the urban architecture of their capitals, including Sultaniyya?

Sultaniyya, the Imperial Capital

Prior to the foundation of Sultaniyya as the capital of Öljeytü, the area was known by two other names in the historical texts: Qunqur Öläng and Sharuyaz. According to Hafiz-i Abru (d. 1430), Qunqur Öläng was the fertile meadow chosen by Arghun as the site of his grand city (*shāh-i bilād*: the king of cities).[3] The name possibly referred to a slightly different district during the time of Öljeytü; the pasture located to the north-west of Sultaniyya rather than the imperial city itself. Similarly, under the rule of Öljeytü and his son Abu Saʿid, Sharuyaz described an area on the edge of the capital, although the exact location of the site is still unknown. For instance, Hafiz-i Abru reports that the coffin of Abu Saʿid was transported to a mausoleum near Sultaniyya called Sharuyaz.[4]

In the spring of 704/1305, Öljeytü completed the construction of the city that had previously been founded by his father Arghun in Qunqur Öläng. He gave it the name Sultaniyya, which means 'The Imperial'.[5] According to Wassaf, a large group of skilled artists and artisans with their families migrated into Sultaniyya and played a significant role in the building of the imperial city.[6] The presence in Sultaniyya of Muslim and non-Muslim artisans and engineers from Tabriz, Baghdad and Mosul is also reported by the Mamluk historian al-Yusufi (d. 1357).[7]

In the literature on Sultaniyya, the general consensus is that the city was composed of two parts: a splendid square citadel located in the centre and the surrounding urban fabric. However, there are some slight discrepancies between different accounts regarding the type of buildings forming each of the two districts. It appears that the citadel accommodated the *abwāb al-birr*. The charitable foundation encompassed different components including the sublime dome (*qubbih* or *gunbad-i ʿālī*), school, mosque, khanqah, *dār al-shafā*, *dār al-ḍīyāfa* (guest house), *dār al-ḥuffāẓ*[8] and *dār al-sīyāda*.[9] The Ilkhan endowed extensive lands to provide an income for the complex and bestowed custodianship (*tawlīyyat*) of the endowments on Rashid al-Din.[10]

The only surviving element of the foundation is the dome, a massive octagonal structure covered with a 50m-tall, rounded roof.[11] The building was possibly built with the purpose of being used as a royal tomb chamber,[12] as there are several references to the burial of Öljeytü himself as well as the members of his court in this building and the adjacent rectangular hall, which is known as *turbat-khānih*.[13] Apart from textual accounts highlighting the date on which the construction campaign of Sultaniyya began, the inscriptions on the tomb contain two dates that could help with the dating of the building, 710/1310–11 and 713/1313–14, which possibly mark completion of the exterior decoration and completion of the first phase of interior decoration respectively.[14] Examination of the building suggests that the rectangular hall and the crypt underneath it were added to the main domed room at some point between 1313/14 and Öljeytü's death in 1316. Perhaps during the same period, the initial decoration of the tomb consisting of brick, terracotta and tile was covered with a layer of tile and painted plaster.[15] There is a third date written on the inscription of the south-east bay, 720/1320–1, which presumably indicates the end of the second phase of decoration. The possible reasons for redecoration of the tomb will be touched on in the final chapter. Despite vivid descriptions of the tomb and its furnishings given by historical texts, no reliable trace of the cenotaphs or the graves has been found up to now.

The picture of the outer city presented in historical sources is less lucid. The remarks on the buildings are random and are sometimes intertwined with the imagination of the chroniclers or travellers who visited the city. In comparison, the archaeologists' findings regarding the area that lay beyond the citadel seem to be more factual, boosting our understanding of the spatial structure of this part, although methodological problems, such as difficulties in obtaining sufficient data as well as interpreting them, should not be overlooked.[16] The limitations of visual, literary and physical evidence necessitate the cross-checking of information from a variety of sources. Thus, it becomes evident that a comprehensive understanding of Ilkhanid Sultaniyya relies on a combined study of archaeological and architectural remnants, along with historical records. This approach enables us to construct a more cohesive and reliable depiction of the citadel and the outer city.

Textual sources on Sultaniyya were partly discussed in the introduction. The most productive phases of excavation of the Ilkhanid city and its surrounding settlements are examined here. The first phase of the archaeological study of Sultaniyya was carried out by Saʿid Ganjavi in the 1970s, focusing mainly on the site of Tappih-nur.[17] In the fall of 1987, Hushang Sobuti dug ten trial trenches inside and outside the tomb of Öljeytü in order to identify the main entrances of the building. The operation threw some light on how the tomb was connected with the neighbouring buildings.[18] 'Ali-'Asghar Mirfattah conducted the second phase of excavation in several locations, including the citadel, the area known as Jum'ih-masjid,[19] Tappih-nur, the site of Dash Kassan (Viar) and a few historical spots spread across the region. According to the historical texts and the field survey done prior to the excavation, these places promised to be archaeologically productive. This phase lasted from 1988 to 2004. Despite the fact that the sixteen excavation seasons yielded significant findings in terms of architectural structures and archaeological artefacts both within the citadel and in the outer city, a substantial portion of these results lack proper documentation and remain predominantly unpublished.[20] Mehrdad 'Asgarian carried out the third phase of excavation in 2005, which was meant to determine the southern confines of the area of Jum'ih-masjid.[21] The last phase was directed by 'Abd al-Reza Muhajerinejad in 2009 across the whole area of Jum'ih-masjid, which spans over eighty hectares, and the site of Tappih-nur (Figures 4.1 and 4.2).[22]

Drawing upon the findings of several excavation seasons and utilising the historical records describing the Ilkhanid city, the following sections aim to reconstruct the imperial city that showcased the remarkable achievements of the Ilkhanids in art and architecture during its heyday. The aim is to create an objective context where one can look for non-Islamic/non-Persian visual and conceptual traditions which were injected into the architectural vocabulary of Sultaniyya.

The Citadel of Sultaniyya

Ilkhanid chroniclers and their Timurid successors have mentioned the foundation of the citadel of Sultaniyya.[23] The contemporary historian of the reign of Öljeytü, Abu al-Qasim Kashani, gives one of the most detailed descriptions of the citadel and the *abwāb al-birr* embracing nineteen edifices, some of which were mentioned earlier.[24] Hafiz-i Abru's account is also a comprehensive report revealing interesting points about the citadel and, more particularly, the tomb of the Ilkhan.[25] Wassaf's brief mention of the construction of Sultaniyya is of great importance since he emphasises that Öljeytü completed the unfinished building that his father Arghun had founded.[26]

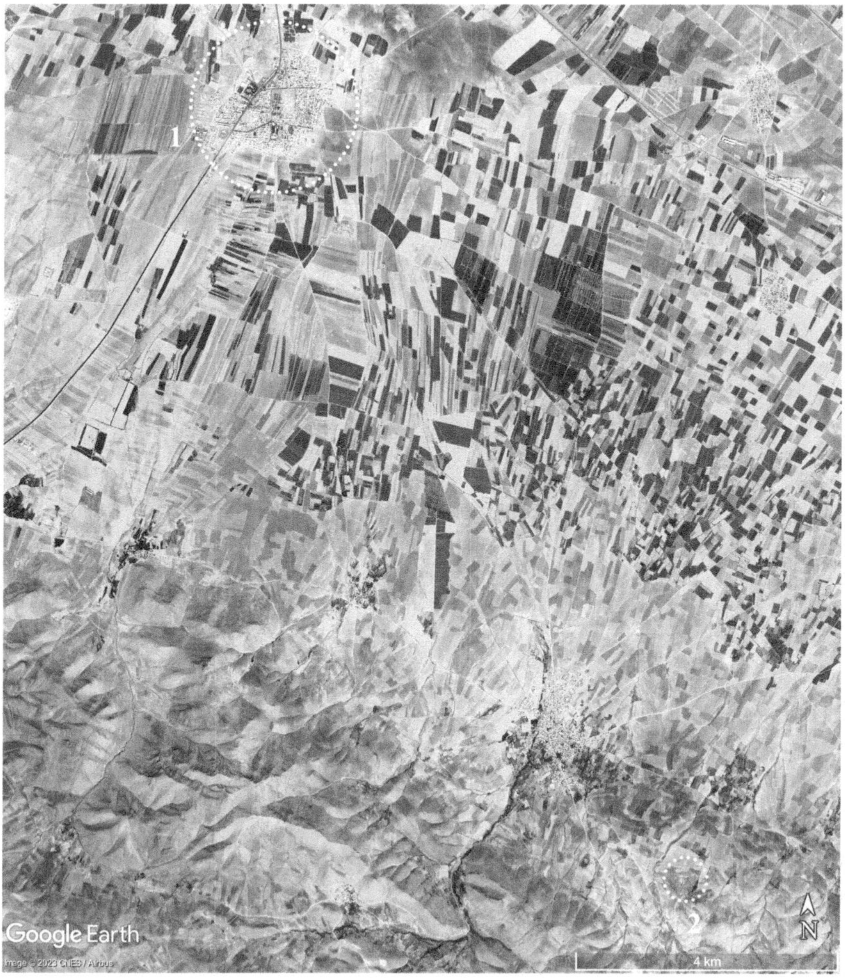

Figure 4.1 Sultaniyya and the site of Dash Kassan (Viar).
1. City of Sultaniyya
2. Dash Kassan (Viar)
Google Earth (imagery date: 24 August 2022)
36° 22′ 59.73″ N, 48° 49′ 13.69″ E, eye alt 11.09 km
CNES/Airbus 2023. Accessed 5 September 2023

Both textual and physical evidence confirm that the citadel was an approximately square area measuring 295 by 315 metres. It was oriented cardinally and enclosed with the walls built of cut stone and fortified with sixteen towers (Figure 4.3).[27] A moat also ran around the citadel. Although historical

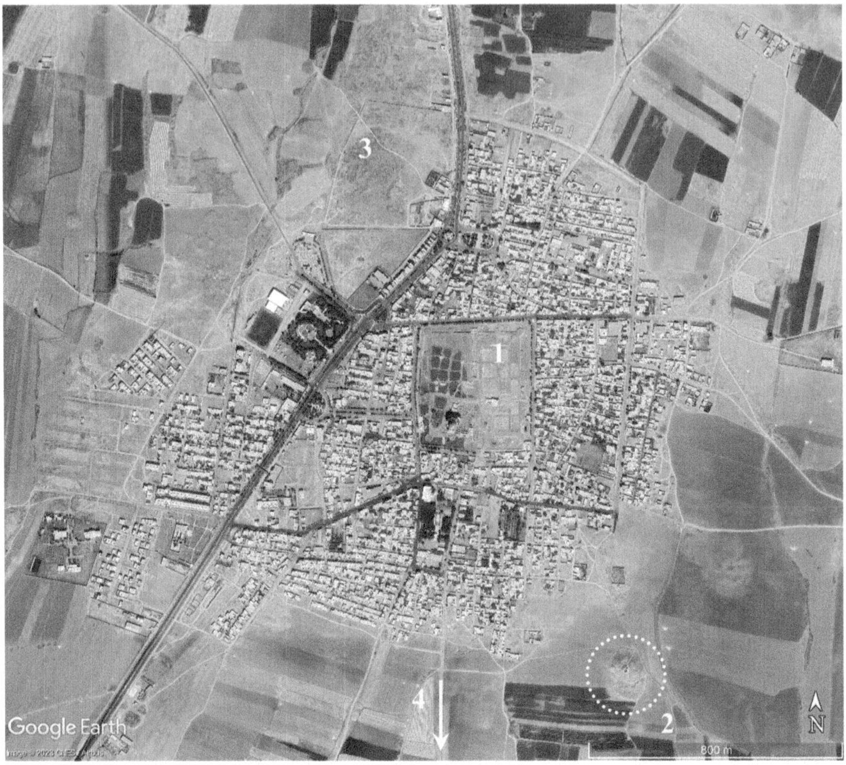

Figure 4.2 Satellite image of Sultaniyya and its surroundings, 2022. The locations of excavated sites are marked on the image.
1. Citadel
2. Tappih-nur
3. Area of Jumʿih-masjid
4. Towards Dash Kassan (Viar)
Google Earth (imagery date: 24 August 2022)
36° 26′ 06.03″ N, 48° 47′ 41.76″ E, eye alt 2.29 km
CNES/Airbus 2023. Accessed 5 September 2023

accounts are silent about the origin of the ramparts, examination of their construction techniques suggests that they were possibly built in two phases under Arghun and his son Öljeytü. The remains of the northern and southern gates, which had been built in alignment with each other, were revealed during the 1990s excavation of the citadel. One can imagine that the axis joining the two gates was part of a grid pattern on which the citadel was laid out. The northern gate seems to be the main entrance to the citadel while the southern gate

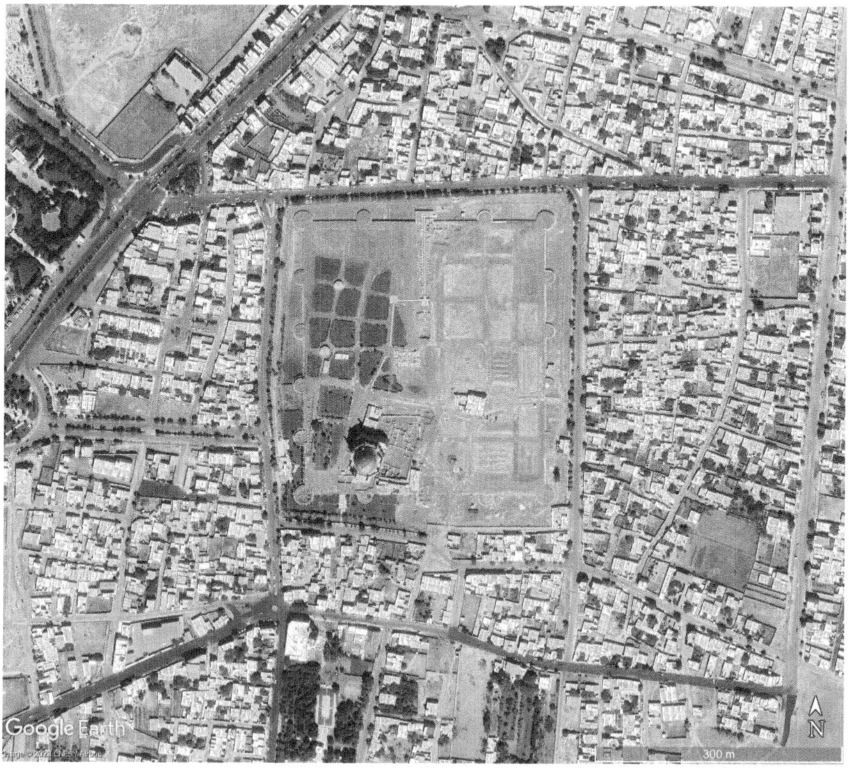

Figure 4.3 Citadel of Sultaniyya surrounded by the residential fabric of modern Sultaniyya. The walls, round towers and Öljeytü's tomb are seen in the image.
Google Earth (imagery date: 24 August 2022)
36° 26′ 04.78″ N, 48° 47′ 48.33″ E, eye alt 881 m
CNES/Airbus 2023. Accessed 5 September 2023

provided private access for the members of the court.[28] Hafiz-i Abru says that after rumours about the execution of Amir Chupan spread, his son Damishq Khwajih fled the citadel through its smaller southern gate with his ten horsemen while Sultan Abu Saʿid was watching the northern gate.[29]

A passageway measuring around three metres in width was uncovered in front of the northern gate during the excavations that were carried out between 2000 and 2002. The relationship between the passage that led through the citadel and other buildings located inside the enclosure is still vague. The passageway ends in a space which seems to be an inner courtyard (Figure 4.4). The partial excavation raises the possibility that the courtyard is the remnant

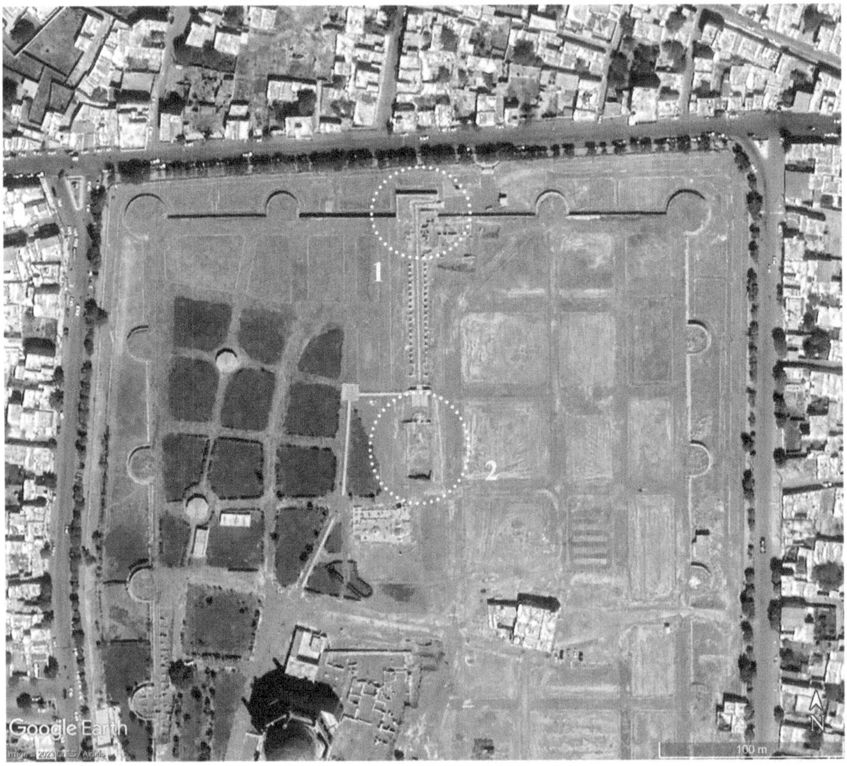

Figure 4.4 A closer view of the northern gate, passageway and inner courtyard within the citadel of Sultaniyya.
1. Northern gate
2. Inner courtyard
Google Earth (imagery date: 24 August 2022)
36° 26′ 08.16″ N, 48° 47′ 48.40″ E, eye alt 393 m
CNES/Airbus 2023. Accessed 5 September 2023

of the structures built during the reign of Arghun, that is, the earlier citadel upon which Öljeytü founded his buildings. Brambilla, on the other hand, suggests that the inner courtyard is part of the constructions dating from the time of Öljeytü, possibly an enclosure accommodating the Ilkhan's harem or his private palace (Figure 4.5).[30] Analysis of the satellite image of the site, however, partly refutes this idea since the unearthed walls of the enclosure barely correspond to the portions of Öljeytü's pious foundation which have been discovered so far. A closer look at the satellite image shows that the former is out of alignment with the latter, and thus possibly belongs to a different

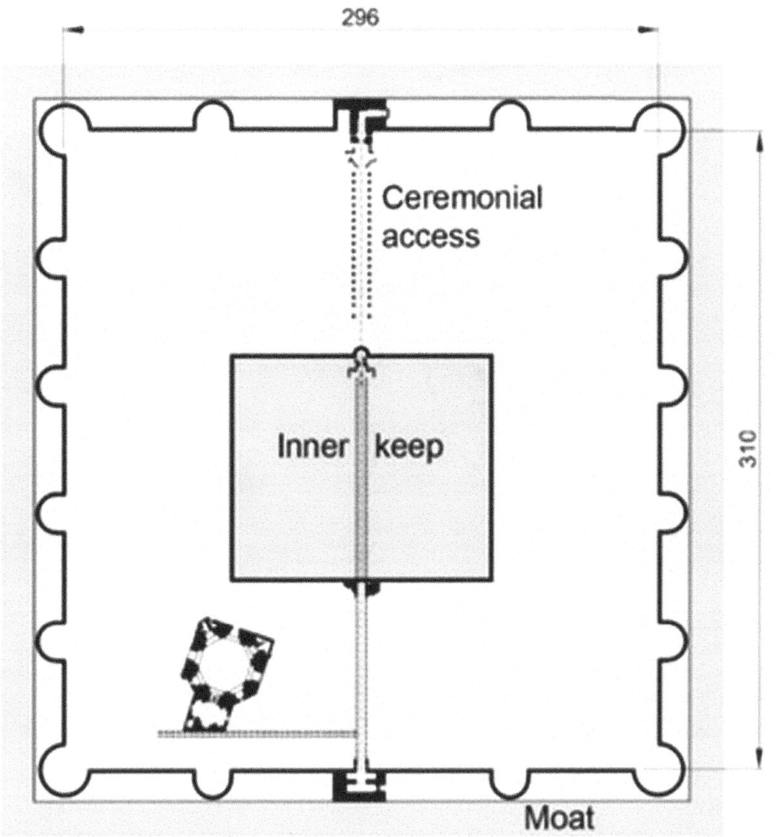

Figure 4.5 Citadel of Sultaniyya, drawing by Marco Brambilla (used with permission). Published in Brambilla, 'Mausoleum of Oljeitu and the Citadel', 132

construction campaign. Further excavation is needed to clarify the layout of the courtyard and its relation to other components of the site.

Remains of some structures attached to the ramparts of the citadel have been found. They possibly connected the walls and towers to the buildings located inside the enclave. For instance, a row of cells built along the western wall seems to have been used as local industrial workshops, as suggested by the artefacts and small kilns found in the rooms (Figures 4.6 and 4.7). Another example is the room built inside tower B with a cruciform layout and the floor paved with bricks (Figure 4.8). The arrangement of the structures adjacent

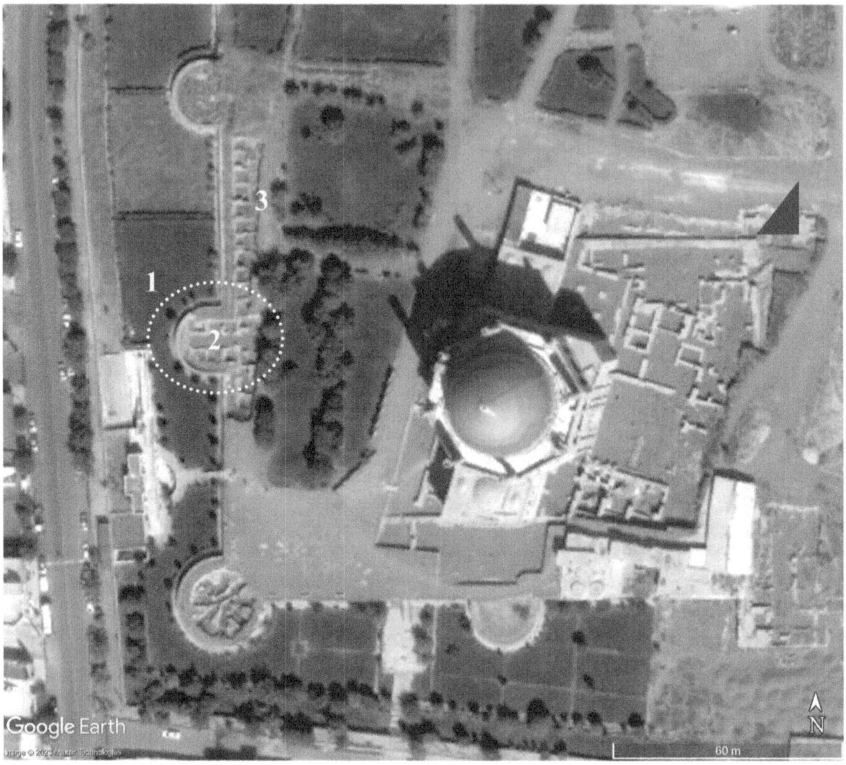

Figure 4.6 A closer view of the south-west corner of the citadel.
1. Tower B
2. Cruciform room
3. A row of cells built along the citadel wall
Google Earth (imagery date: 19 September 2014)
36° 26′ 02.32″ N, 48° 47′ 44.55″ E, eye alt 190 m
Maxar Technologies 2023. Accessed 5 September 2023

to the walls and towers proposes that a passageway parallel to the ramparts rounded the citadel.[31] On the western side of the site, close to the south-west tower, the remnants of a flight of brick stairs, presumably ascending to the top of the tower, have been discovered. The stairs have not been joined to the wall structurally and thus seem to have been built later than the wall.

The northern and eastern façades of the tomb were coated respectively with stucco and tile, as indicated by the remains of decoration on the external walls (Figures 4.9 and 4.10). Since stucco was commonly used as a decorative coating for interior walls, the northern façade might, in fact, have been

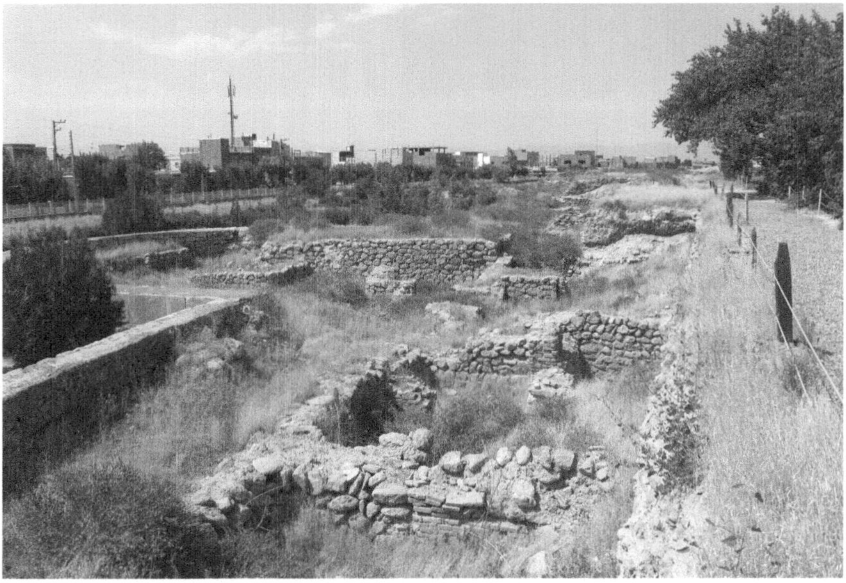

Figure 4.7 Unearthed remains of the row of cells.
© Atri Hatef Naiemi

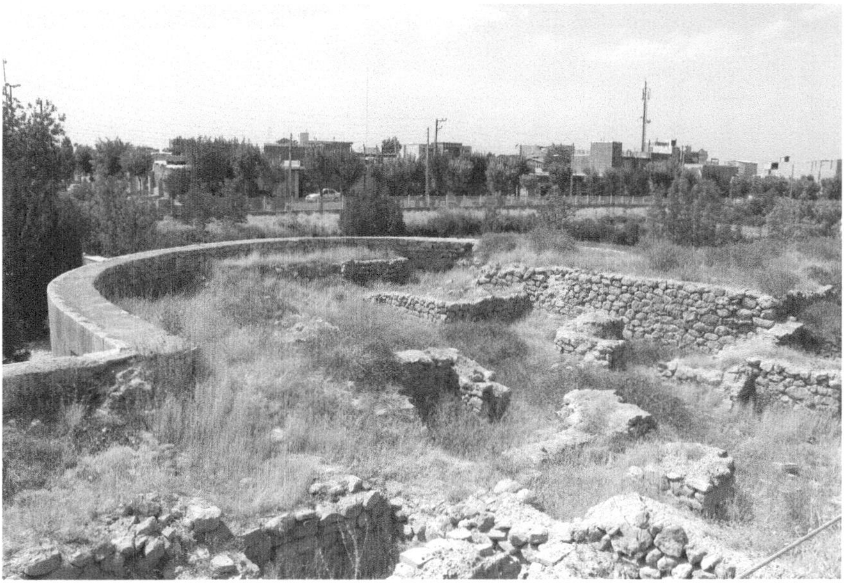

Figure 4.8 Tower B and the remains of the cruciform room.
© Atri Hatef Naiemi

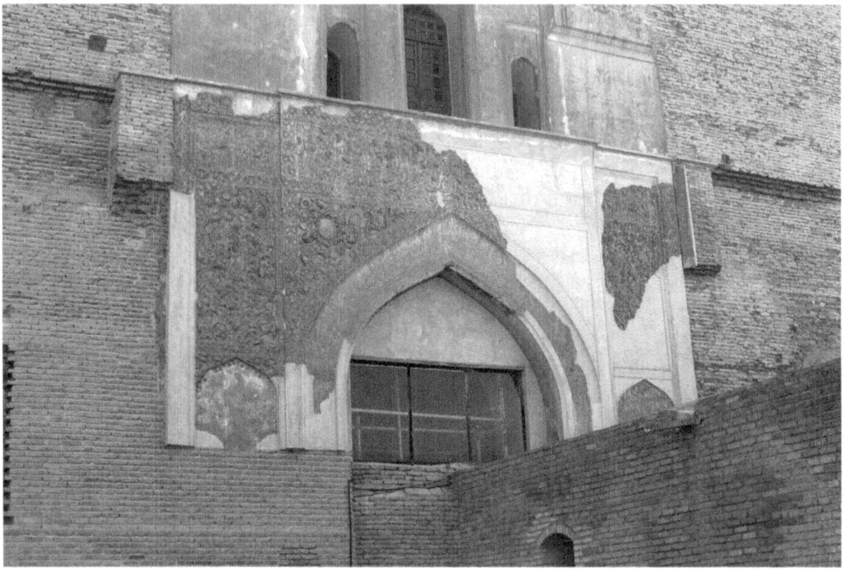

Figure 4.9 Remnants of stucco decoration on the northern façade of the tomb. © Atri Hatef Naiemi

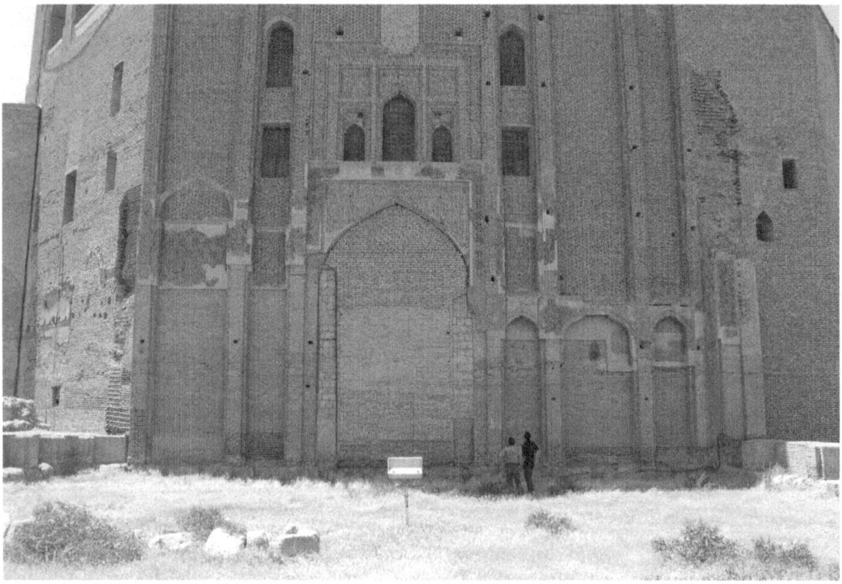

Figure 4.10 Remnants of tile works on the eastern façade of the tomb. © Atri Hatef Naiemi

the interior wall of a now-vanished building (possibly a mosque upon whose pillars a Safavid mosque stands today). In addition to the mosque, the surrounding spaces that are being gradually unearthed suggest that the currently isolated tomb of Öljeytü had been attached to other buildings of the *abwāb al-birr* from other sides too. It is beyond the scope of this chapter to consider all the archaeological findings in the area around the tomb, but it is worth mentioning that the excavations carried out at the eastern side of the tomb revealed the traces of a court with four *iwāns*. The surviving eastern façade decorated with bricks and glazed tiles in an interlaced pattern used to form one of the four sides of the court, and the only access from the tomb to the court was through an opening in this side. Traces of the partially ruined buildings around the tomb are also visible in the drawings left by European travellers who visited Sultaniyya in the nineteenth century.[32]

Some traces of a possibly two-storey catacomb were uncovered in the south of the court. Mirfattah suggests that the crypt had possibly been built before the foundation of the tomb and adjacent structures, on the basis of two pieces of evidence. First, some of the contemporary buildings of Öljeytü's tomb were founded on the top of the underground rooms (Figures 4.11 and 4.12). Second, in addition to pieces of bone and metal objects discovered in the excavation of the crypt, a fragment of a tile was found showing the date of 684/1285 (one year after Arghun's enthronement).[33] The burial cells might be a model for the crypt built later beneath the tomb. Therefore, Mirfattah raises the possibility of the existence of a royal burial place in the south-east corner of the tomb prior to the construction of the pious complex under Öljeytü.[34] The presence of the older crypt explains the choice of the south-west corner of the citadel as the location for the Ilkhan's tomb.

The internal network of passages, partly found in the excavations, proposes that the citadel consisted of four zones with different functions. Öljeytü's tomb was possibly the centre of the religious zone. In the north-east corner of the religious quarter, a room was recently unearthed where a group of pottery shards inscribed with the phrase *waqf-i abwāb al-birr* ('endowed to the *abwāb al-birr*') were found (Figure 4.13). The room presumably worked as a storeroom for keeping endowed objects that belonged to the complex.[35] Apart from the archaeological significance of such findings, the shards reassure us that the structures discovered so far around the tomb were part of the

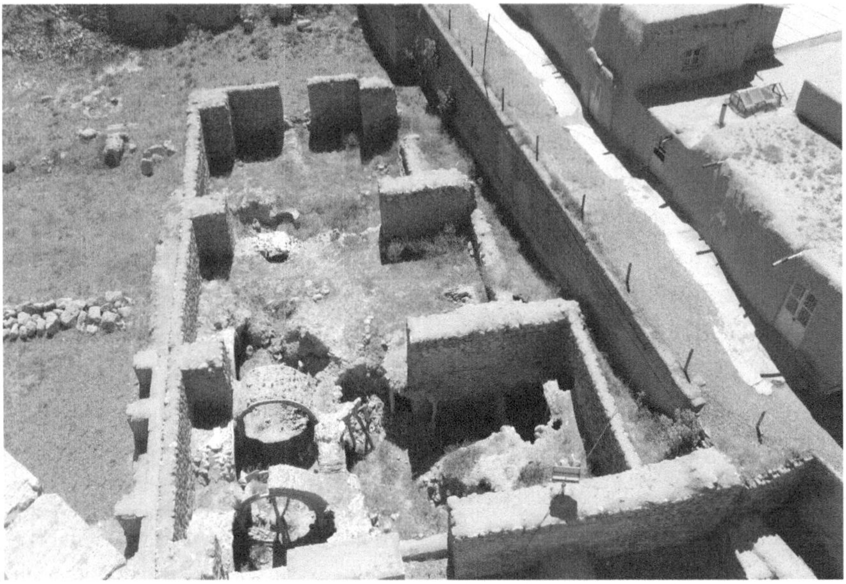

Figure 4.11 Two-storey catacomb (view from the second floor of Öljeytü's tomb). © Atri Hatef Naiemi

charitable complex and validate the historical texts that call Öljeytü's pious foundation the *abwāb al-birr*.

Along with the architectural remains, archaeological findings and written records discussed so far, there is a visual record of medieval Sultaniyya which is worth our attention here. Matrakçi Nasuh's panoramic view of the city, the earliest extant image of Sultaniyya, is an important historical document providing insights into the landscape of Öljeytü's capital. The painting is highly informative and represents more details than written material. It depicts the now-ruined components of Sultaniyya and thus has been widely used by architectural historians in the study of the earlier phases of the city. Nevertheless, it needs to be consulted with caution. The miniature should not be considered a visual reference per se, but rather in its historical context and in relation to the pictorial conventions and limitations with which the painter had to deal.[36]

The image seems to depict the citadel of the city with its wall and towers, as the number of towers corresponds to what archaeologists have found in the excavation (Figure 4.14, a, b). The large monument on the right certainly represents Öljeytü's tomb (Figure 4.14, c). On the left, the massive structure

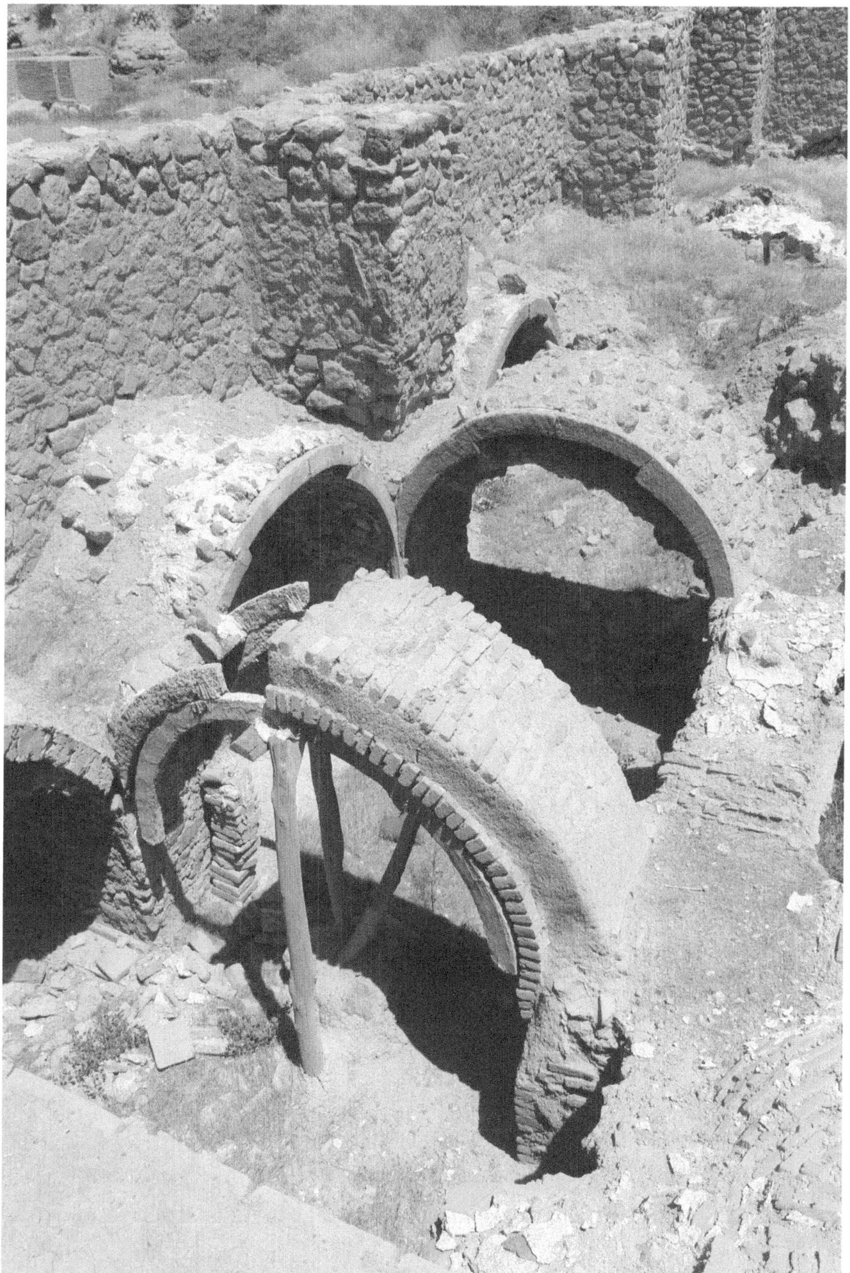

Figure 4.12 Two-storey catacomb.
© Atri Hatef Naiemi

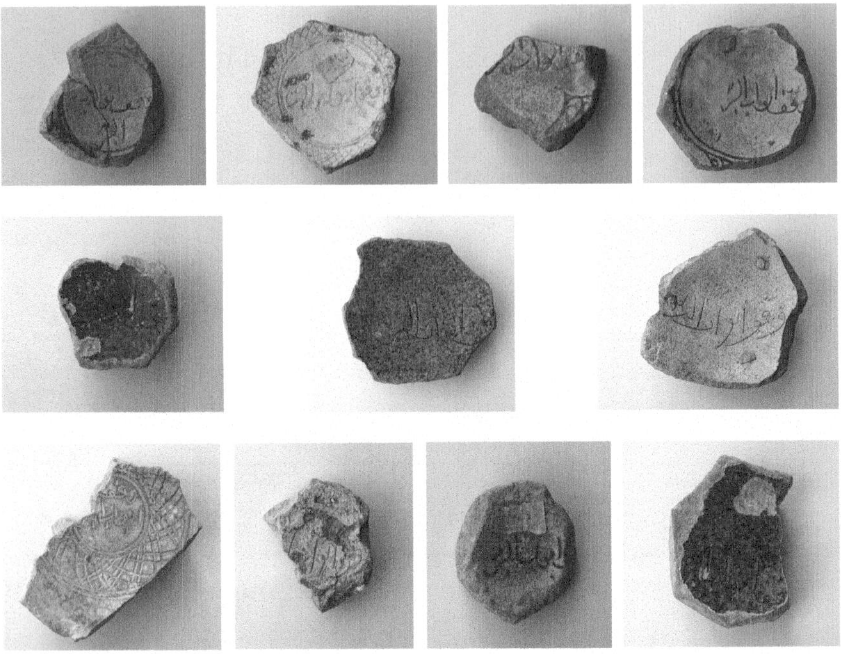

Figure 4.13 Some examples of the pottery shards inscribed with the phrase *waqf-i abwāb al-birr* ('endowed to the *abwāb al-birr*') found during the archaeological excavation in the citadel of Sultaniyya. The shards are preserved in the archaeological archive of ICHTO in Zanjan.
© Atri Hatef Naiemi (courtesy of the ICHTO of Zanjan)

and the long, arcaded building are possibly the congregational mosque built by Öljeytü and the bazaar of the city respectively (Figure 4.14, d, e). Blair refers to Kashani's description of the bazaar,[37] and suggests that the structure in the illustration is the same bazaar as that founded by Taj al-Din 'Ali Shah and repaired by him after the fire of 1312.[38] Interestingly, as discussed earlier, archaeological excavation in the area of Jumʿih-masjid supports the hypothetical location of the bazaar in the outer city close to the congregational mosque.

In another case, Blair identifies the polygonal building with two minarets on the right as Rashid al-Din's pious foundation. The foundation, consisting of a school, hospital and khanqah, alongside a large number of houses (around a thousand houses: *qarīb-i hizār khānih*), was located in a quarter founded by the vizier. The formal features of the building match up with Hafiz-i Abru's

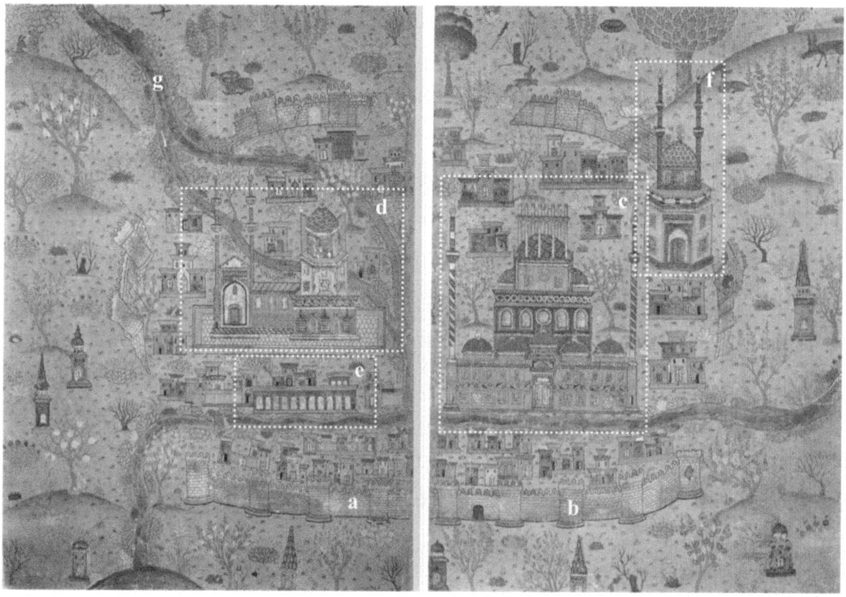

Figure 4.14 Matrakçi Nasuh's miniature of Sultaniyya, sixteenth century. Yildiz T 5964, folios 31b and 32a.
a. Wall of the citadel
b. Towers
c. Tomb of Öljeytü
d. Congregational mosque built by Öljeytü
e. Bazaar of Sultaniyya
f. Rashid al-Din's pious foundation (as suggested by Blair) or the dodecagonal building unearthed at the site of Tappih-nur
g. Surface channel of the *qanāt* of Dar al-Shafa
Courtesy of Istanbul University Library

description of the splendid edifice (*ʿimārat-i ʿālī*) patronised by the vizier.[39] However, considering the recent archaeological findings in the site of Tappih-nur, one can suggest that the polygonal structure in the painting is the same dodecagonal building just unearthed there, the one which is perceived to be Abu Saʿid's mausoleum.

The arrangement of the buildings in the miniature raises the possibility that Matrakçi depicted Öljeytü's tomb as seen from the north. If that is the case, first, the domed structure attached to the tomb in the image must be the now-vanished mosque mentioned earlier; and second, the court and related structures unearthed to the east of the tomb have been overlooked in the painting.

Given our understanding of Ilkhanid Sultaniyya based on available textual and physical evidence, Matrakçi seems to have been more interested in depicting the key components of the city than in placing them in their accurate location or maintaining their topographic relations. As a result, the confines of the citadel and the outer city are blurred, and it is challenging to distinguish between the palatial constructions and the buildings distributed outside the citadel. For example, the rampart in the map resembles the wall enclosing the inner citadel today, but it contains some of the elements which evidently stood in the outer city. Despite the historical significance of Matrakçi's map, it should be considered a collage of buildings connected together on the basis of sketches he made during his journey.[40] The image is not entirely imaginary and somewhat corroborates other literary and material evidence, but it cannot be treated as a model in the thorough reconstruction of the Mongol capital at Sultaniyya.

The Outer City of Sultaniyya

According to Mustawfi, Arghun founded Sulatniyya and built a wall around the city measuring 12,000 paces (7,320 m) in circumference. Öljeytü decided to finish the architectural undertakings of his father, and therefore he expanded the city wall to 30,000 paces (18,300 m). The task remained incomplete due to the death of the sultan. At the heart of the city, he founded a citadel with a perimeter of 2,000 paces (1,220 m).[41] The perimeter of the citadel mentioned in Mustawfi's account roughly matches up with the length of the walls found in the recent excavations. Therefore, we may hypothetically accept that he reports almost the actual dimensions of the walls constructed around the city. On the basis of the discovered citadel walls and Mustawfi's reported dimensions of the city walls, we can estimate the approximate area of Sultaniyya under each of the two Ilkhans, Arghun and Öljeytü. With the tomb of Öljeytü placed in the centre of the capital, the hypothetical area of each phase of the city is indicated on the current map of Sultaniyya (Figure 4.15). According to the map, the area embracing most of the archaeological finds and architectural remains from the Ilkhanid period is the same area as was initially established as the capital of Arghun. This fact suggests that urban development during Öljeytü's reign mainly happened within the boundaries of the older city. Although eye-witness chronicler Mustawfi reports that the Ilkhan intended to

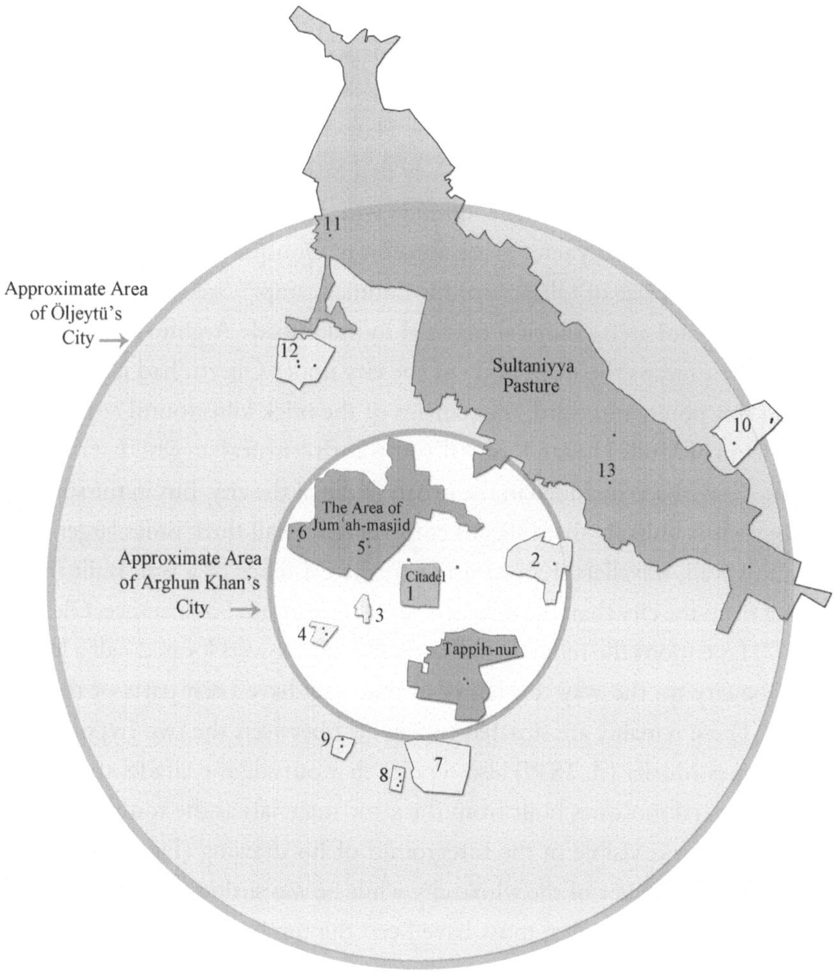

Figure 4.15 Hypothetical area of Sultaniyya under Arghun Khan and Öljeytü.

1. Öljeytü's tomb
2. Site of Finjanabad
3. Maydan lands
4. Shaykh Buraq's tomb and khanqah
5. Cemetery
6. Shrine of Imam-zadih Abdullah
7. Remains of the brick kilns
8. Mausoleum of Mulla Hassan Kashi
9. Area of Qush-khanih
10. Carvan-gah (or Tappih-yi caravanserai)
11. Uch-tappih
12. Tappih-qal'ih
13. Mustafa-Khan plain

© Atri Hatef Naiemi (drawing based on the map of the city of Sultaniyya sourced from the local archive of ICHTO located at the World Heritage Site of Sultaniyya)

build a wall almost three times larger than the one his father had ordered to be built, Öljeytü presumably did not have a chance to fulfil his own aspirations.

Öljeytü definitely expanded the walls; however, the ratio reported by Mustawfi (30,000 paces) and repeated by Hafiz-i Abru may be slightly exaggerated, for three reasons. First, it is unlikely that Sultaniyya Pasture was enclosed by the new walls in order to be combined with the main structure of the city, since the texts frequently refer to the meadow of Qunqur Öläng and Sultaniyya as the favourite place of Öljeytü for his summer camp.[42] Second, the extent of architectural and archaeological material found outside Arghun's wall is very small, which means the main body of the city under Öljeytü had not reached beyond this point; and third, the remains of the brick kilns found around the mausoleum of Mulla Hassan Kashi (fl. fourteenth century) suggest that this area must not have been included in the urban fabric of the city, but in the suburb. Although it is unlikely that Öljeytü constructed a wall three times larger than Arghun's wall, travellers' reports attest to the existence of a wall built much further from the city than the one attributed to Arghun. For instance, Olearius (d. 1671) mentions the remnants of walls, gate and towers located half a league from the city on the way to Hamedan that may have been parts of the city walls.[43] These remains are situated somewhere between the two hypothetical walls. James Morier (d. 1849) also reports that outside the citadel there were ruins of several mosques built from the same materials as the tomb.[44] One of these buildings is visible in the foreground of his drawing (Figure 4.16). He made this general view of the whole city while he was sitting on a small mound in the south. The building must have been the tomb of Shaykh Buraq. The remains of a tall wall and buttresses that were possibly part of the circuit wall of the city can be seen right behind the tomb. Consequently, it would be challenging to determine the exact dimensions of Öljeytü's wall with certainty; the available textual and physical evidence lead us to suggest that the city developed during his reign beyond the limits of Arghun's city, but that the development was probably aborted in its early stages because of the Ilkhan's death.

Although we are still uncertain about the area of Sultaniyya's outer city under Öljeytü and his father, textual records, particularly contemporary accounts of the foundation of Sultaniyya, inform us about a thriving city that extended beyond the citadel.[45] Historical chronicles and descriptive poetry describe architectural projects and related historical events in rich detail.

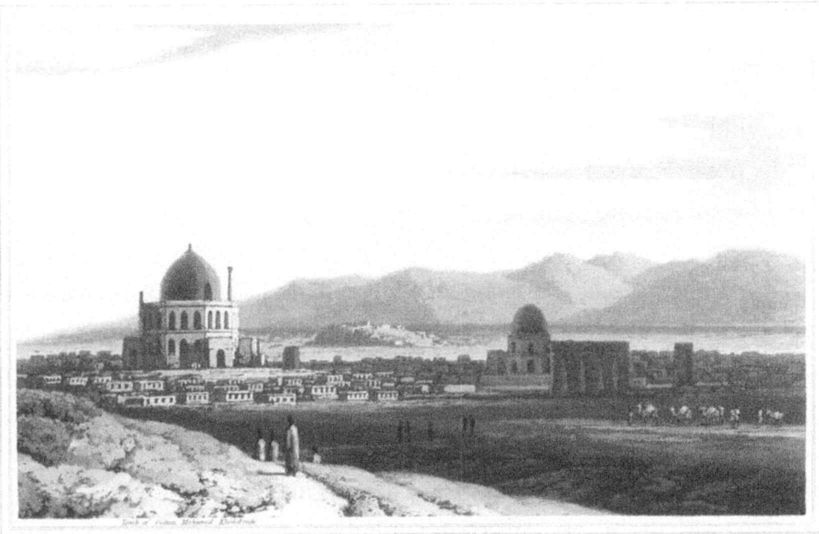

Figure 4.16 James Morier's view of the city of Sultaniyya.
Original painting published in Morier, *Journey through Persia*

They are also valuable sources of information shedding light on the possible location of public buildings within the urban context.

For example, in the *Tarikh-i Öljeytü*, Kashani distinguishes precisely between the buildings founded in the citadel and those built in the outer city. He reports exaggeratedly that the city (he presumably meant the outer city) was prosperous and full of rivers and trees. There were more than ten thousand shops (*afzūn az dah-hizār dukkān*) that presented their exquisite goods, and many mosques and endless (*bī pāyān*) *zawāyā* (s. *zāwīya*)[46] and edifices were erected in the city. The noblemen built splendid palaces and gardens in the city by order of the sultan. Kashani specifically describes the edifice that the vizier ʻAli Shah had built in the immediate vicinity of the entrance (*pīshgāh*) of the citadel.[47] A workshop called Firdaws (*kārkhānih-yi Firdaws*), whose location is still vague, is the other construction ascribed to ʻAli Shah.[48] Kashani also mentions the octagonal tomb attributed to Shaykh Buraq, one of the few buildings that have remained from the Ilkhanid period in modern-day Sultaniyya. The tomb patronised by Öljeytü around 1307, and the adjacent khanqah, built by Khwajih Shams al-Din Muhammad Qazvini in 1333, are located in the south-west of the city.[49]

In addition to the *Tarikh-i Öljeytü*, there are other references to the buildings patronised by Öljeytü as well as his viziers and amirs in Sultaniyya in different chronicles. For instance, in the *Tarikh-i Wassaf*, Wassaf tells us that Rashid al-Din presented Wassaf's book to Öljeytü when the sultan visited the observatory of Sultaniyya, but he does not expand on the location or architecture of the building. Moreover, he mentions the portable school (*madrasa-yi sayyāra*) 'invented' by the two viziers Rashid al-Din and Taj al-Din (*az mukhtariʿāt-i du vazīr ast*). He describes the school as an educational institution held in a sublime tent adjacent to the royal camp in which a group of scholars taught.[50] Hafiz-i Abru also refers to an excellent school built by Öljeytü in Sultaniyya and compares it to the madrasa of Mustansiriya in Baghdad.[51] This building must be the same school as that mentioned by Amuli, an instructor at Öljeytü's pious complex in his capital.[52]

Along with the historical texts containing scattered references to the physical elements of Sultaniyya, examination of the architectural and archaeological remains of the Ilkhanid city can also clarify our picture of its spatial structure. What will be discussed next are two archaeological sites, Jumʿih-masjid and Tappih-nur, which possibly shaped important quarters in the outer city under Öljeytü and Abu Saʿid.

The site of Jumʿih-masjid

Archaeological findings propose that the outer city of Ilkhanid Sultaniyya (or at least part of it) had extended over the area known today as the site of Jumʿih-masjid. In other words, the area of Jumʿih-masjid presumably formed the civilian settlement of the Ilkhanid city where citizens led their daily lives. The site is located in the north-west of modern Sultaniyya. In the archaeological studies conducted by Muhajerinejad at the site in 2009, forty-one trial trenches were dug to estimate the archaeological potential of the site. The location of the suggested trenches was defined on the basis of visible features in the aerial photos of the site taken between 1955 and 2002. The current satellite images overlaid with older aerial photos enabled the archaeologists to choose the location of the trenches more effectively. As a result, almost all the trenches revealed significant finds.[53]

On the basis of data compiled from fieldwork, archival research and artefacts analysis, Muhajerinejad speculates about the distribution of buildings across the site and suggests that the religious buildings were possibly located in the south-east, and that the public spaces, bazaar and cemetery were placed in the south and south-west part of the site.[54] The large amount of tiles of different types scattered throughout the site of Jumʿih-masjid, the good quality of the soil of the region, and the pieces of flint (*sang-i chakhmāq*) found on the ground[55] support the hypothesis that the pottery workshops were distributed across the area of Jumʿih-masjid and the Talibiyya lands. The main *qanāt* channels were built along the north–south axis of the site. While the mounds distributed over the area represent the ruined constructions of the old city, the empty spaces between the hills and mounds were possibly the gardens and urban plazas arranged among the buildings.[56]

Taking into account the buildings' remnants as well as the fragments of architectural decorations, such as glazed bricks and lustre tiles found in some of the trenches, Muhajerinejad raises the possibility that the congregational mosque (*masjid-i Jāmiʿ*) of the city was built in the south-east corner of the site (Figure 4.17, Building A). Aerial photographs and satellite images of the site of Jumʿih-masjid can be used to verify his claim about the location of the mosque. In the aerial photograph taken in 1964 a feature on the ground is recognisable, which seems to be a row of rooms arranged around a large open courtyard. Traces of what is possibly a domed chamber projecting out of the southern wall of the building are also visible. When the 1964 photograph of the site was overlaid with the 2014 satellite image of the same area, the building with the courtyard matched up with 'Building A', the structure which is claimed to be the congregational mosque (Figures 4.18 and 4.19). Furthermore, both the 1964 photograph and the 2014 satellite image show that the building has a deviation from the north–south axis (of around 20°) and almost matches up with the direction of the *qiblih*.[57] Hence, both the layout and the orientation of 'Building A' support the claim that this building must have been the congregational mosque of the city.

To the south-west of 'Building A', the earlier excavations conducted by Mirfattah in the 1990s revealed the remains of an architectural structure, presumably associated with the bazaar of the city, for instance a caravanserai, a *khān* (an inner-town inn for merchants) or a *sarāy* (a warehouse). The spaces excavated behind the eastern side of this building were possibly residential units attached to the bazaar (Figure 4.19, Building B).[58] Part of the excavated

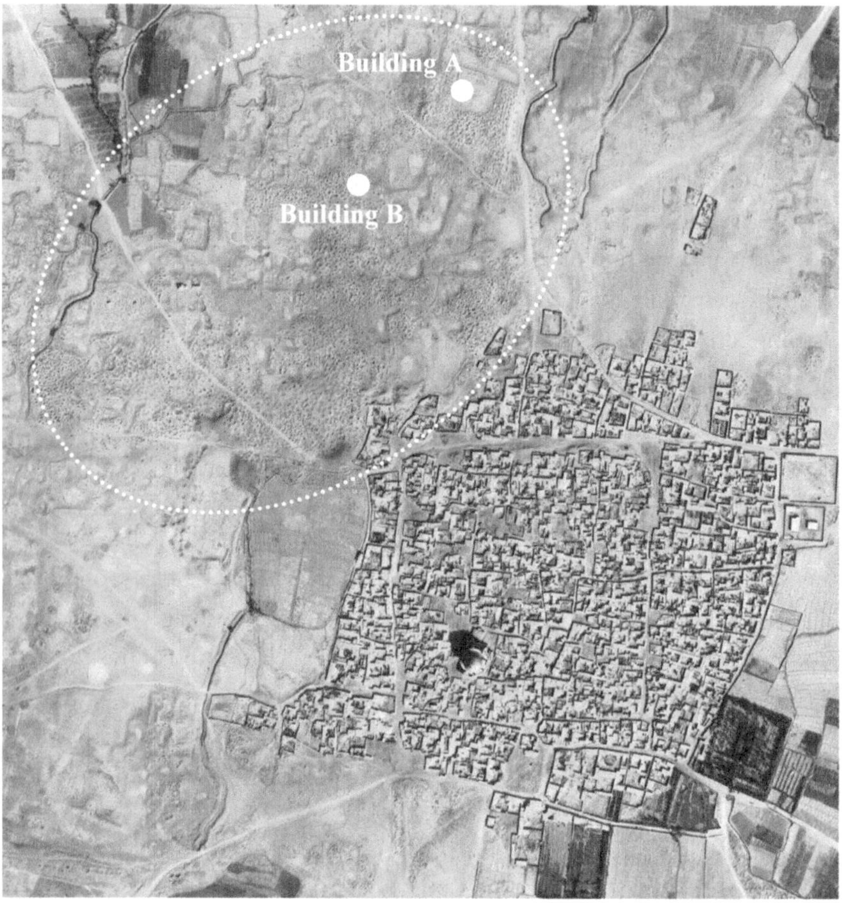

Figure 4.17 Aerial photo of Sultaniyya taken in 1964. The site of Jumʿih-masjid is located north-west of Sultaniyya.
Iran National Cartography Centre

buildings in this phase were covered again at the end of the season and are not visible in more recent satellite images of the site.

Written sources also shed some light on the possible location of the congregational mosque and the bazaar. In the *Nafaʾis al-Funun*, Amuli mentions an excellent congregational mosque (*Jāmiʿī bas ʿālī*) founded by Öljeytü in Sultaniyya.[59] This congregational mosque must have been the same Friday Mosque (*masjid-i Jumʿih*) built of marble and grand tiles that Hafiz-i Abru describes in his chronicle.[60] His report of the siege of the citadel by Amir

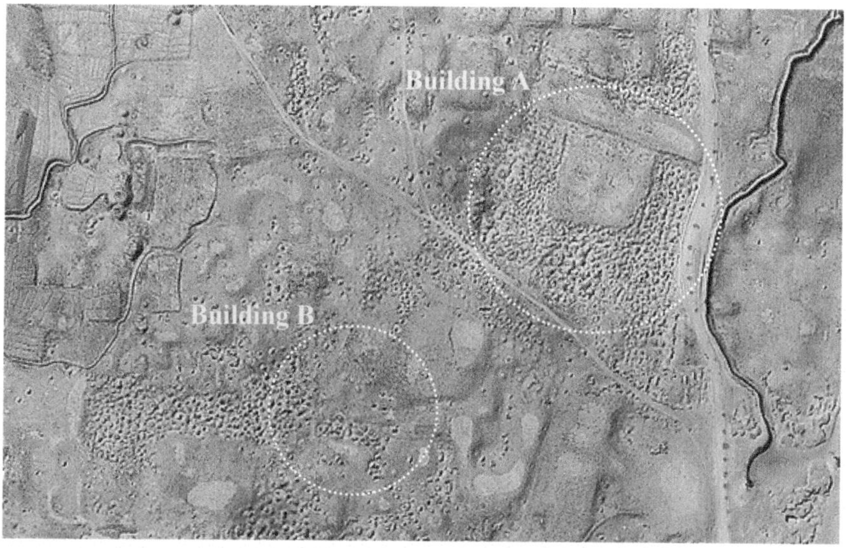

Figure 4.18 Building A and Building B on the 1964 aerial photo of the site of Jumʿih-masjid. Iran National Cartography Centre

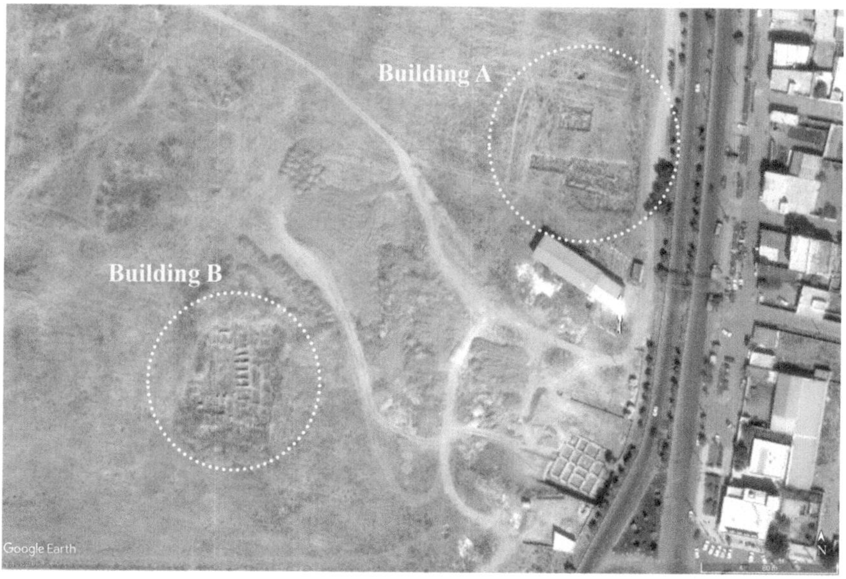

Figure 4.19 Building A and Building B on the 2014 satellite image of the site of Jumʿih-masjid. Google Earth (imagery date: 19 September 2014)
36° 26′ 25.16″ N, 48° 47′ 41.48″ E, eye alt 318 m
Maxar Technologies 2023. Accessed 6 September 2023

Sintay in 1385 also confirms the proximity of the congregational mosque to the bazaars of *qaṣṣābān* (butchers) and *na'l-bandān* (farriers).[61] In a more recent account, Fedot Katof (fl. seventeenth century), a Russian merchant from Moscow who travelled to the Safavid court in Isfahan in 1623 and 1624, gives a view of seventeenth-century Sultaniyya. He says that there was a large mosque in the citadel where the shah had been buried with his son. Katof's account of the mosque implies that he is, in fact, describing the tomb of Öljeytü. He also mentions that a bazaar, a stone caravanserai and a large mosque, which must have been the congregational mosque, with sixteen stone columns were located in the city.[62] The congregational mosque of Sultaniyya was of great importance throughout the Ilkhanid period, since after the accession of each Ilkhan the ruler's name was mentioned in a *khuṭba* (sermon) that occurred there.[63]

The site of Tappih-nur

The area of Tappih-nur lies south-east of the city and consists of several mounds of different size. Many artefacts, ranging from prehistory to the Islamic era, have been unearthed so far. The pottery pieces and architectural remains found on the central mound relate exclusively to the Ilkhanid period.[64] The most significant finding is a dodecagonal building excavated from this mound. Although it resembles a tomb tower, there is still not enough evidence to determine its function (Figures 4.20 and 4.21).[65] The plan and possible dimensions of the structure, as well as the quality of the building material

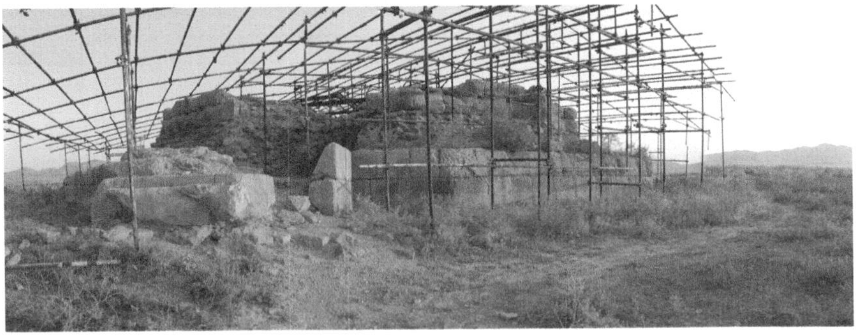

Figure 4.20 Tappih-nur: the ruins of the dodecagonal building.
© Atri Hatef Naiemi

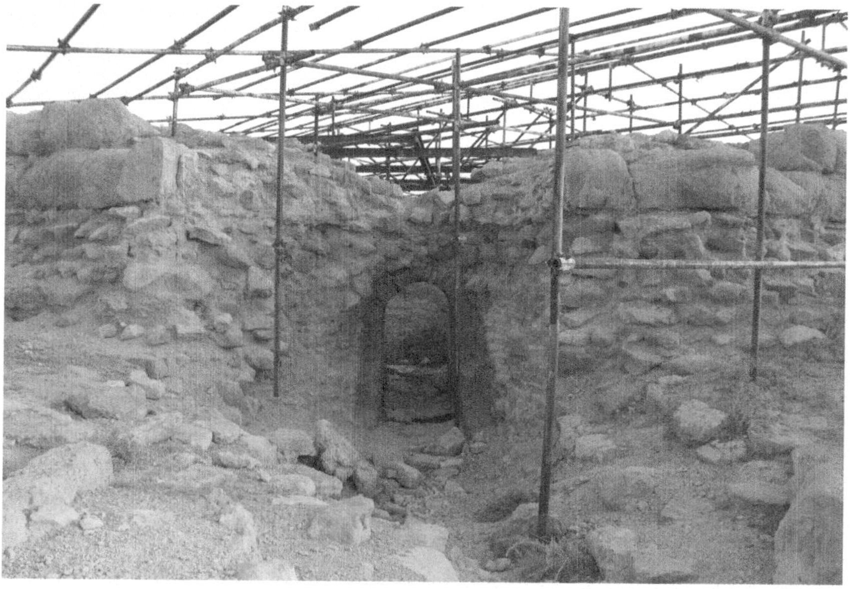

Figure 4.21 Entrance to the dodecagonal building.
© Atri Hatef Naiemi

(for instance, the green tuffite stones installed in the platform or the glazed tiles scattered around the site), propose that the building never was a mere isolated structure on the verge of the Mongol city, but was possibly part of a larger complex. However, there are still some ambiguities in the way in which it interacted with the citadel or the outer city. Among different theories speculating on the function of the monument, that suggested by Brambilla seems more plausible. He proposes that Tappih-nur is the site originally known as Sharuyaz, and the building founded on top of the mound must have been built by Abu Saʿid, Öljeytü's son, as his mausoleum. He raises the possibility that the mausoleum might have been located in the centre of an enclosure while a group of structures within or outside the enclosure encompassed the mausoleum.[66] Clavijo's account of 'an immense mosque and palace of many apartments' that stood some distance outside the city supports Brambilla's claim. He reports that Miran Shah (Tamerlane's son) had demolished the edifice entirely and had thrown out the body of the founder that had been buried there in a magnificent tomb.[67] It is probable that Clavijo refers to the palace and tomb complex of Abu Saʿid at the site of Tappih-nur, since the location and architectural remains of the building match his account. Hafiz-i Abru also relates the funeral of Abu Sa'id and clearly mentions that the coffin of the Ilkhan was carried to the mausoleum (*marqad*) and the city that had been built around Sultaniyya during his lifetime, in a spot called Sharuyaz.[68]

During the reign of Abu Sa'id, different sectors of the kingdom fragmented into independent units. In Fars and Kerman, local governors minted money bearing their own names and patronised several architectural projects. They gradually spread their authority over southern and western Iran. Abu Sa'id died in 1335 at Qarabagh.[69] Following the death of the sultan and the disintegration of the Ilkhanids, in a power vacuum that lasted almost half a century, Sultaniyya became a battlefield where different political groups asserted their claim to reign. However, the city retained its economic centrality throughout this period. For instance, Clavijo's report of Sultaniyya, shortly after Miran Shah's rampage through Sultaniyya and Tabriz in 1399, proves the partial prosperity of the city even after the fall of the Ilkhanids. He says that although Sultaniyya was less populous than Tabriz, it was a more important centre of exchange for merchants and their goods.[70] Many water channels, fine streets and squares and several hostels accommodating merchants are the other urban elements that caught Clavijo's attention.[71] Nevertheless, the dissolution of the Ilkhanids, which had already diminished the political significance of Sultaniyya, resulted in the gradual destruction of the city over the next centuries, in such a way that at the beginning of the twentieth century nothing remained of the former prosperous capital except for a few semi-ruined buildings.

Sultaniyya: A Perso-Islamic Capital City or a Mongol Camp?

In some aspects of the Ilkhans' social life, for instance their adherence to seasonal migrations and their erection of magnificent camps in the environs of their cities, steppe conventions appeared on the surface. In Ilkhanid urban architecture, nevertheless, the interaction between settled and nomadic cultures occurred in some depth, resulting in the formation of forms and meanings that were syntheses of Mongolian and Perso-Islamic concepts. In this regard, and within the scope of the present research, Sultaniyya is an ideal case study representing the Ilkhans' struggles to establish a capital in accordance with the rules of the sedentary world, but which at the same time harmonised with their nomadic roots. Although the architectural undertakings of Öljeytü at Sultaniyya, the pious ensemble in particular, are commonly attributed to his conversion and subsequently to his sincere faith in Islam, there is some textual and physical evidence that suggests otherwise. While in the next chapter we will expand on the idea that Öljeytü's construction projects had part of their origins in the customs of the Mongols, here we briefly argue that it was the Ilkhan's inclination towards such nomadic traditions that to some extent determined the location of his newly founded city.

As we saw earlier, Ghazan Khan established Tabriz as the *dār al-mulk* of the Ilkhanids, but in its vicinity he founded the city of Ghazaniyya with the charitable complex of Shanb-i Ghazan at its heart. The motivations behind the construction of a new city next to the metropolis of Tabriz were discussed in Chapter 3. From the perspective of the nomadic Mongols, the Khans obtained royal charisma and legitimacy through occupying certain lands whose spiritual power had been derived from different sources: for example, an ancestral shrine or an earlier imperial settlement. Like the case of Ghazaniyya, the foundation of Sultaniyya could be explained in connection with the traditional beliefs of the steppe nomads.

In Hafiz-i Abru's account of the building of Sultaniyya, Öljeytü states that he aimed to complete his father's unfinished project in order to keep his name alive. He says:

> I do not build this city and the castle (*qal'ih*) to be my stronghold, God forbid, in the time of hardship or to bring me wealth. The main reason for the building is that Padishah Arghun had founded it and intended to finish it, but life did not give him a chance.[72]

Although Öljeytü had a great desire to construct edifices, he did not trust his power and capabilities, as he himself declares. Nevertheless, he had a motive for doing this job, because the padishah (Arghun) believed in it.[73] In addition to Öljeytü's indebtedness to his father, the fact that he not only completed Arghun's construction but also established it as his main capital suggests that Sultaniyya might have had other significance in the Ilkhan's eyes. One could raise the possibility that Öljeytü aimed to inherit legitimacy and royal charisma from his father through taking the control of a site that had already been occupied by Arghun. But what factors persuaded Arghun to build his capital city in the region and choose a nearby site in Mount Sujas as his burial place known as *quruq-i Arghun*? Apart from some practical reasons such as mild weather, lush pastures and the proximity of the Sultaniyya Pasture to main trade routes,[74] it is possible that, like Shanb, Arghun believed that the primordial good fortune actually existed in Sultaniyya, although the source of this quality is still vague.

In addition to capturing Arghun's legitimacy and royal charisma, the proximity of Öljeytü's *abwāb al-birr*, the pivotal element of the enclave embracing his tomb, to the spot recognised as a royal burial place during the time of Arghun could be explained in relation to the Mongol ideology that acknowledged ancestral shrines as sources of spiritual power. Likewise, the closeness of Öljeytü's capital to the burial site of Arghun in Mount Sujas should be regarded as an attempt to gain this power.[75]

The other factor pointing towards the spiritual significance of the region is an unfinished rock-cut complex known locally as Dash Kassan (Figure 4.22). The site is located near the village of Viar about 30 km south-south-east of Sultaniyya. The structural, stylistic and iconographical features of the complex suggest that it was a Buddhist temple[76] possibly founded by Arghun, who had Buddhist priests brought from India according to Rashid al-Din.[77]

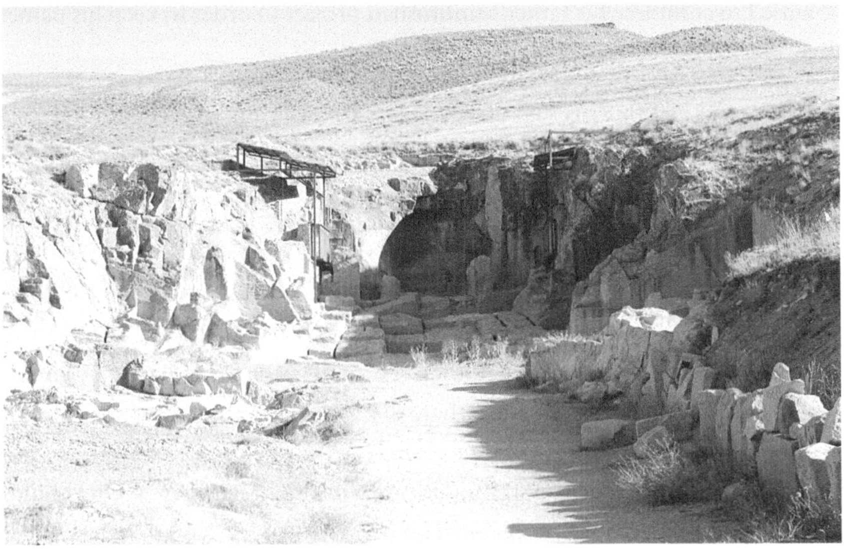

Figure 4.22 Rock-cut complex known as Dash Kassan (Viar) temple. © Atri Hatef Naiemi

Inside the complex, there are two rock-cut panels with the design of Chinese-type dragons (Figure 4.23). The rock resembles the green tuffite stones used in the outer walls of the citadel of Sultaniyya. In addition, several architectural fragments carved and scattered all over the complex seem to have been cut for the purpose of being transferred to and utilised in other sites. Thus, the site might have changed to a carving workshop or even a quarry after the building was left unfinished (Figures 4.24 and 4.25). Interestingly, some pieces carry intriguing marks which possibly belonged to certain carving workshops (Figure 4.26).

A passage from the *Jamiʿ al-Tawarikh* alongside a recently found stone bust at the site of Dash Kassan support the claim that the complex was aimed at being a Buddhist monastery. According to Rashid al-Din, Ghazan Khan destroyed all the idol temples and fire temples following his conversion and forcefully converted most of the Buddhist priests to Islam. When some of the converts pretended to be Muslim but resumed practising Buddhism, the Ilkhan warned them against hypocrisy and threatened to kill them if they rebuilt their temples. Ghazan clarified the following:

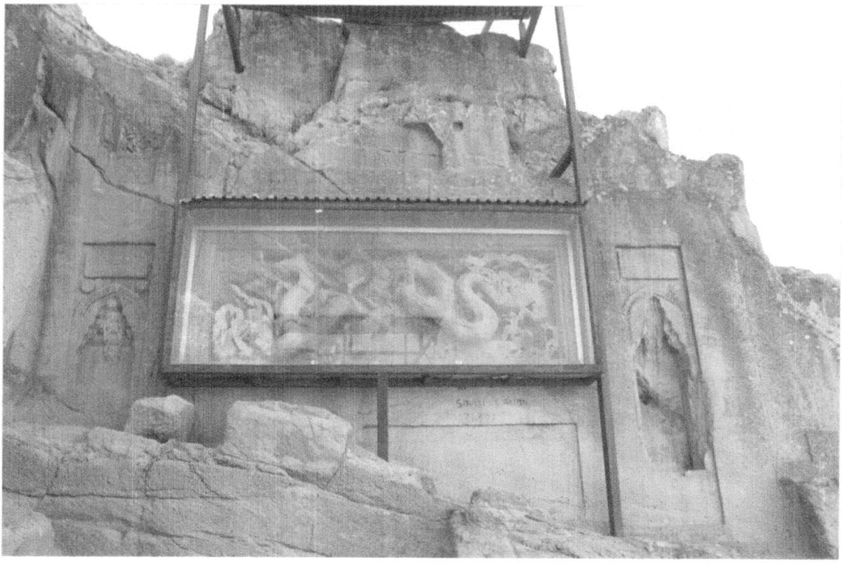

Figure 4.23 Rock-cut panel with the design of dragons flanked by *muqarnas* carvings, Dash Kassan (Viar).

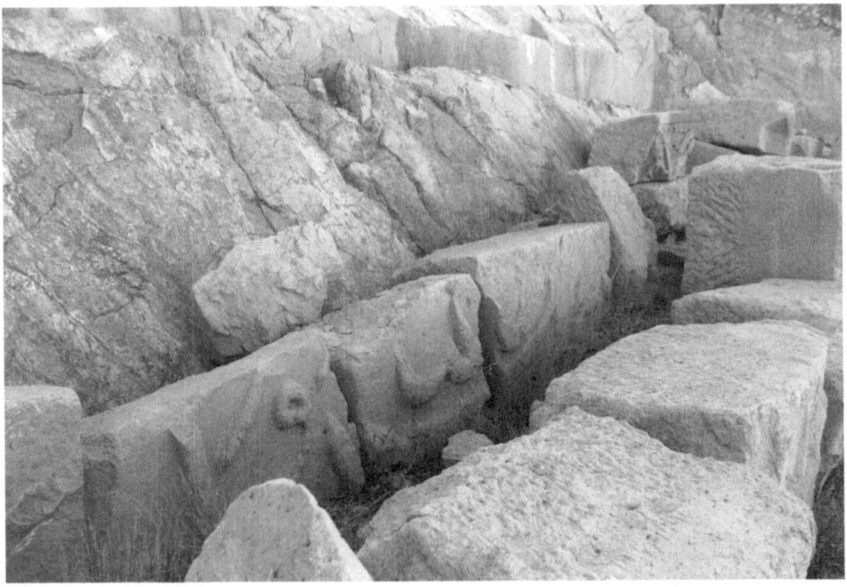

Figure 4.24 An unfinished stone inscription, Dash Kassan (Viar).
© Atri Hatef Naiemi

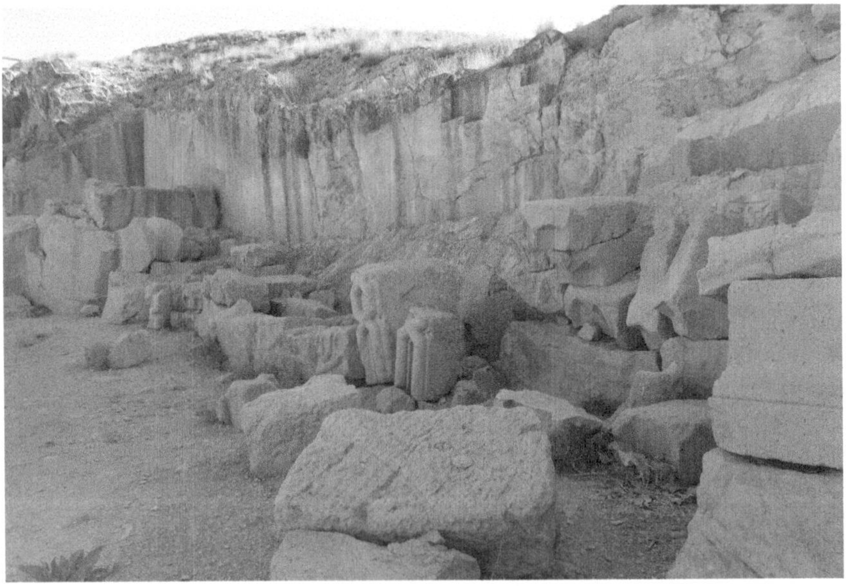

Figure 4.25 Carved fragments scattered all over the complex, Dash Kassan (Viar).
© Atri Hatef Naiemi

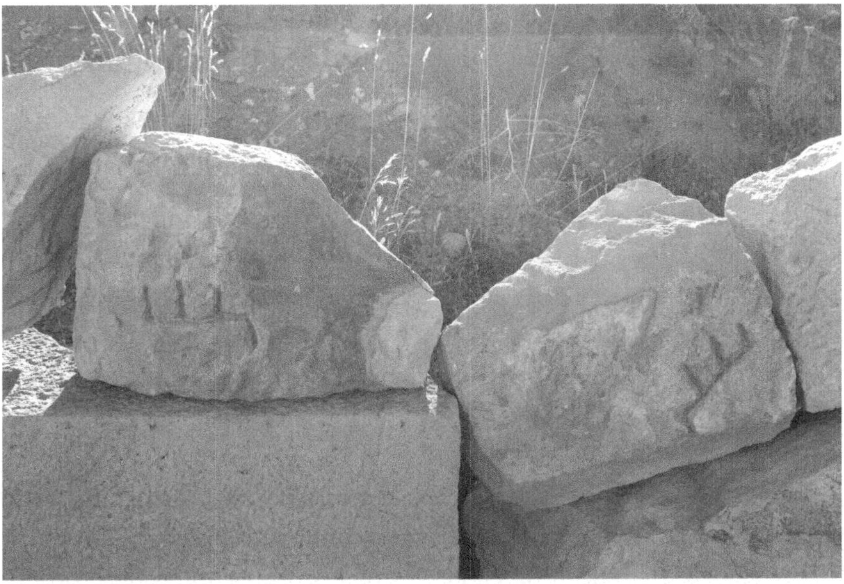

Figure 4.26 An example of marks on the carved fragments possibly inscribed by certain carving workshops.

> My father was an idol worshipper (*but parast*) and remained so until he passed away and he had built himself an idol shrine (*but-khānih*) and a temple (*maʿbad*) and had given endowments to them in the name of that group [*bakhshīyān*: the Buddhist priests], I destroyed that shrine, but if you [*bakhshīyān*] go there and reside, you will be given alms.

A number of Ghazan Khan's amirs and khatuns advised him as follows:

> your father had built a temple and carved (or painted) his face on the walls of the temple (*ṣūrat-i khud bar dīvār-hā-yi ān khānih kardih*), but now since [the building] is in ruins, snow and rain fall on the faces of your father, and he was an idol worshipper. If [*bakhshīyān*] rebuild the temple, it will make your father's soul calm and keep his name alive.[78]

The Ilkhan eventually did not listen to the advice and forbade the priests to repair the temple. The account is not specific about the location of Arghun's temple, but it leads us to suggest that the rock-cut complex still standing in

Dash Kassan is the same building as the aforementioned. The clue is Arghun's face carved on the wall, which hypothetically could be the same stone bust as that discovered in the south-west corner of the main court of the complex (Figure 4.27). If that is the case, Dash Kassan must have been an important spiritual site lying not far from Arghun's city.

I conclude this chapter by addressing the question 'Sultaniyya: A Perso-Islamic capital city or a Mongol camp?', answering that it seems to have simultaneously fulfilled the criteria for both entities. Öljeytü founded his imperial capital in the same place as had already been claimed by his father and therefore achieved legitimacy and royal charisma according to Mongolian native beliefs. On the other hand, within the citadel of the city, he built a multi-functional charitable complex, many elements of which, such as mosque, khanqah and *dār al-ḥuffāẓ*, were devoted to Islamic practices. The outer city of Sultaniyya also embraced the familiar structural components that were observable in other Iranian cities during the medieval period, such as bazaar and congregational mosque. Apart from Sultaniyya's location and overall framework, there are

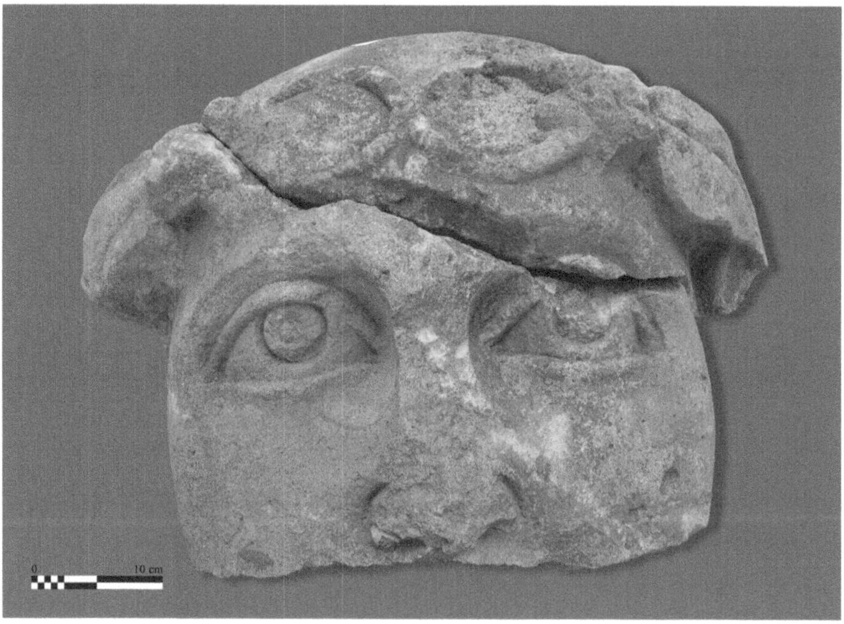

Figure 4.27 Stone bust uncovered in the main court of Dash Kassan (Viar). Courtesy of ICHTO of Zanjan

other arenas where the Ilkhanid city bridges the gap between sedentary notions and nomadic traditions. This idea will be followed in the next chapter, which examines the mechanisms through which the dialogue between the Ilkhans and their Iranian subjects was constructed.

Notes

1. Not all the available sources have been referred to in this chapter, due to the large number of chronicles and their sometimes repetitive accounts. For a list of all visitors to Sultaniyya, see Farnaz Akhavan-Tavakoli, *Kitāb-shināsī-yi Sultaniyya* [A Bibliography of Sultaniyya] (Tehran: Sāzmān-i Mīrāth-i Farhangī-yi Kishvar, 2002), 178–9.
2. This chapter draws on my previously-published article 'The Ilkhanid City of Sultaniyya' and naturally avoids repeating what has already been discussed there.
3. Hafiz-i Abru, *Dhayl-i Jāmiʿ al-Tawārīkh-i Rashīdī*, 67.
4. For the description of the funeral of Abu Saʿid, see Hafiz-i Abru, *Dhayl-i Jāmiʿ al-Tawārīkh-i Rashīdī*, 190–1.
5. Wassaf al-Hazra and Ayati, *Taḥrīr-i Tārīkh-i Wassaf*, 277. For the whole passage, see the Appendix, section 6.

   Although Sultaniyya was established as the capital of the Ilkhanids, it is not necessarily always called '*dār al-mulk*' (the capital) in contemporary accounts of the reign of Öljeytü. For instance, while Mustawfi refers to the city as the *dār al-mulk* of Iran, Kashani frequently calls it the *shahr* (city) of Sultaniyya or the *yaylāq* of Sultaniyya. See Mustawfi, *Nuzhat al-Qulūb*, *passim* and Kashani, *Tārīkh-i Öljeytü*, *passim*.
6. Wassaf al-Hazra and Ayati, *Taḥrīr-i Tārīkh-i Wassaf*, 277.
7. Donald Little, 'The Founding of Sulṭāniyya: A Mamlūk Version', *Iran: Journal of the British Institute of Persian Studies* 16 (1978): 172.
8. *Dār al-ḥuffāẓ* was a place where students memorised and recited the Qur'an.
9. Different historians have described the components of the complex in different ways. See Blair, 'Mongol Capital of Sulṭāniyya', 144.
10. Muhammad ibn Mahmud Amuli, *Nafāyis al-Funūn fī ʿArāyis al-ʿUyūn* [Treasures of Sciences in the Lovely Realm of Sights], ed. Abu al-Hassan Shiʿrani (Tehran: Islamiyya Press, 2002), vol. 2, 257–8. For the whole passage, see the Appendix, section 7.
11. For a detailed description of the architectural features of the tomb, see Blair, 'Monumentality under the Mongols', 113–22.
12. Other possible functions of the sublime dome are discussed in Chapter 5.

13. On the story of the construction of the tomb of Sultaniyya as a place for the bodies of Imam ʿAli and Imam Husayn, see Andre Godard, 'The Mausoleum of Öljeitü at Sulṭāniya', in *A Survey of Persian Art from Prehistoric Times to the Present*, ed. Arthur Pope, Phyllis Ackerman and Theodore Besterman (London; New York: Oxford University Press, 1938), 1,111–13, Blair, 'Monumentality under the Mongols', 126, and Chapter 5, n. 109.
14. Blair, 'Monumentality under the Mongols', 117.
15. Ibid., 119.
16. For further discussion on the methodological problems of historical archaeology, see the Introduction.
17. Ganjavi, 'Kāvush-i Tappih Nur'.
18. Hushang Sobuti, *Miʿmārī-yi Sultaniyya dar Guzar-gāh-i Hunar* [The Architecture of the Dome of Sultaniyya] (Tehran: Pazinih Press, 2001), 32–6.
19. This area is locally called *Jumʿih-masjid*, which is the same as *masjid-i Jumʿih*, or congregational mosque. In the Turkish language spoken in the north-west of Iran, unlike in Persian, the adjective precedes the noun.
20. Only a very small part of the results of the excavations undertaken within the citadel has been published in ʿAli-ʿAsghar Mirfattah, 'Sultaniyya [Sultaniyya]', *Mīrāth-i Farhangī* 13 (1995): 14–25.
21. ʿAsgarian, Muhammadi and Qasemi, *Gamānih-zanī dar Qismatī az Ḥarīm-i Tārīkhī-yi Shahr-i Ghadīm-i Sultaniyya*. The report has not been published. A copy is available at the local archive of the Iran Cultural Heritage, Handicrafts, and Tourism Organization (ICHTO) located at the World Heritage Site of Sultaniyya.
22. Muhajerinejad, *Faṣl-i Avval-i Kāvush-i Muḥavvata-yi Jumʿih-masjid*; Muhajerinejad, *Guzārish-i Gamānih-zanī*. The report has not been published, but a copy is available at the local archive of ICHTO.
23. Blair, 'Mongol Capital of Sulṭāniyya', 139–51.
24. Kashani, *Tārīkh-i Öljeytü*, 45–8.
25. Hafiz-i Abru, *Dhayl-i Jāmiʿ al-Tawārīkh-i Rashīdī*, 67–8.
26. Wassaf al-Hazra and Ayati, *Taḥrīr-i Tārīkh-i Wassaf*, 277.
27. Kashani writes that the walls of the citadel were built of blue stone (*sang-i mīnā rang*). See Kashani, *Tārīkh-i Öljeytü*, 46.
28. Mirfattah, 'Sultaniyya', 16–22.
29. Hafiz-i Abru, *Dhayl-i Jāmiʿ al-Tawārīkh-i Rashīdī*, 169.
30. Marco Brambilla, 'The Mausoleum of Oljeitu and the Citadel of Sultaniyya', in *Iran After the Mongols*, ed. Sussan Babaei (London: I. B. Tauris, 2019), 133.

31. This interpretation was proposed by Mifattah in the unpublished report of the excavation undertaken in Sultaniyya in 2002. Further excavation is needed to verify this analysis.
32. Flandin and Coste's drawings of Öljeytü's tomb (made in 1851 and 1867) depict the ruins of a wall attached to the east side the tomb. Traces of a partially ruined building with collapsed arches are also visible in Dubeux's view of the tomb (made in 1841). For the original drawings, see Eugène Flandin and Pascal-Xavier Coste, *Voyage en Perse* [Journey to Persia] (Paris: Gide et Jules Baudry, 1851); Pascal-Xavier Coste, *Monuments Modernes de la Perse mesurés, dessinés et décrits* [Modern Monuments of Persia Measured, Drawn and Described] (Paris: A. Morel, 1867); M. Louis Dubeux, *La Perse* [Persia] (Paris: Firmin Didot Frères. 1841).
33. The tile is preserved at the archive of ICHTO in Zanjan. Unfortunately, I could not get permission to see it.
34. Mirfattah, 'Sultaniyya', 21.
35. 'Ali-ʿAsghar Mirfattah, *Faṣl -i Chāhārdahum-i Kāvush-i Shahr-i Ghadīm-i Sultaniyya* [The Fourteenth Season of Archaeological Excavation in the Historical City of Sultaniyya], 2002. The report has not been published, but a copy is available at the local archive of ICHTO.
36. The challenges faced by scholars in the interpretation of historical paintings have been discussed in the Introduction. For further discussion on the methodological problems, for instance, see Kathryn Ebel, 'Representations of the Frontier in Ottoman Town Views of the Sixteenth Century', *Imago Mundi* 60, no. 1 (2008): 1–22; Gülru Necipoğlu, 'Plans and Models in 15th- and 16th-Century Ottoman Architectural Practice', *Journal of the Society of Architectural Historians* 45, no. 3 (1986): 224–43.
37. Kashani, *Tārīkh-i Öljeytü*, 122, 136.
38. Blair, 'Mongol Capital of Sulṭāniyya', 146.
39. Hafiz-i Abru, *Dhayl-i Jāmiʿ al-Tawārīkh-i Rashīdī*, 68.
40. For city views in Ottoman manuscripts, see Ebel, 'Representations of the Frontier'.
41. Mustawfi, *Nuzhat al-Qulūb*, 97 (for the whole passage, see the Appendix, section 9). Mustawfi uses *gām* (pace) as the unit of length for the perimeter of the citadel and the city. However, Hafiz-i Abru and the later Timurid historians (Mirkhwand and Khwandmir) use *gaz*. According to Blair (Blair, 'Mongol Capital of Sulṭāniyya', 143), the *gaz* used by Hafiz-i Abru is equal to 42 cm. The citadel measures 295 by 315 m. If we consider the citadel as a square (as the

contemporary texts describe it), the average length of each of the walls will be 305 m, which yields a value of 61 cm for the *gām*. Since Hafiz-i Abru's *gaz* is different from Mustawfi's *gām*, one might suggest that Hafiz-i Abru simply copied the figures from Mustawfi but reported them in a different unit of length. See als Wilber, *Architecture of Islamic Iran*, 44–5.

42. Kashani, *Tārīkh-i Öljeytü*, *passim*.
43. Adam Olearius, *The Voyages and Travells of the Ambassadors Sent by Frederick Duke of Holstein, to the Great Duke of Muscovy, and the king of Persia: Begun in the year M.DC. XXXIII and finish'd in M.DC. XXXIX: Containing a compleat history of Muscovy, Tartary, Persia, and other adjacent countries: With several publick transactions reaching neer the present times: In VII books* (London: publisher not identified, 1669), 186.
44. James Morier, *A Journey through Persia, Armenia, and Asia Minor, to Constantinople, in the Years 1808 and 1809: In which is included, some account of the proceedings of his majesty's mission, under sir Harford Jones, Bart. K.C. to the court of the king of Persia* (London: publisher not identified, 1812), 257–9.
45. Kashani, *Tārīkh-i Öljeytü*, 46; Mustawfi, *Nuzhat al-Qulūb*, 97; Hafiz-i Abru, *Dhayl-i Jāmiʿ al-Tawārīkh-i Rashīdī*, 67–8.
46. *Zāwīya* is a small religious school or monastery where a Sufi shaykh dwelt with his students.
47. Kashani, *Tārīkh-i Öljeytü*, 46–7.
48. In the annotations of the *Dhayl-i Jāmiʿ al-Tawārīkh-i Rashīdī*, Khanbaba Bayani refers to a manuscript of the *Tārīkh-i Öljeytü* in the Bibliothèque Nationale de France in which Sultaniyya is mentioned as the location of Firdaws workshop. In this copy, Kashani writes that 'Khwajih ʿAli Shah organised a splendid feast for the sultan in the workshop of Sultaniyya which was known as *kārkhānih-yi Firdaws*' (Hafiz-i Abru, *Dhayl-i Jāmiʿ al-Tawārīkh-i Rashīdī*, 97, n. 1). However, in another manuscript of the *Tārīkh-i Öljeytü* in the library of Ayasofya in Istanbul, Kashani says that the vizier Saʿd al-Din designated Khwajih ʿAli Shah as the supervisor of *kārkhānih-yi Firdaws* in Baghdad in order to banish him from the royal camp (Kashani, *Tārīkh-i Öljeytü*, 121). Wassaf also tells us that *kārkhānih-yi Firdaws* was one of the constructions built by Taj al-Din ʿAli Shah in Baghdad. He reports that the construction of the workshop in Baghdad was finished in thirteen days, and that the decoration of the building took fewer than forty days to complete. At the opening ceremony of the workshop, ʿAli Shah presented *kārkhānih-yi Firdaws*, Ghiyathiyya School, Shatiyya palaces and *madrasa-yi sayyāra*, along with several precious gifts, to the sultan,

his wives and his commanders (Wassaf al-Hazra and Ayati, *Taḥrīr-i Tārīkh-i Wassaf*, 304).

49. Hushang Sobuti, *Banā-hā-yi Ārām-gāhī-yi Ustān-i Zanjan* [The Shrines of Zanjan Province], Zanjan: Zangan Press, 1998, 54.
50. Wassaf al-Hazra and Ayati, *Taḥrīr-i Tārīkh-i Wassaf*, 304.
51. Hafiz-i Abru, *Dhayl-i Jāmiʿ al-Tawārīkh-i Rashīdī*, 68.
52. Amuli, *Nafāyis al-Funūn*, vol. 2, 258.
53. Muhajerinejad, *Faṣl-i Avval-i Kāvush-i Muḥavvata-yi Jumʿih-masjid*, 11–14.
54. Outside the public cemetery, on the surrounding mounds and hills, there are a few tombs with a distinct appearance that must have been related to the high-ranking Mongols. The particular burial method applied in these graves suggests the association of the buried person with Central Asian religions such as shamanism. See Muhajerinejad, *Faṣl-i Avval-i Kāvush-i Muḥavvata-yi Jumʿih-masjid*, 405.
55. Flint (*sang-i chakhmāq*) is a raw material for pottery production. It is one of the ingredients with which the coating (*laʿāb*) is made.
56. Mirfattah, 'Sultaniyya', 23.
57. In Sultaniyya the direction of the *qiblih* has deviated 29° from the north–south axis, facing the south-west.
58. Mirfattah, 'Sultaniyya', 24.
59. Amuli, *Nafāyis al-Funūn*, vol. 2, 258.
60. Hafiz-i Abru, *Dhayl-i Jāmiʿ al-Tawārīkh-i Rashīdī*, 68.
61. Ibid., 282. The characteristic elements of the physical structure of Sultaniyya mentioned by historical texts correspond not only to the archaeological remains unearthed during the excavation but also to the traditional definition of the Islamic city: 'A city must have a congregational Friday mosque and it must have a market/chief bazaar nearby'. See William Marçais, 'L'Islamisme et la Vie Urbaine [Islamism and Urban Life]', *L'Académie des Inscriptions et Belles-Lêttres, Comptes Rendus* (1928): 86–100, cited in Abu-Lughod, 'Islamic City', 156.
62. Fedot Katof, *Safar-nāmih-yi Fedot Katof* [The Travel Account of Fedot Katof], trans. Muhammad S. Homayunfard (Tehran: Kitāb-Khānih-yi Milliī-yi Iran, 1977), 57–8.
63. Mirfattah, 'Sultaniyya', 22.
64. Ganjavi, 'Kāvush-i Tappih Nur', 163–96; Muhajerinejad, *Guzārish-i Gamānih-zanī*.
65. Marco Brambilla, 'Tepe Nur: An Īlkhānid Monument in Sulṭāniyya', University of Pennsylvania, https://www.sas.upenn.edu/ancient/masons/abstracts/Agudo/M-Brambilla.html (last accessed 21 August 2023).

66. Ibid.
67. Clavijo, *Embassy to Tamerlane*, 162.
68. Hafiz-i Abru, *Dhayl-i Jāmiʿ al-Tawārīkh-i Rashīdī*, 190.
69. Wilber, *Architecture of Islamic Iran*, 26–7.
70. Clavijo, *Embassy to Tamerlane*, 158.
71. Ibid., 161.
72. Hafiz-i Abru, *Dhayl-i Jāmiʿ al-Tawārīkh-i Rashīdī*, 67. For the whole passage, see the Appendix, section 8.
73. Ibid., 67–8.
74. For further discussion on the location of Sultaniyya, see Rezvan and Karimian, *Sultaniyya: Ẓuhūr va Suqūṭ-i Yik Pāytakht*, 85–7.
75. In the *Zubdat al-Tawārīkh*, Hafiz-i Abru uses the term '*quruq-i Sulṭaniyya*'. See Hafiz-i Abru, *Zubdat al-Tawārīkh* [Cream of Histories], ed. Seyed Kamal al-Din Hajseyed Javadi (Tehran: Vizārat-i Farhang va Irshād-i Islāmī, 2001), vol. 3, 41. However, to the best of my knowledge, none of the contemporary historians of the reign of Öljeytü refers to Sultaniyya as a '*quruq*'.
76. Gianroberto Scarcia, 'The "Vihār" of Qonqor-olong: Preliminary Report', *East and West* 25, no. 1/2 (1975): 99.
77. Rashid al-Din, Roshan and Musavi, *Jāmiʿ al-Tawārīkh*, vol. 2, 1179. In addition, Blair raises the possibility that the name of the nearby village, 'Viar', might be associated with the word *vihara*, which is a Sanskrit term for a Buddhist monastery. See Blair, 'Monumentality under the Mongols', 146.
78. Rashid al-Din, *Jāmiʿ al-Tawārīkh*, vol. 2, 1,356–7.

5

Theorising Transcultural Interactions in the Context of Ilkhanid Cities

In earlier scholarship the Mongols were often introduced as barbarian hordes whose extensive campaigns across the continent caused nothing but bloodshed.[1] In the course of time, they were acknowledged as people who facilitated commerce and communication through the creation of a *pax* and through stabilising social, cultural and economic life throughout Eurasia. Uncovering the role of the nomads as cultural mediators, more recent studies, published in the last decade of the twentieth century and the first decades of the twenty-first, have explored 'Mongol agency' in the circulation of artistic forms and styles. Focusing on chinoiserie in Iranian art in the thirteenth and fourteenth centuries, these studies highlight the active role of the Mongols in the adoption, adaptation and/or rejection of Chinese elements in the visual context of Iran and Central Asia.[2] This book nonetheless challenges the idea that the Mongols were 'agents not donors'[3] who merely facilitated the arrival of foreign forms and concepts in Ilkhanid Iran. Rather, it looks for the nomadic traditions and thoughts injected by the Mongols into Iranian urban architecture.[4] Recognising these imported traits might not be easy since, as will be discussed shortly, the merging of foreign and local modes usually happens in those realms where there is more resemblance or commonality. The receiving culture would be receptive to the new items if it could identify them with something already familiar from previous experience.[5] Therefore, the nomadic concepts could have been hidden in the guise of pre-existing similar Islamic/Iranian notions.

The goal of the present research is to uncover the material and conceptual elements of Ilkhanid urban architecture which were borrowed from the

Mongol culture. This goal was set because of a generally accepted thought (particularly held by Iranian scholars) that acknowledges to a large degree (if not exclusively) the role of the society of the Muslim Iranians in the development of different aspects of art and culture under the Ilkhanate.[6] These scholars, of course, admit the encounter of the two great civilisations of Iran and China that resulted in Chinese elements extensively occurring in Iranian art. However, in the context of the Ilkhanid court, they believe that the Mongol rulers of Iran, particularly Muslim Ilkhans, were mesmerised by the splendour of Persian art and the richness of Islam. It is undeniable that the art and culture that flourished during the post-conquest period were largely dependent upon the Islamic teachings absorbed by newly converted Ilkhans on the one hand, and the stylistic and technical achievements of the Iranians in different areas of art and science on the other. Nevertheless, while confirming the importance of the culturally and artistically fertile environment of Iran in the formation of Ilkhanid art and architecture, the previous chapters of this book have looked for the non-Islamic/non-Iranian notions brought in by the Mongol conquerors, which are apart from the motifs and themes generally represented under the umbrella of chinoiserie.

Chinoiserie, and its 'translation' in Persianate visual culture, *khitā'ī*,[7] deal with the occurrence of Chinese motifs and styles in an Iranian context, whereas this study intends to describe the circumstance that caused the emergence of the Mongol concepts (not merely their visual elements) in Ilkhanid urban architecture. It looks at the interaction between the nomadic selfhood of Mongol khans and the established sedentary identity of Muslim sultans or Iranian padishahs, a negotiation which has often been reflected in the architectural projects patronised by the Ilkhans. Building on my previous findings regarding the items transported to Ilkhanid Iran and the agents and mechanism through which they were introduced to the conquered culture, I aim to theorise such intercultural contacts in this chapter.

As a prelude to the discussion, two points need to be clarified here. First, the question of the encounter between the Iranians and the Mongols can be addressed beyond the notion of the encounter between the settled culture and the steppe life. The Ilkhans had passed the stage of nomadic life and established their royal authority in the form of a legitimate dynasty. In sedentary societies, as a rule, the sedentary culture and the traditions of a given dynasty are always learnt and followed by the ruling group of their subsequent dynasty.[8] Therefore, within the scope of our discussion, the adoption of Islamic/Iranian culture by the Mongol conquerors can be conceived in connection with the rule of learning. In the study of Iranian–Mongol relations, if we accept that the Mongols naturally learnt what the sedentary world offered them, we will be able to distance ourselves from the assumption that the process of cultural adoption happened only because of the exceptional assets and traits of the sedentary culture of Iran.

Second, it must be noted that in the study of cultural exchange in Ilkhanid Iran we usually deal with some distinct groups in the society, such as the ruling class or members of the elite who have a bold presence in the literary sources. These groups, as primary patrons of art and architecture, with whom most of the remaining material culture is associated, form our main, and sometimes only, focus of attention. As we saw in the case of Sultaniyya, although conducting archaeological excavations in the residential areas of the cities improves our understanding of the social life of non-elite groups, it is barely enlightening about the quality of their intercultural encounters with foreigners due to the scarcity of evidence. On the other hand, apart from the Ilkhans and the Mongol princes and amirs, we lack a balanced account of the society of the Mongol invaders and their traditional culture. Our data are largely confined to the general description of their rituals in their homeland mainly prior to the campaigns in the thirteenth century,[9] while we are still quite uninformed about the nature of religious and cultural practices among the lower classes of the Mongols in Iran. They were present in the conquered lands, including Iran, and lived beside the local population, who had a different religion, nationality and ethnicity, but are narrowly mentioned in the historical texts. That said, our rather one-dimensional comprehension of Iranian-Mongol society hardly imposes a restriction on the art-historical studies of the period because, apart from providing the labour, the masses did not play a significant role in the production of high art and architecture, and the extant artefacts and monuments barely represent the sociocultural attributes of this group. Our limited knowledge of the culture of ordinary people in Ilkhanid Iran, however, can be problematic when the notion of Iranian–Mongol encounters is examined from an anthropological point of view.[10]

Intercultural Contact and the Complexity of the Terminology

The study of intercultural contact is a broad discipline that includes analysis of a wide range of communication processes across different groups of people from disparate cultural backgrounds, both in modern and pre-modern societies. In the twentieth century, a variety of terms were created in order to explain different aspects of these complex cultural phenomena. Various branches of this discipline (intercultural contact studies) address different forms of encounter that vary in process or outcome. For example, syncretism deals with one type of intercultural contact during which certain forms are transmitted from one culture to the other, while the other forms fall away. The factor of resemblance determines the cultural traits that are adopted in new cultural contexts and are retained there, although in a different form. Syncretism rejects the mere coexistence of different cultural forms as the only result of intercultural encounters and suggests alternative concepts such as adaptation and assimilation. Bricolage is another concept explaining many forms of cultural borrowings in which various traits are combined in novel, and sometimes arbitrary, ways so that the product would be a new whole. The element of 'unmotivated combinations' in bricolage differentiates it from syncretism.[11] Cultural creolisation describes the interaction between two or more cultures in which participants select particular elements, reject others, and create new possibilities that supersede parent/prior cultures.[12] Hybridity predominated for a while in intercultural analyses, mostly because of the cross-disciplinary nature of this concept. In Bhabha's view, hybridity is defined not as the mere combination of two original concepts from which the third emerges, but as the 'third space', which enables other positions to emerge. The product of the process of cultural hybridity would be something different, new and unrecognisable to the participants.[13]

Acculturation is another important type of intercultural contact, referring to changes that take place in individuals as a result of communication with culturally dissimilar people. What differentiates acculturation from similar processes is that it looks at the people who live in countries other than those in which they were born. In the acculturation process, we deal with two opposing concepts: retention of the heritage culture on the one hand and acquisition of the receiving culture on the other. The retention/discarding of the former and the adoption/rejection of the latter can happen to varying degrees, and the outcome, of course, would be different in each case. Among various results, two concepts seem to be more relevant to our discussion: assimilation and enculturation. Assimilation describes a situation in which the practices and values of the receiving culture are adopted while those of the heritage culture are discarded. Enculturation refers to a process in which some elements of both heritage culture and receiving culture are retained or obtained selectively.[14] Acculturation could happen in related but somewhat independent domains or dimensions of cultural practices, values and identifications, and therefore it might not be a singular process that occurs at a single pace.[15] To obtain a comprehensive perception of the process, the three constructs often need to be considered together.

In modern societies, immigrants and refugees are the main targets of acculturation research.[16] Within the scope of the present study, in the medieval society of Ilkhanid Iran, the target group seemed to be slightly different. The Mongols who conquered Iran and gradually settled in their new territory are comparable to the modern immigrants who are settled in their new homeland. In the case of the Mongol conquerors of Iran, who imposed several decades of widespread bloodshed on the Iranians, another factor articulated as the 'unfavourable context of reception'[17] affects the acculturation process. However, it is noteworthy that contexts of reception change over time. The reaction of the Iranians to the Mongol occupiers in the early Ilkhanid period, while they still had a vivid memory of their violence, must have been different from what they felt about the Mongols during the reign of the later Muslim Ilkhans.[18]

Our understanding of acculturation processes is largely dependent on knowing the context in which the interactions occur. This context is formed from the characteristics of the newcomers as well as their hosts, and the religious, socio-political and cultural status of their countries of origin as well as the circumstances of the country in which they settle. The previous chapters of the book have provided different segments of this context, on the basis of which the acculturation process itself will be analysed here. In other words, as Allsen has observed, in order to determine the character, pace and extent of acculturation, different aspects of the societies involved should be scrutinised, both before and after contact. As a result, a cultural 'baseline' would be established against which the assimilation or enculturation process can be measured.[19] It should be noted that there are some other factors affecting the quality and extent of acculturation in the course of contact. An important example of these factors are the agents through whom the circulation and transformation of cultural notions happened. The agents could intervene in these processes and, while having their own political, religious or aesthetic motivations, determine which elements of the heritage culture have priority over others to enter the receiving culture. I will expand on the role of cultural transmission agents shortly.

All the above-mentioned forms of intercultural contact seem to share one common characteristic in their outcome, which is the concept of 'newness'. This notion describes a product, which is not part of the sequence of past and present, but a new element renewing and refiguring the past.[20] In view of this fact, in the process of translation and negotiation of cultural identities, the new identity is constructed not on the basis of the continuities of the nationalist tradition, but according to the national notions translated into foreign forms of culture.[21]

With a more comprehensive understanding of the diverse encounters between different cultures, we can now engage in theorising them. Given the nature of intercultural contact in Ilkhanid Iran and the involved groups, two sets of theories appear to hold particular relevance to our discussion, with a greater focus on the latter: postcolonial theories and the theory of translation.

Postcolonial Theories

Study of theories of colonial discourses would pave the way for a better understanding of postcolonialism. Colonialism addresses the issue of the settlement of one group of people in a new location, usually with the purpose of governing the indigenous inhabitants and exploiting or developing their resources.[22] Colonialism, however, does not concern itself exclusively with the problem of possessing land, but involves the more serious issue of 'colonizing mind and imagination', which is primarily achieved by spreading the dominant languages of power.[23] Postcolonialism, on the other hand, does not describe a new historical era following colonialism, which lacks every sign of the grievous colonial past. Rather, it challenges colonial ways of knowing that are still circulating.[24] Postcolonial theories address the impact of the long periods of forced dependency and hegemony not only on the societies of the colonised but also on those of the colonisers, and examine the hybrid and novel forms of culture that develop during the process of colonialism. These theories go beyond the traditional binary opposition of coloniser versus colonised and define a third concept, hybridity, which is not confined to the simple combination of the two separate cultural forms.[25]

In order to apply postcolonialism in our art/architectural history studies, we should be aware of its defects. This theoretical approach is often criticised because of its inclination, in Liebmann's words, to homogenise colonial encounters while different colonised societies around the world have experienced different forms of colonialism. Postcolonialism is accused of representing the perspectives of European colonisers while its concepts and theories are formed in American universities, rather than that of colonised peoples. Critics claim that postcolonialist scholars ignore the economic and social realities of the societies that are still dealing with the legacy of colonialism. Since the study of material culture shapes an important part of archaeology and architectural research, it can provide a historical and material basis for postcolonial analyses, and thus partly compensates for postcolonialists' ignorance concerning the material aspects of colonialism.[26]

The concept of intercultural contact could be discussed in relation to postcolonial theories, since the theories 'sought to theorise the limits and nature of cultural translation' and develop a set of ideas about the emergence of new cultural forms and practices as the product of circulation, appropriation and translation.[27] Postcolonial theorists who deal with contemporary issues of cross-cultural interaction often focus on some specific areas of the problem (such as defending the rights of the colonised people who have been limited politically and culturally) which are not necessarily the concern of scholarship addressing the pre-modern world. Although the literature on postcolonialism may not provide a methodology that is directly applicable to pre-modern cultures, it has produced a rich interpretive vocabulary, which can also be used to evaluate the cultural impact of dominant power in the ancient and medieval worlds.[28]

Since postcolonial theories deal with the interaction between imperial and indigenous cultures or between coloniser and colonised, they form a component of the conceptual framework of the present book, which aims to analyse the formation of new hybrid identities as the result of the interface between the Mongols as the dominant military power and the Iranians as the subordinate nation. Furthermore, a substantial part of the discourses on postcolonialism explores the ways through which the colonial powers justified their domination and perpetuated their subjugation in the colonised lands. In this regard, these theories would be applicable to our discussion of the nature of the presence of the Mongols in Iran, since, as in many familiar cases of forced colonisation, the Mongols were unwelcome newcomers who initially imposed their presence on the Iranians.[29]

Theory of Translation

The concept of the transportation and translation of culture forms the basis for this research because of the rich history of cultural interactions under the Ilkhanids. The approach adopted here is close in spirit to the theories that extend the notion of translation beyond language to visual and cultural fields. Bhabha considers translation as a way of imitating. In his view, in this process an original is imitated. However, without the priority of the original being emphasised, it can be simulated, copied, transferred and transformed.[30] Acknowledging the global circulation of culture at all times, Akcan defines translation as processes of transformation that happen during the act of movement of people, ideas, objects, technology, information and images among different geographical regions. Akcan's translation method consists of two pivotal elements: items of transportation, including the things that circulate; and channels of transportation including the agents and institutions through which circulation, transformation and, eventually, translation take place.[31] Apart from the complexity of the act of transportation, the same, if not a greater, extent of sophistication is expected in the process of translation in the destination or the 'contact zone'. In this regard, Akcan coins the terms 'appropriating' translation and 'foreignizing' translation, which represent the two ends of a spectrum. The former describes the tendency to absorb foreign ideas and artefacts into the local norms, and the latter refers to the tendency to reveal the differences between domestic and foreign ideas.[32]

Flood considers the notion of translation in relation to different fields of cultural production and defines it as 'both an explanatory metaphor and a dynamic practice through which the circulation, mediation, reception and transformation of distinct cultural forms and practices is effected'.[33] In Flood's view, when different cultures seek to communicate, they need some facilitators that help them to bridge the gap. Appropriation, translation and re-historicisation of cultural signs and their associated meanings are some of the modes of facilitating the communication.[34] When multiple cultures come together, they exchange various cultural elements. As a result of the exchange, the cultural items undergo varying degrees of modification in order to suit the taste and sensibilities of the culture of adoption. This process of encounter and transformation contributes to the emergence of new syntheses or new hybrid identities.

In the process of cultural translation, we are not always dealing with homogeneous original forms and practices transferred from one zone to the other. For instance, under Mongol rule in the thirteenth and fourteenth centuries, due to the multi-directional encounters between different nations and ethnic groups, hybrid motifs and ideas came into being from 'parent' notions which themselves might have been the product of other cultural syntheses; hence those were heterogeneous in nature. Considering the complexity of the process and the multiplicity of the participants, it could be challenging to trace the sources of all the contributors. Locating these origins would be even more problematic in the areas known as 'contact zones', such as Ilkhanid Iran, that witnessed the most complicated forms of cultural exchanges. While transcultural communications affected different regions of the continent during the post-conquest era, some sectors seem to have experienced a higher density of interactions due to their geopolitical circumstances.[35] These regions, best described as 'contact zones', are articulated, in Pratt's words, as 'social spaces where cultures meet, clash and grapple with each other, often in contexts of highly asymmetrical relations of power, such as colonialism and slavery'.[36]

Part of the Chinese ideas, motifs and designs in art and architecture that arrived in Ilkhanid Iran had already been filtered through the Mongols' aesthetic taste and their perceptions of imperial art and architecture in Yuan China. This is particularly the case for those concepts that were associated with the Khaqan himself and his sovereignty over the state: for instance, the visual elements that symbolised royal power. In other words, the Mongols hand-picked their visual vocabulary on the basis of pre-established Chinese imperial language in art and architecture. This claim means that part of this vocabulary that reached Ilkhanid Iran was adopted by the Ilkhans not specifically as Chinese visual material, but as a set of elements that had already been employed by their superiors in the Yuan dynasty in order to exhibit their royal identity as the emperors of China. Cloud patterns, for example, symbolise auspicious good fortune and immortality in Chinese conventions.[37] Kadoi, however, suggests that cloud patterns used in the tile-work of Takht-i Sulayman possibly did not hold any particular symbolic meaning. She associates their usage with either imperial images of Yuan China or the personal taste of the Ilkhans. Sometimes, as in the case of cloud patterns, motifs, objects or architectural forms themselves do not change during transportation, but their meanings can change in their new cultural context. This process is also defined by Akcan as translation.[38]

To add further complexity to the process, we must consider the movement of armies, merchants, travellers, missionaries and, more importantly, craftsmen carrying goods and subsequently various cultural traditions across Eurasia in the first half of the thirteenth century. Large colonies of artisans and their families were captured by the Mongols in northern China and the eastern Iranian world and resettled in the cities of Mongolia and Central Asia.[39] The objects, more particularly precious textiles, produced in the workshops of these cities denote the combination of a wide variety of designs, styles and techniques brought in by the craftsmen from their homelands, and the local themes. In the second half of the thirteenth century, several groups of craftsmen from Central Asia and Mongolia were resettled again in northern China.[40] As a result, luxury textiles woven in northern China in the Mongol period carried the visual vocabulary of Iran, Mongolia, Central Asia and China. The textiles' imagery gradually spread to other mediums, and therefore the same bewildering variety of motifs appeared in different forms of art objects and architectural decorations.

The lengthy and complex process of the circulation of artists and artisans across the vast territories of the Mongols raises the possibility that the eastern and western sectors of the Mongol empire could have shared some common visual traditions through the thirteenth and fourteenth centuries. Therefore, what was perceived by the Yuan dynasty as Chinese imperial art, and appeared in the artistic and architectural projects patronised by the Khaqans in China, might have included some patterns and designs that had already been injected into Chinese visual culture through communication with Western and Central Asian craftsmen in the earlier decades of the thirteenth century.

Part of the Yuan visual vocabulary was absorbed by the Khaqans' cousins in Iran, as is perfectly exemplified by tile works of Takht-i Sulayman.[41] While these exotic motifs are usually deemed to be Chinese-inspired,[42] one can suggest that they might have derived from models that had been current in the eastern Iranian world or Central Asia but were transferred to China by captured artisans, and were gradually attached to the main body of Chinese art. This issue, however, is sometimes overlooked by those scholars who attribute the appearance of non-Iranian elements in Ilkhanid art, more specifically dragons and phoenixes, only to the penetration of Chinese and Mongol visual culture into the artistic traditions of Iran and omit the previous phases of the long journey of the motifs.[43] These studies consider the tile works of Takht-i Sulayman as representing the first appearance of these imperial motifs in Iran, whereas the design could have had its origins in similar motifs that had already existed in the Persian visual vocabulary but were somehow transferred eastwards; for example, the phoenix resembles the *sīmurgh*, the mythical bird in Iranian mythology and literature. As in other examples, one can mention the fashion for dragon decoration in early thirteenth-century Islamic architecture, and more particularly in the architectural decoration in the Jazira, or the dragon theme that developed in Anatolian Seljuq art, although neither of these cases resembled the style or meaning of Chinese dragons.[44]

A fragment of a *kesi* (silk tapestry), woven in Central Asia in the thirteenth century or earlier, represents an interesting example supporting this point (Figure 5.1). The tapestry is designed with dragons chasing flaming pearls among clouds. The design is different from the pattern of animals and birds that was common in the decorative art of eastern Central Asia before the Mongol conquest.[45] The design of dragons on the tapestry shows the influence of a new foreign tradition upon the Central Asian native style. The dense arrangement of the dragons reveals some similarities to another *kesi*, also originating from Central Asia, which exhibits strong Persian elements (Figure 5.2). The common features of the two cases are more noticeable than the similarities between the former and the tapestries attributed to the eastern Central Asian tradition.[46] This tapestry is a good example of the appearance of dragons in a non-Chinese context before the Mongol period, and suggests that the Mongols had possibly met these motifs long before conquering China and being influenced by Chinese visual language in the late thirteenth century.[47]

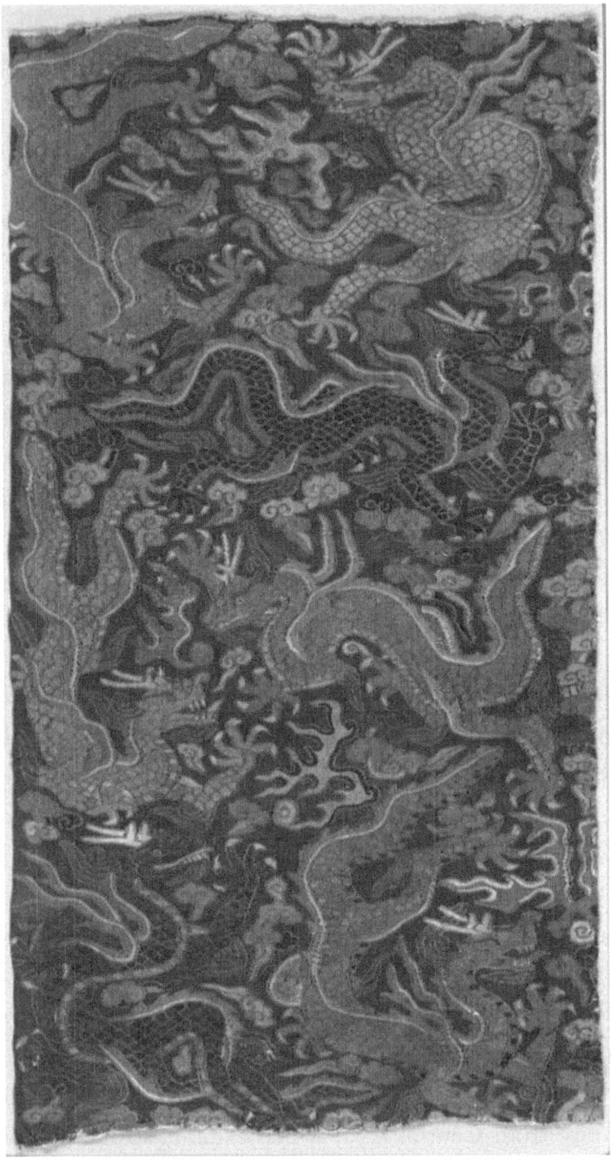

Figure 5.1 *Dragons Chasing Flaming Pearls.*
1200s or earlier
Central China
Tapestry, silk and gold thread
Overall: 60 × 32 cm (23⅝ × 12⅝ in.)
Andrew R. and Martha Holden Jennings Fund 1988.33
Courtesy of the Cleveland Museum of Art

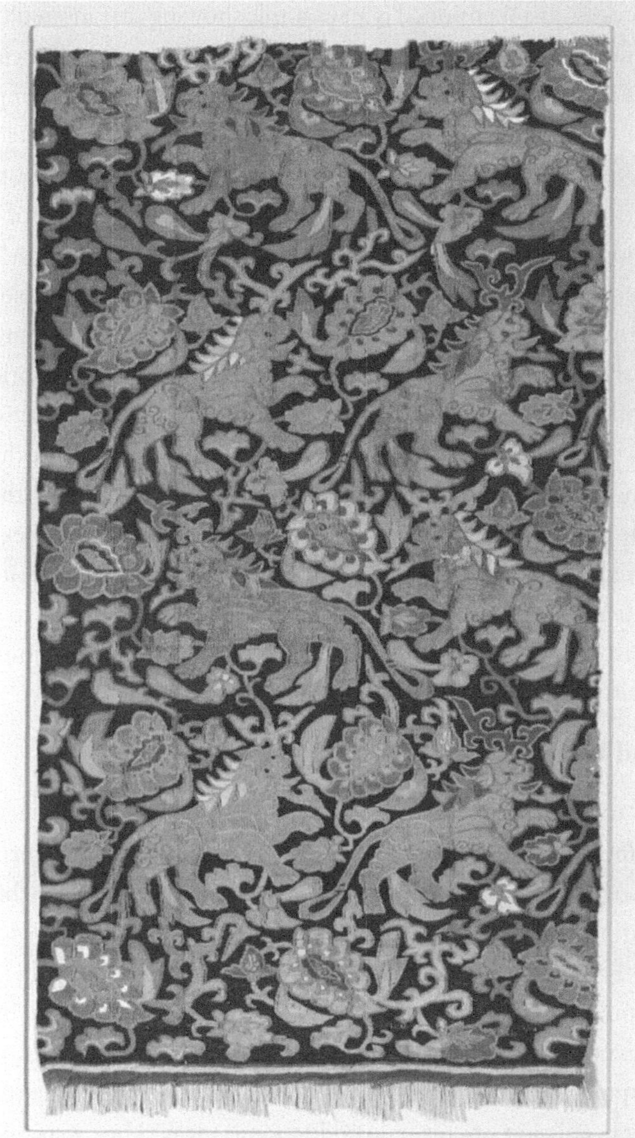

Figure 5.2 *Tapestry with Golden Lions and Palmettes.*
1200s or earlier
Central Asia
Silk, gold thread; tapestry weave
Overall: 63.5 × 34.7 cm (25 × 13 11/16 in.); Mounted: 73.7 × 45.7 cm (29 × 18 in.)
Purchase from the J. H. Wade Fund 1991.3
Courtesy of the Cleveland Museum of Art

The process just mentioned is an example showing that intercultural contacts were not confined to linear interactions between nations. The circulation of material culture across the medieval world was not always as simple as the movement of objects eastwards or westwards. Intercultural contacts could occur in several simultaneous interrelated processes between two or more cultures, and thus it would be challenging to uncover the provenance of the items of circulation or their transmission direction. In this regard the term 'transculturation' is suggested, which represents, according to Flood, a complex process of transformation that develops through extended contact between cultures. Transculturation emphasises that cultural forms are already hybrid and in process, and that cultural exchange could happen in multiple directions. This fact means that 'translation is a dynamic activity that takes place both between and within cultural codes, forms and practices'.[48] Understanding this equips us with the appropriate means to approach the Ilkhanid era and explain the multi-layered dialogues that gave rise to the distinctive art and architecture of this period. Yet, prior to delving into the dialogues, it is essential to elucidate a specific aspect concerning the agents through whom the communications were constituted across post-conquest Eurasia.

Active and Passive Agents of Transportation

Referring to Akcan's translation method, in relation to the network of ideas, themes, motifs and techniques circulated throughout the territory of the Mongols, we are faced with two major issues: items, and channels of transportation. Travel, broadly defined, is one of the major channels of transportation. Following the conquest, different categories of nomadic and sedentary populations including artists, artisans, scholars, travellers, merchants and envoys, who moved across various cultural zones of Eurasia, regardless of the purpose of their journeys, played a substantial role in the transportation and transmission of cultural products and ideas. They were agents who contributed, to varying degrees, to the establishment of the encounter and, subsequently, to the exchange between different groups. They acted not just as messengers, but rather as mediators who became involved in the circulation of signs, concepts and systems. Their views, taste and priorities were influential in determining what was borrowed from a foreign culture or was exchanged between two cultural domains.

The extent to which the agents facilitated this process varied somewhat. One factor via which the nature of their contribution can be evaluated is the level of their intervention in the process of circulation of cultural wares; either they actively observed and adopted the items or they merely (passively) carried them. To realise the difference, one can think of a spectrum with passiveness and activeness at each end. At one end of the spectrum, passive travellers are located who carried objects, patterns and concepts in their unchanged entities across culturally different regions. At the opposite end, active travellers are placed who not only hand-picked objects, patterns and concepts in their lands of origin, but also imposed high degrees of transformation on the items of transportation during their trip. To put it another way, while the transportation of objects and ideas took place through the movement of people anyway, the characteristics of the 'carriers', such as their aesthetic tastes, political and ethnic biases or religious tendencies, worked as filters through which only certain parts of concepts could pass, while undergoing different levels of change.[49]

An example may shed some light on this point. When compared to the other agents, artists and artisans appear to be positioned closer to the 'activeness' end of this spectrum. Those craftsmen, who travelled between various workshops in different regions, encountered local styles and techniques. They absorbed them first and injected their own native taste and knowledge into the visual and technical vocabulary of the regions next. The motifs and techniques transferred by these agents to their home towns were not mere foreign forms and ideas, but the concepts that had been already appropriated by the aesthetic taste and preferences of the artisans and therefore had been assimilated into the destination's visual culture. In addition to the craftsmen themselves, the albums of templates (pattern books) created by them and circulated among local workshops are also significant agents of dissemination of motifs and ideas, although in a more complex way. Persian potters' exposure to Chinese patterns under the Timurids is an interesting example in this regard. It is plausible that some certain groups of Persian potters were given the opportunity of visiting the court collections of Chinese porcelain. Hence, they were able to duplicate Chinese models from different periods and collect their patterns in their albums. The odd side of this imitation was that sometimes a single Persian vessel or a group of contemporary vessels displayed various Chinese patterns and styles from different periods, which have never existed in the bazaar at one time.[50] In other words, although the individual motifs were imitated from Chinese models, their combination was a novel arrangement created by Persian ceramicists. Consequently, making use of the albums of patterns which were not dependent on the factor of time, while it facilitated the transportation of motifs, might add more complexity to the adoption and adaptation of foreign styles.

Encounter and exchange, however, did not always happen between two different cultures. During the Ilkhanid period, in addition to the intercultural transportation of motifs, the availability of paper facilitated the transmission of patterns and designs within the Persian artistic vocabulary, but from one medium to another. Moreover, using paper allowed for a greater homogeneity in the arts since artisans make different works in different cities on the basis of designs on paper, not their memories of works.[51] Drawing on paper also played an important role in the dissemination of designs from Ilkhanid capitals to peripheral regions and in the creation of 'a unified imperial style' patronised by the court.[52]

On the basis of this information, we can infer that the adoption and adaptation of cultural forms and their associated meanings was not the spontaneous and inevitable outcome of the coexistence of Mongol conquerors and their Iranian subjects; rather, it arose from the intentional or unintentional involvement of multiple agents. As we have seen so far, the Ilkhans themselves also acted as conduits for foreign conventions to flow across the continent.[53] Their contributory role in cultural transmission must have been most evident in the areas in which they directly engaged, including their architectural endeavours. With this idea in mind, what will be offered next is a lengthy discussion of different elements of Mongol culture that were introduced at varying levels into Ilkhanid cities.

Dialogues

Tackling the formation of the Ilkhanate as a non-Iranian dynasty, we are presented with two levels of encounter that did not occur necessarily independently from one another. On the first level, the encounter happened between the Iranians' pre-established definitions of sovereignty and the Ilkhans' nomadic perceptions of rulership. On the second level, while the former remained unchanged, the latter was replaced with the Yuan political system consisting of both Mongol beliefs and Chinese values. The notion of kingship over this period was connected, although to varying degrees, with the definition of a Muslim sultan, a Persian padishah, a Mongol Khan and a Chinese emperor. In other words, when the Ilkhans ascended the throne, they fluctuated between four different realms of signs and meanings. In addition to politics, the visual language the Ilkhans used to communicate with their subjects, as well as with the outside world, borrowed many elements from Iranian, Chinese and Mongolian visual culture. Taking the cosmopolitanism fostered in Ilkhanid Iran into consideration, one would be able to uncover fusions of sedentary and nomadic elements spread across Ilkhanid art, architecture and urban planning.

Ilkhanid art, particularly paintings and decorative arts, and to a lesser degree architecture, is usually represented as a synthesis of manifold Eastern and Western ideas and themes. Putting more emphasis on Ilkhanid urban architecture, the present study seeks to uncover the interactions that underlie this syncretic fusion rather than focusing merely on the juxtaposition of various cultural elements. The preceding chapters of the book have proved that these interactions have taken place among individuals and have been manifested in their undertakings. Consequently, they can be delineated in three domains: a dialogue between Khans and sultans/padishahs; a dialogue between tents and buildings; and a dialogue between camps and cities. The first level of communication was previously addressed in the cases of Ghazan Khan and Öljeytü, where we discussed how the words and acts of the two Ilkhans convey an oscillation between being a Mongol Ilkhan and a Muslim sultan. In the following section, the other forms of communication will be contextualised in order to reveal the mechanism through which the negotiation happened.

The dialogue between tents and buildings

Ilkhanid architectural projects consisted of numerous structures financed by royals and notables in their capitals and major urban centres as well as by local officials in smaller cities and towns far from the centre. Within the scope of the present research, the focus is on the constructions of the first group, of which only a few have remained. Among these buildings, to the best of my knowledge, the tomb of Öljeytü is the sole foundation patronised by an Ilkhan himself that has survived in its entirety. The plausible function of the building as the eternal home of Öljeytü would transform it into a truthful representation of the Ilkhan's world view and his aesthetic taste while exhibiting the most remarkable stylistic and technical achievements of his time. As will be discussed at length in the following pages, the architectural design, ornaments and fittings of the building can be considered an arena in which the highest level of negotiation occurred between the Ilkhan's conceptions of his celestial abode, based on his nomadic ideology, and the sedentary world's expectations of the mausoleum of a Muslim sultan/padishah. These various aspects lead us to frame our discussion regarding 'the dialogue between tents and buildings' around Öljeytü's tomb.

Despite the fact that buildings are static, architectural idioms could travel distances through the portability of artisans, architects, and artefacts such as architectural drawings.[54] In the case of Ilkhanid architecture, the semi-nomad Ilkhans themselves, while in the saddle, worked as the agents of architectural transportation. They facilitated the transfer of concepts and ideas not only between Central Asia and Iran, but also within Iran through their seasonal migrations. In the position of patrons and, sometimes, overseers,[55] the Ilkhans were enabled by the memory of their homeland to revitalise what they had left behind on the steppes of Mongolia in their new foundations in Iran. A great portion of their nostalgic feeling about their nomadic lifestyle was fulfilled through the erection of magnificent tents in their seasonal camps, as well as in the vicinity of their permanent capitals.[56] More interesting, however, is the process through which the tents of the Ilkhans, representing their Mongolian heritage, 'negotiated' with their monuments, which symbolised their authority as the legitimate rulers of a sedentary civilisation.[57]

Part of the negotiation happened on the surface. For instance, while the tomb of Öljeytü in Sultaniyya is associated with the tradition of building royal mausoleums in the eastern Islamic world, its external appearance may superficially be compared to that of Turko-Mongol tents.[58] Further, the north-north-east to south-south-west orientation of the octagonal tomb is likely to be in accordance with Mongol convention in which buildings faced south,[59] in spite of Muslim religious custom in which religious buildings face in a south-westerly direction, towards the *qiblih*.[60] Some other points of comparison between Ilkhanid complexes and Mongol tents were discussed in Chapter 2 in the case of the palatial complex at Takht-i Sulayman. However, if we take into account the meanings conveyed by architectural forms and ornaments, it becomes apparent that the greater part of the process of negotiation and translation occurred in some depth, which means that, instead of the amalgamation of nomadic and sedentary cultures in Ilkhanid architecture, we are witnessing a dynamic process in which 'signs and meanings were appropriated, translated, rehistoricised and read anew'.[61]

The ornament with a 'bookish' or 'painterly' quality, as Akbarnia describes it, inspired by manuscript decoration appeared on Ilkhanid buildings as well as portable objects such as ceramics and metalwork. She suggests that the decorative programme of all these architectural monuments and artefacts might have been inspired by a *khitā'ī* idiom created in a virtual *kitāb-khānih*.[62] One of these motifs, extensively used in the second phase of painted decoration in the tomb of Öljeytü, is associated with a Far East motif called cloud collar (i.e. the four-lobed shoulder attachment).[63] The motif appeared in Iran in the early fourteenth century and was gradually applied in different mediums, including architectural decoration. Neither the origin of cloud collars nor their symbolic meaning is certain, though it is plausible that the idea of cloud collars arrived in Iran and China in the course of the Mongol invasions. The Mongols, who possibly had the custom of wearing cloud collars, carried the motifs to Iran during their campaigns. In the tomb, the motif was adapted to fit the architectural limitations of the building (Figures 5.3 and 5.4).[64]

Furthermore, the blue-painted decoration on a white ground resembles the patterns decorating the external surface of Mongol tents, based on the scenes depicted in some historical miniatures, for instance the Diez albums.[65] Besides the visual evidence, the *Yuan Shi* (the official dynastic history of the Yuan dynasty) also reports that for the construction of a new *zongmao dian* (palace of palm) at Shangdu in 1325, two gigantic carpets were woven of *qing-bai yangmao* (blue and white wool).[66] This account suggests that the composition of blue and white was a familiar colour arrangement in Mongol visual culture. On the other hand, blue-painted decoration on a white ground was known as the most traditional scheme for the decoration of Persian mausoleums.[67] Therefore, one might suggest that Far Eastern motifs and designs were transformed from textile to architectural decoration in Ilkhanid Iran under the impact of a local decoration design.

While one should avoid drawing definitive conclusions, the existence of the same colour composition, albeit in a different context, leads us to speculate on

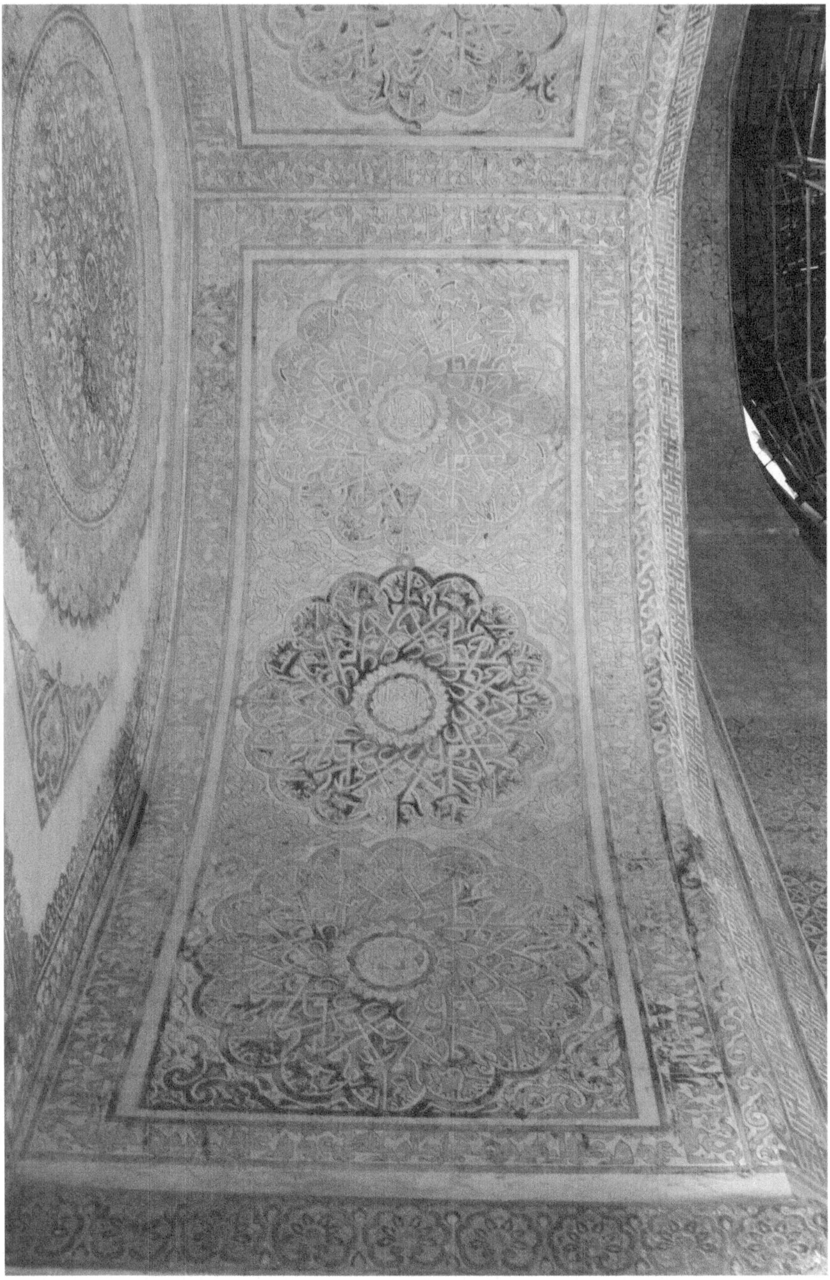

Figure 5.3 Painted plaster, part of the second phase of the interior decoration of Öljeytü's tomb.

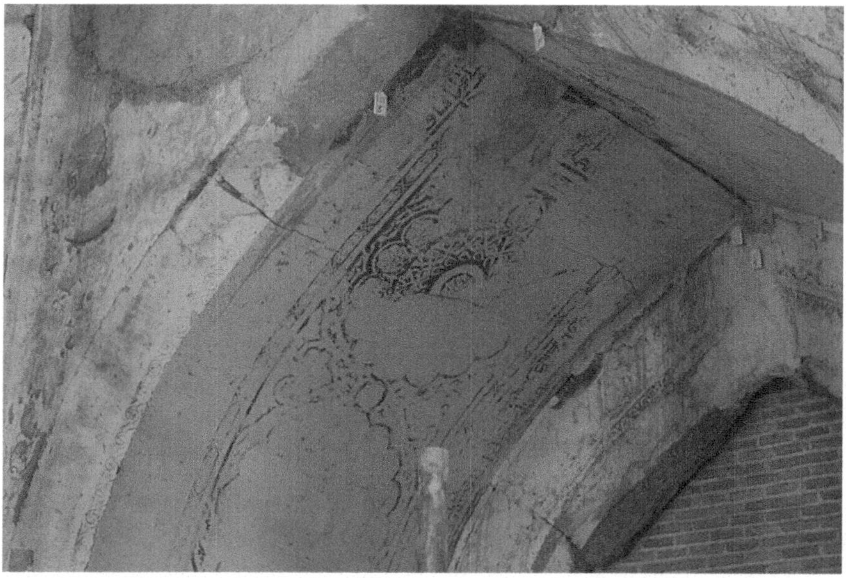

Figure 5.4 Painted plaster, part of the second phase of the interior decoration of Öljeytü's tomb.
© Atri Hatef Naiemi

the symbolic significance of the blue-painted motifs on the white walls of the tomb of Öljeytü. In *The Secret History of the Mongols*, in a dialogue between Chinggis Khan and his adopted brother, Shigi-qutuqu,[68] the Khan says:

> Write down in a blue book a list of the shares into which [you] divide the nation and of the judgements [you] deliver. Unto the seed of [my] seed, let no one alter the blue writing of Shigi-qutuqu, ordained in consultation with me, [written] on white paper in a blue book and made into a register. Anyone who alters it shall be [found] guilty.[69]

The above-mentioned interpretations of the blue-and-white composition in ornaments of the Ilkhan's tomb can be examined in relation to the place of white in Mongol visual culture. In the Eurasian steppe, colours represented particular concepts and meanings. All people of different tribes or ethnic groups who lived in the same historical period were able to understand them.[70] For example, white denotes good fortune in Mongol culture. The banner of Chinggis Khan was a white standard with nine pennants.[71] During the reign of his successors, erecting a white banner indicated the presence of the royal household. *The Secret History of the Mongols* mentions that Chinggis Khan bestowed the rank of *beki* on Old Man Üsün and said that 'he shall wear a white dress and ride a white gelding'. *Beki* possibly meant a high-ranking officer, and white was the colour of esteem.[72]

The Mongols celebrated the New Year with the 'White Festival', which is still a national holiday in Mongolia. In the feast, as Marco Polo describes, 'the great Kaan with all his subjects dress themselves all in white robes ... they do it because white dress seems to them lucky and good, and therefore they wear it at the beginning of their year so that they may take their good and have joy and comfort all the year'.[73] Rabban Sawma writes that in 1303, Mar Yaballaha visited Ghazan Khan in the city of Hilla on the day of the 'White Festival'.[74] This report shows that this Mongol ceremony was still appreciated during the time of the Muslim Ilkhans.

Another mention of the Mongols' symbolic use of white, although in a different sector of the empire, is given by Ibn Battuta. He visited the city of El Khansa in China, a large city which consisted of six smaller cities. During his visit, he was informed of a battle between the Great Khan and some of his relations and nobles. Ibn Battuta recounts the funeral of the Khan and a hundred of his relatives who had been killed in that battle in great detail. He mentions that 'all the people of the city, Chinese, Mohammedans and others, were present on the occasion, and had on their mourning, which consists of a sort of white hood'.[75] Interestingly enough, the picture illustrated by Ibn Battuta in China shares some common characteristics with another funeral depicted in a culturally different context: the *Funeral of Isfandiyar* (Figure 5.5), a folio from the Ilkhanid manuscript of the *Great Mongol Shahnama*. The painting depicts a group of mourners wailing and tearing their hair around Isfandiyar's bier. The Mongol costumes and accessories and the physiognomy of members of the procession are noticeable, suggesting that the ceremony shown in the manuscript is a traditional Mongol burial. Soudavar refers to Rashid al-Din's account of the funeral of Ghazan Khan and proposes that the scene illustrated in this manuscript could be the funeral procession of Öljeytü or Ghazan Khan.[76] Rashid al-Din writes that

> his corpse was mounted on a special carriage accompanied by khatuns and amirs. The procession headed towards Tabriz. Along the way, bareheaded

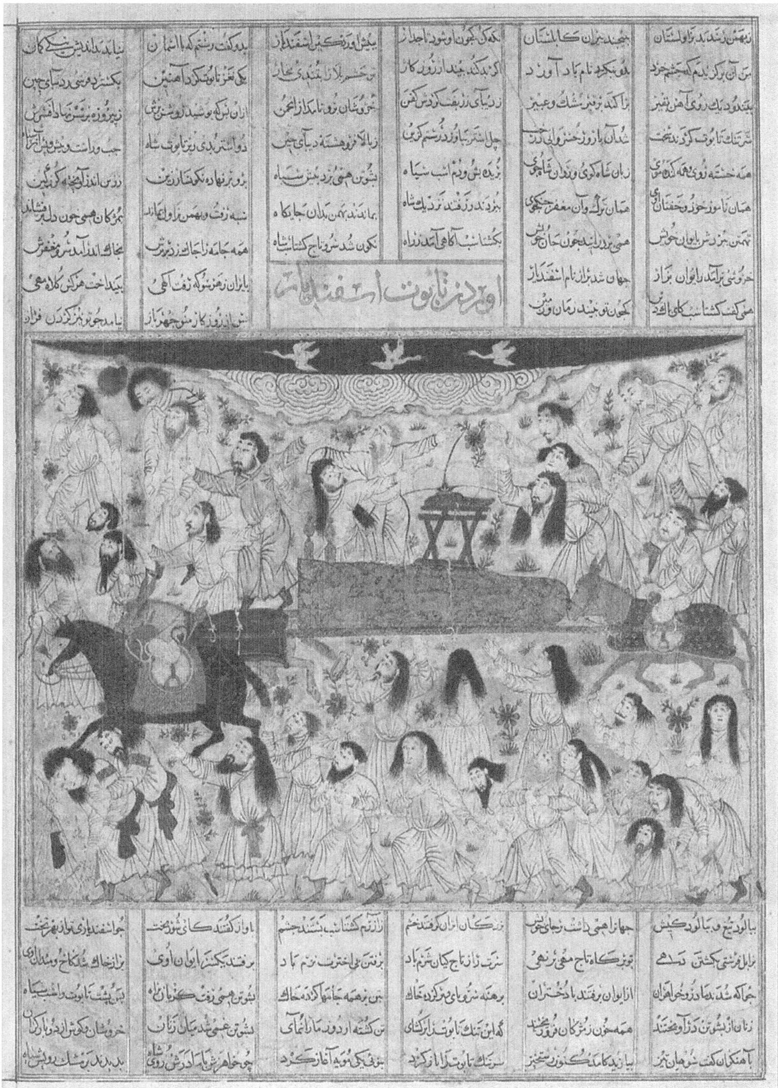

Figure 5.5 The *Funeral of Isfandiyar*: folio from a *Shahnama*, 1330s.
Attributed to Iran, Tabriz
Ink, opaque watercolour and gold on paper
Page: Ht 22$^{13}/_{16}$ in. (58 cm)
W. 15¾ in. (40 cm)
Mat: Ht 24 in. (61 cm)
W. 19½ in. (49.5 cm)
Purchase, Joseph Pulitzer Bequest, 1933
Courtesy of the Metropolitan Museum of Art

> and barefooted men and women came out of cities and villages wearing tattered gowns and wailing in grief ... when the procession reached the suburb of the *dār al-mulk* of Tabriz, the city dwellers dressed in dark (*kabūd*)[77] garments out of misery, and men and women, great and small came out and buried the corpse.[78]

The general atmosphere of Ghazan Khan's funeral in Rashid al-Din's account corresponds with the painting, except for Ghazan's dark-dressed mourners, who are different from Isfandiyar's white funeral procession. The minor discrepancy between the account and the painting can be explained by Ghazan's conversion and acceptance of the Muslim faith. Given that Mongol nomadic customs (including funerals) had an impact on the ceremonial practices of the Ilkhanid court,[79] Soudavar's claim seems plausible. Furthermore, the fact that the manuscript was produced in the court's scriptorium shows that the symbolic importance of the colour white was known to the Ilkhans. In addition to the elements of Mongol native culture appearing in the painting, the Buddhist iconography of the work (e.g. the clouds and the geese bearing the soul to heaven) is also notable.

Apart from the individual motifs transferred from other mediums to the architectural ornaments of the tomb of Öljeytü, the painted decoration of the building, in its entirety, seems to have re-created the colourful textiles hung on the walls of the Mongols' tents[80] or decorating their palaces as a nostalgic vestige of their nomadic past.[81] This resemblance suggests that in the absence of precious wall hangings inside the tomb, the architectural decoration was meant to evoke memories of their ancestral tents. Moreover, the mere fact of using textile-like stuccos and mural paintings points towards the Ilkhans' tendency to reside in tent-like buildings.

In addition to the extensive decoration of the tomb, some smaller fittings found in the environs of the building offer more evidence on the eclectic (if not exclusively nomadic) taste of Öljeytü in the architectural projects undertaken under his patronage. For example, European travellers to the site of Sultaniyya reported observing a lattice metal grille that separated the rectangular hall (*turbat-khānih*) from the main octagonal hall.[82] The grille was formed from bars connected by inlaid brass bosses. One of the bosses possibly used at the tomb complex of Sultaniyya is inlaid with silver and gold and engraved with the design of a Mongol-looking falconer in his traditional robe and hat (Figure 5.6). However, it is rather curious that in the context of the decorative programme of the tomb, with all the Qur'anic quotations and the large collection of *ḥadīth*s, the metalwork represents a scene of royal entertainment.[83] The other example is a ball joint which, despite the inlaid boss, has inscriptions bearing the name of Öljeytü.[84] The formal details of the two bosses are different, however.

Along with the decoration programme of the tomb, it is equally possible that the nomadic beliefs penetrated the layout of the building. As we mentioned earlier, according to Rashid al-Din, Ghazan Khan was inspired by the tomb of Sultan Sanjar at Marv, one of the greatest edifices of the eastern Islamic world, and built a mausoleum for himself that was much more majestic than Sanjar's tomb (Figure 5.7).[85] In view of the fact that Ghazan's tomb was in turn a model for Öljeytü's, one might expect that the architectural characteristics of the tomb at Marv reappeared in the tomb at Sultaniyya. While this is almost the case as regards the general form and layout of Öljeytü's tomb, two features differentiate it from its predecessors: the rectangular hall appended to the domed hall, and the absence of a cenotaph, which still exists in Sanjar's tomb (Figure 5.8).[86] Although the tomb at Sultaniyya was in the tradition of polygonal mausoleums with dome chambers and side galleries that had been constructed in Iran for at least four centuries prior to Sultaniyya,[87] the two above-mentioned points raise the possibility that the tomb might have encompassed some other features that had not been seen in the preceding constructions.

The rectangular hall which is believed to embrace the cenotaph of the Ilkhan was added to the building at the same stage as the domed hall was redecorated. Pietro Della Valle (d. 1652) reports that the cenotaph situated inside the grille in the centre of the sanctuary (the rectangular hall) was covered with precious silk-and-gold cloth.[88] Soudavar also suggests that the *Bier of Alexander*, a folio from the *Great Mongol Shahnama*, represents the inside of the tomb at Sultaniyya where the coffin of Öljeytü had been placed.[89] The other mention of Öljeytü's burial is found in Wassaf's account, where he writes that the Ilkhan was buried in the dome (*qubbih*) of the *abwāb al-birr*.[90] Hafiz-i Abru expands on the funeral of Öljeytü and says that while the nobles, khatuns and amirs were clad in dark colours as a sign of mourning for him, he was buried in the crypt (*sardābih*) of the dome (domed chamber) that he had already built inside

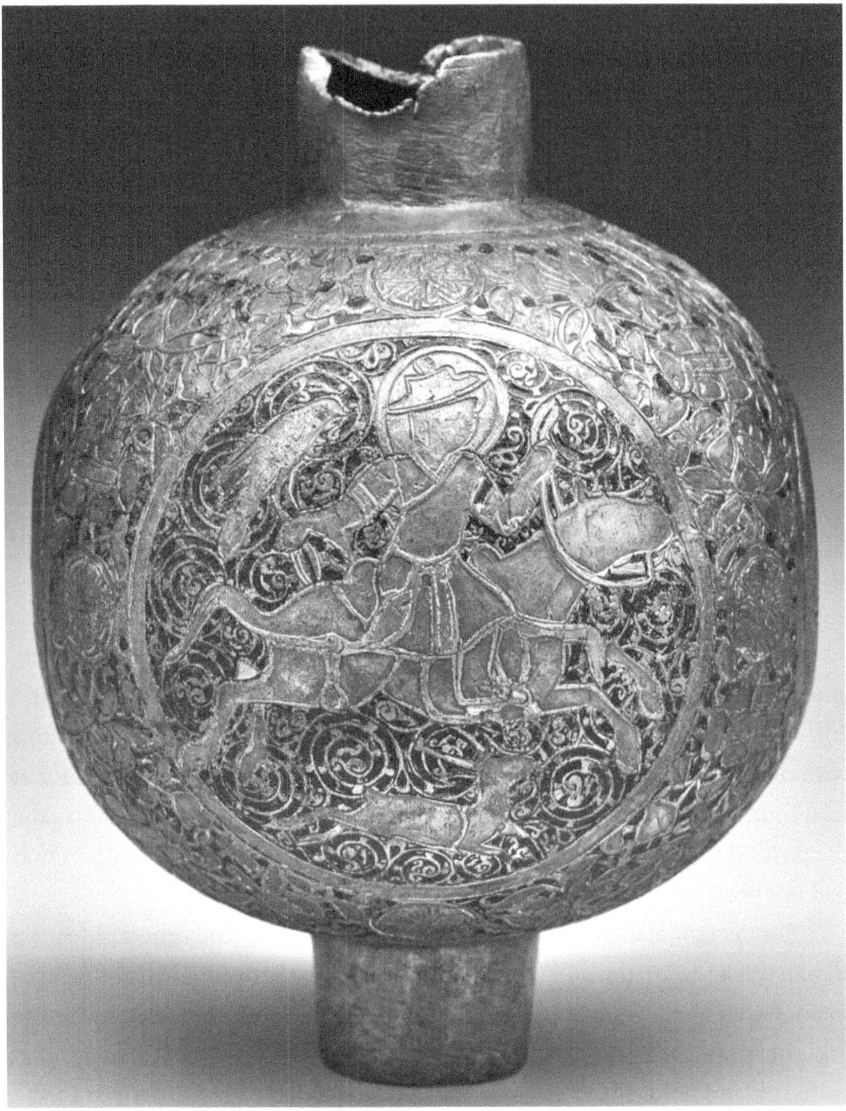

Figure 5.6 Ball joint from a window grill, early. Early fourteenth century
Bronze inlaid with silver, gold and nielloed
3⅞ × 5⅛ × 4 in. (9.84 × 13.02 × 10.16 cm)
The Keir Collection of Islamic Art, on loan to the Dallas Museum of Art

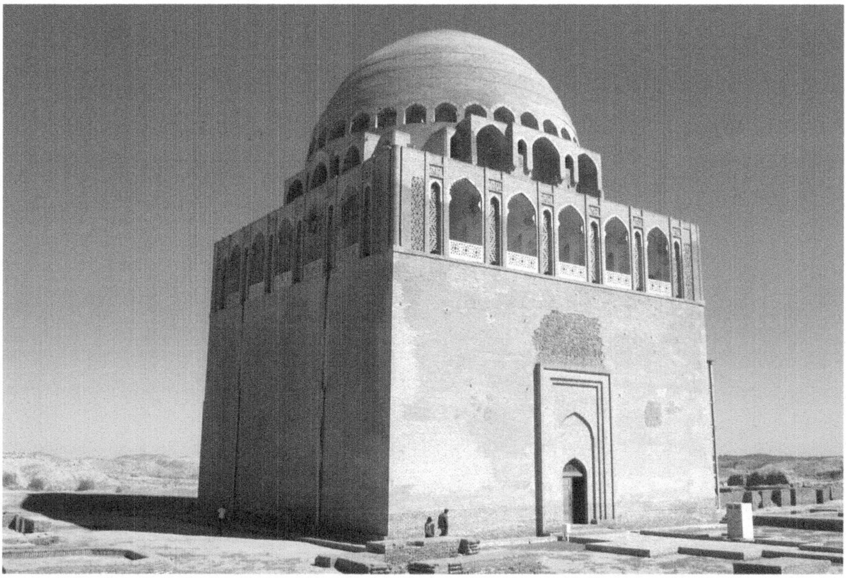

Figure 5.7 Tomb of Sultan Sanjar in Marv.
© Peretz Partensky
Flickr, accessed 9 September 2023, https://www.flickr.com/photos/ifl/3892634354/

the citadel (*qalʿih*) of Sultaniyya. Alongside his corpse a large amount of gold, jewels and precious belongings were buried as if his tomb were a treasure house (*ganj-khānih*).[91] Despite the textual and visual evidence on the existence of the Ilkhan's cenotaph inside the tomb or his burial in the crypt, no trace of the actual grave has been found during the excavations, neither in the domed hall nor in the rooms underneath the rectangular hall.[92] While the texts confirm his burial in the building, the lack of archaeological proof leads us to suggest that in Sultaniyya, Öljeytü combined the Iranian-Islamic practice of constructing monumental tombs with the Mongol custom of burying the dead in a secret location together with his/her valuable possessions.

As discussed in Chapter 4, the tomb was initially decorated with brick, terracotta and tile, but in a few years the decoration was entirely covered with a layer of tile and painted plaster. The first layer of decoration, along with other structural features of the tomb, proposes that the building was originally intended for a palace rather than a funerary monument. The drastic redecoration was conducted with the purpose of making it appropriate for the tomb of

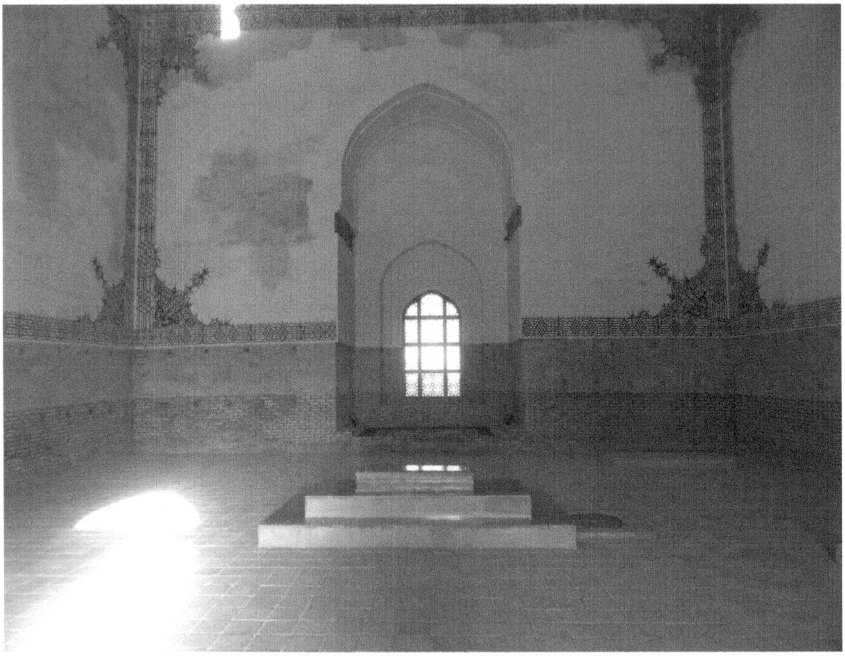

Figure 5.8 Interior of the tomb of Sultan Sanjar in Marv.
© Hans Birger Nilsen
Flickr, accessed 9 September 2023, https://www.flickr.com/photos/110608682@N04/44747314854/in/photostream/

the Sultan. Sims suggests that the architectural and decorative iconography of the building, in the first phase, was inappropriate for a tomb. The largely non-epigraphic decoration of the building, the low legibility of its highly stylised Qur'anic quotations and the dissimilarity between the decoration of the tomb and other contemporary tomb complexes are some of the pieces of evidence supporting her claim.[93] Furthermore, Blair puts forward the argument that the redecoration of the tomb can be seen as part of the development of the shrine complex and the transformation of Öljeytü's single-room tomb working as a family burial place into a multi-chambered place of pilgrimage accommodating larger groups of people.[94] Considering this hypothesis, it is possible that the Ilkhan envisaged his tomb as a destination for both Iranian and Mongol pilgrims, and thus desired the building to communicate – visually and conceptually – with people from diverse ethnic and religious backgrounds. In the same way, the internal decoration of the tomb, borrowing some aspects of

Mongol tents as well as Öljeytü's secret grave in accordance with the tradition of his ancestors, were supposed to indicate that the magnificent tomb with its Perso-Islamic appearance belonged to a Muslim sultan who was also a Mongol khan. All the above-mentioned examples point towards the fact that while the Mongols showed interest in the adoption of the urban concept of rulership through the foundation of monumental buildings, they enjoyed showcasing their nomadic assets in the settled context of these structures. The tomb of Öljeytü strongly exemplifies this eclecticism.

The Ilkhans oscillated not only between settled and nomadic concepts, but among several religious and cultural doctrines presented by the sedentary world. The epigraphic programme of the tomb is an intriguing example in this regard. In the second phase of interior decoration of the tomb the names of the Rashidun (the first four caliphs: Abu Bakr, 'Umar, 'Uthman and 'Ali) emerge in conjunction with some *ḥadīth*s by 'Ali and the names of two Shi'ite imams, Hassan and Husain, reflecting the religious eclecticism of the Mongol period.[95] In fact, besides the negotiation between foreign and local ideas, one should seek another level of encounter between various native motifs and themes in Ilkhanid art and architecture.

Another noteworthy example is a painting possibly extracted from one of the copies of the *Jami' al-Tawarikh* and assembled in the Diez albums.[96] The picture is a notable case vividly representing the interaction and intersection of local modes and foreign idioms. The manuscript depicts two figures dressed in Mongol robes and headgear and seated inside a white tent with blue ornaments. Two men are reading the Qur'an placed on the Qur'an stand. The inscription above the entrance of the tent that reads *al-mulk lillāh* ('All sovereignty belongs to God'), as well as the two Allah-shaped elements on the top of the tent, suggest that the tent must have worked as a portable mosque.[97] While the figures in the painting are usually described as converted Mongol princes in a prayer space, the curious gesture of the man on the left demands further attention. He seems to be gazing in wonder at the Qur'an and revealing his surprise by raising his eyebrows and putting his index finger to his lips. To interpret the gesture, we should look at another painting from the *Jami' al-Tawarikh*, in which Hülegü Khan is depicted with a similar gesture, the *Siege of Alamut*. The painting is accompanied by a short description mentioning that Hülegü bit his finger out of astonishment.[98] Nevertheless, whether the gesture of the figure was meant to show the unfamiliarity of a newly converted or a non-Muslim Mongol prince with the Qur'an, or his admiration for the holy book, is still unclear to us.

This miniature clarifies that the Mongols adopted, whether sincerely or not, the religion of the sedentary world, but still practised it in their familiar nomadic context. In dealing with the rules of the civilised world, the Mongols' preference for these mobile structures was not merely because of their greater compatibility with their semi-nomadic lifestyle that continued through the Ilkhanid period. The tents seem to have shaped a crucial aspect of the Mongols' nomadic identity. In *The Secret History of the Mongols* the creation of the Mongol Empire is marked by the unification of several tribes, which are called 'the people of the felt-walled tents/yurts'.[99] This phrase emphasises that the Mongols did not consider their tents exclusively as a requirement for their seasonal migrations but perceived them as a device that materialised part of their collective identity. Furthermore, the tents visually represented the affiliation of the Mongols in different khanates with the Mongol Empire and its illustrious founder, Chinggis Khan.

The dialogue between camps and cities

Despite the reputation of the Mongols as barbarian hordes and destroyers of civilisations, they had a great influence over Eurasian urbanism.[100] Prior to Chinggis Khan's military campaigns, there was a growing urbanisation throughout Central Asia during the eleventh and twelfth centuries. Several new towns rose on the trade routes or at the meeting points of agricultural and pastoral regions, although these towns are barely comparable with the capital cities founded later by the Mongols in China or Iran.[101] Besides the towns with permanent buildings that existed in Central Asia before the Mongol invasion, seasonal camps came into being at the beginning of the thirteenth century that contained noticeable permanent elements. For instance, Chinggis Khan's Great *Ordu*, discussed in Chapter 1, was possibly located in a permanent place consisting of both temporary and permanent structures. Despite his seasonal migrations between different camps, the fact that Chinggis Khan's Great *Ordu* was erected in a fixed location suggests that neither the Ilkhans nor their counterparts in Yuan China were unfamiliar with the concept of designating a specific place as their capital. This hypothesis is worth considering, because the idea of constructing permanent capitals is usually assumed to be a theme borrowed by the Mongols from the nearby sedentary civilisations.[102]

Apart from the emergence of the camps with increasingly permanent components, during the time of Chinggis Khan's successors the tents imitating the magnificence of monuments arguably lost some of their qualities as portable structures. In written sources there are references to splendid tents pitched at a fixed place which were never taken down. For example, Rashid al-Din mentions that at the summer camp of Ögödei, Chinggis Khan's son, in Örmögatü, his people erected a grand tent (*khargāh-i buzurg*) accommodating 1,000 people, and never removed it (*hargiz bar nimī-giriftand*).[103]

This piece of information regarding the existence of permanent towns as well as the seasonal camps with permanent structures proposes that the Ilkhans' conceptions of built environment and social life were not confined exclusively to their memories of 'felt-walled tents' that traditionally were being erected across the steppes of Eurasia. In other words, the Ilkhans had a sort of settled mentality even before their extensive encounter with the sedentary world following the Mongol conquest of Western Asia. Hence, it would be erroneous to assume that they showed an inclination to found urban centres merely under the influence of their Persian advisors in the sedentary context of Iran.

As regards Ghazaniyya and Sultaniyya, the foundation of cities that fulfilled the requirements of the Ilkhans as the rulers of a sedentary sovereignty was studied earlier in the book. As we have seen, these urban centres distanced themselves from the conventional model of the Iranian/Islamic city in order to satisfy the needs of the Mongols who had retained their semi-nomadic lifestyle. Ilkhanid cities should be conceived, in Haneda's words, as a 'compromise' between the tribesmen's desire to erect their encampments outside the established cities and the Ilkhans' wish to build splendid monuments that impressed their subjects.[104] The outcome of this agreement is the two cases of Ghazaniyya and Sultaniyya, which share some common characteristics: both cities were built in the midst of a lush pasture – where the Ilkhan could encamp contentedly – while having an *abwāb al-birr* at their core embracing the Ilkhan's tomb. This arrangement seems to have constituted an unprecedented type of urban centre in the long tradition of city planning in Iran.

The *abwāb al-birr*s are the most notable architectural projects undertaken during the Ilkhanid period. Several large-scale pious complexes were founded or expanded under the patronage of the Ilkhans and their notables and officials throughout their territory. A charitable ensemble formed at the core of the newly founded city of Ghazaniyya. In their capital in Sultaniyya, a similar *abwāb al-birr* was also the outstanding element around which the citadel and, beyond that, the outer city were shaped. While the fabric of the main body of the cities has largely been overlooked in the contemporary textual and visual material, repeated references to these compounds in historical sources have built a proper context for studying their structural and functional features. Despite the extensive destruction of the two cities and, thus, the scarcity of architectural and archaeological evidence, the spatial structure of Ghazaniyya and Sultaniyya has been partially reconstructed. Nevertheless, in order to scrutinise the negotiation that developed between the Mongols and the Iranians in the context of the built environment of their cities, it was these urban projects (the *abwāb al-birr*s) that were specifically addressed, rather than the whole city, because of their better-described attributes.

It should be underlined that at the pious ensembles of Ghazaniyya and Sultaniyya the tombs were intended to be regarded as a place of pilgrimage following the death of the Ilkhan. The sporadic references to the pilgrimages made by the members of the court to the tombs in the textual sources[105] show that this target was partly met.[106] In this regard, Kashani's mention of Sultaniyya as the destination for pilgrims of the world and the Kaʿba of human beings (*maqṣad-i zuvvār-i ʿālam va Kaʿba-yi maqām-i banī ādam*) is of great importance.[107]

It is intriguing that the spiritual significance of the tombs, as a 'destination for pilgrims', was defined in connection with the Ilkhans themselves. This specific quality of the tombs was in contrast to the tradition of burying notables in the vicinity of the graves of religious figures and Sufi saints in search of blessing that was common throughout the Islamic world.[108] The gesture suggests that the Ilkhans deemed themselves sources of spirituality and religious legitimacy.[109] This perception seems far from the beliefs of a faithful Muslim, who seeks eternal bliss in the afterlife in proximity with the tombs of the religious leaders. On the contrary, it is arguable that the symbolic act of the two Ilkhans had its origin in the Mongol practice of visitation of the ancestors. As discussed earlier, although the Mongols had the custom of secret burials, in the absence of actual graves the encampments of the deceased khans were honoured as shrines. In other words, the departed khans could lend their spiritual power to a spot and sometimes even to the entire region, as was the case for Burkhan Khaldun.

The motives behind the locations of Ghazaniyya and Sultaniyya were examined earlier in the book. The construction of the former in an area that had already been claimed by Arghun, and the foundation of the latter over an earlier imperial city and close to the spot attributed to the burial place of Arghun, seem to have been in accordance with the nomads' ideology in which good fortune was believed to exist permanently in some specific places. The Khans obtained royal charisma and, thus, legitimacy through occupying these lands. This way of conceptualising the major urban centres of Ghazan Khan and Öljeytü substantiates the claim that the Mongol conventions partially survived the process of Islamisation and Persianisation of the Ilkhanid court imposed (or offered) by their Iranian viziers and notables. However, focusing on the primary architectural enterprises of the Ilkhans in the *abwāb al-birr*s of Ghazaniyya and Sultaniyya, we reach the conclusion that certain domains emerged where nomadic traditions and Perso-Islamic conventions converged, such as venerating the memory of spiritual leaders or distributing votive offerings in devotional sites. Consequently, the foundation of a pious compound with the Ilkhan's tomb at its core is justifiable from the perspectives of both Iranians and Mongols.

Being aware of such shared areas prompts speculation that the complexes might not have been built entirely under the influence of Islamic charitable buildings. Despite Rashid al-Din's statement about Ghazan Khan's imitation of the holy shrines of the Shiʿa imams and Sufi shaykhs whom he had visited earlier in Khurasan and Iraq, it is possible that the Mongol patrons had a faint intention of revitalising part of their nomadic traditions in their *abwāb al-birr*s even if these traditions had to be embodied in a typical Islamic/Iranian architectural structure. In this way, a Mongol practice that had a counterpart in the receiving culture was translated into a local and, thus, a more understandable act.

To support this claim, it is important to note that nomadic beliefs could travel far away in distance and time so that even the later Ilkhans seem to have had vivid memories of the cultural and religious practices of their ancestors as well as of the other khanates.[110] In spite of the mass conversion of the Mongols during the Ilkhanid period, there are historical accounts confirming that some of the Muslim Ilkhans and their Mongol amirs still had ambivalent feelings and opinions towards Islam. In the *Tarikh-i Öljeytü*, Kashani writes about an argument between Hanafis and Shafiʿis at Öljeytü's court. The dispute made the Ilkhan so furious that he left the room. Qutlugh-Shah Nuyan, one of the Mongol amirs, addressed the other amirs saying: 'what is this that we have done? We abandoned the *yāsāq* [or *yāsā*: code of laws] and *yūsūn* [customs] of Chinggis Khan and converted into the ancient religion of the Arabs, which is divided into seventy-odd parts.'[111] In a similar anecdote, Kashani writes about a severe thunderbolt that struck Öljeytü's *ordu* and killed a couple of his guards. The Ilkhan got frightened and was told by his amirs that, according to the former rules and the *yāsāq* of Chinggis Khan, he needed to pass through the fire in order to overcome the disaster. They called for Buddhist priests to come and set up the grand fire. The priests told him that the lightning was caused by the infelicity of Islam and by being a Muslim. They advised him to cease his daily prayers and repent of his wrongdoings. He took their advice for about three months. During this period, however, dealing with his uncertain Islamic beliefs, 'the king (padishah) struggled between affirmation and denial, devotion and hatred, resolution and hesitation'.[112] Although this incident eventually resulted in the conversion of Öljeytü from Sunnism to Shiʿism, the story suggests how easily the foundations of the Ilkhans' Islamic ideology could have been shaken, despite the process of Islamisation of the Ilkhanid court being conducted during the later Mongol period in Iran. Given the oscillation of the Ilkhans between different religious opinions and practices, in the case of the charitable complexes, it is not difficult to believe that Mongolian beliefs might have intertwined with Islamic/Iranian concepts of feeding the poor or visiting the shrines of the Shiʿa imams and Sufi shaykhs in the hope of gaining blessing from different sources of spirituality.

Apart from the fact that the Ilkhans continued eagerly to encamp outside their cities, which was deeply rooted in their roving heritage, they brought specific ideas from this culture to the cities and infused them into their architectural endeavours. This chapter has discussed the occasions on which Mongol nomadic forms and practices were transferred to the Perso-Islamic context of Ilkhanid Iran and were translated into the domestic language of architecture. It is noteworthy that in addition to these cases, there must have been numerous instances of confrontation between the two cultures which did not automatically result in negotiation being established and in signs and meanings being exchanged or synthetised. Referring to Berlekamp's statement that 'the fact of encounter is not the same as the fact of exchange',[113] despite the expansion of contact between the Mongols and the Iranians following the conquest, not all cases of encounter were associated with active communication between the two sides, for various reasons. For example, the fact that new ideas were introduced into Ilkhanid Iran does not necessarily mean that they were always conceptually accessible to their new intended audience. The lack of familiar alternatives in the destination culture might have interrupted the process of translation. In this case, although the Mongols' cultural items and elements entered Ilkhanid Iran successfully, they were not fully understood by their new host.

Given the extent of encounter, but also the failed cases of interaction, exploring hybrid signs and meanings representing the occurrence of exchange demands meticulous examination of the material culture produced under the auspices of the Ilkhanid court. This issue could be even more challenging in the case of urban architecture, due to the limited number of extant buildings and the insufficiency of archaeological excavation. In addition, as was discussed earlier in this chapter, the complex nature of cultural syntheses makes it difficult to recognise the fusion and to trace back all the contributors. However, despite all these constraints, the study of individual cases of artefacts, buildings and urban complexes is a credible, and possibly the only, method of analysing the encounter between the two cultural domains and the way in which they exchanged motifs, traditions and thoughts. We can conclude this chapter by pointing out that looking for more examples of various categories of material culture could enrich the present research. Nevertheless, if we theorise the Mongol–Iranian intercultural contacts merely on the basis of material evidence, without considering intangible matters such as religious beliefs or native traditions, we will merely develop a set of ideas about a cultural phenomenon which could be far from the historical reality.

Notes

1. For further discussion on the traditional views about the Mongols, see the Introduction.

2. Allsen, *Commodity and Exchange*; Allsen, *Culture and Conquest*; Akbarnia, '*Khita'i*: Cultural Memory', 1–49; Amitai-Preiss and Biran, *Nomads as Agents*. For further discussion and bibliography on this issue, see the Introduction.
3. Allsen, *Culture and Conquest*, 191.
4. Looking for these forms and concepts would seem to conflict with Allsen's statement about the Mongols, who, 'with some exceptions, were not primarily engaged in transmitting their own ethnic culture to their diverse sedentary subjects'. See Allsen, *Culture and Conquest*, 19.
5. Allsen, *Commodity and Exchange*, 101–2.
6. For instance, Bayani discusses the influential presence of Persian bureaucrats and religious scholars in the Ilkhanid court. She emphasises that these two groups empowered the 'Iranian element' in order to rebuild the administrative and cultural structure of the state. See Bayani, *Dīn va Dawlat*, vol. 2, 383–4. In another study, Bayani argues that Ghazan Khan commenced his comprehensive reforms on the basis of 'Iranian traditions and Islamic teachings'. See Shirin Bayani, *Mughulān va Ḥukūmat-i Īlkhānī dar Iran* [The Mongols and Ilkhanid Rule in Iran] (Tehran: SAMT, 2010), 218–19. Ghafrani also highlights the role of Rashid al-Din in the execution of the reforms of Ghazan Khan and suggests that the Ilkhan himself had not benefited from sufficient education and training to accomplish this grand project. See 'Ali Ghafrani, 'Rashid al-Din Fazlallah va Andīsha-yi Ābād-garī dar Qalamru-yi Īlkhānān [Rashid al-Din Fazlallah and the Concept of Development in the Territory of the Ilkhans]', *Muṭāli'āt-i Islāmī* 71 (2006): 173.
7. Persian adjective for 'Chinese' introduced by Ladan Akbarnia. See Akbarnia, '*Khita'i*: Cultural Memory'.
8. In this regard, the thoughts of Ibn Khaldun (d. 1406) on the transition of dynasties from desert life to sedentary culture are enlightening. See Ibn Khaldun, *The Muqaddimah: An Introduction to History*, trans. Franz Rosenthal (New York: Pantheon, 1958), vol. 1, 347 and 351.
9. See e.g. William Fitzhugh, Morris Rossabi and William Honeychurch, *Genghis Khan and the Mongol Empire* (Washington: Dino Don, 2009), 57–83; Vesna Wallace, *Buddhism in Mongolian History, Culture, and Society* (New York: Oxford University Press, 2015).
10. To the best of my knowledge the question of Iranian–Mongol encounters has not been addressed by anthropologists yet, perhaps because of the scarcity of archaeological data derived from the residential areas of the few Ilkhanid cities that have been excavated so far.

11. Deborah Kapchan and Pauline Turner Strong, 'Theorizing the Hybrid', *The Journal of American Folklore* 112, no. 445 (1999): 240–1.
12. Robin Cohen, 'Creolization and Cultural Globalization: The Soft Sounds of Fugitive Power', *Globalizations* 4, no. 3 (2007): 381.
13. Bhabha, 'The Third Space', 211. Cultural hybridity is different from 'the exoticism of multiculturalism or the diversity of cultures'. For further discussion, see Bhabha, *The Location of Culture*, 38.
14. Seth Schwartz, Jennifer Unger, Byron Zamboanga and José Szapocznik, 'Rethinking the Concept of Acculturation: Implications for Theory and Research', *American Psychologist* 65, no. 4 (2010): 237–9.
15. Ibid., 245.
16. For immigration-based acculturation, see Sylvia Chen, Veronica Benet-Martinez and Michael Bond, 'Bicultural Identity, Bilingualism, and Psychological Adjustment in Multicultural Societies: Immigration-based and Globalization-based Acculturation', *Journal of Personality* 76 (2008): 803–38; Gibson, Margaret, 'Immigrant Adaptation and Patterns of Acculturation', *Human Development* 44 (2001): 19–23; Seth Schwartz, Marilyn Montgomery and E. Briones, 'The Role of Identity in Acculturation among Immigrant People: Theoretical Propositions, Empirical Questions and Applied Recommendations', *Human Development* 49 (2006): 1–30.
17. Schwartz *et al.*, 'Rethinking the Concept', 247.
18. The reaction of the conquered (the Iranians) to the conqueror (the Mongols) during the *acculturation* process can be compared with other historical cases of forced colonisation, for instance Ottoman occupation of the Balkans and Greece. The Ottomans established their universal empire in the fifteenth century. In order to conduct their cosmopolitan regime, they not only had to impose controls on numerous provinces, but also had to leave their own stamp on the conquered lands by shaping a common culture connecting all the provinces together and representing them as the components of an integrated system. On the other hand, they were faced with the issue of the pre-existing structures in the conquered cities, which determined their particular approach to each of their provinces. For further discussion, see Erse Brouskare and Elizabeth Key Fowden, *Ottoman Architecture in Greece* (Athens: Hellenic Ministry of Culture, Directorate of Byzantine and Post-Byzantine Antiquities, 2009); Heath Lowry, *In the Footsteps of the Ottomans: A Search for Sacred Spaces and Architectural Monuments in Northern Greece* (Istanbul: Bahçeşehir University Press, 2009); Machiel Kiel, *Studies on the Ottoman Architecture of*

the Balkans (Aldershot; Brookfield, VT: Variorum, 1990). For further discussion on the forced presence of the Ottomans in the major cities of the Mamluk Sultanate, see Heghnar Zeitlian Watenpaugh, *The Image of an Ottoman City: Imperial Architecture and Urban Experience in Aleppo in the 16th and 17th Centuries* (Boston; Leiden: Brill, 2004); Heghnar Zeitlian Watenpaugh, 'An Uneasy Historiography: The Legacy of Ottoman Architecture in the Former Arab Provinces', *Muqarnas* 24 (2007): 27–43; Çiğdem Kafescioğlu, '"In the Image of Rūm": Ottoman Architectural Patronage in Sixteenth-Century Aleppo and Damascus', *Muqarnas Online* 16, no. 1 (1999): 70–96; Doris Behrens-Abouseif, *Egypt's Adjustment to Ottoman Rule: Institutions, Waqf and Architecture in Cairo, 16th and 17th Centuries* (New York; Leiden: Brill, 1994).

19. Allsen, 'Archaeology and Mid-Imperial History', 94.
20. Bhabha, *The Location of Culture*, 7.
21. Ibid., 38.
22. John McLeod, *Beginning Postcolonialism* (Manchester; New York: Manchester University Press, 2000), 7–8.
23. Ibid., 22.
24. Ibid., 32–3.
25. Liebmann, 'The Intersections of Archaeology', 2, 5. For more discussion on postcolonial theorists of hybridity, see Stuart Hall, 'Cultural Identity and Diaspora', in *Colonial Discourse and Post-Colonial Theory: A Reader*, ed. Laura Chrisman and Patrick Williams (London; New York: Harvester Wheatsheaf, 1994), 227–37; Monika Fludernik, *Hybridity and Postcolonialism: Twentieth-Century Indian Literature* (Tübingen: Stauffenburg, 1998); Arita Balaram, '(Re)theorizing Hybridity for the Study of Identity and Difference', *Social and Personality Psychology Compass* 12, no. 10 (2018): e12413-n/a; Keri Iyall Smith and Patricia Leavy, *Hybrid Identities: Theoretical and Empirical Examinations* (Leiden; Boston: Brill, 2008).
26. Matthew Liebmann, 'Introduction: The Intersections of Archaeology and Postcolonial Studies', in *Archaeology and the Postcolonial Critique*, ed. Matthew Liebmann and Uzma Rizvi (Lanham, MD: AltaMira, 2008), 10–13.
27. Flood, *Objects of Translation*, 8.
28. Canepa, 'Theorizing Cross-Cultural', 10.
29. As was discussed in the case of Ghazan Khan in Chapter 3, negative views on the unwelcome presence of the Mongols were relieved over the course of time, particularly with the efforts of the Persian elite who sought to legitimise the

rule of the Mongols over Iran. Rashid al-Din and ʿAta Malik Juvayni are two influential figures in the legitimisation of the Mongols.

30. Bhabha, 'The Third Space', 210.
31. Akcan, 'Channels and Items of Translation', 145–6.
32. Ibid., 152.
33. Flood, *Objects of Translation*, 8.
34. Ibid., 8.
35. For instance, those regions located at the intersection of trade routes or the ports that worked as entrepôts between east and west possibly encountered a higher density of interactions.
36. Mary Louise Pratt, 'Arts of the Contact Zone', *Profession* (1991): 34.
37. Yuka Kadoi, 'Cloud Patterns: The Exchange of Ideas between China and Iran under the Mongols', *Oriental Art* 48, no. 2 (2002): 29.
38. Akcan, 'Channels and Items of Translation', 149.
39. James Watt and Anne Wardwell, *When Silk was Gold: Central Asian and Chinese Textiles* (New York: Metropolitan Museum of Art in cooperation with the Cleveland Museum of Art, 1997), 127.
40. Ibid., 130.
41. For more discussion on the Ilkhanid phase of Takht-i Sulayman, see Masuya, 'Ilkhanid Phase of Takht-i Sulaimān'; Huff, 'Ilkhanid Palace at Takht-i Sulayman'; Stefano Carboni and Qamar Adamjee, 'Takht-i Sulaiman and Tilework in the Ilkhanid Period', The Metropolitan Museum of Art, http://www.metmuseum.org/toah/hd/khan7/hd_khan7.htm (last accessed 1 March 2023).
42. For instance, Masuya describes the motifs depicted on the tiles in Takht-i Sulayman as 'Chinese dragons and phoenixes'. See Masuya, 'Ilkhanid Courtly Life', 96.
43. For instance, giving lesser attention to the journey of the motifs, Canepa says: 'The first appearance of the dragon and the phoenix in Iran, as well as other images and ornament drawn from Mongol visual culture, occurs in tiles that decorated a ceremonial hall … [in the] site of Taḵt-e Solaymān.' See Canepa, 'Theorizing Cross-Cultural', 18. See also Yolande Crowe, 'Late Thirteenth-Century Persian Tilework and Chinese Textiles', *Bulletin of the Asia Institute* 5 (1991): 157.
44. Kadoi, 'Cloud Patterns', 27. For further discussion on the provenance and symbolic meaning of the pattern of dragon in general, see Giovanni Curatola, 'The Viar Dragon', in *Solṭāniye III, Quaderni del Seminario de Iranistica,*

Uralo-Altaistica e Caucasologia dell'Universita degli Studi de Venezia 9 (Venice: publisher not identified, 1982), 75–81. For further discussion on the dragon motif in areas west of Iran, see Sara Kuehn, *The Dragon in Medieval East Christian and Islamic Art* (Leiden; Boston: Brill, 2011), esp. 21–34.

45. Watt and Wardwell, *When Silk was Gold*, 77.
46. Ibid., 75.
47. See Kuehn's discussion about the westward migration of the dragon iconography from the Western Central Asian regions into Western Asia during the Seljuq period in Kuehn, *Dragon in Medieval East Christian*, 35.
48. Flood, *Objects of Translation*, 9.
49. In this context, the role of the 'carriers' is comparable with that of the language translators. In Rykwert's words, 'the quality and value of a translation from one language to another depends much more on the translator's mastery of the language into which he is translating, on his judgement and skill, and less on his knowledge of the language of the original text'. See Joseph Rykwert, 'Translation and/or Representation', *Arq* 63 (2006): 25. Regardless of the characteristics of the items that were transported, the nature of the act of transportation was largely dependent upon the attributes of the 'carriers'.
50. Lisa Golombek, Robert Mason and Gauvin Bailey, *Tamerlane's Tableware: A New Approach to the Chinoiserie Ceramics of the Fifteenth and Sixteenth Centuries* (Toronto and Costa Mesa: Mazda in association with the Royal Ontario Museum, 1996), 13.
51. Jonathan Bloom, 'Paper: The Transformative Medium in Ilkhanid Art', in *Beyond the Legacy of Genghis Khan*, ed. Linda Komaroff (Leiden: Brill, 2006), 298–302.
52. Gülru Necipoğlu, 'Geometric Design in Timurid/Turkmen Architectural Practice: Thoughts on a Recently Discovered Scroll and its Late Gothic Parallels', in *Timurid Art and Culture: Iran and Central Asia in the Fifteenth Century*, es. Lisa Golombek and Maria Subtelny (Leiden: Brill, 1992), 48.
53. For further discussion on the political agents of cultural transmission in the Ilkhanid court, see Hatef Naiemi, 'Confronting the Foreigner'.
54. For further discussion on different methods of transmission of designs in early Islamic architecture, see Jonathan Bloom, 'On the Transmission of Designs in Early Islamic Architecture', *Muqarnas* 10 (1993): 21–8.
55. This is particularly the case for Ghazan Khan, who is said to have designed the charitable complex of Shanb-i Ghazan himself (*khīshtan ṭarḥ kishīdih*). See Rashid al-Din and Jahn, *Tārīkh-i Mubārak-i Ghāzānī*, 208. Rashid al-Din also

reports that during the construction of Ghazan's tomb in Shanb-i Ghazan, the Ilkhan followed the process enthusiastically. He oversaw the workshop and was sometimes addressed by the master builders about the structural details of the building. See Rashid al-Din and Jahn, *Tārīkh-i Mubārak-i Ghāzānī*, 117.

56. Given the low number of military expeditions in Öljeytü's reign, O'Kane suggests that most of the seasonal movements of the Ilkhan were not dictated by necessity but were due to nomadism. See Bernard O'Kane, 'From Tents to Pavilions: Royal Mobility and Persian Palace Design', *Ars Orientalis* 23 (1993): 249.
57. The issue of the Mongols' tendency to adopt Chinese-style architecture as 'a vehicle of legitimation of rule' has been well studied in the case of the Yuan dynasty. See for instance Steinhardt, 'Imperial Architecture under Mongolian Patronage'; Steinhardt, 'Imperial Architecture along the Mongolian Road'; Steinhardt, *Chinese Imperial City Planning*. Although the political and social context is rather different, the Ilkhans' approach to Iranian-style monuments is comparable with that of their cousins to Chinese-style architecture.
58. Hillenbrand, *Islamic Art and Architecture*, 199. Hillenbrand also draws a comparison between Seljuq tomb towers and the yurt or tent of the Turkic nomads. He calls the tombs 'tents for the afterlife'. See ibid., 107.
59. On the orientation of the Mongols' dwellings (tents), see Ruysbroeck, *Mission of Friar William Rubruck*, 74–5.
60. Blair, 'Monumentality under the Mongols', 113; Jackson, *The Mongols and the Islamic World*, 363.
61. Flood, *Objects of Translation*, 262.
62. This institution was possibly not a central royal library-atelier in which all the models were produced by the court and sent to different regions, but various workshops spread across the state. See Akbarnia, '*Khita'i*: Cultural Memory', 196–7.
63. For a general survey of the cloud collar motif, see Schuyler Cammann, 'The Symbolism of the Cloud Collar Motif', *The Art Bulletin* 33, no. 1 (1951): 1–9.
64. Kadoi, 'Cloud Patterns', 33–4.
65. See e.g. *Preparations for a Festival* (an illustration from the *Jāmiʿ al-Tawārīkh*, Diez A, fol. 70, fourteenth century, Staatsbibliothek Berlin). The Diez albums in the Oriental Department of the Staatsbibliothek at Berlin contain more than four hundred figurative paintings, drawings, fragments and calligraphic works, originating mostly from Ilkhanid, Jalayirid and Timurid workshops. For further discussion on the Diez albums, see Julia Gonnella, Friederike Weis and

Christoph Rauch, *The Diez Albums: Contexts and Contents* (Leiden; Boston: Brill, 2017).

66. Masuya, 'Seasonal Capitals', 241. It is likely that the carpets were woven not to cover the floor of the palace but for the construction of the tent-palace itself. Masuya refers to the term 青白羊毛 used in the *Yuan Shi* (which literally means blue and white wool), but she does not mention the Chinese equivalent for 'carpet'. Therefore, it is not clear whether the wool was used to make 'carpet' or 'felt', as it was widely used by the Mongols for the construction of their felt-walled tents.
67. Eleanor Sims, 'The "Iconography" of the Internal Decoration in the Mausoleum of Ūljāytū at Sultaniyya', in *Content and Context of Visual Arts in the Islamic World: Papers from a Colloquium in Memory of Richard Ettinghausen*, ed. Carol Bier, Priscilla Parsons Soucek and Richard Ettinghausen (University Park: Pennsylvania State University Press for the College Art Association of America, 1988), 150.
68. Shigi-qutuqu was an abandoned baby found by the soldiers of Chinggis Khan. He gave the baby as a prize of war to his mother, Mother Hö'elün. She named him Shigiken-quduqu (Shigi-qutuqu) and raised him. See Onon, *Secret History of the Mongols*, 114.
69. Onon, *Secret History of the Mongols*, 192–3.
70. Allsen, *Commodity and Exchange*, 57.
71. Onon, *Secret History of the Mongols*, 190.
72. Ibid., 207.
73. Moule and Pelliot, *Marco Polo*, vol. 1, 222.
74. Sawma, *Monks of Kublai Khan*, 250.
75. Ibn Battuta, *Travels of Ibn Battuta*, 220.
76. Soudavar, 'The Saga of Abu-Sa'id', 130.
77. Greenish blue.
78. Rashid al-Din, *Jāmiʿ al-Tawārīkh*, vol. 2, 1,325.
79. Kadoi, 'Chinese and Turko-Mongol Elements', 637.
80. For further discussion on the position of textile furnishings in both the indoor and outdoor life of the Mongol princes, see Lisa Golombek, 'The Draped Universe of Islam', in *Content and Context of Visual Arts in the Islamic World*, ed. Priscilla Soucek (University Park: Pennsylvania State University Press for the College Art Association of America, 1988), 30–1.
81. Kadoi, *Islamic Chinoiserie*, 31.
82. The Venetian traveller Barbaro, cited in Blair, 'Mongol Capital of Sulṭāniyya', 143.

83. Blair divides the epigraphic material of the tomb into four categories: pious phrases or sacred names; Qur'anic citations; *ḥadīth*s; and historical references, including dates. See Blair, 'Epigraphic Program of the Tomb', 61. Regarding the internal decoration of the tomb, Sims refers to small-scale geometrical and floral ornament. See Sims, 'Iconography of the Internal Decoration', 143. In accordance with these observations about the decorative programme of the tomb, during my fieldwork in Sultaniyya I found no trace of the ornament resembling the motifs inscribed on the boss.
84. For the image of the ball joint, see Gaston Wiet, *L'Exposition Persane de 1931* [The Persian Exhibition of 1931] (Cairo: Institut Français D'archéologie Orientale, 1933), 45–6.
85. Rashid al-Din, *Jāmiʿ al-Tawārīkh*, vol. 2, 1,376.
86. The cenotaph in Sanjar's tomb dates only from 1906. See Blair, 'Monumentality under the Mongols', 168. However, its mere presence supports the idea that the original cenotaph was possibly located in this exact spot marking the tomb of the sultan underneath the ground.
87. Blair, 'Monumentality under the Mongols', 136–7.
88. Blair, 'Mongol Capital of Sulṭāniyya', 143.
89. Soudavar, 'The Saga of Abu-Saʿid', 143.
90. Wassaf al-Hazra and Ayati, *Taḥrīr-i Tārīkh-i Wassaf*, 355.
91. Hafiz-i Abru, *Dhayl-i Jāmiʿ al-Tawārīkh-i Rashīdī*, 119–20.
92. Mirfattah, 'Sultaniyya', 21–2.
93. The Qur'anic inscriptions of Phase 1 are mostly limited to short *sura*s and do not bear on the function of the building. However, parts of the Throne Verse of *Sura* 2, which is frequently seen in Muslim tombs, can be found among the inscriptions. See Sims, 'Iconography of the Internal Decoration', 149–50.
94. Blair, 'Monumentality under the Mongols', 126–7. Blair also re-examines the inscriptions of the building with regard to contemporary political events of the reign of Öljeytü. She suggests that the inscriptions of the second phase reflect his attempt to capture the Holy Cities. See Blair, 'Monumentality under the Mongols', 125. In her view, the architectural features and the inscriptions both propose that the building in fact symbolised the Ilkhan's 'desired dominance as God's caliph on earth, protector of the holy cities, and lord of the world'. See Blair, 'Epigraphic Program of the Tomb', 73.
95. Blair, 'Epigraphic Program of the Tomb', 60.
96. See *Tent mosque or Mongol princes studying the Quran* (an illustration from the *Jāmiʿ al-Tawārīkh*, Diez A, fol. 70, fourteenth century, Staatsbibliothek Berlin).

97. Komaroff and Carboni, *Legacy of Genghis Khan*, 252. I have not found any reference to such portable mosques in literary sources, although there are some references to portable schools in historical texts; see for instance Wassaf al-Hazra and Ayati, *Taḥrīr-i Tārīkh-i Wassaf*, 304.
98. See the *Siege of Alamut* (an illustration from the *Jāmiʿ al-Tawārīkh*, Bibliothèque Nationale de France). The description says that '[Hülegü Khan] *angusht-i taʿajjub dar dandān-i taḥayyur girift*'. For further studies of the gestures of human figures in medieval paintings, see Anna Contadini, *A World of Beasts: A Thirteenth-Century Illustrated Arabic Book on Animals (the Kitāb Naʿt al-Ḥayawān) in the Ibn Bakhtīshūʿ Tradition* (Leiden; Boston: Brill, 2012).
99. Onon, *Secret History of the Mongols*, 190. There are several references in the historical accounts confirming that the Mongols' tents were literally built of white felt. For instance, when Juvayni refers to Ögedey's tent, Sir Ordu, he describes it as a pavilion whose walls were made of lattice wood, and they were covered with white felt. See Juvayni, *Tārīkh-i Jahāngushāy*, vol. 1, 296. William of Rubruck also describes the dwellings of the Tartars as a hoop of interlaced branches which was covered with white felt. See Ruysbroeck, *Mission of Friar William Rubruck*, 72.
100. Sinor, for instance, mentions that in many Chinese historians' eyes the steppe people were barbarians with no cities or fixed dwellings nor any kind of agriculture. See Sinor, 'Horse and Pasture', 172. For further discussion on these stereotypes, see the Introduction.
101. Michal Biran, 'Rulers and City Life in Mongol Central Asia (1220–1370)', in *Turko-Mongol Rulers, Cities, and City Life*, ed. David Durand-Guedy (Boston; Leiden: Brill, 2013), 257–9.

    Much earlier than the emergence of the Mongol Empire in the thirteenth century, during the period of Uyghur power in Mongolia beginning in the mid-eighth century, several walled settlements were constructed. The Uyghur capital, Khar Balgas, located to the north of Karakorum, is one example of these settlements. Later, during the time of the Khitans in the eleventh century, significant settlements were built; for instance, Kharbukhyn (Kharukhain) Balgas was one of the three centres founded by the Khitans. For further discussion see Daniel Waugh, 'Nomads and Settlement: New Perspectives in the Archaeology of Mongolia', *Silk Road Journal* 8 (2010): 97–123.
102. This hypothesis does not rule out the idea of borrowing from the sedentary civilisations; however, it would indicate that the borrowing took place much

earlier than the period when the Ilkhans in the West and the Yuan in the East conducted their architectural and urban undertakings. For further discussion on Chinese influences in city construction in Mongolia prior to the conquest phase, see Waugh, 'Nomads and Settlement'.

103. Rashid al-Din, *Jāmiʿ al-Tawārīkh*, vol. 1, 671.

104. Masashi Haneda, 'Gāzāniyya in Tabrīz', in *Urbanism in Islam: The Proceedings of International Conference on Urbanism in Islam (ICUIT)* (Tokyo: The Middle Eastern Culture Centre, 1989), vol. 2, 293.

105. In addition to literary sources, some of the inscriptions of the tomb of Öljeytü can also be interpreted with regard to the significance of the building as a centre of pilgrimage and circumambulation. See Blair, 'Epigraphic Program of the Tomb', 67. In my view, the most relevant inscription is the one encircling the dome at the highest level. The inscription contains the Qur'an, 2:127: 'And [mention] when Abraham was raising the foundations of the House and [with him] Ishmael, [saying], Our Lord, accept [this] from us. Indeed, You are the Hearing, the Knowing.'

'English Translation of Sura al-Baqara', King Saud University, https://quran.ksu.edu.sa/index.php?l=en#aya=2_127 (last accessed 23 August 2023).

106. Referring to Kashani's mention of the burial of Öljeytü's wife in his tomb in Sultaniyya, Blair suggests that – comparable with the tomb of Ghazan in Tabriz – Öljeytü had always considered his tomb as a place of pilgrimage. See Kashani, *Tārīkh-i Öljeytü*, 83 and Blair, 'Monumentality under the Mongols', 126. Although I agree with her on the significance of the tomb as a place of pilgrimage, in my view this quality had been more noticeable in the case of Ghazan's tomb in Tabriz, as there are more references to the pilgrimage rituals performed in Shanb-i Ghazan in primary sources; see for instance Rashid al-Din and Jahn, *Tārīkh-i Mubārak-i Ghāzānī*, 209–14. I have addressed the question of the sacredness attributed to Ghazan and Öljeytü themselves as well as their burial places in an as-yet-unpublished article, 'In Search of Blessing: The Veneration of the Tomb of Ghazan Khan from the Ilkhanid Period to the Present'.

107. Kashani, *Tārīkh-i Öljeytü*, 45. To the best of my knowledge, this is the only occasion on which Sultaniyya is called 'Kaʿba' by a medieval historian. In the ode dedicated to Öljeytü, Wassaf calls Sultaniyya 'the fifth heaven of the world (*panjumīn jannat-i dunyā*)'. Although this phrase possibly pointed to the outstanding scenic beauty of Sultaniyya, it also indicated the spiritual importance of the city. See Ayati, 'Qaṣīda-yi Wassaf al-Hazra', 27.

108. On the practice of visiting tombs during the medieval period, see Christopher Schurman Taylor, *In the Vicinity of the Righteous: Ziyāra and the Veneration of Muslim Saints in Late Medieval Egypt* (Leiden; Boston: Brill, 1998).

109. The religious significance of the tomb of Öljeytü may be explained in connection with the story that is told concerning Öljeytü's intention to transfer the bodies of Imam 'Ali and Imam Husayn to his tomb. Sir Percy Sykes writes that 'he [Öljeytü] entertained the project of transporting the bones of 'Ali and Husayn from Najaf and Kerbela respectively and erected a superb building to receive the sacred remains. His plan was never realised, and the building became his own mausoleum.' See Sir Percy Sykes, *A History of Persia* (London: Macmillan & Co., 1915), vol. 2, 235. While Sykes suggests that Öljeytü built the tomb for the bodies of the two imams, Andre Godard considers this idea to be against tradition. He also argues that such a huge building could not have been finished in four years (which is the time period between the conversion of the Ilkhan in 1309 and the dedication of the building in 1313). Godard suggests that the building was originally built as the Ilkhan's tomb, but changed when Öljeytü converted to Shi'ism and decided to bring the bodies to Sultaniyya (Godard, 'Mausoleum of Öljeitü', 1,111–13). Nevertheless, some recent studies analyse the changes in the structure and internal decoration of the tomb in relation to the functional changes of the building as well as to contemporary events in the reign of Öljeytü (briefly discussed earlier in this chapter), without crediting this story: see for instance Sims, 'Iconography of the Internal Decoration' and Blair, 'Monumentality under the Mongols'. To the best of my knowledge, there is no reference to this legend in any source from the period.

110. After the death of Arghun Khan, the Mongols accompanying Ghazan Khan in Semnan removed the feathers of their helmets by order of the Ilkhan, according to a Mongol tradition. See Rashid al-Din, *Jāmi' al-Tawārīkh*, vol. 2, 1230. This is one of many examples of the traditional Mongol way of doing things that was still common under the later Ilkhans.

111. David Morgan, 'The "Great Yāsā of Chingiz Khān" and Mongol Law in the Īlkhānate', *Bulletin of the School of Oriental and African Studies, University of London* 49, no. 1 (1986): 172; Kashani, *Tārīkh-i Öljeytü*, 98.

112. Kashani, *Tārīkh-i Öljeytü*, 99.

113. See Persis Berlekamp, 'The Limits of Artistic Exchange in Fourteenth-Century Tabriz: The Paradox of Rashid al-Din's Book on Chinese Medicine, Part I', *Muqarnas* 27 (2010): 230.

Concluding Remarks
The Study of Ilkhanid Cities: Challenges and Successes

For decades within modern scholarship, the Mongols of Central Asian steppe origin were often characterised solely as barbaric conquerors responsible for the destruction of the cultural accomplishments of settled societies. However, more recent studies have revealed that they held a significant position in enabling transcultural interactions between East and West during the medieval period. Despite the sedentary world's reductive stereotypes, Mongol nomads were not passive mediators of cultural exchange, but rather active agents who facilitated the long journey of commodities and ideas across Eurasia. This book has taken one step further and has suggested that, beyond contributing to the transportation of signs and meanings between the Far East and West Asia, Mongol Ilkhans who felt nostalgic about the customs of their ancestors and had a tendency to revive the traditions of their homeland brought part of their own nomadic system of values to their conquered land, Iran. Although they showed inclinations to adopt Iranian local language in art, religion and politics, they never broke their ties with cultural conventions.

Through examination of the urban centres founded under the patronage of the Ilkhans, this study has attempted to illuminate the dialogue that was established between the Mongol conquerors and the Iranians following the mid-thirteenth-century conquest of Iran. While acknowledging the presence of diverse imported visual conventions, particularly Chinese decorative repertoire in Ilkhanid art, the book has placed greater emphasis on the Mongol nomadic traditions and concepts that penetrated the court-sponsored architectural projects. Conversely, it also looked at the impact of the settled

Iranian-Islamic culture of Iran on the Ilkhans, which was influential in transforming Central Asian nomads into the rulers of the sedentary world.

Theorising of the Iranian–Mongol encounter needs to be grounded in a physical context, which, in this research, is the built environment of their cities. Since the Ilkhans themselves were actively involved in the design and construction of architectural projects, particularly in their major urban centres such as Ghazaniyya and Sultaniyya, these endeavours denoted the political aspirations and religious mindset of their patrons more powerfully than the artefacts and manuscripts crafted in the court's workshops and scriptoriums by artists and scribes. The charitable foundations built under the patronage of Mongol rulers represented their perceptions of life and the afterlife. The constructions symbolising the majesty of their imperial power were also a genuine reflection of how the Ilkhans wished to be judged in their subjects' eyes.

This book has considered Ilkhanid cities within the broader socio-religious political context in which the concept of medieval urbanism evolved. The survey of neighbouring cities in Western and Eastern Asia in Chapter 1 paved the way for a comprehensive examination of the Ilkhans' major political and administrative centres in Chapter 2. The study of a larger number of Ilkhanid urban foundations was followed, in the next two chapters, by a detailed inspection of the most significant architectural projects conducted under Mongol rule in Ghazaniyya and Sultaniyya. This analysis not only served to describe the spatial structure of the two cities, but also shed much light on the question of the encounter between Perso-Islamic concepts and Mongolian nomadic conventions. Elaborating on the previous findings of the book, the final chapter sought to theorise the interactions underlying the syncretic nature of Ilkhanid cities. To this end, the communications were approached at three distinct levels operating between people as well as their undertakings, as follows: a dialogue between Khans and sultans/padishahs; a dialogue between tents and buildings; and a dialogue between camps and cities.

This study also took the question of encounter between the conqueror and the conquered beyond the Ilkhanate. Focusing on the imperial urban foundations of the Yuan dynasty, I discussed how Mongol emperors, as a foreign military group, took advantage of the local language of art and architecture in order to legitimise their rule in the Far East. Whether or not the results of this study are directly applicable to the presence of the Ilkhans in Iran, it provided insights into the approach adopted by Mongol nomads in their interaction with sedentary cultures in the post-conquest period, including that of Iran. A comparative study seems to be most fruitful in the case of the Ilkhans and their relatives in Yuan China, due to their common ethnic and cultural background as well as their partially shared interests. However, the comparison can be appropriately extended to other groups that represented diverse cases of the encounter between native inhabitants and ethnically foreign-origin ruling elites in the medieval world: for example, the Ilkhans' western neighbour, the Mamluk Sultanate,[1] or the Ilkhans' successors, the Timurids (1370–1507), who were also of Turco-Mongol origin. Like their predecessors, the rulers of the Timurid dynasty retained the tradition of erecting royal camps in the vicinity of their cities. Despite the foundation of prosperous cities, such as Samarqand, Timur, the founder of the Timurid Empire and 'a sovereign in transition between nomadic and sedentary living',[2] adhered to his camp outside the city walls where he conducted feasts and festivals, made political and military decisions and received foreign emissaries.[3]

Making a comparison between Mamluk and Ilkhanid cities raises the question of whether the latter can essentially fit into the general framework of 'Islamic urbanism'. Ilkhanid cities, particularly those patronised by the Ilkhans themselves, were built mostly in accordance with the general characteristics of many cities that developed across the Islamic world around the same time. This study, however, has revealed some qualities which are unique to these sites, for instance, the different nature of the concept of the citadel. In medieval Islamic urbanism, including Mamluk cities, a citadel consisting of royal mosques, palaces and places for ruling family and the military was the centre of the power and government of the military elite. In the Ilkhanid city, by contrast, the *abwāb al-birr*, being formed from several charitable buildings encircling the tomb of the Ilkhan and his household, shaped the central core of the city. This book has touched upon the distinguishing feature of the Ilkhanid city, and, to some extent, contributory forces such as the popularity of Sufism in Ilkhanid Iran and the impact of Sufi shrine complexes on the Ilkhans,[4] but further studies are needed, first to clarify the religious, political and administrative significance of these charitable complexes, and second, to explain the Ilkhans' preference for such foundations rather than citadels at the heart of their cities.

In addition to the built environment of Ilkhanid cities, this study has looked into the social dynamics that catalysed the formation of these urban centres. Nonetheless, there are still certain restrictions: for example, the examination of contributory figures was limited here to the members of the royal court and the ruling elite, whereas it could extend to the broader social network which actively participated in the construction of the urban centres. This network is formed from people who indicated a need for buildings, the individuals or groups who financed the construction of buildings, and the architects, builders and overseers who designed, executed and supervised construction projects. It would be challenging to uncover the social structure of Ilkhanid society outside the court, as historical accounts written by court historians contain hardly any information on commoners. The urban areas associated with the general public have also been given less attention, since excavations are often conducted in the urban spaces with a higher concentration of architectural and archaeological remains: for instance, the core of the city embracing the key elements of congregational mosque, bazaar and citadel, rather than the civilian settlement of the cities. The latter is an area that deserves greater attention in future studies.

Addressing the question of Mongol–Iranian transcultural interactions in the context of the architectural landscape of cities, this book has sought to clarify the poorly understood picture of the Ilkhanid city and to remove ambiguities concerning the tangible and intangible forces that formed the architectural identity of the city. Despite having used various sources of evidence, however, we are still struggling with significant deficiencies in different categories of information. For instance, much archaeological evidence has yet to be unearthed in several important Ilkhanid sites, and several non-Persian literary sources, more particularly Mongolian and Chinese texts, have been overlooked owing to language restrictions. Consequently, many questions remain to be answered. In view of the ongoing excavations being conducted in a number of Ilkhanid sites, as well as the larger number of Eastern Asian sources being translated into European languages, it is hoped that the broader availability of physical and textual evidence will pave the way for a more detailed exploration of these cities. Taking into account all the findings in this research, the Ilkhanid city should now be characterised as possessing a hybrid quality, which was injected not only into the physical structure of the city, but also into the world views, motivations and tastes of its patrons.

Notes

1. The Mamluks' adherence to their Inner Asian legacy has been partly examined by Amitai-Preiss in the context of the Mamluk Sultanate of Egypt and Syria. See Amitai-Preiss, 'Echoes of the Eurasian Steppe'. For further discussion on the issue of Mamluk legitimisation using Islamic themes (the religion of their subjects) in relation to their external audience, see Anne Broadbridge, 'Mamluk Legitimacy and the Mongols: The Reigns of Baybars and Qalāwūn', *Mamlūk Studies Review* V (2001): 91–118. See also the sources mentioned by Broadbridge on Mamluk legitimacy in relation to their internal audience (ibid., 91).
2. Gronke, 'The Persian Court', 19.
3. Clavijo, the Spanish ambassador who visited Samarqand in 1404, described Timur's royal camp in detail. See Clavijo, *Embassy to Tamerlane*, 266–77.
4. See Chapter 3, section 'Observing Ghazaniyya and Shanb-i Ghazan from a Perso-Islamic perspective'. For further studies on Sufism in Ilkhanid Iran, see Amitai-Preiss, 'Sufis and Shamans' and Lane, *Early Mongol Rule*, 229–36; on Sufi shrines, see Golombek, 'Cult of Saints'; Sheila Blair, 'Sufi Saints and Shrine Architecture in the Early Fourteenth Century', *Muqarnas* 7 (1990): 35–49.

Appendix

This appendix presents some of the historical accounts which have been mentioned briefly in the book. The aim is to give the reader a better understanding of the original accounts by providing the complete passages as they appear in the primary sources. In each section the account in Persian script is followed by the English translation. Translations of all the passages are by the author.

1 Rashid al-Din's Account of the Presence of the Buddhists in Maraghih (Chapter 2) in Rashid al-Din, *Jāmiʿ al-Tawārīkh*, vol. 2, 1,176–9

(1176) ارغون خان چهارم رمضان سنه ثمان و ثمانین و ستمائه در مراغه نزول فرمود و به تفرج رصد رفت و داروی سیاه خوردن که ذکر آن خواهد آمد آنجا آغاز کرد.

(1179) ارغون خان به غایت معتقد بخشیان و طریقه ایشان بود و همواره آن طایفه را تربیت و تقویت می فرمود. از جانب هند بخشی ای بیامد و دعوی عمر درازی می کرد. از وی پرسید که به چه طریق عمر بخشیان آنجا دراز می گردد. گفت: به دارویی مخصوص. ارغون خان سؤال کرد که آن دارو اینجا یافت شود. گفت: شود. اشارت فرمود تا آن را ترتیب کند. بخشی معجونی بساخت که در آن گوگرد و زیبق بود و قرب هشت ماه آن را تناول می فرمود.

(1176) Arghun Khan arrived in Maraghih on the 4th of Ramaḍan 688 and promenaded towards the observatory and began to eat the black drug (*dārū-yi sīyāh*), which will be mentioned later, there.

(1179) Arghun Khan had great faith in Buddhist priests (*bakhshīyān*) and their way, and always supported those people and encouraged them. A Buddhist priest came from India and claimed that he had lived a long life. [Arghun] asked him how the Buddhist priests had a long life there. He said:

with a special drug. Arghun Khan asked him if the drug could be found here. [He] said: yes. [Arghun] ordered him to arrange that. The priest made an elixir (*maʿjūn*) in which there were sulfur (*gūgird*) and mercury (*sīmāb*), and [Arghun] ate that for about eight months.

2 Rashid al-Din's Account of the Foundation of Ujan (Chapter 2) in Rashid al-Din, *Jāmiʿ al-Tawārīkh*, vol. 2, 1,303–5

(1303) طوی عام فرمودن پادشاه اسلام در اوردوی زرین به موضع باغ اوجان و ختم کردن قرآن در آنجا و بذل عام فرمودن

پادشاه اسلام پیش از آن استادان فاخر و مهندسان ماهر را فرموده بود تا خرگاهی زرین و تختی رزین با آلات و ادوات مناسب سازند و مدت سه سال گروهی انبوه به ترتیب آن مشغول بودند و در این وقت که به دارالملک تبریز رسید تمام شده بود. در اواخر ذی القعده سنه احدی و سبعمائه از تبریز به اوجان حرکت فرمود و در آنجا مرغزاری را به غایت نزه و خرم به جهت نزول مبارک دیوار کشیده و در آنجا رودخانه ها و چشمه های آب روان است و حوض ها و آبگیرهای معظم ساخته اند و انواع طیور در آنجا مأوی گرفته و آن مربع متساوی الاضلاع را به اقسام متساویه بخش کرده و بر دو طرف مرزهای آن درخت بید و سپیدار نشانده تا ممر خلق بر آن مرزها باشد و هیچ آفریده ای در میان مرغزار نگذرد و راه هر طایفه ای معین که از کجا درآیند و از کجا بیرون شوند و در آن (1304) میان کوشک ها و برج ها و حمام و عمارات عالیه ساخته فرمود تا آن خرگاه زرین را در میان آن باغ بزنند با بارگاه و سایه بان ها که بدان مخصوص است. تمامت فراش ها و مهندسان جمع شدند، در مدت یک ماه توانستند زد از غایت عظمت، و تخت مرصع به جواهر و یواقیت بنهادند.

(1303) *Padishah-i Islām* throwing a public feast (*ṭuy-i ʿām*) in the golden encampment (*ordu-yi zarrīn*) at the garden of Ujan and completing the recitation of the Qur'an there, and ordering a public bestowal (*bazl-i ʿām*)

Padishah-i Islām had already ordered excellent masters (*ustādān*) and skilful engineers (*muhandisān*) to build a golden tent (*khargāh-i zarrīn*) and a firm throne (*takht-i razīn*) with all the necessary equipment, and a large group were busy organising that for three years, and when [Ghazan] arrived in the *dār al-mulk* of Tabriz at this time, the construction had finished. In late Dhul Qaʿda 701 [Ghazan] travelled from Tabriz to Ujan, and [they] had built a wall around an extremely pleasing meadow (*marghzār*) for his arrival, and rivers and springs are flowing there, and [they] have built grand pools, and different kinds of birds have nested there, and [they] have divided that square into equal sections and have planted willows and poplars on both sides of its borders to be the path for those who are going past the borders, and no creature (*āfarīdih*) passes through the meadow, and the path of each tribe (family) was clear, from where they can come in and from where they can go out (1304), and [Ghazan] built pavilions, towers, public baths, and magnificent edifices there and ordered [them] to erect the golden tent and its special canopies in that garden. All the handymen (*farrāshān*) and engineers gathered, [they] could set up [the tent] after one month because of its grandness and decorated the throne with jewels and rubies.

3 Mustawfi's Account of the Foundation of Ujan (Chapter 2) in Mustawfi, *Nuzhat al-Qulūb*, 127

(127) بیژن بن گیو بن گودرز ساخت، غازان خان تجدید عمارتش کرد و از سنگ و گچ بارو کشید و شهر اسلام خواند و دارالملک ساخت، دور باروی غازانی سه هزار گام بود ... غله نیکو حاصل دارد و با حاصل شهر به هم به وقف ابواب البر غازانی تعلق دارد.

(127) Bizhan bin Giv bin Gudarz built [Ujan], Ghazan Khan reconstructed it and erected a wall built of stone and plaster and called it Shahr-i Islam (City of Islam) and designated it as *dār al-mulk*. The perimeter of the wall of Ghazan Khan (*bārū-yi Ghāzānī*) was 3,000 paces (*gāms*) ... [Ujan] produces high-grade grain which, together with the income of the city, belong to the endowment of the *abwāb al-birr* of Ghazan Khan (*abwāb al-birr-i Ghāzānī*).

4 Rashid al-Din's Account of the Foundation of Ghazaniyya (Chapter 3) in Rashid al-Din, *Jāmi' al-Tawārīkh*, vol. 2, 1,369–76

(1369) حکایت دوازدهم در عمارت دوستی پادشاه اسلام و تحریض فرمودن مردم بر آن

پیش از این پادشاهان مغول و بعضی از آبا و اجداد پادشاه اسلام خلد سلطانه هوس عمارت داشتهاند و در آن شروع کرده، لیکن کمتر به انجام رسانیده چنانکه مشاهده رفته...

(1372) ... و شهر تبریز که این زمان دار الملک است بارویی مختصر داشت و آن نیز مندرس گشته، و بیرون شهر خانه ها و عمارات بسیار است، فرمود که چگونه شاید که شهری چندین هزار آدمی آنجا ساکن اند و دارالملک است آن را بارویی نسازند؟! ...

(1373) ... فرمود تا بارو بیرون باغات بگردانیدند ... (1374) و شهری دیگر بزرگتر از محوطه تبریز قدیم در موضع شنب، و شم نیز گویند که ابواب البر ساخته بنا فرموده، چنانکه ابواب البر و اکثر باغات آن محیط است و آن را غازانیه نام نهاد و فرمود که تجار که از روم و افرنج رسند بار آنجا گشایند، لیکن تمغاچی آنجا و از آن شهر تبریز یکی باشد تا منازعت نیفتد ...

(1376) ... و چون در دارالملک تبریز [بود] آنجا اختیار فرمود، و خارج شهر در جانب غربی در موضع شنب خویشتن طرح کشیده آن را بنیاد نهاد و این زمان چند سال [است] تا به عمارت آن مشغول اند و از گنبد سلطان سنجر سلجوقی به مرو که معظم‌ترین عمارات عالم است و دیده بود بسیار باعظمت تر بنیاد نهاده ...

(1369) The twelfth anecdote, which is about *Padishah-i Islām*'s interest in construction (*ʿimārat-dūstī*) and encouraging people in this work
Previously, Mongol kings and some of the ancestors of *Padishah-i Islām* – may his kingship last for ever – had a desire for construction and started that, but, as has been observed, [they] have accomplished less ...

(1372) ... The city of Tabriz, which is the *dār al-mulk* at this time, had an insignificant wall, and that also had been damaged, and many houses and edifices are located outside the city. [Ghazan] said, how is it possible that [in] a city in which several thousand people reside and [which] is the *dār al-mulk*, [they] do not build a wall for it? ...

(1373) ... [Ghazan] ordered [them] to build the wall outside of the gardens ... (1374) and [he] has founded another city (*shahr*), larger than the encompassment of Old Tabriz, in Shanb, also called Shamm, where [he] had built the *abwāb al-birr* in such a way that [the city] encompasses the *abwāb al-birr* and most of its gardens, and [he] called it Ghazaniyya, and ordered the merchants, who arrive from Rum and Afranj, to unload there, but the toll-collector (*tamghāchī*) [of Ghazaniyya] and the one of Tabriz should be the same [person] to prevent hostility (*tā munāziʿat nayuftad*) ...

(1376) ... Since [Ghazan] was in the *dār al-mulk* of Tabriz, he made a decision there and himself designed a building (*khīshtan ṭarḥ kishīdih*) and founded it outside the city [of Tabriz] to the west [of Tabriz] in Shanb, and at this time, it has been a few years that [they] have been busy constructing it, and [he] has founded it much more majestic than the tomb of Sultan Sanjar at Marv, which is the grandest edifice of the world and [he] had seen it before.

5 Mustawfi's Account of the Foundation of Ghazaniyya (Chapter 3) in Mustawfi, *Nuzhat al-Qulūb*, 123

(122) چون در عهد مغول آن شهر (تبریز) دارالملک گشت (123) کثرت خلایق در آنجا جمع شدند و بر بیرون شهر عمارات کردند ... غازان خان آن را بارویی کشید چنانکه تمامت باغات و عمارات و دیه ها و ولیان کوه و سنجاران نیز داخل آن بارو بود، جهت وفات او تمام ناکرده بماند و دور باروی غازانی بیست و پنج هزار گام است و شش دروازه دارد ... در زیر شهر به موضعی که شام می خوانند خارج باروی غازانی، غازان خان شهرچه ای برآورده است و جهت خوابگاه خود در آنجا عمارات عالیه کرده چنانکه مثل آن در تمامت ایران نیست.

(122) Since during the Mongol period that city (Tabriz) became the *dār al-mulk* (123) a large population gathered there and built their buildings outside the city ... Ghazan Khan built a wall for it in a way that all the gardens, buildings, villages, Valiyan-kuh and Sanjaran were located inside the wall. [The wall] was left unfinished because of his death, and the perimeter of the wall of Ghazan Khan (*bārū-yi Ghāzānī*) is 25,000 paces and [it] has six gates ... Ghazan Khan founded a small city (*shahrchih*) in the south of the city [of Tabriz] in a place called Sham outside the wall of Ghazan Khan and built magnificent edifices there for his own chamber (*khābgāh*) in such a way that it (the small city) has no equal in Iran.

6 Wassaf's Account of the Construction of Sultaniyya (Chapter 4) in Wassaf al-Hazra and Ayati, *Taḥrīr-i Tārīkh-i Wassaf*, 277

(277) در بهار سال 704 عمارتی را که در مکانی به نام قنقور اولانگ پدر او بنیان نهاده و اکنون ناتمام بود تمام کرد و آن را سلطانیه نامید. مخارج ساختمان و اجناس و آلات آن را بر مالی که از ولایات می رسید حوالت کرد و رسولان برای گردآوری مال به اطراف روان گشتند و بنایان و مهندسان به کار مشغول شدند و گروه کثیری از صنعتگران با زن و فرزند به آنجا کوچ کردند و به کار اتمام آن بنای عظیم مشغول شدند. مرا در وصف بنای سلطانیه قصیده ای است.

(277) In the spring of 704, Öljeytü completed the construction of a city that had formerly been founded by his father Arghun in Qunqur Öläng and was unfinished at this time and named it Sultaniyya. He assigned the money (*māl*), which came from the provinces, for the expenses of construction and

[necessary] goods and tools and [his] messengers moved around to collect the money, and builders (*bannāyān*) and engineers (*muhandisān*) became busy working [there], and a large group of artisans (*ṣan'atgarān*) with their wives and children migrated there and became busy finishing that magnificent construction. I have an ode on the foundation of Sultaniyya.

7 Amuli's Account of the Foundation of Sultaniyya (Chapter 4) in Amuli, *Nafāyis al-Funūn*, vol. 2, 257–8

(257) ... و آثار او (اولجایتو) در جهان از شهرها و قلاع و ابواب خیر و مساجد و مدارس عالی بسیار است. از آن جمله شهر سلطانیه که در شهور سنه اربع و سبعمائة بنیاد نهاد و در مدت ده سال به مرتبه رسانید که از بلاد ربع مسکون معمورتر شد و در وسط سلطانیه قلعه بس عالی به مقدار شهری بنا فرمود، وجهه مرقد خود گنبدی بس عالی هشت منار (258) بر سر آن ساخته و در حوالی آن ابواب خیر از جامع و خانقاه و مدارس و دارالسیاده که هرگز مثل آن در جهان کس ندیده و نشنیده بفرمود و بسیاری از املاک نفیسه بر آنجا وقف کرد چنانچه حاصل آن در عهد دولت او به صد تومان می رسید و چون این جمله به تعلیم و ارشاد وزیر عالم عادل ... خواجه رشیدالدین ... بود نیابت تولیت بدو داد.

(257) ... and his works (the works of Öljeytü) in the world are numerous, including cities and castles and *abwāb-i khayr*s and mosques and excellent madrasas. One of those [is] the city of Sultaniyya that he founded in the months of year 704 and during ten years [the city] reached the point where it became more flourishing than other cities in the world, and in the centre of Sultaniyya [he] founded a great castle, which was the size of a city; on the side of his tomb (*marqad*) [he built] a sublime dome and eight minarets (258) on its top, and around it [he] built the *abwāb-i khayr* consisting of *Jāmi'* mosque and khanqah and madrasas and *dār al-sīyāda*, that no one has ever seen or heard like that in the world, and [he] endowed extensive valuable lands to it (the *abwāb-i khayr*) in such a way that its income reached 100 *tumān*s during his reign, and since all these happened because of the teachings and guidance of the learned and virtuous ... vizier Khwajih Rashid al-Din ..., [Öljeytü] bestowed the custodianship (*tawlīyyat*) [of the endowments] upon him.

8 Hafiz-i Abru's Account of the Foundation of Sultaniyya (Chapter 4) in Hafiz-i Abru, *Dhayl-i Jāmiʿ al-Tawārīkh-i Rashīdī*, 67–8

(67) [سلطان] فرمود که یک روز پیش پدر خود پادشاه ارغون ... حاضر بودم او را داعیه عمارت سلطانیه بر خاطر خطور کرده بود فرمود همچنان که من پادشاه جهانم می خواهم شهری بنا کنم که آن شاه بلاد بود، جماعتی که حاضر بودند بسی مواضع نام بردند و هر یک از آنچه از عیب و هنر دانستند باز نمودند آخرالامر موضع قنقور اولانگ اختیار کردند که ییلاقی به غایت منتزه است ... فرمان فرمود تا طرح شهر برکشیدند و بنای قلعه آن از سنگ تراشیده اشارت فرمود. فاما چون بنیاد عمارت کرد زمانه فرصت نداد که به اتمام رسد اکنون می خواهم که آنچه پدر من بنیاد کرده بود اگر حق سبحانه توفیق بخشد به اتمام رسانم چه فرزند شایسته آن است که پیروی مادر و پدر کند و نام او را زنده دارد ... و این شهر و قلعه نه از برای آن می سازم که اگر نعوذ بالله سختی پیش آید این موضوع مرا مأمنی باشد یا از آن مرا مالی حاصل شود، باعث اصلی برین عمارت آن است که پادشاه ارغون بنیاد کرده بود و می خواست که تمام کند روزگار فرصت نداد ... (68) در اندک زمانی شهری عالی معمور شد و قلعه آن را دیوار از سنگ تراشیده کرده اند ... و اصل قلعه مربع نهاده اند طول و عرض مساوی ... و یک دروازه و شانزده برج دارد ... و در اندرون قلعه هر کس از امرا موضعی عمارت کرده بود و سطان اولجایتو از برای مدفن خود در اندرون قلعه عمارتی ساخته است و آن را ابواب البر نام نهاده و گنبدی مثمن بزرگ عالی که قطر آن شصت گز است ... و ارتفاع آن صد و بیست گز ... و متصل آن گنبد، چند عمارت عالی ساخته است مسجدی به تکلف و دارالضیافه و دارالسیاده و موقوفات بسیار بر آن وقف کرده ... در شهر مساجد بسیار ساخته اند اما مسجد جمعه که سلطان ساخت ... و دارالشفائی دیگر ... و دگر مدرسه عالی بر نمونه مستنصر به بغداد در آن شهر بساخت ...

(67) [Sultan] said: one day I was with my father, Padishah Arghun ... and he had decided to found Sultaniyya. [Arghun] said: I am the padishah of the world, [I] intend to found a city which will be the king of cities (*shāh-i bilād*). The people, who were present there, mentioned different locations and expressed their disadvantage and advantage, eventually [they] chose Qunqur Öläng, which was an extremely pleasurable *yaylāq* (summer camp) ... [Arghun] ordered [them] to design the city and build its castle out of carved stone. But, when [he] founded the building, the universe did not give [him] a chance to finish the work. Now I intend to complete, if God bless me, what my father had founded, because a righteous child is the one

who follows his mother and father and keeps their names alive ... I do not build this city and the castle (*qal'ih*) to be my stronghold, God forbid, in the time of hardship or to bring me wealth; the main reason for the building is that Padishah Arghun had founded it and intended to finish it, but life did not give him a chance ... (68) within a short space of time [Sultaniyya] became an excellent thriving city, and [they] built the wall of the castle out of carved stone ... and [they] designed the castle as a square with four sides of equal length ... and [the castle] has a gate and sixteen towers ... and inside the castle each of the amirs had founded a building, and Sultan Öljeytü has built an edifice inside the castle for his own tomb (*madfan*) and has named it *abwāb al-birr*, and [has built] a sublime large octagonal dome (*gunbad-i muthammin-i buzurg-i 'ālī*) which is 60 *gaz* in diameter ... and 120 *gaz* in height ... and adjacent to that dome, [Sultan] has built a few splendid buildings [such as a] magnificent mosque and *dār al-ḍīyāfa* and *dār al-sīyāda* and established substantial endowments for it ... [they] built many mosques in the city but the *Jāmi'* mosque was built by Sultan ... and another *dār al-shafā* ... and another grand mosque resembling the one that Mustansir built in Baghdad.

9 Mustawfi's Account of the Foundation of Sultaniyya (Chapter 4) in Mustawfi, *Nuzhat al-Qulūb*, 97

(97) ارغون خان بن ابقای خان بن هولاکوخان مغول بنیاد فرمود. پسرش اولجایتو سلطان ... به اتمام رسانید و به نام خود منسوب کرد ... دور باروش که ارغون بنیاد کرده بود و از ده هزار گام. و آنکه اولجایتو سلطان می ساخت و به سبب وفات او تمام ناکرده ماند سی هزار گام. و درو قلعه ای است از سنگ تراشیده که خوابگاه اولجایتو سلطانست و دیگر عمارات در آنجاست و دور آن قلعه دو هزار گام بود.

(97) Arghun Khan bin Abqay Khan bin Hülegü Khan-i Mughul founded [Sultaniyya]. His son Öljeytü Sultan ... finished it and named it after himself ... the perimeter of the wall, which had been built by Arghun, was 10,000 paces, and the one that Öljeytü built and was left unfinished due to his death [was] 30,000 paces. And inside it, there is a castle (*qal'ih*) built of carved stone, which is the chamber (*khābgāh*) of Öljeytü Sultan, and there are other edifices there, and the perimeter of that castle was 2,000 paces.

Bibliography

Persian Primary Sources

Amuli, Mahmud. *Nafāyis al-Funūn fī 'Arāyis al-'Uyūn* [Treasures of Sciences in the Lovely Realm of Sights], 3 volumes. Edited by Abu al-Hassan Shiʿrani. Tehran: Islamiyya Press, 2002.

'Ata Malik Juvayni. *Tārīkh-i Jahāngushāy* [The History of The World Conqueror], 3 volumes. Edited by Muhammad Qazvini. Tehran: Hermes, 2008.

Banakati, Davood. *Tārīkh-i Banākatī* [Banakati's History]. Edited by Jaʿfar Shuʿar. Tehran: Anjuman-i Āthār-i Millī, 1969.

Evliya Çelebi. 'The Sīyāḥat-nāmih of Evliya Çelebi [Travel Account of Evliya Çelebi]'. Translated by Haj Husayn Nakhjavani. *Nashrīyih-yi Dānishkadih-yi Adabīyyāt-i Tabriz Nashrīyih-yi Dānishkadih-yi Adabīyyāt-i Tabriz* (1959): 261–301.

Hafiz-i Abru. *Dhayl-i Jāmiʿ al-Tawārīkh-i Rashīdī* [The Continuation of Rashid Al-Din's Jāmiʿ al-Tawārīkh]. Edited by Khan-Baba Bayani. Tehran: Anjuman-i Āthār-i Millī, 1971.

Hafiz-i Abru. *Zubdat al-Tawārīkh* [Cream of Histories], 4 volumes. Edited by Seyed Kamal al-Din Hajseyed Javadi. Tehran: Vizārat-i Farhang va Irshād-i Islāmī, 2001.

Hakim-i Nishapuri. *Tārīkh-i Nishābūr* [The History of Nishapur]. Edited by Muhammad R. Shafiei Kadkani. Tehran: Agah Press, 2005.

Ibn Battuta and H. A. R. (Hamilton Alexander Rosskeen) Gibb. *The Travels of Ibn Battuta, A. D. 1325–1354*, 5 volumes. Abingdon: Routledge, 2016.

Ibn Hawqal. *Ṣūrat al-'Arḍ* [The Face of the Earth]. Edited and translated by Jaʿfar Shuʿar. Tehran: Amir Kabir Press, 1987.

Kashani, Abu al-Ghasim. *Tārīkh-i Öljeytü* [The Chronicles of Öljeytü]. Edited by Mahin Hambly. Tehran: Bungāh-i Tarjuma va Nashr-i Kitāb, 1969.

Khwandmir. *Tārīkh-i Ḥabīb al-Sīyar fī Akhbār Afrād al-Bashar* [The Beloved of Careers Reporting on the Multitudes of People], 4 volumes. Edited by Jalal al-Din Humayi. Tehran: Khayyam Press, 2001.

Mustawfi, Hamdallah. *Nuzhat al-Qulūb* [Hearts' Bliss]. Edited by Muhammad Dabir-Siyaqi. Qazvin: Hadith-i Imruz, 2002.

Mustawfi, Hamdallah. *Tārīkh-i Guzīdih* [Excerpt History]. Edited by ʿAbd al-Husayn Navaei. Tehran: Amir Kabir Press, 1985.

Nakhjavani, Muhammad. *Dastūr al-Kātib fī Taʿyīn al-Marātib*, 2 volumes. Edited by Abd al-Karim Alizadih. Moscow: Oriental Institute of Azerbaijan, 1964.

Rashid al-Din Fazlallah Hamadani. *Jāmiʿ al-Tawārīkh* [Compendium of Chronicles], 4 volumes. Edited and with a commentary by Muhammad Roshan and Mustafa Musavi. Tehran: Alburz Press, 1994.

Rashid al-Din Fazlallah Hamadani, *Tārīkh-i Mubārak-i Ghāzānī* [The Blessed History of Ghazan]. Edited by Karl Jahn. Hertford: Stephen Austin, 1940.

Rashid al-Din Fazlallah Hamadani, Mujtaba Minuvi and Iraj Afshar, *Waqf Nāmih-yi Rabʿ-i Rashīdī* [The Endowment Deed of Rabʿ-i Rashīdī]. Tehran: Anjuman-i Āthār-i Millī, 1971.

Shahzadih Nadir Mirza. *Tārīkh va Jughrāfīyā-yi Dār al-Salṭanih-yi Tabriz* [History and Geography of the Dār al-Salṭanih of Tabriz]. Edited by Muhammad Mushiri. Tehran: Iqbal Press, 1981.

Tattavi, Qazi Ahmad and Asef Khan Qazvini. *Tārīkh-i Alfī* [Millennial History], 8 volumes. Edited by Ghulam-Reza Tabatabaei Majd. Tehran: Intishārāt-i ʿIlmī va Farhangī, 2003.

Wassaf al-Hazra and ʿAbd al-Muhammad Ayati. *Taḥrīr-i Tārīkh-i Wassaf* [Wassaf's History, Rewritten]. Tehran: Bunyād-i Farhang-i Iran, 1967.

Yaqut al-Hamawi. *Muʿjam al-Buldān* [Dictionary of Countries], 2 volumes. Edited by Alinaqi Munzavi. Tehran: Sāzmān-i Mīrāth-i Farhangī-yi Kishvar, 2001.

Non-Persian Primary Sources

Coste, Pascal-Xavier. *Monuments Modernes de la Perse mesurés, dessinés et décrits* [Modern Monuments of Persia Measured, Drawn and Described]. Paris: A. Morel, 1867.

Dubeux, M. Louis. *La Perse* [Persia]. Paris: Firmin Didot Frères. 1841.

Flandin, Eugène and Pascal-Xavier Coste. *Voyage en Perse* [Journey to Persia]. Paris: Gide et Jules Baudry. 1851.

González de Clavijo, Ruy and Guy Le Strange. *Embassy to Tamerlane, 1403–1406.* London: G. Routledge, 1928.

Ibn al-Fuwati. *Majmaʿ al-Ādāb fī Muʿjam al-ʾAlqāb*, 7 volumes. Edited by Muhammad al-Kazim. Tehran: Ministry of Culture and Islamic Education, 1995.

Ibn Khaldun. *The Muqaddimah: An Introduction to History*, 3 volumes. Translated by Franz Rosenthal. New York: Pantheon, 1958.

Marco Polo. *The Book of Ser Marco Polo, the Venetian, Concerning the Kingdoms and Marvels of the East*, 2 volumes. Translated and edited by Colonel Henry Yule. London: John Murray, Albemarle Street, 1871.

Morier, James. *A Journey through Persia, Armenia, and Asia Minor, to Constantinople, in the Years 1808 and 1809: In which is included, some account of the proceedings of his majesty's mission, under Sir Harford Jones, Bart. K.C. to the court of the king of Persia*. London: publisher not identified, 1812.

Nasir-i Khusraw. *Nāṣer-e Khosraw's Book of Travels: Safarnāma*. Translated by Wheeler M. Thackston. Albany, NY: The Persian Heritage Foundation, Bibliotheca Persica, 1986.

Olearius, Adam. *The Voyages and Travells of the Ambassadors Sent by Frederick Duke of Holstein, to the Great Duke of Muscovy, and the king of Persia: Begun in the year M.DC. XXXIII and finish'd in M.DC. XXXIX: Containing a compleat history of Muscovy, Tartary, Persia, and other adjacent countries: With several publick transactions reaching neer the present times: In VII books*. London: publisher not identified, 1669.

Ruysbroeck, Willem van. *The Mission of Friar William of Rubruck: His Journey to the Court of the Great Khan Möngke, 1253–1255*. Translated by Peter Jackson. Indianapolis, IN: Hackett, 2009.

Sawma, Rabban. *The Monks of Kublai Khan, Emperor of China*. Translated by Sir E. A. Wallis Budge. London; New York: I. B. Tauris, 2014.

Sykes, Sir Percy. *A History of Persia*, 2 volumes. London: Macmillan & Co., 1915.

Xun, Xiao. *Gugong Yilu* [Record of the Remains of the Imperial Palace]. Taibei: Shijie Press, 1963.

Yuan Shi [History of the Yuan]. Edited by Song Lian, 15 volumes. Beijing: Zhonghua Press, 1976.

Secondary Sources

Abu-Lughod, Janet. 'The Islamic City: Historic Myth, Islamic Essence, and Contemporary Relevance'. *International Journal of Middle East Studies* 19 (1987): 155–76.

Abu-Lughod, Janet. 'What is Islamic about a City? Some Comparative Reflections'. In *Urbanism in Islam: The Proceedings of International Conference on Urbanism in Islam (ICUIT), Volume 1*, 193–217. Tokyo: The Middle Eastern Culture Center, 1989.

Akbarnia, Ladan. '*Khita'i*: Cultural Memory and the Creation of a Mongol Visual Idiom in Iran and Central Asia'. PhD diss., Harvard University, 2007.

Akcan, Esra. 'Channels and Items of Translation'. In *Art History in the Wake of the Global Turn*, edited by Jill H. Casid and Aruna D'Souza, 145–59. Williamstown, MA: Sterling and Francine Clark Art Institute, 2014.

Akhavan-Tavakoli, Farnaz. *Kitāb-shināsī-yi Sultaniyya* [A Bibliography of Sultaniyya]. Tehran: Sāzmān-i Mīrāth-i Farhangī-yi Kishvar, 2002.

Akimushkin, Oleg and Anatol Ivanov. 'The Art of Illumination'. In *The Arts of the Book in Central Asia, 14th–16th Centuries*, edited by Oleg Akimushkin and Basil Gray, 35–57. London: Serindia, 1979.

'Aliasl, Parviz and Shahram Yusefifard. 'Ghazaniyya-yi Tabriz: Namād-i Taḥavvul-i Farhangī-yi Mughulān [Ghazaniyya of Tabriz: The Symbol of the Cultural Revolution of the Mongols]'. *Tārīkh va Tamaddun-i Islāmī* 13 (2011): 65–82.

Allsen, Thomas. 'Archaeology and Mid-Imperial History: The Chin and Yuan'. In *Soviet Studies of Pre-Modern China: Assessments of Recent Scholarship*, edited by Gilbert Rozman, 81–95. Cambridge: Cambridge University Press. Ann Arbor, MI: Center for Chinese Studies, University of Michigan, 1984.

Allsen, Thomas. 'Biography of a Cultural Broker: Bolad Ch'eng-Hsiang in China and Iran'. In *The Court of the Il-khans, 1290–1340*, edited by Julian Raby and Teresa Fitzherbert, 7–22. Oxford: Oxford University Press, 1996.

Allsen, Thomas. 'Changing Forms of Legitimation in Mongol Iran'. In *Rulers from the Steppe: State Formation on the Eurasian Periphery*, edited by Gary Thomas Seaman and Daniel Marks, 223–41. Los Angeles: Ethnographics Press, Center for Visual Anthropology, University of Southern California, 1991.

Allsen, Thomas. *Commodity and Exchange in the Mongol Empire: A Cultural History of Islamic Textiles*. Cambridge: Cambridge University Press, 1997.

Allsen, Thomas. *Culture and Conquest in Mongol Eurasia*. Cambridge: Cambridge University Press, 2001.

Allsen, Thomas. 'Notes on Chinese Titles in Mongol Iran'. *Mongolian Studies* 14 (1991): 27–39.

Allsen, Thomas. 'Spiritual Geography and Political Legitimacy in the Eastern Steppe'. In *Ideology and the Formation of Early States*, edited by Henri J. M. Claessen and Jarich G. Oosten, 116–35. Leiden; New York; Cologne: Brill, 1996.

Amirahmadi, Bahram. 'Ujan 1 [Ujan 1]'. *Rushd-i Āmuzish-i Jughrāfīyā* 25 (1991): 49–53.

Amirahmadi, Bahram. 'Ujan 2 [Ujan 2]'. *Rushd-i Āmuzish-i Jughrāfīyā* 26 (1991): 50–6.

Amitai-Preiss, Reuven. 'Echoes of the Eurasian Steppe in the Daily Culture of Mamluk Military Society'. *Journal of the Royal Asiatic Society* 26, no. 1–2 (2016): 261–70.

Amitai-Preiss, Reuven. 'Ghazan, Islam and Mongol Tradition: A View from the Mamlūks Sultanate'. *Bulletin of the School of Oriental and African Studies* 59, no. 1 (1996): 1–10.

Amitai-Preiss, Reuven. 'New Material from the Mamluk Sources for the Biography of Rashid al-Din'. In *The Court of the Il-khans, 1290–1340*, edited by Julian Raby and Teresa Fitzherbert, 23–37. Oxford: Oxford University Press, 1996.

Amitai-Preiss, Reuven. 'Sufis and Shamans: Some Remarks on the Islamization of the Mongols in the Ilkhanate'. *Journal of the Economic and Social History of the Orient* 42, no. 1 (1999): 27–46.

Amitai-Preiss, Reuven. 'Turko-Mongolian Nomads and the Iqṭāʿ System in the Islamic Middle East (c. 1000–1400 AD)'. In *Nomads in the Sedentary World*, edited by Anatoly Khazanov and André Wink, 152–71. Richmond, Surrey: Curzon, 2001.

Amitai-Preiss, Reuven and Michal Biran (eds). *Nomads as Agents of Cultural Change: The Mongols and their Eurasian Predecessors*. Honolulu: University of Hawaii Press, 2015.

ʿAsgarian, Mehrdad, Ibrahim Muhammadi and Parastou Qasemi. *Gamānih-zanī dar Qismatī az Ḥarīm-i Tārīkhī-yi Shahr-i Ghadīm-i Sultaniyya* [The Report of the Trial Trenching in the Historical City of Sultaniyya]. Zanjan: Sāzmān-i Mīrāth-i Farhangī-yi Kishvar, 2005.

Avni, Gideon. '"From Polis to Madina" Revisited – Urban Change in Byzantine and Early Islamic Palestine'. *Journal of the Royal Asiatic Society* 21, no. 3 (2011): 301–29.

Ayati, ʿAbd al-Muhammad. 'Qaṣīda-yi Wassaf al-Hazra dar Vaṣf-i Sultaniyya [The Ode of Wassaf al-Hazra describing Sultaniyya]'. *Nāmih-yi Anjuman* 15 (2004): 23–30.

ʿAli, Abulfazl. *Guzārish-i Faṣl-i Duvvum-i Barrisī va Shināsāyī-yi Abhar and Khurram-darra* [The Report of the Second Season of the Field Survey of Abhar and Khurram-darra]. Zanjan: Sāzmān-i Mīrāth-i Farhangī-yi Kishvar, 2006.

Bakhtiyari-Shahri, Mahmud. *Guzārish-i Thabtī-yi Shahr-i Īlkhānī-yi Aq Qalʿih dar Fihrist-i Āthār-i Millī* [The Inscription Report of the Ilkhanid City of Aq Qalʿih for Iran National Heritage List]. Place of publication not identified: Sāzmān-i Mīrāth-i Farhangī-yi Khurasan, 1996.

Balaram, Arita. '(Re)theorizing Hybridity for the Study of Identity and Difference'. *Social and Personality Psychology Compass* 12, no. 10 (2018): e12413-n/a.

Ball, Warwick. 'Some Rock-Cut Monuments in Southern Iran'. *Iran: Journal of the British Institute of Persian Studies* 24 (1986): 95–115.

Ball, Warwick. 'Two Aspects of Iranian Buddhism'. *Bulletin of the Asia Institute of Pahlavi University*: (1976): 1–4.

Baqiri, Muhammad. *Az Samarqand bi Kashan: Nāmih-hā-yi Ghiyath al-Din Jamshid Kashani bi Pidarash* [From Samarqand to Kashan: The Letters of Ghiyath al-Din Jamshid Kashani to his Father]. Tehran: Intishārāt-i 'Ilmī va Farhangī, 1996.

Barthold, V. V. and J. M. Rogers. 'The Burial Rites of the Turks and the Mongols'. *Central Asiatic Journal* 14, no. 1/3 (1970): 195–227.

Baugher, Sherene, Douglas Appler and William Moss (eds). *Urban Archaeology, Municipal Government and Local Planning: Preserving Heritage within the Commonwealth of Nations and the United States*. New York: Springer, 2017.

Bausani, A. 'Religion under the Mongols'. In *The Cambridge History of Iran*, edited by J. A. Boyle, 5: 538–49. Cambridge: Cambridge University Press, 1968.

Bayani, Shirin. *Dīn va Dawlat dar Iran-i 'Ahd-i Mughul* [Religion and Government in Iran during the Time of the Mongols], 2 volumes. Tehran: Tehran: Markaz-i Nashr-i Dānishgāhī, 2002.

Bayani, Shirin. *Mughulān va Ḥukūmat-i Īlkhānī dar Iran* [The Mongols and Ilkhanid Rule in Iran]. Tehran: SAMT, 2010.

Behrens-Abouseif, Doris. *Cairo of the Mamluks: A History of the Architecture and its Culture*. London; New York: I. B. Tauris, 2007.

Behrens-Abouseif, Doris. *Egypt's Adjustment to Ottoman Rule: Institutions, Waqf and Architecture in Cairo, 16th and 17th Centuries*. New York; Leiden: Brill, 1994.

Behrens-Abouseif, Doris. 'The Mamluk City'. In *The City in the Islamic World*, edited by Salma Khadra Jayyusi, Renata Holod, Attilio Petruccioli and André Raymond, 295–316. Leiden: Brill, 2008.

Bemmann, Jan and Susanne Reichert. 'Karakorum, the First Capital of the Mongol World Empire: An Imperial City in a Non-Urban Society'. *Asian Archaeology* 4, no. 2 (2021): 121–43.

Bemmann, Jan, Sven Linzen, Susanne Reichert and Lkh Munkhbayar. 'Mapping Karakorum, the Capital of the Mongol Empire'. *Antiquity* 96, no. 385 (2022): 159–78.

Bemmann, Jan, Ulambayar Erdenebat and Ernst Pohl. *Mongolian–German Karakorum Expedition, Volume 1: Excavations in the Craftsmen Quarter at the Main Road*. Wiesbaden: Reichert Verlag, 2010.

Berlekamp, Persis. 'The Limits of Artistic Exchange in Fourteenth-Century Tabriz: The Paradox of Rashid al-Din's Book on Chinese Medicine, Part I'. *Muqarnas: An Annual on the Visual Culture of the Islamic World* 27 (2010): 209–50.

Bhabha, Homi. *The Location of Culture*. London; New York: Routledge, 1994.

Bhabha, Homi. 'The Third Space'. In *Identity: Community, Culture, Difference*, edited by Jonathan Rutherford, 207–21. London: Lawrence & Wishart, 1990.

Bier, Carol. 'The Decagonal Tomb Tower at Maragha and its Architectural Context: Lines of Mathematical Thought'. *Nexus Network Journal* 14, no. 2 (2012): 251–73.

Biran, Michal. 'Rulers and City Life in Mongol Central Asia (1220–1370)'. In *Turko-Mongol Rulers, Cities, and City Life*, edited by David Durand-Guedy, 257–83. Boston; Leiden: Brill, 2013.

Bivar, A. D. H. *Excavation at Ghubayra, Iran*. London: School of Oriental and African Studies, 2000.

Blair, Sheila. 'The Coins of the Later Ilkhanids: A Typological Analysis'. *Journal of the Economic and Social History of the Orient* 26, no. 3 (1983): 295–317.

Blair, Sheila. 'The Epigraphic Program of the Tomb of Uljaytu at Sultaniyya: Meaning in Mongol Architecture'. *Islamic Art: An Annual Dedicated to the Art and Culture of the Muslim World* 2 (1987): 43–96.

Blair, Sheila. 'Ilkhanid Architecture and Society: An Analysis of the Endowment Deed of the Rabʿ-i Rashīdī'. *Iran: Journal of the British Institute of Persian Studies* 22 (1984): 67–90.

Blair, Sheila. *The Ilkhanid Shrine Complex at Natanz, Iran*. Cambridge, MA: Harvard University, Center for Middle Eastern Studies, 1986.

Blair, Sheila. 'The Mongol Capital of Sulṭāniyya, "The Imperial"'. *Iran: Journal of the British Institute of Persian Studies* 24 (1986): 139–51.

Blair, Sheila. *The Monumental Inscriptions from Early Islamic Iran and Transoxiana*. Leiden; New York: Brill, 1992.

Blair, Sheila. 'Monumentality under the Mongols: The Tomb of Uljaytu at Sultaniyya'. In *Text and Image in Medieval Persian Art*, edited by Sheila Blair, 112–71. Edinburgh: Edinburgh University Press, 2014.

Blair, Sheila. 'Patterns of Patronage and Production in the Ilkhanid Iran: The Case of Rashid al-Din'. In *The Court of the Il-khans, 1290–1340*, edited by Julian Raby and Teresa Fitzherbert, 39–62. Oxford: Oxford University Press, 1996.

Blair, Sheila. 'The Religious Arts of the Ilkhanids'. In *The Legacy of Genghis Khan: Courtly Art and Culture in Western Asia, 1256–1353*, edited by Linda Komaroff and Stefano Carboni, 105–34. New York; New Haven: Metropolitan Museum of Art, 2002.

Blair, Sheila. 'Sufi Saints and Shrine Architecture in the Early Fourteenth Century'. *Muqarnas: An Annual on the Visual Culture of the Islamic World* 7 (1990): 35–49.

Blair, Sheila. 'Tabriz: International Entrepôt under the Mongols'. In *Politics, Patronage and the Transmission of Knowledge in 13th–15th Century Tabriz*, edited by Judith Pfeiffer, 321–56. Leiden; Boston: Brill, 2014.

Blair, Sheila, Jonathan Bloom and Richard Ettinghausen. *The Art and Architecture of Islam 1250–1800*. New Haven, CT: Yale University Press, 1994.

Blair, Sheila and Rashid al-Din. *A Compendium of Chronicles: Rashid al-Din's Illustrated History of the World*. London: Nour Foundation in association with Oxford University Press, 1995.

Blessing, Patricia. 'Building a Frontier: Architecture in Anatolia under the Ilkhanid Rule'. In *Cultural Encounters in Anatolia in the Medieval Period: The Ilkhanids in Anatolia, Symposium Proceedings, 21–22 May 2015, Ankara*, edited by Suzan Yalman, Filiz Yenişehirlioğlu, Alev Ayaokur and Defne Karakaya, 65–85. Ankara: Vehbi Koç Ankara Studies Research Center, 2019.

Blessing, Patricia. *Rebuilding Anatolia after the Mongol Conquest: Islamic Architecture in the Lands of Rum, 1240–1330*. London: Routledge, 2016.

Bloom, Jonathan. 'On the Transmission of Designs in Early Islamic Architecture'. *Muqarnas: An Annual on the Visual Culture of the Islamic World* 10 (1993): 21–8.

Bloom, Jonathan. 'Paper: The Transformative Medium in Ilkhanid Art'. In *Beyond the Legacy of Genghis Khan*, edited by Linda Komaroff, 289–302. Leiden: Brill, 2006.

Bonine, Michael. *The Middle Eastern City and Islamic Urbanism: An Annotated Bibliography of Western Literature*. Bonn: Ferd. Dümmlers Verlag, 1994.

Bosworth, Clifford Edmund. *The New Islamic Dynasties: A Chronological and Genealogical Manual*. New York: Columbia University Press, 1996.

Bosworth, Clifford Edmund. 'Nishapur: Historical Geography and History to the Beginning of the 20th Century'. *Encyclopædia Iranica*. http://www.iranicaonline.org/articles/nishapur-i (last accessed 28 June 2023).

Boyle, John Andrew. 'Bīrūnī and Rashīd al-Dīn'. *Central Asiatic Journal* 21, no. 1 (1977): 4–12.

Boyle, John Andrew. 'Dynastic and Political History of the Il-Khāns'. In *The Cambridge History of Iran*, edited by J. A. Boyle, 5: 303–421.

Boyle, John Andrew. 'The Seasonal Residences of the Great Khan Ögedei'. *Central Asiatic Journal* 16, no. 2 (1972): 125–31.

Brambilla, Marco. 'The Mausoleum of Oljeitu and the Citadel of Sultaniyya'. In *Iran After the Mongols*, edited by Sussan Babaei, 129–42. London: I. B. Tauris, 2019.

Brambilla, Marco. 'Tepe Nur: An Īlkhānid Monument in Sulṭāniyya'. University of Pennsylvania. https://www.sas.upenn.edu/ancient/masons/abstracts/Agudo/M-Brambilla.html (last accessed 21 August 2023).

Broadbridge, Anne. 'Mamluk Legitimacy and the Mongols: The Reigns of Baybars and Qalāwūn'. *Mamlūk Studies Review* V (2001): 91–118.

Brouskare, Erse and Elizabeth Key Fowden. *Ottoman Architecture in Greece*. Athens: Hellenic Ministry of Culture, Directorate of Byzantine and Post-Byzantine Antiquities, 2009.

Bulliet, Richard. 'Medieval Nishapur: A Topographic and Demographic Reconstruction'. *Studia Iranica* 5 (1975): 67–89.

Bulliet, Richard. *The Patricians of Nishapur: A Study in Medieval Islamic Social History*. Cambridge, MA: Harvard University Press, 1972.

Cammann, Schuyler. 'The Symbolism of the Cloud Collar Motif'. *The Art Bulletin* 33, no. 1 (1951): 1–9.

Canepa, Matthew. 'Preface: Theorizing Cross-cultural Interaction among Ancient and Early Medieval Visual Cultures'. *Ars Orientalis* 38 (2010): 7–29.

Carboni, Stefano and Qamar Adamjee. 'Takht-i Sulaiman and Tilework in the Ilkhanid Period'. The Metropolitan Museum of Art. http://www.metmuseum.org/toah/hd/khan7/hd_khan7.htm (last accessed 1 March 2023).

Chan, Hok-lam. 'Exorcising the Dragon: A Legend about the Building of the Mongolian Upper Capital (Shangdu)'. *Central Asiatic Journal* 55, no. 1 (2011): 1–32.

Chan, Hok-lam. *Legends of the Building of Old Peking*. Seattle; Hong Kong: University of Washington Press, 2008.

Chan, Hok-lam. 'Liu Ping-chung (1216–1274)'. In *In the Service of the Khan: Eminent Personalities of the Early Mongol-Yüan Period (1200–1300)*, edited by Igore de Rachewiltz, Hok-lam Chan, Hsiao Ch'i-sh'ing and Peter Geier, 245–69. Wiesbaden: Harrassowitz Verlag, 1993.

Chan, Hok-lam. 'Liu Ping-chung: A Buddhist-Taoist Statesman at the Court of Khubilai Khan'. *T'Oung Pao* 53, no. 1/3 (1967): 98–146.

Chan, Hok-lam and Wm. Theodore De Bary. *Yüan Thought: Chinese Thought and Religion under the Mongols*. New York, Columbia University Press, 1982.

Chen, Sylvia, Veronica Benet-Martinez and Michael Bond. 'Bicultural Identity, Bilingualism, and Psychological Adjustment in Multicultural Societies: Immigration-based and Globalization-based Acculturation'. *Journal of Personality* 76 (2008): 803–38.

Chrisman, Laura and Patrick Williams. *Colonial Discourse and Post-Colonial Theory: A Reader*. London; New York: Harvester Wheatsheaf, 1993.

Cohen, Robin. 'Creolization and Cultural Globalization: The Soft Sounds of Fugitive Power'. *Globalizations* 4, no. 3 (2007): 369–84.

Contadini, Anna. *A World of Beasts: A Thirteenth-Century Illustrated Arabic Book on Animals (the Kitāb Naʿt al-Ḥayawān) in the Ibn Bakhtīshūʿ Tradition*. Leiden; Boston: Brill, 2012.

Cowley, David, Charles Moriarty, George Geddes, Georgina Brown, Tom Wade and Caroline Nichol, 'UAVs in Context: Archaeological Airborne Recording in a National Body of Survey and Record', *Drones* 2, no. 1 (2018): 1–16.

Crowe, Yolande. 'Late Thirteenth-Century Persian Tilework and Chinese Textiles'. *Bulletin of the Asia Institute* 5 (1991): 153–61.

Crowe, Yolande. 'Some Timurid Designs and their Far Eastern Connections'. In *Timurid Art and Culture: Iran and Central Asia in the Fifteenth Century*, edited by Lisa Golombek and Maria Subtelny, 168–78. Leiden: Brill, 1992.

Curatola, Giovanni. 'The Viar Dragon'. In *Solṭāniye III, Quaderni del Seminario de Iranistica, Uralo-Altaistica e Caucasologia dell'Universita degli Studi de Venezia 9*, 71–89. Venice: publisher not identified, 1982.

Danti, Michael. *The Ilkhanid Heartland: Hasanlu Tepe (Iran) Period I*. Philadelphia: University of Pennsylvania Museum of Archaeology and Anthropology, 2004.

Demoule, Jean-Paul. 'Rescue Archaeology: A European View'. *Annual Review of Anthropology* 41 (2012): 611–26.

De Nicola, Bruno. 'The Economic Role of Mongol Women: Continuity and Transformation from Mongolia to Iran'. In *The Mongols' Middle East: Continuity and Transformation in Ilkhanid Iran*, edited by Bruno De Nicola and Charles Melville, 79–105. Leiden; Boston: Brill, 2016.

De Nicola, Bruno. 'Letters from Mongol Anatolia: Professional, Political and Intellectual Connections among Members of a Persianised Elite'. *Iran: Journal of the British Institute of Persian Studies* 56, no. 1 (2018): 77–90.

De Nicola, Bruno. 'On the Outskirts of the Ilkhanate: The Mongols' Relationship with the Province of Kastamonu in the Second Half of the 13th Century'. In *Cultural Encounters in Anatolia in the Medieval Period: The Ilkhanids in Anatolia, Symposium Proceedings, 21–22 May 2015, Ankara*, edited by Suzan

Yalman, Filiz Yenişehirlioğlu, Alev Ayaokur and Defne Karakaya, 117–35. Ankara: Vehbi Koç Ankara Studies Research Center, 2019.

De Nicola, Bruno. *Women in Mongol Iran: the Khātūns, 1206–1335*. Edinburgh: Edinburgh University Press, 2017.

DeWeese, Devin. *Islamization and Native Religion in the Golden Horde: Baba Tükles and Conversion to Islam in Historical and Epic Tradition*. University Park: Pennsylvania State University Press, 1994.

Di Cosmo, Nicola. 'Black Sea Emporia and the Mongol Empire: A Reassessment of the Pax Mongolica'. *Journal of the Economic and Social History of the Orient* 53, no. 1/2 (2010): 83–108.

Ebel, Kathryn. 'Representations of the Frontier in Ottoman Town Views of the Sixteenth Century'. *Imago Mundi* 60, no. 1 (2008): 1–22.

Elman, Benjamin and Martin Kern. *Statecraft and Classical Learning: The Rituals of Zhou in East Asian History*. Leiden; Boston: Brill, 2010.

Endicott-West, Elizabeth. 'The Yuan'. In *Soviet Studies of Pre-Modern China: Assessments of Recent Scholarship*, edited by Gilbert Rozman, 97–110. Cambridge: Cambridge University Press. Ann Arbor, MI: Center for Chinese Studies, University of Michigan, 1984.

Ettinghausen, Richard. *Arab Painting*. Geneva: Skira, 1962.

Ettinghausen, Richard and Oleg Grabar. *The Art and Architecture of Islam 650–1250*. London; New Haven, CT: Yale University Press, 1994.

Falahat, Somaiyeh and M. Reza Shirazi. 'New Urban Developments in Safavid Isfahan: Continuity or Disjuncture?' *Planning Perspectives* 27, no. 4 (2012): 611–24.

Fehérvári, Géza. *Ceramics of the Islamic world: In the Tareq Rajab Museum*. London; New York: I. B. Tauris, 2000.

Fitzhugh, William, Morris Rossabi and William Honeychurch. *Genghis Khan and the Mongol Empire*. Washington: Dino Don, 2009.

Flood, Finbarr Barry. *Objects of Translation: Material Culture and Medieval 'Hindu–Muslim' Encounter*. Princeton: Princeton University Press, 2009.

Fludernik, Monika. *Hybridity and Postcolonialism: Twentieth-Century Indian Literature*. Tübingen: Stauffenburg, 1998.

Foltz, Richard. *Religions of the Silk Road: Overland Trade and Cultural Exchange from Antiquity to the Fifteenth Century*. New York: Palgrave Macmillan, 1999.

Fragner, Bert. 'Ilkhanid Rule and its Contributions to Iranian Political Culture'. In *Beyond the Legacy of Genghis Khan*, edited by Linda Komaroff, 68–80. Leiden: Brill, 2006.

Franke, Herbert. 'Chinese Historiography under Mongol Rule: The Role of History in Acculturation'. *Mongolian Studies* 1 (1974): 15–26.

Frenkel, Yehoshua. 'Baybars and the Sacred Geography of Bilād al-Shām: A Chapter in the Islamization of Syria's Landscape'. *Jerusalem Studies in Arabic and Islam* 25 (2001): 153–70.

Funari, Pedro Paulo, Martin Hall and Siân Jones (eds). *Historical Archaeology: Back from the Edge*. London; New York: Routledge, 1999.

Ganjavi, Saʿid. 'Kāvush-i Tappih Nur [The Excavation of Tappih-nur]', *Barrisīhā-yi Tārīkhī* 62, no. 1 (1976): 163–96.

Gascoigne, Alison. 'The Water Supply of Tinnis: Public Amenities and Private Investments'. In *Cities in the Pre-Modern Islamic World: The Urban Impact of State, Society and Religion*, edited by Amira K. Bennison and Alison L. Gascoigne, 161–76. New York: Routledge, 2007.

Gaube, Heinz. *Iranian Cities*. New York: New York University Press, 1979.

Gaube, Heinz. 'Iranian Cities'. In *The City in the Islamic World, Volume 1*, edited by Salma Jayyusi, Renata Holod, Attilio Petruccioli and André Raymond, 159–80. Leiden; Boston: Brill, 2008.

Ghafrani, ʿAli. 'Rashid al-Din Fazlallah va Andīsha-yi Ābād-garī dar Qalamru-yi Īlkhānān [Rashid al-Din Fazlallah and the Concept of Development in the Territory of the Ilkhans]', *Muṭāliʿāt-i Islāmī* 71 (2006): 167–90.

Gibson, Margaret. 'Immigrant Adaptation and Patterns of Acculturation'. *Human Development* 44 (2001): 19–23.

Godard, Andre. 'The Mausoleum of Öljeitü at Sulṭāniya'. In *A Survey of Persian Art from Prehistoric Times to the Present*, edited by Arthur Pope, Phyllis Ackerman and Theodore Besterman, 1,103–18. London; New York: Oxford University Press, 1938.

Golden, Peter. 'Courts and Court Culture in the Proto-urban and Urban Developments among the Pre-Chinggisid Turkic Peoples'. In *Turko-Mongol Rulers, Cities, and City Life*, edited by David Durand-Guedy, 21–73. Leiden; Boston: Brill, 2013.

Golombek, Lisa. 'The Cult of Saints and Shrine Architecture in the Fourteenth Century'. In *Near Eastern Numismatics: Iconography, Epigraphy and History: Studies in Honor of George C. Miles*, edited by George Carpenter Miles and Dickran Kouymjian, 419–30. Beirut: American University of Beirut, 1974.

Golombek, Lisa. 'The Draped Universe of Islam'. In *Content and Context of Visual Arts in the Islamic World*, edited by Priscilla Soucek, 25–38. University Park: Pennsylvania State University Press for the College Art Association of America, 1988.

Golombek, Lisa. 'Urban Patterns in Pre-Safavid Isfahan'. *Iranian Studies* 7, no. 1/2 (1974): 18–48.

Golombek, Lisa, Robert Mason and Gauvin Bailey. *Tamerlane's Tableware: A New Approach to the Chinoiserie Ceramics of the Fifteenth and Sixteenth Centuries.* Toronto and Costa Mesa: Mazda in association with the Royal Ontario Museum, 1996.

Golombek, Lisa and Donald Wilber. *The Timurid Architecture of Iran and Turan.* Princeton, NJ: Princeton University Press, 1988.

Gonnella, Julia, Friederike Weis and Christoph Rauch. *The Diez Albums: Contexts and Contents.* Leiden; Boston: Brill, 2017.

Grabar, Oleg. 'The Architecture of the Middle Eastern City from Past to Present: The Case of the Mosque'. In *Middle Eastern Cities: A Symposium on Ancient, Islamic, and Contemporary Middle Eastern Urbanism*, edited by Ira Lapidus, 26–46. Berkeley: University of California Press, 1969.

Grabar, Oleg. *The Great Mosque of Isfahan.* New York: New York University Press, 1990.

Grabar, Oleg and Sheila Blair. *Epic Images and Contemporary History: The Illustrations of the Great Mongol Shahnama.* Chicago: University of Chicago Press, 1980.

Green, Nile. *The Persianate World: The Frontiers of a Eurasian Lingua Franca.* Oakland: University of California Press, 2019.

Gronke, Monika. 'The Persian Court between Palace and Tent: From Timur to 'Abbas I'. In *Timurid Art and Culture: Iran and Central Asia in the Fifteenth Century*, edited by Lisa Golombek and Maria Subtelny, 18–22. Leiden: Brill, 1992.

Grube, Ernst. *Persian Painting in the Fourteenth Century: A Research Report.* Naples: Istituto Orientale di Napoli, 1978.

Guzman, Gregory. 'European Captives and Craftsmen among the Mongols, 1231–1255'. *The Historian* 72, no. 1 (2010): 122–50.

Hall, Stuart. 'Cultural Identity and Diaspora'. In *Colonial Discourse and Post-Colonial Theory: A Reader*, edited by Laura Chrisman and Patrick Williams, 227–37. London; New York: Harvester Wheatsheaf, 1994.

Hamblin, William. 'Egypt: Mamluk Dynasty (1250–1517): Army and Iqta' System'. In *Encyclopedia of African History, Volume 1*, edited by Kevin Shillington, 444–5. New York; London: Fitzroy Dearborn, 2004.

Hamza, Hani. *The Northern Cemetery of Cairo.* Costa Mesa, CA: Mazda, 2001.

Haneda, Masashi. 'Gāzāniyya in Tabrīz'. In *Urbanism in Islam: The Proceedings of International Conference on Urbanism in Islam (ICUIT), Volume 2*, 283–99. Tokyo: The Middle Eastern Culture Center, 1989.

Haneda, Masashi. 'An Interpretation of the Concept of Islamic City'. In *Islamic Urban Studies: Historical Review and Perspectives*, edited by Masashi Haneda and Toru Miura, 1–10. London: Kegan Paul International, 1994.

Haneda, Masashi. 'The Pastoral City and the Mausoleum City: Nomadic Rule and City Construction in the Eastern Islamic World'. In *Islamic Urbanism in Human History: Political Power and Social Networks*, edited by Sato Tsugitaka, 142–70. London: Kegan Paul International, 1997.

Hanson, William and Ioana Oltean. *Archaeology from Historical Aerial and Satellite Archives*. New York: Springer, 2012

Hatef Naiemi, Atri. 'Confronting the Foreigner: Common Policies of Rashid al-Din and Liu Bingzhong on Mongol Rule in Iran and China'. *Journal of the Royal Asiatic Society* 32, no. 3 (2022): 613–33.

Hatef Naiemi, Atri. 'The Ilkhanid City of Sultaniyya: Some Remarks on the Citadel and the Outer City'. *Iran: Journal of the British Institute of Persian Studies* 60, no. 1 (2022): 91–120.

Hillenbrand, Robert. 'The Art of the Books in Ilkhanid Iran'. In *The Legacy of Genghis Khan: Courtly Art and Culture in Western Asia, 1256–1353*, edited by Linda Komaroff and Stefano Carboni, 135–67. New York; New Haven: Metropolitan Museum of Art, 2002.

Hillenbrand, Robert. *The Art of the Saljūqs in Iran and Anatolia: Proceedings of a Symposium Held in Edinburgh in 1982*. Costa Mesa, CA: Mazda, 1994.

Hillenbrand, Robert. *Islamic Art and Architecture*. London: Thames & Hudson, 1999.

Hillenbrand, Robert. 'Mamluk and Ilkhanid Bestiaries: Convention and Experiment'. *Ars Orientalis* 20 (1990): 149–87.

Hoffmann, Brigitt. 'The Gates of Piety and Charity: Rašīd al-dīn Faḍl Allāh as Founder of Pious Endowments'. In *L'Iran Face à la Domination Mongole*, edited by Denise Aigle, 189–201. Tehran: Institut Français de Recherche en Iran, 1997.

Hoffmann, Brigitt. 'In Pursuit of Memoria and Salvation: Rashīd al-Dīn and his Rabʿ-i Rashīdī'. In *Politics, Patronage and the Transmission of Knowledge in 13th–15th Century Tabriz*, edited by Judith Pfeiffer, 171–85. Leiden; Boston: Brill, 2014.

Hoffmann, Brigitt. 'Speaking about Oneself: Autobiographical Statements in the Works of Rashīd al-Dīn'. In *Rashid al-Din: Agent and Mediator of Cultural Exchanges in Ilkhanid Iran*, edited by Anna Akasoy, Charles Burnett and Ronit Yoeli-Tlalim, 1–14. London: Warburg Institute, 2013.

Hope, Michael. *Power, Politics, and Tradition in the Mongol Empire and the Īlkhānate of Iran*. Oxford: Oxford University Press, 2016.

Hourani, Albert Habib and Samuel Stern (eds). *The Islamic City: A Colloquium*. Oxford: Bruno Cassirer and University of Pennsylvania Press, 1970.

Huff, Dietrich. 'The Ilkhanid Palace at Takht-i Sulayman: Excavation Results'. In *Beyond the Legacy of Genghis Khan*, edited by Linda Komaroff, 94–110. Leiden: Brill, 2006.

Huff, Dietrich. 'Taḵt-e Solaymān'. *Encyclopædia Iranica*. http://www.iranicaonline.org/articles/takt-e-solayman (last accessed 14 October 2022).

Humphreys, Stephen. 'The Expressive Intent of the Mamluk Architecture of Cairo'. *Studia Islamica* 35 (1972): 69–120.

Humphreys, Stephen. *From Saladin to the Mongols: The Ayyubids of Damascus, 1193–1260*. Albany: State University of New York Press, 1977.

Hüttel, Hans-Georg. 'The Search for Khara Khorum and the Palace of the Great Khan'. In *Genghis Khan and the Mongol Empire*, edited by William Fitzhugh, Morris Rossabi and William Honeychurch, 146–9. Washington: Dino Don, 2009.

Isfahanian, Davood and Alireza Khaza'ili. 'Shahr-hā-yi Tāza Bunyād dar Dura-yi Īlkhānī [The Ilkhanid New Cities]'. *Nāmih-yi Anjuman* 6 (2002): 60–70.

Isfahanian, Davood and Alireza Khaza'ili. ''Umrān-i Shahrī dar Iran-i 'Aṣr-i Mughul [Urban Development in Iran during the Time of the Mongols]'. *Jughrāfīyā va Barnāmih-Rīzī* 12 (2003): 9–34.

Iyall Smith, Keri and Patricia Leavy. *Hybrid Identities: Theoretical and Empirical Examinations*. Leiden; Boston: Brill, 2008.

Jackson, Peter. 'The Mongols and the Faith of the Conquered'. In *Mongols, Turks, and Others: Eurasian Nomads and the Sedentary World*, edited by Reuven Amitai-Preiss and Michal Biran, 245–90. Leiden; Boston: Brill, 2005.

Jackson, Peter. *The Mongols and the Islamic World: From Conquest to Conversion*. London; New Haven: Yale University Press, 2017.

Ja'fari, Qadir. 'Takht-i Sulayman ya Sughūrlūq dar Zamān-i Mughul va Ba'd az Ān [Takht-i Sulayman or Sughūrlūq during the Mongol Period and Afterwards]'. *Vahīd* 215 (1977): 33–6.

Jam, Pedram. 'Qiydar-i Nabi: Īlkhān-i Būdāyī dar kisvat-i Payāmbar-i Ibrāhīmī [Qiydar-i Nabi: A Buddhist Ilkhan in the Guise of an Abrahamic Prophet]'. *Pazhūhish-hā-yi Tārīkh-i Iran va Islam* 15 (2014): 85–104.

Johnson, Matthew. 'Rethinking Historical Archaeology'. In *Historical Archaeology: Back from the Edge*, edited by Pedro Paulo Funari, Martin Hall and Siân Jones, 23–36. London; New York: Routledge, 1999.

Kadoi, Yuka. 'Chinese and Turko-Mongol Elements in Ilkhanid and Timurid Arts, Part 1: The Mongols (c. 1250–1350)'. In *A Companion to Islamic Art and*

Architecture, 2 volumes, edited by Finbarr Barry Flood and Gülru Necipoğlu, 636–51. Oxford: Wiley-Blackwell, 2017.

Kadoi, Yuka. 'Cloud Patterns: The Exchange of Ideas between China and Iran under the Mongols'. *Oriental Art* 48, no. 2 (2002): 25–36.

Kadoi, Yuka. *Islamic Chinoiserie: The Art of Mongol Iran*. Edinburgh: Edinburgh University Press, 2009.

Kafescioğlu, Çiğdem. '"In the Image of Rūm": Ottoman Architectural Patronage in Sixteenth-Century Aleppo and Damascus'. *Muqarnas Online* 16, no. 1 (1999): 70–96.

Kamaly, Husayn. 'Isfahan: Medieval Period'. *Encyclopædia Iranica*. 2023, http://www.iranicaonline.org/articles/isfahan-vi-medieval-period (last accessed 10 July).

Kamola, Stefan. *Making Mongol History: Rashid Al-Din and the Jami' Al-Tawarikh*. Edinburgh: Edinburgh University Press, 2019.

Kapchan, Deborah and Pauline Turner Strong. 'Theorizing the Hybrid'. *The Journal of American Folklore* 112, no. 445 (1999): 239–53.

Kasayi, Nurallah. 'Isfahan and the Nizamiyya Madrasa [Isfahan va Madrasa-yi Nizamiyya]', *Farhang-i Isfahan* 4 (1996): 6–12.

Katof, Fedot. *Safar-nāmih-yi Fedot Katof* [The Travel Account of Fedot Katof]. Translated by Muhammad S Homayunfard. Tehran: Kitāb-Khānih-yi Milliī-yi Iran, 1977.

Katouzian, Homa. *The Persians: Ancient, Mediaeval and Modern Iran*. New Haven, CT: Yale University Press, 2009.

Keall, Edward. 'Some Thoughts on the Early Eyvan'. In *Near Eastern Numismatics, Iconography, Epigraphy, and History: Studies in Honor of George C. Miles*, edited by Dickran Kouymjian, 123–30. Beirut: American University of Beirut, 1974.

Kennedy, David and Robert Bewley. 'Aerial Archaeology in Jordan'. *Antiquity* 83 (2009): 69–81.

Kennedy, David, Robert Bewley and F. Radcliffe. 'Aerial Archaeology in the Middle East, Progress and Achievements in Jordan (1997–2008) and the Future'. *Aerial Archaeology: Studies in Archaeological Aerial Photography* 4–5 (2010): 333–7.

Kennedy, David and M. C. Bishop. 'Google Earth and the Archaeology of Saudi Arabia: A Case Study from the Jeddah Area'. *Journal of Archaeological Science* 38 (2011): 1,284–93.

Kenney, Ellen. *Power and Patronage in Medieval Syria: The Architecture and Urban Works of Tankiz al-Nāṣirī*. Chicago: Middle East Documentation Center, 2009.

Khaza'ili, Alireza. 'Rushd va Zivāl-i Shahr-hā-yi Iran dar dura-yi Ilkhānān [The Development and Fall of the Iranian Cities during the Ilkhanid Period]'. PhD diss., University of Tabriz, 2003.

Kiel, Machiel. *Studies on the Ottoman Architecture of the Balkans*. Aldershot; Brookfield, VT: Variorum, 1990.

Kiselev, Sergei. *Drevnemongol'skie goroda* [Ancient Mongolian Cities]. Moscow: Nauka, 1965.

Komaroff, Linda and Stefano Carboni (eds). *The Legacy of Genghis Khan: Courtly Art and Culture in Western Asia, 1256–1353*. New York; New Haven: Metropolitan Museum of Art, 2002.

Korn, Lorenz. 'Saljuqs: Art and Architecture'. *Encyclopædia Iranica*. 2023, http://www.iranicaonline.org/articles/saljuqs-vi (last accessed 15 August).

Kosso, Peter. 'Epistemic Independence between Textual and Material Evidence'. In *Methods in the Mediterranean: Historical and Archaeological Views on Texts and Archaeology*, edited by David Small, 177–96. New York Leiden: Brill, 1995.

Kosso, Peter. *Knowing the Past: Philosophical Issues of History and Archaeology*. Amherst, NY: Humanity Books, 2001.

Kuehn, Sara. *The Dragon in Medieval East Christian and Islamic Art*. Leiden; Boston: Brill, 2011.

Lane, George. *Early Mongol Rule in Thirteenth Century Iran: A Persian Renaissance*. New York: Routledge Curzon, 2003.

Lapidus, Ira. *Muslim Cities in the Later Middle Ages*. Cambridge, MA: Harvard University Press, 1967.

Lashkari, Arash, Hamid Khatib Shahidi and Somaye Muhajer Vatan. 'A Preliminary Report of Excavations at Aveh Plain, Islamic Period'. *Iranian Journal of Archaeological Studies* 3 (2013): 21–37.

Leisten, Thomas. *Excavation of Samarra. Volume 1: Architecture. Final Report of the first Campaign, 1910–1912*. Mainz am Rhein: Von Zabern, 2003.

Lentz, Thomas and Glenn Lowry. *Timur and the Princely Vision: Persian Art and Culture in the Fifteenth Century*. Los Angeles: Los Angeles County Museum of Art, 1989.

Le Strange, Guy. *The Lands of the Eastern Caliphate; Mesopotamia, Persia, and Central Asia, from the Moslem Conquest to the Time of Timur*. Cambridge: Cambridge University Press, 1905.

Liebmann, Matthew. 'Introduction: The Intersections of Archaeology and Postcolonial Studies'. In *Archaeology and the Postcolonial Critique*, edited by Matthew Liebmann and Uzma Rizvi, 1–20. Lanham, MD: AltaMira, 2008.

Little, Donald. 'Diplomatic Missions and Gifts Exchanged by Mamluks and Ilkhans'. In *Beyond the Legacy of Genghis Khan*, edited by Linda Komaroff, 30–42. Leiden: Brill, 2006.

Little, Donald. 'The Founding of Sulṭāniyya: A Mamlūk Version'. *Iran: Journal of the British Institute of Persian Studies* 16 (1978): 170–5.

Lowry, Heath. *In the Footsteps of the Ottomans: A Search for Sacred Spaces and Architectural Monuments in Northern Greece*. Istanbul: Bahçeşehir University Press, 2009.

Lubo-Lesnichenko, E. I. 'Historical and Archaeological Investigation of the City of Khara Khoto [in Russian]'. *SNV* 6 (1968): 115–24.

Lubo-Lesnichenko, E. I. 'Porcelain Artifacts from Khara Khoto [in Russian]'. *SNV* 18 (1976): 199–208.

Mackie, Louise. *Symbols of Power: Luxury Textiles from Islamic Lands, 7th to 21st Century*. Cleveland, OH; New Haven, CT: Cleveland Museum of Art, 2015.

Mahdizadih, Bihzad and Husayn Nasiri. 'Banā-hā-yi Waqfī-yi Maraghih dar Dura-yi Īlkhānī [The Endowed Buildings of Maraghih during the Ilkhanid Period]', *Waqf Mīrāth-i Jāvīdān* 89 (2015): 49–72.

Marçais, Georges. 'L'Urbanisme Musulman [Muslim Urbanism]'. *5e Congrès de la Fédération des Sociétés Savantes de l'Afrique du Nord*. Algiers, 1940. The article was reprinted on pp. 219–31 of the collection of his works, *Mélanges d'Histoire et d'Archéologie de l'Occident Musulman*, tome I, articles et conférences de Georges Marçais. Algiers, 1957.

Marçais, William. 'L'Islamisme et la Vie Urbaine [Islamism and Urban Life]', *L'Académie des Inscriptions et Belles-Lêttres, Comptes Rendus* (1928): 86–100.

Marsh, Peter and Myagmar Saruul-Erdene. 'I Conquer like a Barbarian! Genghis Khan in the Western Popular Imagination'. In *Genghis Khan and the Mongol Empire*, edited by William Fitzhugh, Morris Rossabi and William Honeychurch, 278–81. Washington: Dino Don, 2009.

Masuya, Tomoko. 'Ilkhanid Courtly Life'. In *The Legacy of Genghis Khan: Courtly Art and Culture in Western Asia, 1256–1353*, edited by Linda Komaroff and Stefano Carboni, 75–103. New York; New Haven: Metropolitan Museum of Art, 2002.

Masuya, Tomoko. 'The Ilkhanid Phase of Takht-i Sulaimān'. PhD diss., New York University, 1997.

Masuya, Tomoko. 'Seasonal Capitals with Permanent Buildings in the Mongol Empire'. In *Turko-Mongol Rulers, Cities, and City Life*, edited by David Durand-Guedy, 223–56. Leiden; Boston: Brill, 2013.

Matthee, Rudi. 'The Safavids under Western Eyes: Seventeenth-Century European Travelers to Iran'. *Journal of Early Modern History* 13, no. 2 (2009): 137–71.

McLeod, John. *Beginning Postcolonialism*. Manchester; New York: Manchester University Press, 2000.

Melville, Charles. 'Earthquakes in the History of Nishapur'. *Iran: Journal of the British Institute of Persian Studies* 18 (1980): 103–20.

Melville, Charles. 'The Mongols in Iran'. In *The Legacy of Genghis Khan: Courtly Art and Culture in Western Asia, 1256–1353*, edited by Linda Komaroff and Stefano Carboni, 37–61. New York; New Haven: Metropolitan Museum of Art, 2002.

Melville, Charles. 'Pādshāh-i Islām: The Conversion of Sultān Maḥmūd Ghāzān Khān'. *Pembroke Papers* 1 (1990): 159–77.

Milwright, Marcus. 'Early Islamic Urbanism'. Unpublished.

Milwright, Marcus. 'Imported Pottery in Ottoman Bilad al-Sham'. *Turcica* 40 (2008): 121–52.

Milwright, Marcus. *An Introduction to Islamic Archaeology*. Edinburgh: Edinburgh University Press, 2010.

Mirfattah, 'Ali-'Asghar. *Faṣl-i Chāhārdahum-i Kāvush-i Shahr-i Ghadīm-i Sultaniyya* [The Fourteenth Season of Archaeological Excavation in the Historical City of Sultaniyya]. Unpublished. [A copy of the report is available at the local archive of the Iran Cultural Heritage, Handicrafts, and Tourism Organization (ICHTO) located at the World Heritage Site of Sultaniyya.]

Mirfattah, 'Ali-'Asghar. 'Pāytakht-hā-yi Īlkhānīyān: Maraghih, Tabriz va Sultaniyya [The Ilkhanid Capital Cities: Maraghih, Tabriz and Sultaniyya]'. In *Pāytakht-hā-yi Iran* [The Capitals of Iran], edited by Muhammad Y. Kiani, 517–63. Tehran: Sāzmān-i Mīrāth-i Farhangī-yi Kishva, 1995.

Mirfattah, 'Ali-'Asghar. 'Sultaniyya [Sultaniyya]'. *Mīrāth-i Farhangī* 13 (1995): 14–25.

Morgan, David. 'The "Great Yāsā of Chingiz Khān" and Mongol Law in the Īlkhānate'. *Bulletin of the School of Oriental and African Studies, University of London* 49, no. 1 (1986): 163–76.

Morgan, David (ed.). *Medieval Historical Writing in the Christian and Islamic Worlds*. London: University of London, School of Oriental and African Studies, 1982.

Morgan, David. *The Mongols*. New York; Oxford: Blackwell, 1986.

Morgan, David. *The Mongols*, 2nd edition. Oxford: Blackwell, 2007.

Morgan, David. 'Rašīd al-dīn and Ġazan Khan'. In *L'Iran Face à la Domination Mongole*, edited by Denise Aigle, 179–88. Tehran: Institut Français de Recherche en Iran, 1997.

Morgan, Peter. 'New Thoughts on Old Hormuz: Chinese Ceramics in the Hormuz Region in the Thirteenth and Fourteenth Centuries'. *Iran: Journal of the British Institute of Persian Studies* 29 (1991): 67–83.

Morgan, Peter. 'Some Far Eastern Elements in Coloured-Ground Sultanabad Wares'. In *Islamic Art in the Ashmolean Museum Part 2*, edited by James Allan, 19–43. Oxford: Oxford University Press, 1996.

Moule, Arthur Christopher and Paul Pelliot. *Marco Polo: The Description of the World*, 2 volumes. London: Routledge, 1938.

Muhajerinejad, 'Abd al-Reza. *Faṣl-i Avval-i Kāvush-i Muḥavvata-yi Jumʿih-masjid* [The First Season of Archaeological Excavation in the Area of Jumʿih-masjid]. Zanjan: Sāzmān-i Mīrāth-i Farhangī-yi Kishvar, 2009.

Muhajerinejad, 'Abd al-Reza. *Guzārish-i Gamānih-zanī Jahat-i Taʿyīn-i Ḥarīm-i Muḥavvata-yi Tappih-nūr* [The Report of the Trial Trenching in the Area of Tappih-nur]. Zanjan: Sāzmān-i Mīrāth-i Farhangī-yi Kishvar, 2009.

Mulder, Stephennie. *The Shrines of the 'Alids in Medieval Syria: Sunnis, Shi'is and the Architecture of Coexistence*. Edinburgh: Edinburgh University Press, 2014.

Muradi, Amin, Rasul Musavi-Haji and Behruz 'Umrani. 'Bāz-Shināsī-yi Furm-i Miʿmārī-yi Ārām-gāh-i Ghazan dar Majmūʿa-yi Abwāb al-birrī-yi Ghazaniyya [Re-identification of the Tomb of Ghazan in the Abwāb al-birr of Ghazaniyya]'. *Bāgh-e Nazar* 42 (2016): 33–44.

Mutarjim, 'Abbas and Yaʿqub Muhammadifar. 'Pīshnahādī Barāy-i Taʿyīn-i Maḥall-i Shahr-i Īlkhānī-yi Sultanabad-i Chimchal (Baghdad-i Kūchak) dar Bisotun-i Kermanshah [Some Speculations on the Location of the Ilkhanid City of Sultanabad-i Chimchal (Little Baghdad) in Bisotun, Kermanshah]'. *Payām-i Bāstān-shinās* 3 (2005): 95–104.

Nassar, Nahla. 'Saljuq or Byzantine: Two Related Styles of Jazīra Miniature Painting'. In *The Art of Syria and the Jazīra 1100–1250*, edited by Julian Raby, 85–98. Oxford: Oxford University Press, 1985.

Necipoğlu, Gülru. 'Geometric Design in Timurid/Turkmen Architectural Practice: Thoughts on a Recently Discovered Scroll and its Late Gothic Parallels'. In *Timurid Art and Culture: Iran and Central Asia in the Fifteenth Century*, edited by Lisa Golombek and Maria Subtelny, 48–66. Leiden: Brill, 1992.

Necipoğlu, Gülru. 'Plans and Models in 15th- and 16th-Century Ottoman Architectural Practice'. *Journal of the Society of Architectural Historians* 45, no. 3 (1986): 224–43.

Neglia, Giulia Annalinda. 'Some Historiographical Notes on the Islamic City with Particular Reference to the Visual Representation of the Built City'. In *The City in the Islamic World, Volume 1*, edited by Salma Jayyusi, Renata Holod, Attilio Petruccioli and André Raymond, 3–46. Leiden; Boston: Brill, 2008.

Northedge, Alastair. *The Historical Topography of Samarra*. London: British School of Archaeology in Iraq, 2005.

O'Kane, Bernard. 'From Tents to Pavilions: Royal Mobility and Persian Palace Design'. *Ars Orientalis* 23 (1993): 249–68.

Onon, Urgunge. *The Secret History of the Mongols: The Life and Times of Chinggis Khan*. Taylor & Francis e-Library, 2005.

Orser, Charles. *Encyclopedia of Historical Archaeology*. New York; London: Routledge, 2002.

Orser, Charles. *Historical Archaeology*. 3rd edition. New York: Routledge, 2017.

Orser, Charles. 'Historical Archaeology as Modern-world Archaeology in Argentina'. *International Journal of Historical Archaeology* 12, no. 3 (2008): 181–94.

Ostrowski, Donald. *Muscovy and the Mongols: Cross-Cultural Influences on the Steppe Frontier, 1304–1589*. Cambridge: Cambridge University Press, 1998.

Paul, Jürgen. 'The Seljuq Conquest(s) of Nishapur: A Reappraisal'. *Iranian Studies* 38, no. 4 (2005): 575–85.

Pauty, Edmond. 'Villes Spontanées et Villes Crées en Islam'. *Annales de l'Institut d'Études Orientales* 9 (1951): 52–75.

Peacock, A. C. S. 'Two Sufis of Ilkhanid Anatolia and their Patrons: Notes on the Works of Mu'yyid al-Din Jandi and Da'ud al-Qasari'. In *Cultural Encounters in Anatolia in the Medieval Period: The Ilkhanids in Anatolia, Symposium Proceedings, 21–22 May 2015, Ankara*, edited by Suzan Yalman, Filiz Yenişehirlioğlu, Alev Ayaokur and Defne Karakaya, 11–28. Ankara: Vehbi Koç Ankara Studies Research Center, 2019.

Pentz, Peter. *The Medieval Citadel and its Architecture*. Copenhagen: Nationalmuseet, 1997.

Petrushevsky, Ilya. 'Rashīd al-Dīn's Conception of the State'. *Central Asiatic Journal* 14, no. 1/3 (1970): 148–62.

Petrushevsky, Ilya. 'The Socio-Economic Condition of Iran under the Il-Khans'. In *The Cambridge History of Iran, Volume 5*, edited by John Boyle, 483–537. Cambridge: Cambridge University Press, 1968.

Pfeiffer, Judith. 'Reflections on a "Double Rapprochement": Conversion to Islam among the Mongol Elite during the Early Ilkhanate'. In *Beyond the Legacy of Genghis Khan*, edited by Linda Komaroff, 369–89. Leiden: Brill, 2006.

Pratt, Mary Louise. 'Arts of the Contact Zone'. *Profession* (1991): 33–40.

Preiser-Kapeller, Johannes. '*Civitas Thauris*. The Significance of Tabriz in the Spatial Frameworks of Christian Merchants and Ecclesiastics in the 13th and 14th Centuries'. In *Politics, Patronage and the Transmission of Knowledge in 13th–15th Century Tabriz*, edited by Judith Pfeiffer, 251–99. Leiden; Boston: Brill, 2014.

Pugachenkova, G. A. 'A Monument of Islamic Architecture in Khara Khoto [in Russian]'. *SA* 3 (1965): 258–62.

Quade-Reutter, Karin. 'Qotloḡ Tarkān Ḵātun'. *Encyclopædia Iranica*. 2023, http://www.iranicaonline.org/articles/qotlogh-tarkan-khatun (last accessed 28 July).

Rabbat, Nasser. *The Citadel of Cairo: A New Interpretation of Royal Mamluk Architecture*. New York; Leiden: Brill, 1995.

Rabbat, Nasser. 'The Militarization of Taste in Medieval Bilād al-Shām'. In *Muslim Military Architecture in Greater Syria: from the Coming of Islam to the Ottoman Period*, edited by Hugh Kennedy, 84–105. Leiden; Boston: Brill Academic, 2006.

Rante, Rocco. 'Nishapur: Archeology'. *Encyclopædia Iranica*. http://www.iranicaonline.org/articles/nishapur-06-archeology (last accessed 29 July 2023).

Rante, Rocco and Ghadir Afround. *Rayy: From its Origins to the Mongol Invasion: An Archaeological and Historiographical Study*. Leiden; Boston: Brill, 2015.

Rante, Rocco and Annabelle Collinet. *Nishapur Revisited: Stratigraphy and Ceramics of the Qohandez*. Oxford: Oxbow Books, 2013.

Razavi, Abulfazl. 'Sākhtār-i Ḥayāt-i Shahrī dar 'Aṣr-i Īlkhānān [The Structure of Urban Life during the Ilkhanid Period]', *Kitāb-i Māh-i Tārīkh va Jughrāfīyā* 123 (2008): 4–17.

Rezvan, Homayun and Hassan Karimian. *Sultaniyya: Ẓuhūr va Suqūṭ-i Yik Pāytakht* [Sultaniyya: The Emergence and the Decline of a Capital]. Tehran: Sāzmān-i Jahād-i Dānishgāhī-yi Tehran, 2016.

Riyazikesheh, Muhammad-Reza. 'Nishabur from an Archaeological Perspective [Nishabur az Dīdgāh-i Bāstān-Shināsī]', *Bāstān-Shināsī va Tārīkh* 1, 2 (1990): 20–30.

Rogers, Michael. 'Samarra: A Study in Medieval Town-Planning'. In *The Islamic City: A Colloquium*, edited by Albert Hourani and Samuel Miklos Stern, 119–56. Oxford: Cassirer; [Philadelphia]: University of Pennsylvania Press, 1970.

Rossabi, Morris. 'The Mongols and their Legacy'. In *The Legacy of Genghis Khan: Courtly Art and Culture in Western Asia, 1256–1353*, edited by Linda Komaroff and Stefano Carboni, 13–35. New York; New Haven: Metropolitan Museum of Art, 2002.

Rossabi, Morris. *Voyager from Xanadu: Rabban Sauma and the First Journey from China to the West*. Berkeley: University of California Press, 2010.

Rozman, Gilbert. *Soviet Studies of Pre-Modern China: Assessments of Recent Scholarship*. Ann Arbor, MI: Center for Chinese Studies, University of Michigan, 1984.

Rykwert, Joseph. 'Translation and/or Representation'. *Arq* 63 (2006): 22–5.

Saliba, George. 'Horoscopes and Planetary Theory: Ilkhanid Patronage of Astronomers'. In *Beyond the Legacy of Genghis Khan*, edited by Linda Komaroff, 357–68. Leiden: Brill, 2006.

Scarcia, Gianroberto. 'The "Vihār" of Qonqor-olong: Preliminary Report'. *East and West* 25, no. 1/2 (1975): 99–104.

Schwartz, Seth, Marilyn Montgomery and E. Briones. 'The Role of Identity in Acculturation among Immigrant People: Theoretical Propositions, Empirical Questions, and Applied Recommendations'. *Human Development* 49 (2006): 1–30.

Schwartz, Seth, Jennifer Unger, Byron Zamboanga and José Szapocznik. 'Rethinking the Concept of Acculturation: Implications for Theory and Research'. *American Psychologist* 65, no. 4 (2010): 237–51.

Seaman, Gary and Daniel Marks (eds). *Rulers from the Steppe: State Formation on the Eurasian Periphery*. Los Angeles: Ethnographics Press, Center for Visual Anthropology, University of Southern California, 1991.

Shani, Raya. *A Monumental Manifestation of the Shī'ite Faith in Late Twelfth-Century Iran: The Case of the Gunbad-i 'Alawyān, Hamadān, Volume 11*. Oxford: Oxford University Press for the Board of the Faculty of Oriental Studies, University of Oxford, 1996.

Sharifian, Shakiba and Sadeq Khudaparast. 'Nigāhī bar Gunbad-i Kabūd-i Maraghih [The Examination of Gunbad-i Kabud of Maraghih]'. *Kitāb-i Māh-i Hunar* 180 (2013): 72–6.

Shikari-Niri, Javad. 'Kankāsh dar Baqāyā-yi Raṣad-khānih-yi Maraghih [The Examination of the Architectural Remains of Maraghih Observatory]', *Pazhūhish-hā-yi Tārīkh-i Iran va Islam* 2 (2006): 61–80.

Shikari-Niri, Javad. 'Ta'yīn-i 'Amalkard va Ṭarḥ-i Mi'mārī-yi Vāḥid-hā-yi Nujūmī-yi Makshūfa dar Raṣad-khānih-yi Maraghih [Suggesting the Function and

Architectural Design of the Unearthed Astrological Units in Maraghih Observatory]', *Muṭāli'āt-i Bāstān-shināsī* 8, no. 2 (2016): 91–109.

Shiraishi, Noriyuki. 'Avraga Site: The "Great Ordū" of Genghis Khan'. In *Beyond the Legacy of Genghis Khan*, edited by Linda Komaroff, 83–93. Leiden: Brill, 2006.

Shiraishi, Noriyuki. 'Seasonal Migrations of the Mongol Emperors and the Peri-Urban Area of Kharakhorum'. Translated by Tomoko Masuya and Gaynor Sekimori. *International Journal of Asian Studies* 1, no. 1 (2004): 105–19.

Shoshan, Boas. *Popular Culture in Medieval Cairo*. Cambridge: Cambridge University Press, 1993.

Sims, Eleanor. 'The "Iconography" of the Internal Decoration in the Mausoleum of Ūljāytū at Sultaniyya'. In *Content and Context of Visual Arts in the Islamic World: Papers from a Colloquium in Memory of Richard Ettinghausen*, edited by Carol Bier, Priscilla Parsons Soucek and Richard Ettinghausen, 139–55. University Park: Pennsylvania State University Press for the College Art Association of America, 1988.

Sims, Eleanor. 'Thoughts on a *Shāhnāma* Legacy of the Fourteenth Century: Four Īnjū Manuscripts and the Great Mongol *Shāhnāma*'. In *Beyond the Legacy of Genghis Khan*, edited by Linda Komaroff, 269–86. Leiden: Brill, 2006.

Sinor, Denis. 'Horse and Pasture in Inner Asian History'. *Oriens Extremus* 19, no. 1/2 (1972): 171–83.

Skaff, Jonathan and William Honeychurch. 'Empire Building before the Mongols: Legacies of the Türks and Uyghurs'. In *Genghis Khan and the Mongol Empire*, edited by William Fitzhugh, Morris Rossabi and William Honeychurch, 85–9. Washington: Dino Don, 2009.

Sobuti, Hushang. *Banā-hā-yi Ārām-gāhī-yi Ustān-i Zanjan* [The Shrines of Zanjan Province]. Zanjan: Zangan Press, 1998.

Sobuti, Hushang. *Mi'mārī-yi Sultaniyya dar Guẕar-gāh-i Hunar* [The Architecture of the Dome of Sultaniyya]. Tehran: Pazinih Press, 2001.

Soucek, Priscilla. 'Ceramic Production as Exemplar of Yuan-Ilkhanid Relations'. *RES: Anthropology and Aesthetics* 35, no. 35 (1999): 125–41.

Soudavar, Abolala. 'The Saga of Abu-Sa'id Bahādor Khān, the Abu-Sa'idnāmé'. In *The Court of the Il-khans, 1290–1340*, edited by Julian Raby and Teresa Fitzherbert, 95–188. Oxford: Oxford University Press, 1996.

Steinhardt, Nancy. *Chinese Imperial City Planning*. Honolulu: University of Hawaii Press, 1990.

Steinhardt, Nancy. 'Imperial Architecture along the Mongolian Road to Dadu'. *Ars Orientalis* 18 (1988): 59–93.

Steinhardt, Nancy. 'Imperial Architecture under Mongolian Patronage: Khubilai's Imperial City of Daidu'. PhD diss., Harvard University, 1981.

Steinhardt, Nancy. 'The Plan of Khubilai Khan's Imperial City'. *Artibus Asiae* 44, no. 2/3 (1983): 137–58.

Steinhardt, Nancy. 'Toward the Definition of a Yuan Dynasty Hall'. *Journal of the Society of Architectural Historians* 47, no. 1 (1988): 57–73.

Tabbaa, Yasser. 'Circles of Power: Palace, Citadel, and City in Ayyubid Aleppo'. *Ars Orientalis* 23 (1993): 181–200.

Tabbaa, Yasser. *Constructions of Power and Piety in Medieval Aleppo*. University Park: Pennsylvania State University Press, 1997.

Tabbaa, Yasser. *The Transformation of Islamic Art during the Sunni Revival*. Seattle: University of Washington Press, 2001.

Talmon-Heller, Daniella. *Islamic Piety in Medieval Syria: Mosques, Cemeteries and Sermons under the Zangids and Ayyūbids (1146–1260)*. Leiden; Boston: Brill, 2007.

Taylor, Christopher Schurman. *In the Vicinity of the Righteous: Ziyāra and the Veneration of Muslim Saints in Late Medieval Egypt*. Leiden; Boston: Brill, 1998.

Thompson, Jon. *Silk: 13th to 18th Centuries, Treasures from the Museum of Islamic Art*. Doha: Museum of Islamic Art, 2004.

Tsalkin, V. I. 'Fauna from the Excavations at Khara Khorum [in Russan]'. *Kratkie Soobshcheniia Instituta Arkheologii* 114 (1968): 16–23.

Varjavand, Parviz. *Kāvush-i Raṣad-khānih-yi Maraghih va Nigāhī bi Pīshīna-yi Dānish-i Sitāra-shināsī dar Iran* [The Excavation of Maraghih Observatory and A Brief Study of the History of Astrology in Iran]. Tehran: Amir Kabir Press, 1987.

Velayati, Rahim. *Guzārish-i Khabarī-yi Faṣl-i Avval-i Shahr-i Tārīkhī-yi Ujan* [The Report of the First Season of Excavation in the Historical City of Ujan]. Tehran: University of Tehran, 2017.

Velayati, Rahim, Behzad Mahdizadih and Hamid Khanali. 'Makān-yābī-yi Shahr-i Tārīkhī-yi Ujan bar Asās-i Manābiʿ-i Tārīkhī va Barrisī-hā-yi Bāstān-shinākhtī [Locating the Ilkhanid City of Ujan on the Basis of Historical Sources and Archaeological Surveys]'. *Bagh-e Nazar* 34 (2015): 83–92.

Velayati, Rahim, Homayun Rezvan and Qadir Ibrahimi. 'Miʿmārī-yi Īlkhānī dar Bastara-yi daw Shahr-i Tārīkhī Islāmī-yi Ujan va Sultaniyya [Ilkhanid Architecture in the Historical Cities of Ujan and Sultaniyya]'. *Bagh-e Nazar* 55 (2017): 17–28.

Vladimirtsov, Boris Yakovlevich. *Niẓām-i Ijtimāʿī-yi Mughulān* [The Social System of the Mongols]. Translated by Shirin Bayani. Tehran: Intishārāt-i ʿIlmī va Farhangī, 2007.

Wallace, Vesna. *Buddhism in Mongolian History, Culture, and Society*. New York: Oxford University Press, 2015.

Wardwell, Anne. 'Panni Tartarici: Eastern Islamic Silks Woven with Gold and Silver (13th and 14th Centuries)'. *Islamic Art: An Annual Dedicated to the Art and Culture of the Muslim World* 3 (1988–9): 95–173.

Watenpaugh, Heghnar Zeitlian. *The Image of an Ottoman City: Imperial Architecture and Urban Experience in Aleppo in the 16th and 17th Centuries*. Boston; Leiden: Brill, 2004.

Watenpaugh, Heghnar Zeitlian. 'An Uneasy Historiography: The Legacy of Ottoman Architecture in the Former Arab Provinces'. *Muqarnas* 24 (2007): 27–43.

Watt, James. *The World of Khubilai Khan: Chinese Art in the Yuan Dynasty*. New Haven; London; New York: Metropolitan Museum of Art, 2010.

Watt, James and Anne Wardwell. *When Silk Was Gold: Central Asian and Chinese Textiles*. New York: Metropolitan Museum of Art in cooperation with the Cleveland Museum of Art, 1997.

Waugh, Daniel. 'Nomads and Settlement: New Perspectives in the Archaeology of Mongolia'. *Silk Road Journal* 8 (2010): 97–123.

Wei Jian. *Yuan Shangdu* 元上都 [Shangdu site of the Yuan Dynasty]. Beijing: publisher not identified, 2008.

Whaley, Mark. 'A Rendering of Square Script Mongolian on the Îlkhân Ghâzân Maḥmûd's Coins'. *Mongolian Studies* 26 (2003–4): 39–88.

Wheatley, Paul. *The Places Where Men Pray Together: Cities in Islamic Lands, Seventh through the Tenth Centuries*. Chicago: University of Chicago Press, 2001.

Wiet, Gaston. *L'Exposition Persane de 1931*. Cairo: Impr. de l'Institut français d'archéologie orientale, 1933.

Wilber, Donald. *The Architecture of Islamic Iran: The Il Khānid Period*. New York: Greenwood Press, 1969.

Wilkinson, Charles. *Nishapur: Some Early Islamic Buildings and their Decoration*. New York: The Metropolitan Museum of Art, 1986.

Wing, Patrick. '"Rich in Goods and Abounding in Wealth": The Ilkhanid and Post-Ilkhanid Ruling Elite and the Politics of Commercial Life at Tabriz, 1250–1400'. In *Politics, Patronage and the Transmission of Knowledge in 13th–15th Century Tabriz*, edited by Judith Pfeiffer, 301–20. Leiden; Boston: Brill, 2014.

Wolper, Ethel. *Cities and Saints: Sufism and the Transformation of Urban Space in Medieval Anatolia*. University Park: Pennsylvania State University Press, 2003.

Wolper, Ethel. 'Islamic Architecture and Institutions in the Late Medieval City'. *History Compass* 12 (2014): 912–23.

Yalman, Suzan, Filiz Yenişehirlioğlu, Alev Ayaokur and Defne Karakaya (eds). *Cultural Encounters in Anatolia in the Medieval Period: The Ilkhanids in Anatolia, Symposium Proceedings, 21–22 May 2015, Ankara*. Ankara: Vehbi Koç Ankara Studies Research Center, 2019.

Zadneprovsky, Y. A. 'Early Developments in Central Asia'. *Iran: Journal of the British Institute of Persian Studies* 33 (1995): 155–9.

Index

Note: *italic* indicates figure

EU Authorised Representative:
Easy Access System Europe Mustamäe tee 50, 10621 Tallinn, Estonia
gpsr.requests@easproject.com

Printed and bound by CPI Group (UK) Ltd, Croydon, CR0 4YY
03/08/2026
02185304-0003